OCCUPHONORS

EDUCATION

OCCUPY HONORS EDUCATION

Edited by **Lisa L. Coleman,**
Jonathan D. Kotinek,
and **Alan Y. Oda**

Series Editor | Jeffrey A. Portnoy
Georgia State University

National Collegiate Honors Council
Monograph Series

Manufactured in the United States

National Collegiate Honors Council
1100 Neihardt Residence Center
University of Nebraska-Lincoln
540 N. 16th Street
Lincoln, NE 68588-0627
www.nchchonors.org

Production Editors | Cliff Jefferson and Mitch Pruitt
Wake Up Graphics LLC

Cover and Text Design | 47 Journals LLC

Earthrise cover photo, a composite image of pictures taken by
NASA's Lunar Reconnaissance Orbiter on October 12, 2015,
courtesy of NASA/Goddard/Arizona State University.

International Standard Book Number
978-0-9911351-6-5

TABLE OF CONTENTS

TABLE OF CONTENTS

ACKNOWLEDGEMENTS

The editors wish to acknowledge the following for their role in bringing this monograph to print:

First, we thank the authors of each essay. Your brilliant insights and diligent work are an important contribution to honors education and the mission of inclusive excellence. We are especially appreciative of your patience; readers should understand that some of these essays were first submitted in 2012.

Second, Jonathan Kotinek and Alan Oda wish to thank Lisa Coleman for her careful shepherding, tireless encouragement, and dogged determination to see this project through.

For her part, Lisa Coleman extends gratitude to her co-chairs and co-editors for their friendship, support, sense of humor, and contributions to this volume. She also thanks her co-authors, Rachel Childers, Sam Faudree, and Jake Martin, for their camaraderie inside and outside the classroom and for their insightful contributions. She and her co-authors are grateful to Shawn Alfrey, who provided them with a much-needed and incisive first review of their chapter. Thanks also go to Kameron Dunn, Matt Slaten, and Emilie Cox, who gave Coleman permission to quote from their papers. She also thanks current and past administrators, faculty, and staff campus-wide at Southeastern Oklahoma State University (SE) for their support over many years. Heartfelt thanks go to friends and colleagues Tim Boatmun and Lyndi Standefer-Scarberry, who made directing the SE Honors Program a true joy. Finally, with deep gratitude and love, she thanks her husband, Ronnie; his family; her students at Southeastern; and the place that is Native America for their inspiration.

Jon Kotinek thanks his sons, Noah and Samuel, and his friend, Russ, for giving him the opportunity to work out the ideas related to perspective and communication that he used as examples in his chapter. He extends thanks as well to Dr. Alex Hernandez for their rich conversations on culture, to Dr. Finnie Coleman for his guidance on paradigmatic thinking, and to Dr. Yvonna Lincoln for introducing him to constructivist thinking. Jon thanks his wife, Ashley, for her ongoing support and inspiration.

Alan Oda thanks his students, Sarah (Wentworth) Spafford, Jillian Haag, Katelyn Nakama, Grantham Jones, Sarah Brackbill, Lauren Carlo, and Alec Brunk, who, along with his co-authors Ye Eun (Grace) Oh and Hyun Seo (Hannah) Lee, have been invaluable in his research efforts. He also thanks Dr. Melvin Shoemaker, who first invited him to join the honors faculty at his school. Finally, Alan is grateful to his wife, Donna, and sons, Peter and Andrew, who had to witness him on his laptop at all hours of the night.

Together, we sincerely thank Jeffrey A. Portnoy, General Editor of the National Collegiate Honors Council (NCHC) Monograph Series, for his support and enthusiasm for this project as well as for his unstinting copy editing skills.

We also thank the members of the NCHC Committee on Diversity Issues as well as the other members of the honors community who have tirelessly assisted in crafting the call for proposals for the Diversity Forum each year. By doing so, they helped to generate some of the essays in this volume.

Lastly, the editors wish to thank the NCHC Publications Board members for their patience with our project as well as for the thoughtful reviews and suggestions that have helped to draw out the best this monograph has to offer.

Lisa L. Coleman

Jonathan D. Kotinek

Alan Y. Oda

Why *Occupy Honors Education?*

Jonathan D. Kotinek
Texas A&M University

The title of this monograph, *Occupy Honors Education*, refers to the Occupy Movement that originated in the United States in New York's Zuccotti Park in 2011 and to the principles that informed the movement and its resistance to an economic status quo benefitting the top one percent in America. Contributors Aaron Stoller and Finnie D. Coleman cover these principles in considerable detail in the first and last chapters of this volume. Importantly, however, the editors encourage readers to note that the concerns articulated by the Occupy Movement about diversity, access, and inclusion parallel the formulation provided earlier by Finnie D. Coleman in "The Problem with Diversity: Moving Past the Numbers," the closing chapter of the first NCHC diversity monograph, *Setting the Table for Diversity*, edited by Lisa L. Coleman and Jonathan D. Kotinek, and published in 2010.

By 2012, Lisa L. Coleman, Jonathan D. Kotinek, and Alan Y. Oda, co-chairs of the NCHC Committee on Diversity Issues, had already begun discussing the need for a second monograph on diversity when the theme for the 2012 NCHC conference, "Challenging Structures," provided an opportunity to use the Forum on Diversity to engage these parallel concerns. The theme reads as follows:

> During the American Revolution, Boston's citizens sought independence from arbitrary authority while preserving interdependence and community. Reflecting similar values, the honors revolution has challenged the structure of undergraduate education. Honors faculty foster

independent thought, motivation, and scholarship in students while encouraging collaboration within a community of scholars. As we gather in Boston, we will highlight the scholarship of teaching and learning while reexamining our practices, pedagogy, and communities to extend the challenge of the honors revolution in education.

Our call for proposals for the 2012 Forum on Diversity, which we titled "Occupy Honors Education," roughly coincided with the one-year anniversary of the Occupy Movement. The high-profile evictions from Occupy encampments as well as the police pepper-spraying of student protestors in late fall 2011 raised questions about the erosion of constitutionally enshrined free speech. Thus in formulating the 2012 call, key questions asked how honors education could challenge existing structures as well as structure challenges to prepare our students to change their worlds.

An unstated assumption in this formulation included an understanding that educated people, and especially honors students who may have the benefit of a richer educational experience, are responsible for using that education in the service of a larger community. Consequently, we conceived of education generally, and honors education specifically, to be bound up with preparing our graduates to engage the democratic process productively. The questions of who is represented in that educated population, whether or not there are differences in access, and who is included in decision-making processes are integral to the honors mission. The Occupy Movement articulated principles for action that highlight how traditional structures in our culture are inadequate to address these concerns. The "Challenging Structures" theme proved to be particularly rich ground to mine for how these lessons might be applied. Indeed both Aaron Stoller's and Shawn Alfrey's contributions to this monograph, with their discussions of the value of *engagement* in the honors education enterprise, were developed from the presentations they gave in Boston.

If it is true that culture is a story we tell ourselves about ourselves, we felt it imperative to plumb the rich scholarly literature that NCHC has produced about diversity, access, and inclusion. As is appropriate for any scholarship, the essays that follow have developed as a conversation among the editors, authors, and the existing literature. This conversation has taken a considerable amount of time, but it has proven to be a rich source of insight. During the past five years, we have learned that diversity requires paying attention to individual, representative voices. Further, diversity asks that we cultivate the ability to hear and see how the particular relates to the whole.

Our Earthrise cover is instructive here. This composite image of pictures, taken by NASA's Lunar Reconnaissance Orbiter on October 12, 2015, vividly renders the particular-to-whole relationship diversity asks us to foster. It also mirrors the seismic shift in perspective the monograph *Occupy Honors Education* advocates, in which diversity serves as inspiration and catalyst for inclusive excellence in honors education.

The voices highlighted in this monograph add depth and value to the conversation about diversity in honors and provide a vision for how honors can lead the way in achieving inclusive excellence. We encourage our readers to follow the conversation below in sequence, beginning with the introduction, in which Lisa L. Coleman expertly pulls at the necessary thread of engagement that ties the conversation together. We hope that by following this thread, readers will realize the full impact of the themes that emerge and the imperative nature of the clarion call to action this monograph sounds.

Occupying Naïve America:
The Resistance to Resistance

Lisa L. Coleman
Southeastern Oklahoma State University

On June 28, 2016, four days after Brexit, on *Morning Joe,* the MSNBC political news show, guest Jon Meacham, the Executive Editor of Random House, said to Tony Blair, former Prime Minister of Great Britain: "The intellectual arguments seem to be won for globalization, the visceral argument seems to be in . . . worse shape. He then asked, "Would you agree with that and how do you . . . bridge that?" Blair responded:

> I think that's absolutely right. I think . . . for people like myself who are in the center ground of politics and who think center left and center right can cooperate and work together, who don't like this sort of insurgent populism because we think it's not really gonna deliver for the people. . . , I think there's a big responsibility on us in the center to get our act together and to work out radical but serious solutions to the problems people face.
>
> But I think the center ground have got to become the people of change again and not the guardians of the status quo. (Blair)

A few weeks earlier in May, deep into working on the chapter "Occupying Native America" for this monograph, I was on a plane returning from a National Collegiate Honors Council conference planning meeting in Seattle to the Dallas/Fort Worth airport when I entered the chapter title with a typo, leaving out the "t" in "Native."

My Microsoft Word program helpfully added the umlaut over the "i," emending my title to read "Occupying Naïve America." I was going to fix the typo when I was stopped in my tracks by the compelling nature of the title my mistake had created. Putting work on the chapter aside, I opened a new page in my Word program and placed the newly minted title "Occupying Naïve America" at the top. Adding a colon and a subtitle, "The Resistance to Resistance," I knew I had the title for our introduction. I also recognized I had a task in front of me more challenging than any I had anticipated when I took on the co-editorship of this volume.

Although I would officially retire after twenty-two years at Southeastern Oklahoma State University (SE) as of June 1, 2016, I had no intention of retiring from honors education, but this typo underscored my certainty that whatever relationship I had with a cause that has directed my trajectory for so long, the course I charted now would not be identical to the one I have pursued thus far. Rather than stepping back or stepping down as one might do at the end of a career, I had to step up. I had to deliver a message that might be hard for some in our audience to hear.

On November 9, 2016, the day after the United States' historic election in which Hillary Clinton was unexpectedly defeated by Donald Trump, the so-called populist, I was further galvanized in the mission I proposed for honors when I was fine-tuning this introduction in late September. The argument I make here is that each of us in honors in America is naïve if we believe that honors does not have to change integrally, significantly, if we are to continue to be productive players on the world stage as well as on the campuses of our home institutions. Thus, in what one might think of as the twilight of my career, I am asking for a spotlight on engagement, diversity, equity, and inclusion in honors, and I am sending out a call to each reader of this monograph and the previous diversity monograph, *Setting the Table for Diversity*, that for social justice to exist, diversity, equity, and inclusion for all must become what we in honors are about, centrally, obsessively, perennially. This has to be our mission, the dawn of our new morning. We cannot remain in mourning instead for a dream of honors as an exclusive domain, nor can we remain with a vision of our home honors programs or honors colleges as doing enough simply by maintaining a philosophical status quo in regard to whatever we have already achieved in honors on our home campuses. There are no laurels sufficient for us to rest upon.

Even in the face of the Brexit vote in favor of Britain's exit from the European Union and the defeat of Hillary Clinton by Donald Trump, echoing Tony Blair, but directing my call to the honors community, we have "a big responsibility . . . to get our act together and to work out radical but serious solutions to the problems people face" (Blair). In a conversation reflecting on the results of the U.S. election and the great divide between the voters in the United States, historian Doris Kearns Goodwin stated on *Morning Joe* on Thursday, November 10, 2016:

> People are experiencing modernity and changes and globalization and technology in very different ways. People in cities on the coasts, who are used to living with immigrants, are used to jobs coming okay to them, are feeling one way about all the changes in the world. People living in Trumpland are having a different experience with change.
>
> And the problem is—I do think the problem is—one of empathy. We have to understand how people are reacting differently. We have to feel that sense of fellow feeling. Teddy Roosevelt said democracy will never work unless we understand the other. We've made other people the "other," whether it's immigrants on one side or whether it's the rustbelt people on the other. And the country can't last unless we feel a sense of each other's identity and feel an empathy for what we're going through together.

How do we develop this empathy in ourselves and in our students—this desire to understand those who are not responding to the sorts of change Goodwin mentions in the same way?

In order to facilitate this sort of understanding, honors programs and honors colleges must work together and with other groups, including the National Collegiate Honors Council (NCHC), the Association of American Colleges and Universities (AAC&U), the National Association of African American Honors Programs (NAAAHP), the Association of Jesuit Colleges and Universities (AJCU), to establish best practices. Honors must broaden the base of students who qualify for honors and then facilitate the best means possible, curricular and otherwise, to develop opportunities for conversations that both contribute to global-mindedness in our students and underscore the importance and value of becoming more knowledgeable about the nation and the home communities to which we and they have ties.

By global-mindedness I do not mean that we simply ensure that our students travel or study abroad. Kwame Anthony Appiah's notion of "rooted cosmopolitanism" applies here ("Cosmopolitan" 22). Although we must diligently work to be sure the opportunity to study abroad exists, we must be certain that students know that their personal point of view on this world and its problems is not the only one or necessarily the best one. Further, leaders of honors programs and colleges on their home campuses must be humble enough to realize that while they promote global mindedness, they must also ensure access to resources in their particular community, on campus and off, that will enable their students to have an educational experience deepened and broadened by an understanding of the relationship of the local and the national to a global—even planetary—perspective (Coleman, Childers, Faudree, and Martin 259–60; see Basu 138; see Brown and Cope 108–09).

One major task of the honors community is determining which practices for achieving these ends might be the best. How might we and our students come to understand that to focus simply on bettering ourselves or our own home institution or even our country alone is simply not enough? To reiterate, whatever needs to be done to give us and our students a sense of ourselves as global citizens who concomitantly desire to learn about, honor, and cultivate our roots in our own nation and home communities, we should support those teaching, mentoring, and curricular choices. In other words, the empathy that Goodwin notes, which all Americans should extend to one another, must extend as well from institutions of higher learning and their practitioners to their student bodies and to their expanded base of students, whether American or not, if those students are going to be successful. As Frank Harris, III, and Estela Mara Bensimon note in "The Equity Scorecard": "Lack of cultural knowledge may keep us from noticing the ways in which we, unknowingly and . . . [unintentionally] create the conditions that prevent students from behaving according to our expectations" (80).

As Brexit and the 2016 United States election have underscored, realizing these goals will be no simple exercise. Nevertheless, the concession speech offered by Hillary Clinton, which she also emailed as a "thank you" to her supporters, suggests some ways to begin:

> Our constitutional democracy demands our participation, not just every four years, but all the time. So let's do all we can to keep advancing the causes and values we hold dear: making our economy work for everyone, not just those at the top; protecting our country and protecting our planet; and breaking down all the barriers that hold anyone back from achieving their dreams. (Clinton)

Higher education professionals must understand, as Harris and Bensimon note, that those barriers may well include "the failure to recognize that one's best practices may not be effective with students who are not familiar with the hidden curriculum of how to be a successful college student" (80). In my estimation, the chapters in this monograph offer a variety of paths that intersect with Clinton's call for civic participation. The authors also provide various curricular means through which local, national, and global citizenship, which includes and celebrates the values of diversity, equity, excellence, inclusion, and justice, can be taught and practiced. The first NCHC monograph on diversity, *Setting the Table for Diversity* (2010), laid the groundwork for this one, and I encourage readers to take up that monograph in tandem with this new publication to explore and then join the conversations that take place between them, adding your voices to ours. I am not unmindful of the provocative nature of the claims made in the first monograph and neither are the contributors to this one, each of whom, in various ways, has taken note of the local and global divide in our country and in the world and the resistance that exists throughout society to see from the perspective of those with whom we disagree or with whom we are unfamiliar.

In the chapter by Aaron Stoller, for example, a polemical piece that kicks off this monograph, the very title, "Theory and Resistance in Honors Education," echoes these concerns. Stoller argues, by way of Paulo Freire, against a banking model of education and for a model of honors education informed by the concerns of the critical pedagogue, à la Henry A. Giroux (2001), who argues that "[r]ather than celebrating objectivity and consensus, teachers must place the notions of critique and conflict at the center of their pedagogical models" (Giroux 62 qtd. in Stoller 18). By so doing, critique "breaks through the mystifications and distortions that 'silently' work behind the labels and routines of school practice" (Giroux 62; qtd. in Stoller 18). Stoller advocates against what he names the "neoliberal paradigm," one that views and assesses education by way of a business model, and advocates instead for a critical pedagogy of resistance (12–19). The prescient nature of Stoller's work depicts the 2017 American political scene inside and outside the context of higher education.

Stoller defines resistance by way of the Occupy Movement that began in September 2011 and is still ongoing and being joined by new forms of resistance. The methods of this movement in raising awareness concerning social injustice and pay inequity, for example, have been employed in 2016 politics by way of presidential candidate Bernie Sanders' democratic socialism. Stoller sees the form of resistance practiced by the Occupy Movement as a method to be employed by professors and students alike to challenge the status quo. Ultimately, Stoller supports honors education informed by an understanding of "the primary concerns for the critical pedagogue" (19). These concerns include:

1. "Power/Knowledge" (see also F. Coleman, "Blueprint" 341–43; L. Coleman, Childers, Faudree, and Martin 264–65; Dsziesinski, Camarena, and Homrich-Knieling 83–84 and 91–92);

2. the "Agency of Learners";

3. "Academic and Administrative Freedom";

4. "Participatory Structures and Pedagogies" (see also Alfrey 219–23; L. Coleman et al., 245–54);

5. "Freedom through Justice"; and

6. "Pedagogy as a Form of Friendship" (Stoller 19–20).

David M. Jones' chapter, "From Good Intentions to Educational Equity in an Honors Program: Occupying Honors through Inclusive Excellence," demonstrates Stoller's thesis that theory can be applied practically within the context of what Jones styles an "*occupation*" of honors (36). Jones' opening gambit points to the "I, Too, Am Harvard" project, launched on Tumblr in 2014, in which non-traditional Harvard students visually protest racial discrimination at that institution. Jones then points to a parallel between Harvard and the honors community as two places of "high attainment" (34) and asks: "Are diverse students served equitably in these high-value settings?" (34). To address this question, Jones defines two key terms that informed his professional development work with Estela Bensimon at the University of Southern California's Center for Urban Studies: "equity-mindedness" and "inclusive excellence." "Equity-mindedness" focuses on student success and "responds proactively to systematic social inequalities" rather than focusing on poor student outcomes (39). "Inclusive excellence" speaks both to "numerical diversity" and the "full participation of all student communities in high-value campus activity (inclusion)" such as honors programs (Jones 40). In turn it focuses on student support to help them "reach their academic potential (excellence)" (Jones 40).

Detailing the professional development work done toward creating inclusive excellence in the University of Wisconsin system as a whole by way of the "Equity Scorecard" (Center for Urban Education, University of Southern California) that assesses the equity mindedness of given institutions and practitioners, Jones argues for inclusive excellence in honors education, providing evidence from five years of research and statistical data gathering from the University of Wisconsin at Eau Claire Honors Program that show the results of incorporating inclusive excellence as a value. Additionally, Jones offers four steps in a set of actions to "move equity mindedness and inclusive excellence to the foreground of honors education" (43). These steps include the following:

1. Review and revise honors admissions criteria toward more "holistic . . . protocols" (Jones 43);

2. "Review curricula and implement faculty development strategies" that will "develop student talent from all communities . . ." (Jones 43);

3. "Infuse honors programs with high-impact practices . . . including models for increasing intercultural literacy" (Jones 43);

4. "Review and revise NCHC's guiding document 'Basic Characteristics of a Fully Developed Honors Program' to institutionalize support for inclusive excellence" (Jones 43).

In keeping with Stoller's critical theory-inspired themes of social justice and cultural critique and juxtaposing Jones' insistence that "without inclusion there is no true excellence" (AAC&U qtd. in Jones 36), the authors of "A Privilege for the Privileged? Using Intersectionality to Reframe Honors and Promote Social Responsibility" argue that the honors community has a responsibility to become a force for social change rather than a place only for the privileged, a term they note as relative to context. Amberly Dziesinski, Phame Camarena, and Caitlin Homrich-Knieling claim, for example, that "few honors programs are found in the most elite institutions" (83). At the same time, they also posit that "within the same institution [in which an honors program *does* exist], the honors students are still more likely to come from backgrounds of relative privilege as compared to their non-honors peers" (Dziesinski, Camarena,and Homrich-Knieling 83). They further claim that because these students' "backgrounds of relative privilege" give them more likely access to honors, their privilege as honors students is often "unearned" (Johnson qtd. in Dziesinski, Camarena, and Homrich-Knieling 83).

Asserting that "Vision and Mission Matter," the authors point to the Central Michigan University Honors Scholar Program's new vision statement to "serve the university by fostering a diverse community of scholars committed to academic excellence, intellectual engagement, and social responsibility" and its mission, a commitment to "the greater good" ("Mission and Core Values" qtd. in Dziesinski, Camarena, and Homrich-Knieling 85). Such aspirations require that the program teach the language of critique (see Stoller 13–14), including the theory of "intersectionality," which posits that the outcomes of interactions between human beings and a given society are affected by characteristics such as a person's gender, race, or sexual orientation and the power or lack thereof that is accorded to that person as a result of the institutions and ideologies of that culture (Dziesinski, Camarena, and Homrich-Knieling 91). The authors provide case studies of first-generation, ethnic minority, and LGBTQ group members that highlight conflicts between group membership and group identification and reveal that conversations about identity negotiation and renegotiation may be made more possible by an honors program that "explicitly states its priorities and practices related to social justice" (92).

The theme of resistance, also highlighted by Stoller, shows up in a different guise for Stephanie Brown and Virginia Cope, who build their students' honors experience on the value of global-minded citizenship. "Cosmopolitan Courtesy: Preparing for Global Citizenry" chronicles their efforts at Ohio State University at Newark to develop community-service initiatives coupled with domestic and international travel. The two recount specific, unsettling cross-cultural interchanges that occured in their early international forays as well as during a trip to New Orleans in 2009. Their description of these unsettling events, described as "disorienting dilemmas," present the challenges they faced when students demonstrate resistance to new experiences or inappropriate behavior in their first unfamiliar cross-cultural interactions (see Mezirow (1991) xvi; qtd. in Brown and Cope 112).

To better prepare students with the tools to respond to unforeseen circumstances, Brown and Cope develop lessons in what they call "cosmopolitan courtesy" (108). In so doing, Brown and Cope offer one model for the "intercultural literacy" called for by Jones (43). One lesson includes explicitly teaching the theory of cosmopolitanism put forward by Immanuel Kant, who argues for respect for visiting foreigners and respect for the home and cultural practices of the places one visits (Brown and Cope 115). The authors share a number of lessons they learned and strategic steps they took in their teaching approaches to help their students—and actually anyone—develop the ability to adjust and respond more thoughtfully in the moment to experiences that challenge their personal cultural backgrounds and coping abilities.

In her chapter, "Cosmopolitanism and New Racial Formations in a Post-9/11 Honors Curriculum on Diversity," Lopamudra Basu demonstrates a commitment to cosmopolitanism on the local and global stage shared by Brown and Cope. Basu chronicles her effort to create and then teach the course she calls "After 9/11: American Literature of Trauma and Public Crisis." Basu draws upon a number of recent texts, including chapters in Martha C. Nussbaum's *For Love of Country?* as well as Nussbaum's controversial opening chapter in that work, "Patriotism and Cosmopolitanism," to which her other contributors respond. In that piece Nussbaum advocates for the cosmopolitan perspective over that of the national and the nationalist.

Basu grapples with the many complicated human and political aftereffects of the 9/11 events that resulted in the Patriot Act as well as various permutations of ethnic categorization and stereotyping.

Her chapter includes a discussion of several works of post-9/11 literature that address such themes as who counts as a person worthy of being mourned and the plight of undocumented workers. Finally, she addresses the challenges of various university curricular guidelines regarding diversity at the University of Wisconsin-Stout and offers a commentary on how the very notion of diversity and diversity studies must be readdressed and revised in a post-9/11 world to make clear that we must "bring the local and the global to productive synthesis" (Basu 138).

The synthesis of the local and the global is also the focus of Alan Y. Oda, Ye Eun (Grace) Oh, and Hyun Seo (Hannah) Lee in "Family Issues of Diversity and Education for Asian American Immigrants: How Universities, Colleges, and Honors Programs Can Understand and Support the 1.5 and Second Generation." In this piece, the authors explain that Asian Americans were once labeled what Bob H. Suzuki (2002) calls a "Model Minority" (Suzuki 21 qtd. in Oda, Oh, and Lee 177), a designation that implied the group was exceptionally able to fit into their new culture and perform at academic levels greater than other American immigrants. Current research indicates this stereotype still holds despite the fact that the representation is inaccurate and fraught with pitfalls for students and their advisors alike. In addition to their research on Asian American immigrants in general, the authors research multigenerational Korean Americans in particular, finding that the family dynamics of both groups present challenges to the students' abilities to negotiate between their collectivist home cultures and the individualist American culture.

The authors describe what is called the 1.5 generation, a term typically attributed to immigrant Korean Americans and other 1.5 immigrants who arrived in the United States before adulthood and the various ways in which their acculturation to American culture takes place. This group is different from second-generation Korean Americans, particularly in terms of their relationship to the English language; they are often bilingual, while the second generation often is not. But the 1.5 generation has attributes that differ from the second generation. One of the findings by Oda, Oh, and Lee is that despite these differences, the 1.5 Korean Americans do not always identify with the 1.5 sub-group.

The authors note, as a number of studies have demonstrated, that Asians often have a deeply engrained desire for educational success; they speculate, based on related data, however, that the academic success of Asian students in education in general and in honors in particular does not necessarily mean they are psychologically and socially well adjusted. The expected lifelong reverence for their elders, which is also a part of their cultural context, means they are under pressure from the first generation to succeed. Oda, Oh, and Lee maintain: "While knowing the idiosyncratic characteristics of each minority group on the campus may be challenging, making the effort is important. But what is even more crucial, especially as first steps, is accepting and acknowledging their presence and the particularity of their diversity" (192).

The arguments of Basu and Oda, Oh, and Lee are applicable to the immigration discussions that went on in the 2016 presidential campaigns of Hillary Clinton and Donald Trump and to current issues concerning who can or cannot successfully occupy space in the United States, a question pertinent to the Trump presidency. This discussion of place and space is taken up by Nancy M. West in "Inclusivity Versus Exclusivity: Re-Imagining the Honors College as a Third Place." As West explains, to get to the heart of the matter with our own honors programs, we have to consider the nature of the spaces/places/buildings we occupy and the relationships of those spaces/places/buildings to our "others," whoever they may be (201–04). To occupy a space such that it becomes a place is something that living beings do, as a number of West's sources discuss, in particular Georg Simmel. The "third place" that West advocates for honors programs and colleges is a concept developed by Ray Oldenburg in *The Great Good Place* that refers to a place people are happy to frequent for the community, conversation, and social leveling they find and enjoy there (22–42).

West's reflections on space and place also speak to the worth of the cosmopolitan perspective (see Brown and Cope; Basu; and

Coleman, Childers, Faudree, and Martin), the question of inclusivity and exclusivity in relation to honors recruitment and eligibility (see Jones and Dziesinski, Camarena, and Homrich-Knieling), and to human and social justice issues also commented on by our monograph contributors. Further, West's observation that elitism is often considered undemocratic focuses attention once again on the local and on the importance of conversation and public education writ large. Finally, her observations could be helpful in shedding light on the very question of what is "other" in relation to honors education.

The notion of turning space into place is an idea developed within the honors context by Bernice Braid in terms of mapping out in the field and in the original National Collegiate Honors Council City as Text™ monograph. In the second edition of that monograph, *Place as Text: Approaches to Active Learning*, co-edited by Bernice Braid and Ada Long, in the section titled "Honors Semesters: An Architecture of Active Learning," Braid describes Honors Semesters as "a semester-long immersion into local life that attempts to answer the questions 'How do people who live here transform the space they occupy into the place in which they live?' and, equally important, 'What is it about how I myself observe them that shapes my conclusions?'" (20). These concepts of place, space, and perspective, developed for NCHC by Braid and Long and augmented by the contributors above, as well as many other authors who appear in other NCHC publications, will also be developed and commented upon again in the last four chapters.

In Shawn Alfrey's "Engaging the Bard: Honors, Engagement, and a New Chautauqua," for example, space, place, and context are once again central. Drawing on her own Denver University (DU) course, "Engaging the Bard: DU Students and the Denver Public School's Shakespeare Festival," as a case study, Alfrey's chapter explores how the reflective thinking championed by John Dewey, a facet of critical thinking she sees as central to honors education, can result from the "'situatedness' of service or community-engaged learning . . . " (215; see also Kotinek 285–86).

Alfrey's central illustration is the engagement of the entire Denver educational community with Shakespeare and Denver's annual Shakespeare festival, where the DU students who take her class mentor elementary-age students who perform at the festival. Her chapter points also to what becomes a theme in this monograph: Americans learned to become American; they were taught what it meant through their engaged experience. Alfrey connects this enterprise of engagement to the work of John Dewey, the American champion of experiential learning, and to John Keats' notion of "negative capability" (217–18), a state of mind in some measure the antithesis of the "disorienting dilemma" described by Brown and Cope (Brown and Cope 112). "Negative capability" is the capacity to be open and receptive to, perhaps even revel in, what might be called a state of paradox, or "competing contexts and claims" (Alfrey 218; see also Kotinek 286–87). Alfrey ultimately ties the historic commitment of honors to educational innovation and engagement to the American Chautauqua movement. Thus Alfrey's text speaks, as do those of the rest of our contributors, to the importance of experiential education and the value of community, communication, and civic engagement with regard to diversity and inclusion.

"Occupying Native America" chronicles Lisa L. Coleman's experience devising a Place/City as Text first-year experience for her students and herself at Southeastern Oklahoma State University (SE). Inspired by an NCHC Institute, contributors to *Occupy Honors Education*, and the NCHC monograph *Setting the Table for Diversity*, Coleman determined that "Native America," the slogan on Oklahoma's license plate, would be the site of their exploration, and the story of the Choctaw and Chickasaw tribes, removed to southeastern Oklahoma when it was still Indian Territory, would be its focus. She called the course "Native America: What Does It Mean to Live, Learn, and Work Here?"

Coleman and her co-authors, students Rachel Childers, Samantha Faudree, and Jake Martin, comment on the complicated nature of their relationship with Native America and the degree to which they had to separate themselves from it to see it at all. In particular, the chapter highlights the historical resistance of America and its people, including Coleman and her students, to telling, hearing, and understanding the stories of Native America and its inhabitants. Their chapter also comments on other kinds of resistance in the 2017 news, such as that of the disparate group of water protectors who protested the oil pipeline on the Sioux reservation at Standing Rock.

Drawing on Kant's "Perpetual Peace," and Kwame Anthony Appiah's *Cosmopolitanism: Ethics in a World of Strangers* (texts suggested by the work of Basu and Brown and Cope in this volume), as well as on walkabouts in Oklahoma, Chicago, and later in Ireland, Wales, and London, Faudree and Childers describe the importance of a cultural education and the value of cosmopolitanism. Martin, for his part, discusses the invisibility of Native cultures as well as the tendency of Americans to create versions of Indian cultures that are imaginary at best and stereotypical and demeaning at worst, a perspective shared by Native writer Sherman Alexie.

In addition to Alexie and Martin, the chapter puts a number of Native and non-native thinkers in conversation with one another, including philosopher Martin Heidegger and poet and novelist Linda Hogan, both of whom emphasize "dwelling" and "world" in their writing (see Coleman, Childers, Faudree, and Martin 240–41). The chapter concludes with lessons in perspective for the future from Harper Lee's *To Kill a Mockingbird* and Joy Harjo's *The Woman Who Fell From the Sky: Poems*.

In the provocatively titled penultimate chapter, "What is Truth? Teaching the Constructivist Perspective for Diversity," Jonathan D. Kotinek argues that critical thinking is central to honors education and that to think critically requires the active engagement of perspectives that differ from each other. By comparing and contrasting the philosophical concepts of "positivism" and "constructivism" (281), two approaches to modes of knowing (epistemology) and being (ontology and what counts as "real") (286–87), Kotinek argues for the value of constructivism even in the post-Enlightenment light of the privilege accorded to positivism in terms of how anything can be known or any "fact" be considered "real," "true," or "verifiable" (291–97). Constructivism, Kotinek argues, is an approach to knowing informed by hermeneutics and dialectical reasoning and is useful for qualitative knowledge that values belief and the subjective perspective.

Kotinek draws on James Herbert's "Thinking and Rethinking: The Practical Value of an Honors Education," which was recently reprinted in 2015 as the lead essay in *JNCHC*, where Herbert asserts that "thoughts actually are something that people can have in common" (Herbert 8; qtd. in Kotinek 298). The process of "thinking and rethinking" Herbert describes requires careful listening, restating, and willingness to find common ground (Kotinek 298; see Herbert 5–7). By virtue of Herbert's assertions, Kotinek maintains that teaching constructivist thought provides learners a framework for recognizing their own biases; prepares them to develop their own areas of expertise; and encourages them to seek out, consider, and appreciate the perspectives and expertise of others, thereby becoming "curators of the particular" (297–302; see also Oda, Oh, and Lee 192) and thus contributing to the mission of diversity, equity, and inclusion in honors.

In the final chapter of the monograph, Finnie D. Coleman, who wrote in *Setting the Table for Diversity* on the importance of diversity, equity, and inclusion (see F. Coleman, "The Problem with Diversity: Moving Past the Numbers"), reflects here on the Occupy Movement, a topic introduced by Stoller at the beginning of this volume and touched on as a theme throughout. Coleman's "A Blueprint for Occupying Honors: Activism in Institutional Diversity, Equity, Inclusion, Social Justice, and Academic Excellence" argues that the Occupy Movement began as protests that led to the Arab Spring and the fall of dictators who had been in power in the Middle East for many years. In 2011, the permutation of these protests against economic and cultural oppression surfaced in the United States as an occupation of Wall Street and the 1% that swelled out across the United States, even including higher education and protests against crippling costs and rising student debt. Coleman argues that these same forces were alive in the 2016 presidential race, and I would argue in the Brexit vote in the United Kingdom.

Coleman asserts that honors has much to learn from the kind of activism practiced by the Occupy Movement and encourages all members of the honors community to become activists in the cause of diversity in honors. Coleman notes that while we often think of diversity in terms of numbers and race ("structural diversity") (319–20), diversities other than ethnicity remain hidden by a majority power agenda that cannot be denied (341–43). To name and address this majority power agenda that both works to resist and obfuscate diversity in all its forms, Coleman carefully lays out what he describes as the four pillars of diversity—from the "structural" diversity (320) that he spoke on at length in the earlier monograph, to the "categorical," the "transactional," and the "universal" (320–24). Each of these pillars of diversity supports and promotes "transformational" diversity (324) as diversity's ultimate goal and "manifestation" (Coleman 320). Transformational diversity celebrates the unique contributions each one of us brings to the honors table, thereby making equity, inclusion, and excellence essential to the honors project.

In the last third of his chapter, Coleman takes the questions asked in the original Call for Papers for this monograph and reworks them to reflect on what they suggest and assume: what lies under the questions. By rewording or reformulating these questions altogether, Coleman strikes at the heart of diversity in honors and underscores the point that diversity is not a set of actions only or the things we do; rather, diversity is a state of mind and being that must be actively taken on (Coleman 332–33). Ultimately he proposes a celebratory and respectful occupation of honors in which the blueprint for each program or college will be singular and yet the result of many activists working together in common cause.

The editors urge readers to engage each of these chapters in the order in which they appear, as they do, indeed, speak to one another. The textual conversations they create will amplify the important and truly imperative discussion that we in honors must have on engagement, equity, access, inclusion, and social justice.

REFERENCES

Alfrey, Shawn. "Engaging the Bard: Honors, Engagement, and a New Chautauqua." Coleman, Kotinek, and Oda 215–31.

Appiah, Kwame Anthony. "Cosmopolitan Patriotism." Nussbaum 21–29.

—. *Cosmopolitanism: Ethics in a World of Strangers*. New York: Norton, 2006. Print.

Association of American Colleges and Universities. "Board Statement on Diversity, Equity, and Inclusive Excellence." *About AAC&U*. Association of American Colleges and Universities, 27 June 2013. Web. 29 Aug. 2013.

Basu, Lopamudra. "Cosmopolitanism and New Racial Formations in a Post-9/11 Honors Curriculum on Diversity." Coleman, Kotinek, and Oda 135–76.

Blair, Tony. Interview by Jon Meacham. *Morning Joe*. MSNBC. 28 June 2016. Television.

Braid, Bernice. "Honors Semesters: An Architecture of Active Learning." *Place as Text: Approaches to Active Learning*. 2nd ed. Ed. Bernice Braid and Ada Long. Lincoln: National Collegiate Honors Council, 2010. 19–27. NCHC Monograph Series. Print.

Brown, Stephanie, and Virginia Cope. "Cosmopolitan Courtesy: Preparing for Global Citizenry." Coleman, Kotinek, and Oda 107–34.

Center for Urban Education | USC. "An Overview of the Equity Scorecard™ Process." University of Southern California, 2011. Web. 22 Nov. 2016.

Clinton, Hillary. "Thank you to Supporters." 09 Nov. 2016. Email.

Coleman, Finnie D. "A Blueprint for Occupying Honors: Activism in Institutional Diversity, Equity, Inclusion, Social Justice, and Academic Excellence." Coleman, Kotinek, and Oda 311–52.

—. "The Problem with Diversity: Moving Past the Numbers." *Setting the Table for Diversity*. Ed. Lisa L. Coleman and Jonathan D. Kotinek. Lincoln: National Collegiate Honors Council, 2010. 239–49. NCHC Monograph Series. Print.

Coleman, Lisa L., Rachel Childers, Samantha Faudree, and Jake Martin. "Occupying Native America." Coleman, Kotinek, and Oda 233–79.

Coleman, Lisa L., Jonathan D. Kotinek, and Alan Y. Oda, eds. *Occupy Honors Education*. Lincoln: National Collegiate Honors Council, 2017. NCHC Monograph Series. Print.

Dziesinski, Amberly, Phame Camarena, and Caitlin Homrich-Knieling. "A Privilege for the Privileged? Using Intersectionality to Reframe Honors and Promote Social Responsibility." Coleman, Kotinek, and Oda 81–106.

Giroux, Henry A. *Theory and Resistance in Education: Towards a Pedagogy for the Opposition*. 1983. Westport, CT: Bergin and Garvey, 2001.

Goodwin, Doris Kearns. Interview by Joe Scarborough. *Morning Joe*. MSNBC. 10 Nov. 2016. Television.

Harjo, Joy. *The Woman Who Fell from the Sky: Poems*. New York: Norton, 1994. Print.

Harris, Frank, III, and Estela Mara Bensimon. "The Equity Scorecard: A Collaborative Approach to Assess and Respond to Racial/Ethnic Disparities in Student Outcomes." *New Directions for Student Services* 20 (Winter 2007): 77–84. Print.

Heidegger, Martin. "Building Dwelling Thinking." *Poetry, Language, Thought*. Trans. and Intro. Albert Hofstadter. New York: Harper and Row, Publishers, 1971. 145–61. Print.

Herbert, James. "Thinking and Rethinking: The Practical Value of an Honors Education." Reprinted in "Forum on the Value of Honors." *Journal of the National Collegiate Honors Council: 50th Anniversary Issue* 16.2 (Fall/Winter 2015). Web. 29 Dec. 2016.

INTRODUCTION

Hogan, Linda. *Dwellings: A Spiritual History of the Living World*. New York: Norton, 1995. Print.

Johnson, A. G. *Privilege, Power, and Difference*. Boston: McGraw-Hill, 2006. Print.

Jones, David M. "From Good Intentions to Educational Equity in an Honors Program: Occupying Honors through Inclusive Excellence." Coleman, Kotinek, and Oda 33–79.

Kant, Immanuel. "Perpetual Peace." *Kant: Political Writings*. Second Edition. Ed. Hans Reiss. Trans. H. B. Nisbett. Cambridge: Cambridge University Press, 1991. 93–130. Print.

Kotinek, Jonathan D. "What is Truth? Teaching the Constructivist Perspective for Diversity." Coleman, Kotinek, and Oda 281–309.

Lee, Harper. *To Kill a Mockingbird*. New York: Grand Central Publishing, 1960. Print.

Mezirow, Jack. *Transformative Dimensions of Adult Learning*. San Francisco, CA: Jossey-Bass, 1991, Print.

"Mission and Core Values." Honors Program. Central Michigan University. 16 Nov. 2016. Web.

Nussbaum, Martha C. *For Love of Country?* Ed. Joshua Cohen. Boston: Beacon Press, 2002. Print.

—. "Patriotism and Cosmopolitanism." Nussbaum 3–17.

Oda, Alan Y., Ye Eun (Grace) Oh, and Hyun Seo (Hannah) Lee. "Family Issues of Diversity and Education for Asian American Immigrants: How Universities, Colleges, and Honors Programs Can Understand and Support the 1.5 and Second Generation." Coleman, Kotinek, and Oda 177–98.

Oldenburg, Ray. *The Great Good Place: Cafes, Coffee Shops, Bookstores, Bars, Hair Salons and Other Hangouts at the Heart of a Community*. Philadelphia: Da Capo Press, 1997. Print.

Stoller, Aaron. "Theory and Resistance in Honors Education." Coleman, Kotinek, and Oda 3–32.

xxxii

Suzuki, Bob H. "Revisiting the Model Minority Stereotype: Implications for Student Affairs Practice and Higher Education." *New Directions for Student Services* 97 (2002): 21–32. Print.

West, Nancy M. "Inclusivity Versus Exclusivity: Re-Imagining the Honors College as a Third Place." Coleman, Kotinek, and Oda 199–213.

OCCUPY HONORS EDUCATION

We must see that diversity is much more than a series of practices, processes, and acts: *it is a way of thinking and being that deserves to be conscientiously woven into the fabric of our daily operations and interactions.*

—Finnie D. Coleman
"A Blueprint for Occupying Honors" (332–33)

Theory and Resistance in Honors Education

AARON STOLLER

COLORADO COLLEGE

The cure for the ailments of democracy is more democracy.
—John Dewey (1927/1984) *The Public and Its Problems*

INTRODUCTION

Occupy Wall Street is the name of the political protest that started in New York, New York, in September 2011, and morphed into an ongoing global political action movement. Occupy seeks not simply to shift the content of political discourse but to reframe the way in which American democracy is structured as a more participatory process, representative of the diversity of voices that constitute society. It intends to replace traditional political hierarchies with participatory structures that enable community members to actualize their unique voice and contribute to social change. According to its website, the Occupy Movement has articulated the following Principles of Solidarity underpinning its actions:

- Engaging in direct and transparent participatory democracy;

- Exercising personal and collective responsibility;

- Recognizing individuals' inherent privilege and the influence it has on all interactions;

- Empowering one another against all forms of oppression;

- Redefining how labor is valued;

- The sanctity of individual privacy;

- The belief that education is human right; and

- Making technologies, knowledge, and culture open to all to freely access, create, modify, and distribute. (Principles of Solidarity, 2012)

As a self-described leaderless movement, Occupy challenges citizens to engage in democracy in robust and direct ways, and, as a result, to reconceptualize their relationship with and responsibility to society. It also questions and actively seeks to dismantle the deep influence of corporate capitalism and the neoliberal logic of commodification, self-interest, and profit in democratic life, arguing that these forces are antithetical to the goals of democratic participation, free thought, and both individual and communal justice.

Raising the question of how we might occupy honors education in transformative and revolutionary ways is a complex and challenging question, which includes examining traditional ways of organizing the micro-contexts of education, including classroom design, teacher-student relationships, curricular structures, testing and grading expectations, and course content. It also levies critiques regarding the macro-contexts of education, such as research ethics and the role of higher education in culture. The goal of this essay is to problematize the structures and infrastructures of the traditional university from the standpoint of the Occupy Movement as a way to open up space for re-imagining the functions, purposes, and structures of honors education. I will first describe neoliberalism and its influence on the philosophy and structure of traditional schooling. I then offer a critique of traditional approaches to education and consider the role and impact of honors education in light of this critique.

NEOLIBERAL LOGIC

Any critical analysis of schooling must pay close attention to the logic of the larger social structure in which the university is embedded. In the United States, particularly since the late 1970s and early 1980s, that wider structure has been governed by the logic of neoliberalism, which is an interconnected system of political and economic policies and practices that seeks to establish deregulated, privatized, and competitive markets in all domains of society. It is this very neoliberal paradigm that Occupy attempts to resist, and it is one that is swiftly encroaching on systems of education throughout the United States.

Neoliberalism, the logic of post-industrial, global capitalism, serves as the principle by which all social and political relations are structured. Neoliberal thought is a reconceptualization of classical liberalism, but it differs in important ways. Both classical liberalism and neoliberalism share a number of presuppositions, including a belief that individuals are ultimately self-interested and share a desire to support marketplace economics, a commitment to limiting state regulation, and an emphasis on free trade. Yet, as Mark Olssen and Michael Peters (1995) argue:

> Whereas classical liberalism represents a negative conception of state power . . . neoliberalism has come to represent a positive conception of the state's role in creating the appropriate market. . . . [I]n neoliberalism the state seeks to create an individual that is an enterprising and competitive entrepreneur. (p. 315)

In contrast, classical liberalism relies on a boundary and balance between, on one hand, public institutions and civic life and, on the other, the capital market. This relationship is expressed through the concept of the social contract. Here, the marketplace is viewed as contained within the economic domain of society, as a way of guaranteeing all individuals equal access to the fundamental rights and freedoms of all other dimensions of citizenship.

5

Classical liberalism holds there are dimensions of civic life that exist outside the marketplace to which the market is indebted, as expressed via a tax system supporting the public sphere. Neoliberalism, on the other hand, seeks the elimination of the social contract, as well as the reduction of all dimensions of citizenship to marketplace values via the privatization of the public sphere. According to Erik Malewski and Nathalia Jaramillo (2011), neoliberal thinking results in "a blend of increased privatization, government cutbacks, deregulation of business and industry, and increased international trade" (p. 13). This mindset "underwrites the conditions by which those who utilize entitlement programs . . . are demonized without regard for the subject positions available to them" (p. 13). Here, civic rights, viewed from the logic of profit, become "entitlements" stolen from society by the economically unproductive. Further, in the context of neoliberalism, all non-marketplace activities are not only considered suspect but also as an opportunity for commodification and profit.

The neoliberal paradigm of commodification, self-interest, and profit considers itself to be a value-neutral space that should be imposed on all domains of society. Ironically, while market-based principles are imagined as operating in a "free," self-regulating space, a neoliberal regime relies on the active management of legislative policies by corporate interests. As Graham Burchell (1996) argues, "the rational principle for regulating and limiting governmental activity must be determined by reference to *artificially* arranged and contrived forms of free, *entrepreneurial* and *competitive* conduct of economic-rational individuals" (pp. 23–24, emphasis in original). The goal of such management is to benefit persons and institutions in power through reducing competition, maximizing corporate profit, and reducing worker and citizen empowerment, while offering the illusion of free choice and individual agency. As Olssen and Peters (1995) argue, markets "were traditionally important in classical economics, and formed as an essential part of the welfare state, for regulating private entrepreneurial conduct in the public sphere of society. Under neoliberalism, markets have become a new technology by which control can be effected and performance enhanced, in the public sector" (p. 316). Neoliberalism views the accumulation of capital as both the process and goal of society. As a result, it reduces all human relations and constructions to a simple economic exchange value, believing that economic utility is the sole indicator of value. This reduction has the further, and perhaps more dangerous, effect of reducing democracy to capitalism.

THE NEW MANAGERIALISM

While the market is imagined as a place for the free exchange of ideas that fosters creativity and divergent thinking, neoliberalism depends on administrating society in such a way that the system and its intellectual, economic, and political underpinnings are not subject to critique or interrogation. In this system, creativity, intelligence, and persons serve as capital commodities whose sole purpose is to extend the scope of the institutions they serve. As Olssen and Peters (1995) state further: "the end goals of freedom, choice, consumer sovereignty, competition and individual initiative, as well as those of compliance and obedience, must be constructions of the state acting now in its positive role through the development of the techniques of *auditing, accounting,* and *management*" (pg. 315, emphasis in original). Neoliberalism requires a kind of new managerialism of employees, which, on one hand classifies persons in a system and, on the other hand, constitutes a set of methods that ensures the progress of this social ordering. The common language of such managerial approaches stresses concepts such as outputs, outcomes, accountability, measurement, improvement, and quality. For Olssen and Peters, the core dimensions of this logic include flexibility (i.e., the elimination of the long-term obligation of the employer to the employee), clearly defined objectives (i.e., behavioral outputs that benefit the institution), and a results orientation (i.e., the measurement of worker production for the purposes of profit) (pp. 322–24). The goal of such a system is to limit critical and creative thinking to that which supports the system as a whole. Thus mobility and freedom become domesticated.

As a result of neoliberal policies and practices, the university increasingly serves the interest of the corporate sector and is modeled in its image. As Daniel Saunders (2010) argues, it has transformed the guiding logic of the university from serving the public good through knowledge production and the cultivation of an informed citizenry to a marketplace mentality organized in the same way as a traditional business, with faculty becoming knowledge workers and students becoming knowledge consumers (p. 54).

This business model has created a new pattern of employment, such as fixed-term contracts and new forms of accountability, in which employee products are more clearly defined and frequently reviewed. The emphasis on management, transparency, and accountability signals an overt acknowledgement of one of the central premises of the neoliberal system: a distrust of professional practitioners who might critique or overturn the system. The classical liberal system allowed and, in fact, encouraged professions to become institutional communities that maintained and cultivated field-specific knowledge and were grounded in self-governing systems. By contrast, in the neoliberal system, as Olssen and Peters (2005) maintain, governance is structured between principles and agents, which not only erodes, but actively seeks to prohibit an autonomous space for the emergence of theory, criticism, and new forms of practice (p. 324).

THE KNOWLEDGE ECONOMY

The rise of neoliberal logic emerged concurrently with the shift from an industrial to a knowledge economy. As a result, major research universities are now viewed as an emerging source of capital rather than as institutions serving the public good. According to Peters (2009), state and federal policies increasingly emphasize university practices that develop closer relationships between education and industry (pp. 1–2), and Olssen and Peters (2005) identify this realignment as catalyzed by research produced by think tanks and economic development agencies such as the World Bank and the International Monetary Fund (p. 333).

The World Bank, for example, maintains a "Knowledge for Development" program and describes the four pillars of the knowledge economy as follows:

- An economic and institutional regime that provides incentives for the efficient use of existing and new knowledge and the flourishing of entrepreneurship.

- An educated and skilled population that can create, share, and use knowledge well.

- An efficient innovation system of firms, research centers, universities, think tanks, consultants, and other organizations that can tap into the growing stock of global knowledge, assimilate and adapt it to local needs, and create new technology.

- Information and Communication Technologies (ICT) that can facilitate the effective communication, dissemination, and processing of information. (World Bank, 2013)

To support this process, the World Bank (2013) has developed the Knowledge Economy Index (KEI), which, its website notes, "measures a country's ability to generate, adopt and diffuse knowledge and also whether the environment is conducive for knowledge to be used effectively for economic development." Knowledge exists as a commodity appraised exclusively by its exchange value. Further, knowing and knowledge production become entrepreneurial skills and forms of capital to be deployed only within the context of the free market.

HONORS AS AN OCCUPATION

The role of honors within the context of an increasingly neoliberal university system is complex and paradoxical. From one perspective, honors develops and reinforces neoliberal ideology in the context of the university. Honors students often represent the privileged class on our campuses, who are chosen (at least in part) based on their ability to excel relative to normative academic standards.[1] Honors students are (metaphorically and often literally) the 1%. As part of their experience, they receive special sets of services and privileges not available to the wider campus, which

9

is particularly paradoxical on public campuses whose mission is to serve students equally. Honors might also be viewed simply as a method to incentivize student-consumers attending the university. Here, honors becomes the way in which colleges and universities recruit and retain top candidates, an academic showpiece reduced to the tangible benefits afforded to select candidates at the university. Lastly, if top undergraduate students are placed into narrowly defined research activities without providing a sustained critique of the social, political, and ethical implications of university research, honors might be doing little more than fueling the educational-industrial complex.

Yet, on the other hand, honors may be one of the few spaces left within the context of mass education where students have the opportunity to experience a transformational education. This is possible because honors often stands outside otherwise deeply entrenched university structures as it seeks to maintain a focus on academic discourse, personal engagement with ideas, and the understanding of relationships between and among disciplinary modes of knowing. It also actively cultivates meaningful relationships between faculty and undergraduate students, which is increasingly rare on college campuses. Rather than consisting of a standard curriculum for generic knowers, it often actively works to cultivate critical capacity for unique learners. In this scenario, honors becomes a site of resistance to an otherwise utilitarian education.

The tension facing honors in the university is similar to that of Occupy in culture, yielding a strong family resemblance between the two. Both attempt to create a space for the rich growth of unique individuals within a system increasingly focused on the domestication and exploitation of the talents, skills, and goals of individuals. Both struggle with the paradox of having to resist the neoliberal logic of the system while being forced to operate within that logic in order to survive and thrive.

Occupy does not simply seek to innovate within a pre-determined democratic ordering system but instead to critique and actively resist the platform on which current political action occurs. In doing so, it aims to overturn systems of oppression masked as agents of democracy. Similarly, if honors understands itself as a laboratory that pushes the university forward, then this call to occupy honors education is about much more than simply creating innovative course content; rather, it demands that honors actively re-imagine the entire context and structure of university education. Otherwise, the call for innovation in honors remains domesticated, at the beck and call of the larger, neoliberal ordering of the system.

Occupy has refused the governing logic of the system and instead worked to develop new logics and new modes of participation. According to Peter Cohan (2011), this is why the media has repeatedly struggled to classify Occupy and to understand its critique within the context of the existing social and political order. Occupy has also developed creative ways to use the logic of the system in order to form pockets of resistance and create spaces for freedom and justice. For example, a recent initiative of Occupy is the Rolling Jubilee, in which Occupiers purchase outstanding medical debts traded on the debt market. Typically, agencies that enforce the debt collection purchase these debts at a fraction of the cost, creating a kind of legal bondage of the debtor to the agent. Instead of collecting the debt it purchases, Occupy abolishes it. The goal of the Rolling Jubilee (2013) project is to "liberate debtors at random through a campaign of mutual support, good will, and collective refusal. Debt resistance is just the beginning." As of the writing of this chapter, the Rolling Jubilee has abolished nearly $15,000,000 dollars in debt at a cost of $700,000 dollars.[2] The Rolling Jubilee serves as an example of the kind of creative resistance to which honors should aspire.

Similarly, honors educators should work to resist the neoliberal logic encroaching on education in order to restore scholarly professionalism and to create systems in which rich, democratic education might occur. This aspiration is, in fact, already part of the culture of honors. The "Basic Characteristics of a Fully Developed Honors Program, " listed on the National Collegiate Honors Council (NCHC) website (NCHC 2010) include the notion that honors can and should serve "as a laboratory within which faculty feel welcome to experiment with new subjects, approaches, and pedagogies. When proven successful, such efforts in curriculum and pedagogical development can serve as prototypes for initiatives that can become institutionalized across the campus." Here, honors views itself as a site of innovation and creativity within the context of the wider university. Yet, the call to creative resistance requires not simply innovation within the context of the current system, but actively generating theories of resistance as a community of scholar-practitioners in order to develop practices and participatory structures that seek to encourage, enable, and empower students to take ownership over their education and become critically conscious.

HONORS AS CRITICAL PEDAGOGY

The immediate and perhaps most difficult challenge of this call to occupation is not the lack of human or financial resources in most honors programs but the lack of theoretical resources. University faculty often, though not always, assume that educational and pedagogical practices do not require the same level of theoretical engagement as research within the context of their discipline. Such a perspective, according to Garrison (1995), views pedagogy as a form of "telling" the plain facts in which the teacher plays the role of a conduit between disciplinary knowledge and the awaiting learner (p. 727). To an even greater degree, according to Stoller (2016), administration is viewed as a non-theoretical space where the daily, habitual tasks of management are carried out (pp. 39–46).

Yet if we hope to develop practical forms of resistance and to generate productive forms of participatory inquiry in honors, deeper and more nuanced theories of post-secondary systems are needed. It is the theoretical that allows us to clarify, articulate, and begin to change the practical. In the context of honors, this means that administrators must approach their appointments with the same level of scholarly and theoretical gravity as disciplinary-specific research. Here, the shift from disciplinary scholar to honors administrator requires a shift in scholarly activities.

Honors literature and conference proceedings, like most administrative networks, skew heavily toward presenting practical applications divorced from theoretical grounds. The reasons why particular practices work in a given context, or how those practices can be reconstructed for use on divergent campuses, remain submerged. It is only through thoughtful theoretical analysis that we will be able to discriminate between "best practices" and those that are simply the most used. It is also the only way to develop a language of resistance to the neoliberal structures that are both infiltrating post-secondary systems and antithetical to the goals of deep education. Here, I offer critical pedagogy as one potential entry point for this type of scholarly theorizing and engagement.

Critical pedagogy emerges from within the larger body of critical theory literature. Critical theory attempts not simply to describe the patterns, norms, and ordering principles of societies and social institutions but to go beyond the descriptive to the normative. It attempts not simply to describe society but to critique its structures as a vehicle toward citizen empowerment and social justice. As Henry Giroux (1997) argues, critical pedagogies "are not simply concerned with how teachers and students view knowledge; they are also concerned with the mechanisms of social control and how these mechanisms function to legitimate the beliefs and values underlying wider society institutional arrangements" (p. 4). They seek not simply to transmit what is known about the world but to empower the creative capacities of students in such a way that every person has an equal opportunity to be free.

Some core assumptions that might generally be held by critical theorists include the beliefs that:

- patterns of thought and disciplinary paradigms, including those of the natural sciences, are governed by power relations, that themselves are historically contingent;

- facts can never be isolated from values; therefore there is no such thing as value-neutral data;

- language is central to the formation of subjectivity; therefore linguistic and theoretical resources shape consciousness;

- in any system particular groups are privileged over others, and oppression is most dangerous when oppressed groups uncritically accept their status as a form of the natural ordering of society;

- traditional forms of research often reproduce or reinforce systems of oppression or unjust societies.

From a critical theoretical perspective, the university has been seduced and co-opted by a kind of technocratic and utilitarian rationality, devoid of concern for the human condition, and we have only ourselves to blame. We have participated in and reproduced the process through which, as Giroux (1997) argues, the notion of progress "was stripped of its concern with ameliorating the human condition and became applicable only to the realm of material and technical growth. What was once considered humanly possible, a question involving values and human ends, was now reduced to the issue of what was technically possible" (p. 8).

Unless we intervene, this logic will continue to erode our institutions as rich, democratic spaces and will eventually deprofessionalize our fields, transforming the university into a domesticated resource serving an economic production function.[3]

Critical pedagogy becomes an approach to education that analyzes and actively challenges systems of domination, including empowering students to become critically conscious about the culturally and historically conditioned beliefs, practices, and systems that oppress and restrict their thoughts, choices, and actions. Critical pedagogy was first articulated by Paulo Freire in his 1970 text *Pedagogy of the Oppressed*, where he argued that traditional forms of schooling are based on the idea that pedagogy is simply a transmission of information (i.e., positive, objective facts) between teacher and learner. While this mode of pedagogy has traditionally been viewed as a value-neutral act, Freire argues otherwise. Freire labels traditional pedagogical thinking as the *banking system* of education.

In the banking environment, "knowns" (e.g., data, theories, skills) are assumed to be separate, autonomous, and discrete from the knower. The learner is positioned as a consumer of context-free and objective factoids, and emphasis is placed on the ability of the learner to reproduce those factoids as the sole marker of educational success. Reciprocally, teachers perceived as data managers are expected to deliver educational content in the most efficient manner possible. In this model, Freire (1970/2000) argues:

> Education thus becomes an act of depositing, in which students are the depositories and the teacher is the depositor. Instead of communicating, the teacher issues communiqués and makes deposits which the students patiently receive, memorize, and repeat. This is the "banking" concept of education, in which the scope of action allowed to the students extends only so far as receiving, filing, and storing the deposits. (p. 72)

In the banking model, learning is defined exclusively as behavior modification for an external reviewer, such as that expressed by the assessment movement in post-secondary education in which faculty members are required to design their classes around predetermined "learning outcomes."[4]

Establishing the goals of learning at the outset sets up a type of instructional teleology in which Shirley Grundy (1987) argues "the product will conform to the *eidos* (that is, the intentions or ideas) expressed in the original objectives" (p. 12). The result is a teaching environment free of experimental inquiry, risk, failure, and creativity, but which produces the behavior modifications demanded by outside administrators, legislators, and corporate stakeholders. Here, the teacher-student relationship is viewed as top-down and one-directional. Knowledge is viewed as a collection of dislocated facts, information, or skills that are "deposited" by the expert on the ignorant student.[5]

In the banking model, as David Granger (2003) argues, "the inherently uncertain process of teaching and learning, or interacting with concrete human beings" becomes "carefully controlled artificial conditions" in which "individual learning, discrete facts, standards, high-stakes paper-and-pencil tests, and other paraphernalia of positivism hold sway" (p. 151). The aim of the banking model, then, has nothing to do with critical awareness, creative thinking, exploration, or democratic citizenship but, instead, with the socialization of citizen-workers. This is because, as Giroux (1983/2001) maintains, "in the guise of objectivity and neutrality, [knowledge] is fixed and unchanging in the sense that its form, structure, and underlying normative assumptions appear to be universalized beyond the realm of historical contingency or critical analysis" (p. 178). Students come to see the world and knowledge as something to be digested in obedience to a teacher for whom they are made to perform. The danger, according to Freire (1970/2000), is that "in the last analysis, it is the people themselves who are filed away through lack of creativity, transformation, and knowledge" (p. 72). The banking model is not only incorrect in its thinking about teaching and learning, but also—and more importantly—actually harms students who are alienated from their own creative capacities (i.e., dehumanized) in the very process of schooling.

Here it is important to clarify that this is not a critique of the traditional classroom lecture, although that pedagogical method often embodies the problems of the banking model education. In fact, it is not a critique of any particular pedagogical method, but instead it is a critique of the *guiding logic* of the system that produces pedagogical methods. The issue, then, is with a view of "knowledge" as a body of static data-sets and knowing as a kind of mental state that allows for the reproduction of those facts. It is a problem both with the disconnection of knowledge from inquiry and knowing from embodied action. Dewey (1916/1980) identifies the consequences of this paradigm:

> "Knowledge," in the sense of information, means the working capital, the indispensable resources, of further inquiry; of finding out, or learning, more things. Frequently it is treated as an end in itself, and then the goal becomes to heap it up and display it when called for. This static, cold-storage ideal of knowledge is inimical to educative development. It not only lets occasions for thinking go unused, but it swamps thinking. No one could construct a house on ground cluttered with miscellaneous junk. Pupils who have

16

stored their "minds" with all kinds of material which they have never put to intellectual uses are sure to be hampered when they try to think. They have no practice in selecting what is appropriate, and no criterion to go by; everything is on the same dead static level. (p. 165)

In most traditional schooling environments, learning is understood as a generic act of cognition having nothing to do with inquiry, transformation, or change because knowledge is viewed as a reified object, universally available to all learners regardless of their contexts, goals, or capacities. Thus the end-goal of education becomes knowledge (e.g., information, data) rather than transformation emerging from communal action.

As a critique of pedagogical *logic* rather than *method,* it is important to note that many (though not all) of the experiential and experimental pedagogies already being cultivated in honors resist what Freire describes as banking-style education. The problem is that without a clearly articulated theoretical ground, faculty deploying those pedagogies do not always have a critical language to guide their methodological decision-making. It is also possible (and perhaps likely) that even pedagogically innovative honors faculty might actually be participating in what Freire would describe as acts of oppression if they view pedagogy as an act of telling rather than co-creation.

While the banking system creates persons who might hold an arbitrary body of skills or knowledge, as Freire (1970/2000) argues, those persons are "alienated like the slave in the Hegelian dialectic" (p. 72). This result happens because freedom, in the neoliberal sense, is a form of self-interest. It is the freedom *not* to participate, or *not* to be invested in the concerns of the community. Freire rejected this notion of freedom, instead arguing that true freedom is understanding and having the capacity to overcome the terms of one's own subjectification. Freedom is coming to critical consciousness about how the system restricts, disempowers, and directs the flow of persons and knowledge. Freedom is also working to change the system so that all persons might have the capacity to be free. Freedom is, therefore, both a form of and the result of political action.

17

Far from being value-neutral, Freire understands the banking system as a form of ideology and oppression. The banking model virtually eliminates the dialogue and relationality necessary for developing the critical consciousness that would allow students and teachers to become aware of the hegemonic structures of domination. The banking model does not simply keep students from becoming aware of hegemony, it actively reinforces systems of domination and oppression.

Freire believes that the banking system does not simply trap students, but it also entangles teachers because it erases the dialectical relationality that leads to critical consciousness and continued growth for students and teachers alike. To the contrary, as Freire (1970/2000) argues, teachers' "efforts must coincide with those of the students to engage in critical thinking and the quest for mutual humanization. . . . To achieve this, they must be partners of the students in their relations with them" (p. 75). This dialogical encounter as pedagogy goes far to erase the system of power on which traditional schooling is based and, in turn, creates a system based on love, because, as Freire (1970/2000) argues, "love is an act of courage, not of fear, love is commitment to others. No matter where the oppressed are found, the act of love is commitment to their cause—the cause of liberation" (p. 89).

As Giroux (1983/2001) argues, school should be a "site for creating a critical discourse around the forms a democratic society might take and the socioeconomic forces that might prevent such forms from emerging" (p. 116). Therefore, critical pedagogy must "connect learning to social change, scholarship to commitment, and classroom knowledge to public life" (p. 117). Giroux calls, then, for a pedagogy for the opposition:

> Rather than celebrating objectivity and consensus, teachers must place the notions of critique and conflict at the center of their pedagogical models. Within such a perspective, greater possibilities exist for developing an understanding of the role power plays in defining and distributing the knowledge and social relationships that mediate the school and classroom experience. Critique must become a vital

pedagogical tool not only because it breaks through the mystifications and distortions that "silently" work behind the labels and routines of school practice, but also because it models a form of resistance and oppositional pedagogy. (p. 62)

Giroux calls for schools in which students resist increasingly neo-liberal policies and practices that support the view that schools are businesses designed to create skilled workers; he urges that schools and teachers instead embrace a model of critical consciousness raising.

PRIMARY CONCERNS FOR THE CRITICAL PEDAGOGUE

In the remainder of this chapter, I will attempt to articulate some of the primary concerns for the critical pedagogue. Here I am not restricting the concept of pedagogy simply to the limited venue of the formal classroom space. Instead, pedagogical thinking should be the organizing principle of the entire educational paradigm, particularly within the context of honors education. Critical pedagogy extends well beyond the classroom environment and becomes a lens through which all educational activity, including administrative and co-curricular activity, can be viewed. In this final section, I outline these concerns in six parts:

- Part 1, **Power/Knowledge**, articulates how honors must be sensitive to and, as much as possible, expose the powerladenness of knowledge and knowing.

- Part 2, **The Agency of Learners**, argues that in order for students to emerge as democratically engaged citizens, they must be given opportunities to take active, engaged, and risk-filled stances within their own educative process.

- Part 3, **Academic and Administrative Freedom**, claims that honors faculty must demand forms of educational freedom in all domains of their practice.

19

- Part 4, **Participatory Structures and Pedagogies**, argues that honors must strive for educational environments and shared decision-making processes that include a diversity of voices and standpoints.

- Part 5, **Freedom through Justice**, claims that the working out of human freedom can only be accomplished through tying inquiry and educative practice to a striving for social and environmental justice.

- Part 6, **Pedagogy as a Form of Friendship**, argues that this kind of applicability to human need can only be held as a value within an environment that encourages the diverse expression of experience grounded in meaningful relationships.

PART 1: POWER/KNOWLEDGE

Critical pedagogy is sensitive to the relationship between power and knowledge. It also actively works to dismantle systems of oppression created by the relationship between the two. For critical theorists, the creation of a disinterested expert culture, including the hierarchy of expertise, can quickly become antithetical to the goals of deep democracy and critical consciousness. Further, the creation of such a culture is intertwined with the emergence of the modern research university and the nature of increasingly narrow disciplinary cultures.[6]

Yet the powerladeness of knowledge is rarely, if ever, made overt within the context of the classroom or within university hierarchy and policymaking, in part because it would disrupt the managerial culture of the university. Therefore, we must find ways to center educational practice (e.g., pedagogy, the co-curriculum, and administrative decision-making) on creating democratically engaged environments that include shared decision-making and problem-based practices that expose systems of oppression embedded in and supported by university practices. We must also investigate and work to change university practices that create and sustain systems of domination and oppression. For example, we must place questions of justice at the center of our university

20

discourse: Are all university employees paid a living wage? Does university research ultimately benefit the democratic public rather than corporate or private interests? Are university holdings, including its endowment and pensions, invested in areas committed to ethical, sustainable practices? Is the campus representative and supportive of diverse groups and practices?

In the context of pedagogical practice, knowledge must always be connected to form larger sets of social, cultural, ethical, and political contexts. Constructing democratic pedagogies in this way requires that teachers include students in the process of knowledge creation in order to develop their own creative capacities and expose students to the cultural and social implications of knowledge, requiring them both to participate as *stance takers* within that process.

PART 2: THE AGENCY OF LEARNERS

The question of agency is a complex concern that draws together the role of the teacher, the capacities of learners, and the place of democracy as an organizing principle within education.

Critical pedagogy challenges the banking view that the role of students is to be passive consumers and that education is something enacted upon them. To the contrary, developing a participatory pedagogy necessitates that all participants must be empowered to have a voice and an active role in all decisions that affect them. This requires that students be given opportunities to take stances within their own educative process, including on things like course and curriculum development, participatory research opportunities, and support and credit for activities outside the boundaries of formal systems. It is important here to note that giving students agency is not the same thing as allowing them to dictate the terms of their education (i.e., viewing them as educational consumers), but instead it means democratizing pedagogical spaces in ways that emphasize dialogue, debate, and reconstruction.

This charge calls into question the role of the teacher, viewing teachers and learners as participating within and operating in the same spectrum of creative inquiry. Rather than the distinct concepts

21

of "teacher" and "learner," it would be better to imagine students as "novice learners" and faculty as "master learners." This redistribution of power is a two-way street, and, as Freire (1970/2000) argues, "It is essential for the oppressed to realize that when they accept the struggle for humanization they also accept, from that moment, their total responsibility for their struggle" (p. 68). In this way, giving students agency is more closely related to empowered mentorship through shared struggle.

This charge also is a call toward developing deeper and more intentional communities of inquiry at the university rather than viewing faculty and student life as ontologically separate spaces. Instead, university life should be centered on common problems and emerge through communal forms of inquiry. Yet, in order for these communal forms of inquiry to take place, tenure and promotion processes, pedagogies, and departments must be reimagined from competitive to cooperative structures.

PART 3: ACADEMIC AND ADMINISTRATIVE FREEDOM

The powerladenness of knowing and knowledge also requires that, both in terms of its administrative and research activities, honors educators resist discourses and practices that serve the institutional structures that construct and reinforce systems of oppression. This resistance requires that honors educators call for academic freedom in ways that reach beyond the increasingly narrow lines drawn by neoliberal policies that result in a domesticated form of academic freedom.[7]

Without this call for academic freedom, developing participatory educational structures is not possible. Practices of academic freedom might then include, but are not limited to, developing active and creative forms of resistance to the contemporary assessment movement, which is grounded in neoliberal social ordering. Assessment demands that educational systems justify their existence in the terms of a reductionist, economic input-output model, which is antithetical to the goals of participatory and inquiry-based pedagogies. Like the model of the Rolling Jubilee, a new assessment model might take the form of revisioning simplistic outcomes-based assessment as a form of action research in order to fuse the research and practice-based missions embedded in most honors programs.[8]

Administrative freedom also means actively developing the scholar-practitioner model for honors faculty and staff. All faculty and staff positions in honors should embody the life of the mind in both scope and practice through an equal balance of innovative and ongoing teaching, continual research and publication, and the creative administration of educational environments.

PART 4: PARTICIPATORY STRUCTURES AND PEDAGOGIES

For critical pedagogues, schools should be fundamentally democratic spheres. In order for school to serve the interests of a pluralistic, participatory democracy, we must first acknowledge, as Giroux (1997) does, that "schools are 'reproductive' in that they provide different classes and social groups with forms of knowledge, skills, and culture that not only legitimate the dominant culture but also track students into a labor force differentiated by gender, racial, and class considerations" (p. 119). Secondly, we must actively work to create forms of consciousness raising and democratic practices within its structures, including both pedagogical and administrative spaces.

In doing so, we must strive for educational environments and decision-making processes that are heterogeneous. Heterogeneity is a concept that attempts to reach beyond the contemporary notion of "diversity," which is often conceptualized as simple exposure to difference. (For additional definitions of diversity, see F. Coleman in this volume, pp. 320–24.) Heterogeneity, on the other hand, is a much richer and more difficult concept. It attempts to embed difference within communities of knowers, theories of understanding, and *processes of* knowledge creation and decision-making. It is not just something discussed as a form of enrichment, but something that is practiced in teaching and research activities. It also demands that exposure to difference must include discussions of structured inequality, power, and oppression, as well as engaged, justice-seeking action on our campuses and in our communities.

Heterogeneity is a primary constituting element of authentic democratic life. Helen Longino (1994) writes that we must resist a world where "difference must be ordered, one type chosen as the standard and all others seen as failed or incomplete versions" (p. 447). Instead, we must view difference as fertile ground. In this way, as Longino (1994) writes, heterogeneity "permits equal standing for different types, and mandates investigation of the details of such difference" (p. 477). Heterogeneity is also an overt rejection of standardized and managerial forms of schooling that force unique persons into generic curricula.

Charlene Haddock Seigfried (1993) sees heterogeneity as striving for a kind of "principled pluralism" (p. 2). For John Dewey (1925/1981) the view that knowledge is stable and universal

> demands a rationalistic temperament leading to a fixed and dogmatic attitude. Pluralism, on the other hand, leaves room for contingence, liberty, novelty, and gives complete liberty of action to the empirical method, which can be indefinitely extended. It accepts unity where it finds it, but it does not attempt to force the vast diversity of events and things into a single rational mold. (p. 8)

In order to create generative educational environments, this kind of balance, as much as possible, must be maintained and bring forward, rather than silence, the deep differences already embedded in classrooms and the wider university community.

PART 5: FREEDOM THROUGH JUSTICE

For critical theory, education is ultimately about humanization, the construction of critical consciousness, and the freedom of persons. Here, freedom is neither one's buying power nor an endowed capability located at the core of the individual, but freedom is something for which one strives through an ongoing process of construction and reconstruction of the self and the world. Freedom is the lifelong practice of education. Freire (1970/2000) writes:

> One of the gravest obstacles to the achievement of liberation is that oppressive reality absorbs those within it and thereby acts to submerge human beings' consciousness. Functionally, oppression is domesticating. To no longer be prey to its force, one must emerge from it and turn upon it. This can be done only by means of the praxis: reflection and action upon the world in order to transform it. (p. 51)

Education must be grounded in reflective, intelligent action in the world. This is the only way for knowledge to yield a transformation. To know something is both to have transformed it and to be transformed by it in the process. The implication is that human freedom can only be accomplished through tying inquiry and educative practice to striving for social and environmental justice. In order to move toward critical forms of education, pedagogies and educational practices must emerge out of and demonstrate applicability to human and environmental need.

Just as Dewey understood knowledge as *emerging from* the lived experiences of human beings in the world, he also believed that whenever any theory was separated from the entrenched realities of lived experience, it fundamentally misunderstood the problem on which it is focused. Knowledge is, then, rooted in the lived experience of human beings transacting in their environment. It is also distributed across multiple ways of understanding and making meaning. This diversity becomes best actualized in a democratic system.

PART 6: PEDAGOGY AS A FORM OF FRIENDSHIP

Applicability to human need can only be held as a value within a pedagogical environment that encourages the diverse expression of experience grounded in meaningful relationships. This includes going beyond advising students or administrating courses and toward developing authentic mentoring relationships among students, faculty, and staff, as well as creating environments and cultures where relationships can be fostered in meaningful ways.

It was Dewey's contention that meaning, knowing, and, in fact, being were all intersubjective concepts that take shape within the context of a community of inquiry. This kind of relational structure is not simply cognitive, it is intuitive, emotional, and felt. It is grounded not simply in justice viewed as the reduction or redistribution of power but also constituted by authentic friendship.

Here, we must ask ourselves if the temporal and physical architectures of our universities support the cultivation of truly authentic friendships and mentoring relationships. I contend that neoliberalism demands overly structured and managed forms of interaction among students, faculty, and administrators, which are now so ubiquitous in most universities they have become normalized. Reciprocally, the rich, serendipitous moments of democratic relationship may only rarely occur. More often, faculty and student interactions must be organized via programming models and assessed to ensure they occur. In this way, these interactions may become mechanical, stale, and lifeless.

Critical pedagogy argues that we must work to cultivate organic friendships via the construction of spaces where serendipitous relationships may occur. This first requires the creation of public spaces (e.g., coffee houses, reading rooms) where such interactions might take place. (See West in this volume pp. 199–213.) It also requires the reconceptualization of faculty and staff time so that time spent dialoguing with students is again viewed as a meaningful and necessary part of our roles. Most importantly, meaningful friendships can only occur in an educative culture grounded in true curiosity and empowered learning, where dialogue becomes a vehicle to student growth. In the strictly neoliberal university, which is centered on academic performance, time to degree, and what it labels "student success," this kind of interaction has no place. Yet, for honors, it should be the very process and goal of education.

CONCLUSION

To occupy honors education is to practice and theorize in the manner of the Occupy Movement itself. Neoliberalism as an ideology and cultural movement is swiftly encroaching on American universities, constricting and commodifying the educational process of students and the knowledge-building and teaching activities of university faculty. Thus a parallel exists between the work of Occupy in culture and the work of honors in the university. If honors education hopes to critique, resist, and ultimately overturn neoliberal forces, it must develop a theoretical language to ground its practice. Critical pedagogy, as both a theory and method, begins this task through the six central concerns of critical pedagogues outlined above.

Neoliberalism is not a passing educational fad. It will ultimately dismantle the deeply democratic and human elements of higher education if we, as faculty, do not see ourselves as having a responsibility to resist its presence in our institutions and culture. This is not a naïve attempt to reclaim an imagined and idealized past in university education but a call for faculty to understand their responsibility, in a very concrete way, to the campuses and institutions in which they are embedded. It is a call to construct new forms of education that move beyond cold knowing to empathy, compassion, mutual understanding, freedom, and justice.

NOTES

[1]According to Grissmer (2000), the effectiveness of standardized tests like the SAT for predicting college aptitude or intellectual ability has repeatedly been questioned (p. 224). Yet, honors programs continue to rely on such scores as a valid method of screening applicants, often not allowing students who rank below pre-determined numerical scores to apply. For an alternative view on admissions criteria, see Jones in this volume, pp. 33–79. For more on "honors privilege," see Dziesinski, Camarena, and Homrich-Knieling in this volume, pp. 81–106.

[2]For the most current figures, see <http://rollingjubilee.org>.

[3]This logic is manifested, for example, in the debate about the purpose and viability of the humanities within the university (see American Academy of Arts and Sciences, *The Heart of the Matter*, 2013). In particular, the humanities are often forced to articulate

themselves in terms of economic utility in order to prove their value, rather than being accepted as a necessary part of a healthy democracy. Another example can be found in the increased use of learning outcomes and assessment measures designed to guarantee to shareholders (i.e., legislators, outside administrators, business leaders, parents, students) a return on investment.

[4]With limited space available in this essay, I am regrettably unable to offer a full critique of the destructive effects of learning outcomes on students and student learning. For more on the issue of learning outcomes, I refer readers to Bennett and Brady, 2012; Hussey and Smith, 2002; Hussey and Smith, 2003; Rees, 2004.

[5]One might argue that constructivist approaches to education require the very thing Freire critiques: a solid factual "base" on which students can develop an understanding of a subject or phenomenon. Freire and John Dewey (referenced below) offer a view of learning that provides an alternative to the traditional constructivist paradigms that dominate mainstream views on and approaches to education and pedagogy. Freire's epistemology questions the power structures that establish and facilitate "correct" knowledge or growth. Freire also argues one cannot truly know until a literal, material praxis (action-reflection) in culture has occurred. For a deeper articulation of Freire's epistemology, see Au, 2007.

From a Deweyan perspective, constructivist paradigms are grounded in cognitive psychological models that retain troubling elements of philosophical foundationalism. Dewey's most important articulation of the difference between his own theory and that of traditional strands in cognitive and behavioral psychology is outlined in his essay "The Reflex Arc Concept In Psychology" (Dewey, 1897/1972). For an extended discussion on the differences between Dewey's epistemology and contemporary constructivist paradigms, please refer to Garrison, 1995; Phillips, 1995; and Vanderstraeten, 2002.

[6]From a critical theoretical perspective, a potential danger to democracy presented by the emergence of the academy and its specialized disciplines is the separation of knowledge from the

public sphere. This separation has the potential to present knowledge and knowing as a form of activity reserved for an elite class. To the contrary, Judith Green (1999) argues that philosophy, for example, should be understood not as a "narrowly specialized academic discipline, but rather [as] *a set of public tasks* undertaken for the transformative purpose of *human liberation and well-being* by those who share *an overlapping set of skills and techniques*" (p. 218, emphasis in original).

[7]What I mean by "increasingly narrow lines" is the narrowing scope of the category of academic freedom itself. The notion of "academic freedom" is generally allowable for social, cultural, and political critique published inside academic journals because it is a sort of quasi-private domain that does not generally impact public activity. Yet, that same notion of academic freedom is not extended in other, more public domains. This narrowing of freedom includes the restriction of public scholarship activities (see Moxley, 2013). In this way, the notion of "academic freedom" becomes domesticated because it does not apply equally to all domains of scholarly activity, particularly the public sphere. Instead, scholars are allowed to engage critically so long as those critiques do not disrupt the public sphere, a domain that includes the activities and choices of the academy itself.

[8]Action research is a participatory form of community-based research that intends to yield more direct change than traditional forms of research and scholarship. In this way, it is situated somewhere between critical theory and academic extension. It intends both to critique structures and find solutions to problematic community-based situations.

REFERENCES

American Academy of Arts and Sciences. (2013). *The heart of the matter: The humanities and social sciences for a vibrant, competitive, and secure nation.* Retrieved from <http://www.humanitiescommission.org/_pdf/hss_report.pdf>

Au, W. (2007). Epistemology of the oppressed: The dialectics of Paulo Freire's theory of knowledge. *Journal for Critical Education Policy Studies, 5*(2). <http://www.jceps.com/?pageID=articleandarticleID=100>

Bennett, M., and Brady, J. (2012). A radical critique of the learning outcomes assessment movement. *Radical Teacher, 94*(1), 34–47.

Burchell, G. (1996). Liberal government and techniques of the self. In Barry, A., Osborne, T., and Rose, N. (Eds.), *Foucault and political reason.* (pp. 19–36). Chicago: University of Chicago Press.

Cohan, P. (2011, October 11). What is Occupy Wall Street? *Forbes.* Retrieved from <http://www.forbes.com/sites/peterco han/2011/10/10/what-is-occupy-wall-street>

Dewey, J. (1972). The reflex arc concept in psychology. In J. A. Boydston (Ed.), *John Dewey: The Early Works, 1882–1898*, Vol. 5 (pp. 96–109). Carbondale: Southern Illinois University Press (Original work published in 1896).

Dewey, J. (1980). Logical objects. In J. A. Boydston (Ed.), *John Dewey: The Middle Works, 1899–1924*, Vol. 10 (pp. 89–97). Carbondale: Southern Illinois University Press (Original work published in 1916).

Dewey, J. (1981). *Experience and nature.* In J. A. Boydston (Ed.), *John Dewey: The Later Works, 1925–1953*, Vol. 1, (pp. 1–326). Carbondale: Southern Illinois University Press (Original work published in 1925).

Dewey, J. (1984). *The Public and its Problems.* In J. A. Boydston (Ed.), *John Dewey: The Later Works, 1925–1953*, Vol. 2, (pp. 235–372). Carbondale: Southern Illinois University Press (Original work published in 1927).

Freire, P. (2000). *Pedagogy of the oppressed.* New York, NY: Continuum International Publications Group. (Original work published 1970).

Garrison, J. (1995). Deweyan pragmatism and the epistemology of contemporary social constructivism. *American Educational Research Journal, 32*(4), 716–40.

Giroux, H. (1997). *Pedagogy and the politics of hope: theory, culture, and schooling.* Boulder: Westview Press.

Giroux, H. (2001). *Theory and resistance in education: Towards a pedagogy for the opposition.* Westport, CT: Bergin and Garvey. (Original work published in 1983).

Granger, D. (2003). Positivism, skepticism, and the attractions of "paltry empiricism": Stanley Cavell and the current standards movement in education. *Philosophy of Education Archive,* 146–54.

Green, J. M. (1999). *Deep democracy: Community, diversity, and transformation.* Lanham, MD: Rowman and Littlefield Publishers.

Grissmer, D. W. (2000). The continuing use and misuse of SAT scores. *Psychology, Public Policy, and Law, 6*(1), 223.

Grundy, S. (1987). *Curriculum: Product or praxis?* London: Falmer Press.

Hussey, T., and Smith, P. (2002). The trouble with learning outcomes. *Active learning in higher education, 3*(3), 220–33.

Hussey, T., and Smith, P. (2003). The uses of learning outcomes. *Teaching in Higher Education, 8*(3), 357–68.

Longino, H. E. (1994). In search of feminist epistemology. *The Monist, 77*(4), 472–85.

Malewski, E., and Jaramillo, N. (Eds.). (2011). *Epistemologies of ignorance in education.* Charlotte, NC: Information Age Publishing, Inc.

Moxley, T. (2013, August 30). Virginia Tech professor's 'troops' remark stirs up anger. *Roanoke Times.* Retrieved from <http://www.roanoke.com/news/education/2187706-12/virginia-tech-professors-troops-remark-stirs-up-anger.html>

National Collegiate Honors Council. (2010). Basic characteristics of a fully developed honors program. Retrieved from
<http://nchchonors.org/faculty-directors/basic-characteris
tics-of-a-fully-developed-honors-program>

Olssen, M., and Peters, M. (2005). Neoliberalism, higher education
and the knowledge economy: From the free market to knowledge capitalism. *Journal of Education Policy*, *20*(3), 313–45.

Peters, M. (2009). National education policy constructions of the
'knowledge economy': Towards a critique. *The Journal of Educational Enquiry*, *2*(1), 1–22.

Phillips, D. C. (1995). The good, the bad, and the ugly: The many
faces of constructivism. *Educational Researcher*, *24*(7), 5–12.

Principles of Solidarity. (2012). Retrieved from <http://www.nycga.
net/resources/documents/principles-of-solidarity>

Rees, C. (2004). The problem with outcomes-based curricula in
medical education: Insights from educational theory. *Medical
Education*, *38*(6), 593–98.

Rolling Jubilee. (2013). Retrieved from <http://rollingjubilee.org>

Saunders, D. (2010). Neoliberal ideology and public higher education in the United States. *Journal for Critical Education Policy
Studies*, *8*(1), 41–77.

Seigfried, C. H. (1993). Shared communities of interest: Feminism
and pragmatism. *Hypatia*, *8*(2), 1–14.

Stoller, A. (2016). The theory gap in higher education. *Research in
Education*, *96*(1), 39–45.

Vanderstraeten, R. (2002). Dewey's transactional constructivism.
Journal of Philosophy of Education, *36*(2), 233–46.

World Bank. (2013). *Knowledge for Development (K4D) FAQ*.
Retrieved July 13, 2013 from <http://goo.gl/Sm8ZB>

From Good Intentions to Educational Equity in an Honors Program: Occupying Honors through Inclusive Excellence

DAVID M. JONES

UNIVERSITY OF WISCONSIN AT EAU CLAIRE

PART I: OCCUPYING HONORS

Three News Items

News Item 1: March 7, 2014: The "I, Too, Am Harvard" project was launched on Tumblr by Kimiko Matsuda-Lawrence, featuring students at Harvard University determined to speak out against the clear and present realities of institutional racism. For the project, Harvard students appear in photographs holding dry erase boards with written statements that illustrate racial discrimination they have encountered on and off the nation's most prestigious campus. The following dialogic statements appear in individual photos:

"'I don't see color . . .' Does that mean you don't see Me?"

"'You're lucky to be black . . . so easy to get into college.' Childhood friend."

"Surprise! My application to Harvard wasn't just a picture of my face." (*I, Too, Am Harvard*)

The "I, Too" project demonstrates the reality that even on a selective and highly resourced university campus, deeply embedded assumptions about racial identity, intelligence, and earned merit persist and greatly affect the quality of students' educational experience.

I see an instructive parallel between the challenges being confronted at Harvard and challenges we face in our honors enterprise. As Harvard symbolizes high attainment across United States higher education, honors symbolizes high attainment at individual United States campuses. Are diverse student populations served equitably in these high-value settings?

News Item 2: On March 1, 2014, Suzanne Mettler published an editorial in the *The New York Times* highlighting class divides within the United States system of higher education. Declining public support for colleges and universities, escalating costs of attendance, shrinking financial aid resources, unequal access to selective institutions, overrepresentation of lower-income students at for-profit universities—all of these factors contribute to what Mettler describes as "a caste system, separate and unequal for students with different family incomes" (Mettler). To illustrate economic barriers that correspond to financial status, Mettler describes the significant increases in college costs at public universities in recent decades. About 75% of the nation's students attend public universities, which are still widely regarded as the best means of improving social mobility:

> These institutions still offer the best bargain around, yet even there, tuition increases have bred inequality. For those from the richest fifth, the annual cost of attending a public four-year college has inched up from 6 percent of family income in 1971 to 9 percent in 2011. For everyone else, the

change is formidable. For those in the poorest fifth, costs at State U have skyrocketed from 42 percent of family income to 114 percent. (Mettler)

Honors programs at public universities have often served as a cost-effective way for underserved first-generation students to gain the benefits of high-impact pedagogies such as undergraduate research, smaller class sizes, and the like. Mettler serves as a professor at Cornell, a private college with twice the undergraduate enrollment of the University of Wisconsin at Eau Claire (UWEC), where I work, but according to Bill Steele of the *Cornell Chronicle*, Cornell has an endowment 136 times larger than UWEC's; therefore, at a comprehensive public campus like ours, honors is particularly important to students who would like extraordinary preparation for professional life, graduate studies, and citizenship. And yet, as I reflect on Mettler's essay and on the photo project by Harvard students of color, I am left again to wonder: how are underserved students actually faring on our own campuses, in our own signature programs? Mettler argues that political polarization and a lack of will are preventing changes that would address unequal access to higher education. She also asserts a need for greater oversight over large and politically connected for-profit universities, which "receive on average 86 percent of their revenues from federal student aid" (Mettler), despite low rates of timely degree completion, high rates of student loan default, and the individual stories of low-income students who take on additional debt without gaining the benefit of stronger career prospects.

Beyond the political polarization that has negatively impacted the public investment in higher education, what are we prepared and willing to do as honors educators to improve the access and attainment of underserved students in signature programs on our own campuses? According to Adam Vaccaro, the student creators of the photo project at Harvard have been admitted to a university with a $32 billion dollar endowment and a total student body of 21,000 to serve. Harvard's endowment fund, according to *U.S. News College Compass,* is about 888 times as large as our fund at UWEC, but their photo project reminds us that while equitable access to

Harvard admission is vitally important, admission alone is not enough. Even on a campus where there are financial resources aplenty for financial aid and high-value academic and co-curricular programming, the consequences of inequality persist and are reflected in the experiences of underrepresented students. In light of these realities, the end goal of our collective work must be inclusion: equitable opportunities for learning and growth for all students and freedom from the burdens of bias in the daily life of underserved students. Educators must respond to persistent inequality with persistent dedication to the task of insuring that signature programs are accessible to a diverse range of qualified students and characterized by an inclusive climate that features diversity as an educational priority, even as our pursuit of this priority requires us to re-imagine how we operate and to modify how we invest our time and expertise on campuses.

News Item 3: On August 15, 2013, the Association of American Colleges and Universities (AAC&U) issued a policy statement on diversity, equity, and inclusive excellence, asserting "without inclusion there is no true excellence" (AAC&U). As a guiding national voice for liberal education reform in higher education, the AAC&U made this declaration to encourage stronger institutional commitments to successfully serve all student communities. The statement challenges educators "to focus with new urgency on helping higher education provide a liberal *and* liberating education for *all college students*, including and especially those students from groups historically underserved by the American educational system at all levels" (AAC&U, emphasis in original). With this declaration, the AAC&U heightened its own commitment to educational reforms that identify and change longstanding patterns of exclusion in higher education.

As an educator who strives to attain a standard of equity-mindedness, I find the AAC&U's declaration to be timely and motivating. I believe it requires an *occupation* to bring new urgency to the mission of serving diverse students equitably. Such an occupation needs to include honors programs. There are hard questions to be raised during this occupation that can only be addressed by unflinchingly honest responses: is honors prepared and willing to bring a new urgency to the education of historically underserved students? What knowledge base, professional dispositions, and personal values do honors educators need in order to serve all student communities effectively? How have the stated missions, curricula, and administration of honors programs evolved over time, and have honors program reforms in recent years met the need to serve diverse learners more effectively? As honors educators, how earnestly have we confronted our own assumptions and even our biases as to what constitutes academic merit and valid qualifications when it comes to honors program access and participation?

Inclusive Excellence as an Honors *Occupation*: Statement of Purpose

In this chapter, I *occupy* honors as an equity-minded educator of color, asserting a critical need to pursue inclusive excellence in honors education, envisioning more equitable access and fuller engagement of underserved students in honors. The voice that I bring to this occupation blends multiple ways of assessing the state of honors, encouraging readers to treat the issues of access and equity with all due urgency. Here in my occupation narrative, I share philosophical points, personal reflections, data tracking, and practical examples from more than ten years of service in honors at UWEC. My work in honors has been guided by what Patricia Gurin calls the "compelling need for diversity in higher education," a need that is amplified in a public university enrolling more than 90% white students (Gurin). Among the underserved student populations on campus, UWEC enrolls significant proportions of first-generation students, veterans, and Hmong American students, many of whom are second- and third-generation citizens after family migrations from Laos, Vietnam, and Thailand in the aftermath of United States military involvement in Indochina. The presence of these varied student communities on campus reminds us that no single strategy can serve Gurin's "compelling need for diversity" in all university operations, magnifying the challenge before us (Gurin).

The 2013 *Factbook* from UWEC's Institutional Research Office provides specific data on student demographics on campus. In fall

2013, 1,838 of the 2,017 entering first-year students were white (91.1%). Among the largest U.S. ethnic minority groups, 39 of 2,017 students admitted were Hispanic/Latino (1.9%), and 4 of 2,017 students were African American (.1%). Hispanic/Latino and African American populations in Wisconsin are 6.2% and 6.5% of the total state population. Thus our recent campus numbers indicate inequitable access to UWEC and its programs for these populations. About 3.3% of the 2013–14 class identifies as Asian, the largest single ethnic group among students of color, continuing a trend of modest enrollment growth. Even at a university with a strong regional reputation across Wisconsin and in neighboring states, the most recent enrollment trends suggest mixed success, at best, in recruiting underrepresented students of color (Institutional Research Office, UWEC).

Over the last five years (2010–2015), our honors administrative team at UWEC has had some success in implementing innovative and measurably effective strategies to recruit and engage a more diverse student population. Honors students represented approximately 8.4% of the 2013 incoming class of freshmen at UWEC, and by 2015, we achieved a rough parity between students of color enrolled at the university (8.9%) and students of color enrolled in honors (approximately 9.3%), meaning that no equity gap exists in honors program access. These numbers suggest that honors is having some success in engaging an ethnically diverse range of students in a high-value program, with students of color participating in honors in proportions that at least reflect the university population. It remains the case, however, that the vast majority of students on campus do not participate directly in honors. Where honors can have perhaps its greatest impact is by serving as a rigorous, persistent, and public advocate for change in how diversity, inclusion, and equity are perceived, enabling honors to model for other campus programs ways of implementing inclusive excellence. My personal goal as an honors educator is helping to demonstrate that universities can and must serve the goals of *inclusion* and *excellence* successfully, simultaneously, and sustainably. Just as in past decades honors programs were central to the development of student-faculty research, service learning, and capstone experiences as high-impact, high-value pedagogies, I urge us as honors educators to align our work closely with the national movement emphasizing equity, diversity, and inclusion in all institutional operations.

Whenever individual honors programs attain notable success in serving diverse student populations, they have the potential to inform and inspire other honors programs to follow suit if they are willing to make a spirited public case for inclusive excellence in honors. We have had recent successes at UWEC in fostering a spirit of equity-mindedness that connects honors and other units charged with diversity-related outcomes, but the metaphor of *occupation* is still an appropriate one for imagining all stakeholders at a common table, resolving to serve all students equitably, and embarking on a sustained course of action. In that spirit, my chapter will end with a suggestion for how the National Collegiate Honors Council (NCHC) document "Basic Characteristics of a Fully Developed Honors Program" can be *occupied* by new statements of commitment to inclusive excellence as a foundational component of honors education.

Occupation Strategy: Equity-Mindedness and Inclusive Excellence in a Vision of Change

Two terms from recent literature on educational reform and student success occur often in this chapter and require definitions. The first of these terms, "equity-mindedness," describes an administrative philosophy that values the success of all students and responds proactively to systematic social inequalities that impact higher education outcomes. As described by the Center for Urban Education, equity-minded educators are "aware of the socio-historical context of exclusionary practices and racism in higher education, and the impact of power asymmetries on the roles they and their colleagues play and the responsibility they share for helping students succeed" (Center for Urban Education). Honors leaders need to recognize and respond to the patterns of exclusion and inequality in higher education that impact entire campuses, including honors. Of course, equity-mindedness requires attention to both process and outcomes.

The term "inclusive excellence" also requires defining in the context of honors reform. Implicitly, the term references a need for greater numerical diversity in high-value programs. By numerical diversity, I mean the proportional enrollment and educational attainment of all student populations, reflecting broader demographics across our society. Beyond numerical diversity, inclusive excellence also calls for full participation and engagement of all student communities in high-value campus activity (inclusion) and supports students fully in striving to reach their academic potential (excellence). Both the theory and practice of inclusive excellence are continually evolving in their articulation and implementation in colleges and universities across the country. The University of Wisconsin System describes the fundamental purposes of inclusive excellence in the following ways:

> Inclusive Excellence is a change-oriented planning process that encourages us to continue in our diversification efforts albeit with a greater intentionality and attentiveness of how they serve the needs of our students. Informed by a well-established body of empirical research as to the institutional contexts, practices, and cultures that contribute to the establishment of a diverse learning environment, Inclusive Excellence represents a shift not in the essence of our work but how we approach it and carry it out. Above all, Inclusive Excellence asks us to actively manage diversity as a vital and necessary asset of collegiate life rather than as an external problem. ("Inclusive Excellence," University of Wisconsin System)

The University of Wisconsin System's characterization of inclusive excellence emphasizes the need for intentionality in planning and implementing strategies related to diversity and greater use of empirical evidence to guide institutional change. The System statement, however, also holds that the move toward inclusive essence is not "*a shift in the essence of our work*" (emphasis added). In my

40

view, the italicized language understates the magnitude of the institutional changes required to foster full engagement of all learners in colleges and universities. The University of Denver's Center for Multicultural Excellence describes additional tenets of inclusive excellence that clarify the multi-dimensional challenges we face in serving diverse student populations effectively:

> a community or institution's success is dependent on how well it values, engages, and includes the rich diversity of faculty, staff, student, and alumni constituents and all the valuable social dimensions that they bring to the campus, including but not limited to race/ethnicity, sexual orientation, gender identity, gender expression, religion, nationality, age and disability. More than a short-term project or single office initiative, this comprehensive approach requires a fundamental transformation of the institution by embedding and practicing Inclusive Excellence in every effort, aspect, and level of a college or university. Stated differently, the goal is to make Inclusive Excellence a habit that is implemented and practiced consistently throughout an institution. ("About CME")

Because honors is broadly understood as a high-value program where curricular innovation is welcome, honors programs are uniquely positioned to assist institutions in the strengthening of diversity-related outcomes. If inclusive excellence is sought and attained in honors, the broader campus is more likely to conclude that inclusion and excellence can be simultaneously and successfully attained in other programs.

The vocabularies developed by Estela Bensimon at the Center for Urban Education (CUE) at the University of Southern California (USC) and educational leaders at the AAC&U have great potential to guide practical projects in equity-minded reform; these vocabularies have certainly inspired UWEC's honors reform efforts. CUE's public call for greater inclusivity can be viewed on USC's home page, along with summaries of their ongoing partnerships with institutions that are taking action locally in support of inclusivity. One of the tools available to institutions through CUE is the Equity Scorecard developed by Bensimon, which is a method of assessing equity in a campus or university system, planning interventions, and evaluating the success of interventions. The Scorecard directs a campus toward data collection and analysis of its own diversity-related outcomes to identify any existing institutional patterns whereby students are underserved. While no single solution is available that can work in all contexts, the next section of this chapter illustrates how the Equity Scorecard consultancy at UWEC has informed changes in honors program practices and afforded measurable improvements in outcomes. Personally, my involvement with the Scorecard has proved equally useful for both professional development and honors program reform.

Also at this institutional moment, UWEC remains engaged in a liberal education reform process in conjunction with a national movement known as the LEAP Initiative (Liberal Education, America's Promise), and in fact, the University of Wisconsin System was the AAC&U's first statewide partner in this reform effort. The LEAP initiative may be familiar to readers as AAC&U's research-driven efforts to lead higher education toward inclusive excellence and outcome-based educational models, especially as related to liberal education (general education) core requirements. In the time since the first launch of the LEAP initiative in 2005, the AAC&U has built an increasingly persuasive and public case for inclusive excellence as a necessary condition for liberal educational reform, particularly if new academic practices are to be of equal benefit to underserved students.

Thus, a good place to begin an honors *occupation* on behalf of underserved students is to draw from models that emphasize inclusive excellence and equity-mindedness in language and practice, building stronger ties between honors programs and campus reform initiatives that explicitly seek equity and inclusion. Such collaborations are necessary to bring about a paradigm shift: elevating the pursuit of equitable student outcomes to a place of prominence in all university operations. An equity-minded occupation of honors will require essential changes in practice: renewing our understandings of diversity and student development based on current research, launching new models for organizational collaboration, and developing personal allies who can sustain us through a season of change.

I will summarize Part I with a set of actions that can be taken to move equity-mindedness and inclusive excellence to the foreground of honors education:

1. Review and revise honors admissions criteria with an *equity-minded* lens, resulting in fuller implementation of holistic admissions protocols and greater access to honors programs among underserved student communities.

2. Review curricula and implement faculty development strategies in honors to meet ongoing needs to develop student talent from all communities and to advocate inclusive excellence campus-wide.

3. Infuse honors programs with high-impact practices related to diversity, including multiple models for increasing intercultural literacy.

4. Review and revise NCHC's guiding document "Basic Characteristics of a Fully Developed Honors Program" to institutionalize support for inclusive excellence in honors and across higher education.

The upcoming parts of this chapter provide UWEC and national perspectives on holistic admissions and diverse student access to high-value programs, faculty disposition and development in honors, intercultural learning models in honors, and related topics, culminating in Part V, which suggests specific revisions of the Basic Characteristics document that can help honors programs attain inclusive excellence.

PART II: DATA COLLECTION AND HONORS PROGRAM CHANGE

Measuring Student Access and Success

No one-size-fits-all method exists for achieving greater equity in student outcomes within honors; however, a five-year intense period of honors program reform at UWEC has demonstrated how honors can contribute productively toward inclusive excellence and equity-mindedness across a single campus. One might say that our ongoing honors reforms started with an *occupation*—or at minimum, a rigorous internal critique of enrollment patterns in honors from an equity-minded perspective, grounded in an Equity Scorecard consultancy. Honors at UWEC underwent a leadership transition in 2009, with one immediate priority being a programmatic response to the Interim Report on Excellence (2009) by the Equity Scorecard Team. This internal report assessed student participation in the honors program in relation to ethnicity, working from Equity Scorecard methodologies and collecting data on student enrollments in high-impact programs across campus. The report's findings highlighted unequal honors participation among majority students and students of color. After complimenting the opportunities for "distinct intellectual challenge" provided by honors at UWEC, the Report continues:

> It is important for the institution to exercise intense vigilance to make sure students of color are not disproportionately denied admission to the program. Current enrollments in the Honors program [sic] are not particularly encouraging in this regard. Recent data show that of the 392 students officially enrolled in the program, only 7 are known to be students of color: 4 Asian or Asian American students and 3 Hispanic/Latino(a) students. (Another 4 students are reported as "Not reported/Other.") No African American students and no American Indian students are reported at this time. It seems likely that current admissions criteria for the Honors Program unfairly disadvantage students of color. (Equity Scorecard Team)

At the time of the report, 97% of the 397 honors students at UWEC identified as white, compared to 92.3% of the student body as a whole. In addition to the 4.7% gap in honors participation among students of color compared to white student peers, the presence of an overwhelmingly white student body created practical difficulties in maintaining a climate where a very small number of students of color (7 out of 397, 1.7%) are fully integrated into honors program activity and peer networks (Equity Scorecard Team).

In this context, we, as honors administrators, began work on a multi-year review of our program's admissions procedures, curricula, student demographics, and success measures. Our most recent honors program data from 2015 shows a significant increase in diverse student enrollment over six years, with 9.3% of nearly 700 current honors students being of color. Progress toward inclusive excellence has been steady, at least as reflected in this single metric of ethnic diversity in a signature program. Progress toward equity in the UWEC Honors Program is grounded in an approach to honors education that

1. collects data about student experiences for strategic use in decision-making;

2. seeks energetically to address gaps in persistence among student populations; and

3. identifies equity-minded educators on our campuses who can contribute to reform efforts.

Data collection, storage, and distribution have been central to the honors reform process at UWEC, enabling us to hypothesize about the effectiveness of equity-minded honors reform over a five-year period, academic years 2009–10 through 2013–14. The following findings are noteworthy:

- Retention and graduation rates for entering honors cohorts over a full decade (2004–2013) show a trend toward improved persistence in honors and at the university in the wake of equity-minded honors reform initiatives.

- During the last four years, students admitted to honors through a holistic process (based on a diversity-aware review of multiple measures of academic performance) have performed similarly to students admitted through automatic admission based solely on ACT score/class rank, with holistic admissions having the additional benefit of diversifying the potential pool of students who can benefit from high-impact experiences in honors.

The practice of holistic admissions has been a centerpiece of the reforms that have enabled progress toward equity in honors student enrollment. Historically, the path to honors at UWEC has centered on automatic admission based on the following metrics: ACT 28 or higher and top 5% rank in high school class (RIC), 29 ACT and 10% RIC, or 30 ACT and 15% RIC. Initially, these metrics were selected not because they were known as valid predictors of student success, but because they served as a tool for enrollment management. Starting in 2010, we implemented holistic admissions as a proactive response to a campus and community need to serve a greater range of well-prepared students. The policy currently serves as a supplement but not a replacement for automatic admissions.

Through holistic admissions, all admitted students who meet one of several benchmarks receive additional screening by a team of application readers from Admissions, Honors, Multicultural Affairs, and other units. One of three benchmarks must be met for a student to be considered for holistic admissions: ACT score of 26 or higher, top 10% of high school class, or 3.75 GPA. Strength in several additional criteria and multiple readers of the student applications are required to qualify for holistic admissions, and our data show a strong rate of retention in honors among holistically admitted students, particularly in the second and third academic years after initial implementation of the process.

A broad view of program trends is illustrated by Table 1, which is a cumulative snapshot of student retention and graduation rates for fall admissions in the UWEC Honors Program, Academic Year 2004–05 through 2013–14. The table reports student retention on a semester-by-semester basis (Continuing), student withdrawals from the university (Dropped), and students who eventually attain their degrees (Cum Degree). Noted in the table is significant growth in the size of the honors cohort over time, from 116 entering students in 2004 to 170 entering students in 2013 (the peak size was an incoming class of 186 in 2012). The trend toward larger incoming cohorts in honors is notable starting in 2010, which is the first year that access to honors increased with the implementation of holistic admissions.

The findings show that during the years of intensive program reform (2009–2014), rates of program retention among students from the first semester through the fourth semester have been quite strong, especially in the most recent four years (over 90% for four consecutive years) in comparison to the first four pre-reform years (less than 80% from 2004–05 to 2007–08). Four-year graduation rates (as highlighted in the Term 8 data) have stabilized at nearly 50% for participating honors students. While identifying a single definite cause for these trends is not possible, we have increased our collection of qualitative data through student surveys and other means to help identify what factors may impact our retention and graduation metrics.

Table 2 illustrates recruitment and retention trends in honors holistic admissions for the first four incoming cohorts, including graduation rates for the one cohort (2010–11) where those figures are currently available. That the size of incoming holistic cohorts has increased from 14 in the initial year (2010–11) to 53 in 2014–15 is notable, with the rates of first-to-second-year retention reaching 88.2% or higher for the three most recent cohorts.

Figure 1 highlights four-year graduation rates for selected cohorts of incoming honors students. Based on only one year of findings, the 35.7% four-year graduation rate for holistically admitted honors students is higher than either non-honors students or all UWEC students in the comparison years, but the first cohort of holistically admitted honors students graduated at a lower overall rate than was characteristic of the entire entering 2010 honors class (35.7% vs. 49.4%). This finding indicated to us a need to refine our processes of holistic admissions over time as well as to

TABLE 1. HONORS RETENTION AND GRADUATION RATES

		All Honors Students by Cohort Year—Percen			
					New
		2004–05	2005–06	2006–07	2007–08
	Grand Total	**116**	**99**	**96**	**135**
Term 2	Continuing	99.1	97.0	99.0	98.5
	Dropped	0.9	3.0	1.0	1.5
Term 3	Continuing	91.4	93.9	89.6	88.9
	Dropped	8.6	6.1	10.4	11.1
Term 4	Continuing	78.4	78.8	79.2	72.6
	Dropped	21.6	21.2	20.8	27.4
	Cum Degree				
Term 5	Continuing	80.2	89.9	86.5	85.9
	Dropped	19.8	10.1	13.5	14.1
	Cum Degree				
Term 6	Continuing	73.3	87.9	82.3	86.7
	Dropped	25.0	11.1	16.7	12.6
	Cum Degree	1.7	1.0	1.0	0.7
Term 7	Continuing	75.9	76.8	78.1	85.9
	Dropped	19.0	17.2	15.6	11.9
	Cum Degree	5.2	6.1	6.3	2.2
Term 8	Continuing	41.4	38.4	35.4	41.5
	Dropped	18.1	15.2	15.6	12.6
	Cum Degree	40.5	46.5	49.0	45.9
Term 9	Continuing	27.6	18.2	18.8	23.7
	Dropped	18.1	14.1	16.7	13.3
	Cum Degree	54.3	67.7	64.6	63.0
Term 10	Continuing	4.3	5.1	4.2	5.2
	Dropped	19.8	13.1	16.7	11.9
	Cum Degree	75.9	81.8	79.2	83.0
Term 11	Continuing	0.9	1.0	2.1	1.5
	Dropped	19.0	15.2	14.6	13.3
	Cum Degree	80.2	83.8	83.3	85.2
Term 12	Continuing	1.7	1.0	0.0	0.0
	Dropped	18.1	14.1	15.6	12.6
	Cum Degree	80.2	84.8	84.4	87.4

Source: Office of Institutional Research, University of Wisconsin at Eau Claire

tage Retention and Graduation Rates by Term					
Freshmen Honors Fall Entrance Year					
2008–09	2009–10	2010–11	2011–12	2012–13	2013–14
111	134	154	167	186	170
100.0	99.3	98.7	98.2	99.5	98.8
0.0	0.7	1.3	1.8	0.5	1.2
93.7	94.8	94.2	92.2	95.2	93.5
6.3	5.2	5.8	7.8	4.8	6.5
82.0	94.0	91.6	90.4	93.5	
18.0	6.0	8.4	9.0	6.5	
			0.6		
91.9	91.0	84.4	88.6	89.2	
8.1	9.0	15.6	10.8	10.2	
			0.6	0.5	
89.2	86.6	84.4	87.4		
9.9	9.0	14.3	10.2		
0.9	4.5	1.3	2.4		
83.8	79.9	74.7	79.6		
10.8	10.4	18.2	11.4		
5.4	9.7	7.1	9.0		
32.4	32.1	31.2			
11.7	9.7	19.5			
55.9	58.2	49.4			
15.3	16.4	22.1			
13.5	9.7	20.8			
71.2	73.9	57.1			
2.7	3.0				
14.4	9.0				
82.9	88.1				
0.9	2.2				
14.4	9.0				
84.7	88.8				
0.9					
12.6					
86.5					

think about potential barriers in our curriculum and co-curricular programming.

We are confident that Figure 2 suggests that retention and graduation rates among holistically admitted students will show improvement over time. The key finding is the comparison between honors students who are actively taking courses in honors (REHN) vs. honors students who have stopped taking courses in the program (RHON).

In our most recent figures from Spring 2015, 105 (93%) of our 113 holistically admitted honors students at the university are actively taking courses (REHN group). This figure compares to 411 (84%) of 489 automatically admitted students who are actively taking honors courses. While we once again hesitate to reach firm conclusions based on snapshots of program data, it is reasonable

TABLE 2. RETENTION AND GRADUATION RATES BY TERM—HONORS PROGRAM, HOLISTIC ADMISSIONS

		New Freshmen Holistic Honors Fall Entrance Year			
		2010–11	2011–12	2012–13	2013–14
Grand Total		14	17	33	38
Term 2	Continuing	92.9	100.0	97.0	97.4
	Dropped	7.1	0.0	3.0	2.6
Term 3	Continuing	85.7	88.2	90.9	89.5
	Dropped	14.3	11.8	9.1	10.5
Term 4	Continuing	85.7	88.2	87.9	
	Dropped	14.3	11.8	12.1	
Term 5	Continuing	85.7	88.2	87.9	
	Dropped	14.3	11.8	21.2	
Term 6	Continuing	85.7	88.2		
	Dropped	14.3	11.8		
Term 7	Continuing	85.7	88.2		
	Dropped	14.3	11.8		
Term 8	Continuing	50.0			
	Dropped	14.3			
	Cum Degree	35.7			
Term 9	Continuing	50.0			
	Dropped	14.3			

Source: Office of Institutional Research, University of Wisconsin at Eau Claire

to hypothesize that so far, with the increased access to honors through holistic admissions, we have managed to sustain a level of engagement and participation that is similar to or stronger than automatically admitted students. Compared to automatic admission invitations, greater attention is paid to individual student profiles during the application process for holistic admissions, and it is possible that this hands-on process is a more effective way to assess preparation for and predict success in our honors program.

Through continuing program assessment, we hope to clarify further how programmatic actions can contribute to more diverse enrollments. Implementing holistic admissions within our program has been a significant positive change, but, over time, we hope to assess the impact of intercultural immersions, the recruitment of outstanding faculty of color to teach in honors, enhanced efforts to engage students equitably in undergraduate research, and the integration of courses on diversity-related topics and civic engagement in honors. We believe this kind of multi-year, multi-pronged effort

FIGURE 1. GRADUATION AT TERM 8 (4-YEAR GRADUATION RATES) FOR SELECTED COHORTS AND CAMPUS POPULATIONS

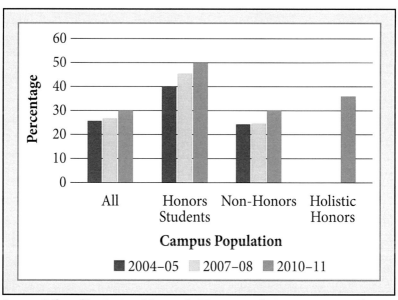

Source: Office of Institutional Research, University of Wisconsin at Eau Claire

is required to move resolutely toward inclusive excellence. The data we have compiled provide multiple means of assessing our work so far and planning new interventions to support honors student success. Of course, as a humanities professor, I recognize that these numbers reflect an instructive but limited range of measurable results. They tell only a part of the story; they constitute a single episode in an epic tale.

The next part of this chapter provides narrative commentary on my personal path toward an *occupation* of honors, followed in Part IV by detailed *occupation strategies* that can embed inclusive excellence into the common practices of honors education.

FIGURE 2. PROGRAM STATUS BY ADMISSION METHOD (AUTOMATIC VS. HOLISTIC), SPRING 2015 SNAPSHOT

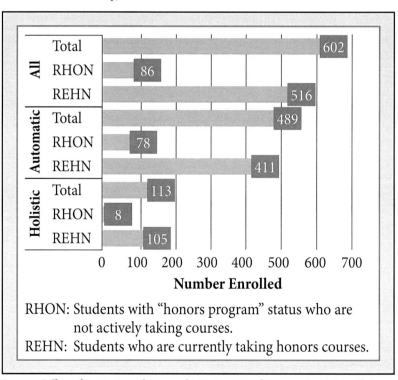

RHON: Students with "honors program" status who are not actively taking courses.
REHN: Students who are currently taking honors courses.

Source: Office of Institutional Research, University of Wisconsin at Eau Claire

PART III: EQUITY-MINDEDNESS

Personal Origins of an Honors Career

To illustrate the rewards and challenges of pursuing inclusive excellence in honors, this section highlights my personal journey to honors leadership. My passion for inclusive excellence in honors stems in part from my cultural identity as a first-generation college graduate and a faculty member of color serving at a predominantly white university. Among many other inspirations, remembering my parents' lives and legacies helps me maintain my commitment to social justice in honors teaching. My mother was born in 1927 as the third of ten children in a family living in poverty in Forrest City, Arkansas, a town named after Confederate general and Ku Klux Klan member Nathaniel Bedford Forrest. Amid systematic legal discrimination against African Americans across the economic and educational systems, my mother valued education highly and served as an educator in several capacities through her life despite not having an opportunity to earn a four-year degree. At age 80, she was recognized as Grandmother of the Year at a Head Start program where she worked long after her first retirement. Earlier in her life, her tireless effort enabled the successful rearing of her children through many years as a single parent. During his service in World War II, my father survived a boat attack in the Pacific Ocean and, eventually, made his way to Omaha, Nebraska, to a military hospital where he was treated for Post Traumatic Stress Disorder (PTSD). He was never able, however, to benefit from the GI Bill or join a local union to leverage his military experience into a civilian trucking job, and he was not a stable member of our family by the time I came of age. Nevertheless, I remain inspired by the extraordinary experiences of both of my parents in persistently seeking opportunities for education and employment against the backdrop of institutional racism. These family stories are a constant reminder to me that barriers to educational attainment still exist and continue to affect the lives of first-generation students.

Inspired by my mother and my siblings (all three of my siblings have earned a bachelor's degree or higher), I became interested early on in U.S. cultural history, an interest that culminated in a focus on the Black Arts Movement in my dissertation research. Studying this extended effort among activists during the 1950s, 1960s, and 1970s to increase economic and political independence and to create art that expressed the culture and consciousness of Black people was instructive. My interest in cultural history was complemented by years of participation in debate as a youth and a cultivated interest in public policy. These elements led to an interest in population demographics, which I find continually useful for considering how well public resources granted to universities are used equitably to serve all student communities.

When I think back on what it took for me to acquire sufficient resources and sustain the personal drive to earn a PhD as a first-generation student, I am reminded that structural barriers can make a degree-seeking path difficult. These barriers can be financial, or they may stem from the climate at a particular university. These barriers can also correlate with the availability or exclusivity of high-impact programs: undergraduate research, study abroad, internships, participation in honors, or other activities that strengthen engagement and add value to the degree. To enroll in many of these programs, students need to be confident in seeking out opportunities and must be able to build strong relationships with faculty. I believe it is common for underserved students to begin their student careers with limited information about these opportunities and how to access them.

Equity-Minded Teaching in Honors: Courses, Themes, and Faculty Identity

While I did not participate in honors as an undergraduate student, I began teaching honors courses early in my university teaching career, which I greatly enjoyed. Honors provided an opportunity to go beyond the standard curriculum by offering courses that allowed greater exploration of research interests. Teaching in honors at UWEC enabled me to go beyond my primary graduate research area of African American literature; I could teach courses that examined broader social problems and social justice strategies.

For instance, these themes were integrated into a section of an honors umbrella course, "Political Ideas in Literature: Literature and War." When first teaching this course around 2006 (during the second Gulf War), I felt strongly that more of the honors curriculum should provide perspectives on current events and the large human questions that were being played out daily in our common lives.

Teaching "Literature and War" moved me out of my comfort zone through the necessity of integrating topics such as Just War Theory and soldiers' memoirs during wartime. The content I developed over time in this course was useful for additional studies of trauma and incarceration in subsequent courses. In more recent courses in literature and even in first-year honors composition, I have engaged students in some of the interdisciplinary literature on mass incarceration, aggressive masculinity, and mass media framing of crime incidents. I make a point of discussing stories of resilience in response to acts of violence and invite guests to class who have personal experience related to these issues. Explorations of this content strengthen my students' preparation for future work and life in a diverse world, given that many of their careers and lives will be touched by survivors of trauma, not to mention that the students themselves may be trauma survivors. An additional benefit of examining these topics in the classroom has been an improved relationship with student affairs units that respond to everyday traumas experienced by students. Units such as residence life, counseling, and campus police all play essential roles in creating a safe and supportive learning environment. I have made it a personal goal to sustain strong relationships with campus professionals in these areas and to collaborate with them to support student success.

I mention these formative experiences to suggest that mutually fruitful relationships can be developed through the greater inclusion of faculty of color in honors. The curricular flexibility within our UWEC honors program has been crucial to my personal development as an educator of color. I would encourage honors administrators in other settings to actively review their programs to see if contributions from faculty of color as well as equity-minded faculty are reflected in the curriculum and across the program.

The Value of Administrative Collaboration in Honors: A Personal Account

Close and effective collaboration with an administrative colleague, former UWEC Honors Program Director Jeff Vahlbusch, has been a signature experience in aligning the goals of inclusivity and excellence in the program. When I joined Dr. Vahlbusch as Honors Faculty Fellow in 2009, I brought to the table an administrative disposition that welcomes calculated risk-taking and innovative change. Collaborating with Vahlbusch has nurtured honors as a setting on our campus where new ideas can be vetted and piloted on a reasonably short calendar, where crossing disciplinary boundaries is viewed with appreciation rather than suspicion, and where student academic development and personal development are equally respected and aligned in program design. Over the course of a multi-year collaboration, Vahlbusch and I have maintained a willingness to work closely over extended days, months, and years to develop common understandings that can be leveraged into program change. Sustaining mutual openness and honest expression of opinion when it comes to highly charged issues of equity, diversity, and inclusion can be challenging, but if honors is going to be a leading enterprise in a move toward inclusive excellence, honors leaders need an extraordinary willingness to give and receive constructive feedback and a never-failing persistence to seek new strategies for the improvement of diversity-related outcomes. That Vahlbusch and I are similar in terms of age, gender, academic affiliations in language studies and the humanities, and a commitment to honors education is an advantage. And yet, our differences in personality and background and our ability to apply these different strengths to the practical challenges we have faced in honors leadership have also contributed significantly to our reform efforts. I would encourage other honors programs to consider how deeply the practices of inclusion are embodied by and within their leadership.

Based on my experiences, I believe that an honors program benefits from the presence of administrators and faculty who persistently question how well established practices in higher education serve all students. My own questioning perspective leads me at times to express skepticism when I encounter broad philosophical assertions on the value of a liberal arts degree that are not supported by data on diverse student experiences. Certainly the aggregate numbers reveal that a liberal arts degree adds value annually to one's earning power and enables access to social mobility, but we often hesitate to weigh the impact of our programs on the 30–35% (or more!) of our students who do not attain a degree within six or more years. Persistent gaps in retention and graduation among underserved students are common across many campuses, and while we know that high-impact practices such as undergraduate research, internships, and other honors programs experiences can narrow gaps in attainment between first-generation students and their peers who are second or third generation, these high-value experiences should be accessed equitably across generational characteristics. Frequent collection and review of relevant data are also crucial for tracking student success and patterns of exclusions in accessing high-value campus experiences.

PART IV: CHALLENGING ASSUMPTIONS

Toward Diversity-Related Outcomes

In a similar vein, an honors leadership team must be willing to confront deficit-minded assumptions about diversity in higher education that are expressed not only by the broader public but also by faculty and administrators. As a working definition, deficit-mindedness can be understood as on- and off-campus perceptions that undergraduate students of color are at fault for being underprepared for rigorous educational experiences, a perception that also stigmatizes other diverse student communities such as non-traditional students, English language learners, and students participating in programs designed to expand college access. Such perceptions become a first line of resistance to equity-minded change in educational practices and are often expressed through the following sentiments:

1. a deficit-minded belief that implementing holistic admissions means lowering standards;

2. a deficit-minded belief that students of color benefit disproportionately from preferential treatment in admissions;

3. a common assumption that success in teaching a diverse student population does not require professional development and personal transformation;

4. a belief that the study of human diversity, including U.S. multiculturalism, lacks academic content and rigor; thus, faculty expertise and service work on diversity and equity issues are undervalued compared to more established disciplinary research and publishing.

I have encountered these forms of resistance often in the context of administrative work in and out of honors, and I strongly feel that equity-minded educators need both a language and a willingness to speak forthrightly to ensure that these assumptions are challenged. Having presented this list, however, I wish not to be overly categorical; I would like to stress that many educators and institutions recognize the urgency of the moment and are taking action to achieve more equitable outcomes. In my more generous moments, I am able to be patient and to appreciate trends in support of greater inclusion and student success. On other days, I am not so patient. After all, in the context of *occupation,* impatience can be a virtue, an impetus to make changes that boldly address the climate of inequality faced by underserved students.

Several theoretical and practical responses to deficit-mindedness may prove beneficial over the shorter and longer term. First, honors leaders must challenge assumptions that holistic admissions means lowering standards and benefiting students of color disproportionately. As a proactive administrative response to these assumptions, honors leaders may implement a faculty development model that emphasizes current research on demographic trends in the school age population, equity in college admissions, standardized testing, and limited access to high-impact programs among enrolled students. Literature on the limited validity of standardized exams in predicting college success, recent U.S. Supreme Court cases on admissions practices, and studies of the efficacy of diversity-related experiences on campus in strengthening student learning would all be useful in an honors faculty development context. Administrators and faculty whose training may not be in education studies or related fields may not be able to maintain a high level of disciplinary expertise in these vast areas of research, but it is important to allow this literature to contribute to what Ernest Boyer describes as "scholarship of application" where honors practitioners review the literature on inclusive excellence, then ask: "How can [this] knowledge be responsibly applied to consequential problems?" (Boyer 21). Rethinking honors in relation to inclusive excellence is just the sort of practical problem that Boyer references.

Second, honors leaders must challenge the assumption that established pedagogy works equally well for all students and that additional professional training is not necessary to work successfully with diverse student populations. To this end, faculty development models can integrate literature on diverse student engagement in honors, including research on program designs that have demonstrated potential for supporting intercultural literacy. An understanding of such literature can help honors leaders reframe the association of honors with elitism and assert the usefulness of honors for fully engaging diverse student communities. Students from underserved communities may not initially identify themselves as elite in terms of their academic skills and thus may not recognize how honors can be beneficial: honors leaders must carefully use language to reframe these assumptions for the benefit of a diverse student community. Reading through the literature on diversity in honors provides a theoretical foundation to help answer a practical question we must address collectively: how does (and how can) honors education contribute to the outcome of inclusive excellence? As equity-minded honors practitioners, we can all model ways of engaging with literature on honors student diversity and applying it to program administration and faculty development.

Third, honors leaders must challenge the assumptions that topics of multiculturalism, equity, and diversity lack rigor as academic discourses, which means, therefore, a limited role for these topics is acceptable within high-value programs. Challenging these assumptions successfully will require review and revision of mission statements and programmatic practice to centralize the goal of inclusive excellence in honors. This process will be difficult, and it may require an infusion of expertise from on- and off-campus practitioners in the area of student diversity to institute equity-minded change in honors. If we are earnest, however, in advocating for equity and inclusion across higher education, including in honors, we must evaluate our daily work with the following questions in mind:

- At a rank and file level, among faculty and administrators on any given day on campus, what level of institutional commitment, faculty development, administrative support, and strategic coordination is given to the pursuit of equity in student recruitment, retention, graduation, and engagement in campus life?

- How has our work in honors assisted in these pursuits?

- Have our honors faculty and administrators been leaders, followers, sideliners, or resisters in relation to the pursuit of equity in educational outcomes?

Ultimately, if we are to attain inclusive excellence in honors, language related to diversity, equity, and inclusion also needs a prominent presence in the NCHC policy document "Basic Characteristics of a Fully Developed Honors Program," which is discussed in Part V below.

Demographic Shifts and Honors Program Development: Challenges and Opportunities

An honors *occupation* requires us not only to cultivate an equity-minded disposition but also to immerse ourselves in the literature of student success and to apply this literature to ongoing honors work.

The modest but measurable improvements in diversity-related outcomes that we have achieved in the UWEC Honors Program have been made possible by significant administrative time dedicated to the close study of shifting conditions in the current higher education environment. Specifically, this meant finding ways that honors could thrive in an environment in which the number of honors-eligible student applications to our university was declining because fewer applicants could meet the automatic admissions criteria of 28 ACT/top 5% rank in class, 29/10%, 30/15%). Emerging demographic trends have continually underscored the need for greater retention and engagement among students who are increasingly diverse. For an occupation to succeed in strengthening inclusive excellence in honors, honors educators must maintain a strong practical understanding of these trends.

Our effort to increase access to honors at UWEC demonstrates in microcosm some of the reforms that will need wider implementation in response to demographic characteristics of the emerging U.S. population. In coming years and decades, prospective students will be more diverse in terms of race, ethnicity, class, age, and other identities, and thus curricula, pedagogy, and program administration need to support the success of these populations. In 2012, the *Washington Post* reported Census Bureau figures showing that "50.4 percent of children younger than one last year were Hispanic, black, Asian American or in other minority groups" (qtd. in Morello and Mellnik). Sociologist and former Census Bureau Director Steve H. Murdock adds to the demographic picture of largely negative population growth across several ethnic groups: "There are virtually no major regions of the country where non-Hispanic birth numbers are not getting lower. . . . Basically, all groups besides Hispanics have birthrates lower than replacement" (qtd. in Lipka A26).

While some faculty and many administrators are aware of this population shift, the impact of these shifts on recruitment, retention, student engagement, and program array has yet to be fully considered. In a prescient 2010 statement about the impact of upcoming population shifts in Texas on honors recruitment, Michael DeLeon observes: "When honors practitioners in Texas and elsewhere take the time to reflect, they should ask if institutions and programs are structured to accommodate the largest demographic paradigm shift ever to occur in the western hemisphere" (72). Related to this, Eric Hoover observes that among current high school graduates: "the nation's already seeing a sharp rise in first-generation and low-income graduates—the very students whom selective four-year institutions have long struggled to serve" (A26). Most certainly, these demographic trends heighten the need for honors programs to recruit, to admit, to engage, to retain, and to graduate underserved students at equitable rates of success.

Inclusive Excellence and Admissions Criteria: National Debates with Honors Implications

Literature on student equity can have immediate rhetorical and practical usefulness in honors program reform efforts, enabling us to address the perception that using holistic admissions criteria in honors amounts to lowering standards. Reviewing educational research on the predictive value and cultural bias in standardized exams as well as recent U.S. Supreme Court cases on admissions policies will clarify the legality, the utility, and the ethicality of holistic admissions criteria. As an introduction to the vast literature on these subjects, I have considered observations by Joseph Soares, who has criticized the intractability of "old regime" formulas that screen initially with standardized testing, using such scores "to draw the boundaries of the pool" before most holistic admission processes even begin (66). A more liberating and just philosophical approach to admissions might also follow from Soares' reasoning, to be mindful of "the need for admissions to be realigned with the broad mission of colleges to educate youths to flourish beyond the classroom. Our visions of admissions have been too often blinkered by numbers with dubious diagnostic value" (66).

Honors programs represent a clear embodiment and test case for the validity of standard measures of academic merit: exceptional high school rank in class (RIC) and SAT/ACT scores being securely established as criteria for honors admissions. As a national debate continues on the efficacy and the ethics of relying solely or predominantly on RIC and SAT/ACT benchmarks for selective college admissions, we encourage all honors practitioners to ask directly: how do our established admissions benchmarks influence the range of students who have access to the benefits of honors?

It does take time to arrive at a program-wide consensus on how student engagement and full participation should be defined and demonstrated, as well as to consider how admissions, curriculum, and pedagogy might all be leveraged in pursuit of inclusive excellence. Where might we start our review and revision of honors operations—by thinking predominantly about compositional or structural diversity (student demographics), or by assessing curricula to see how well faculty and course content reflect diverse perspectives across bodies of knowledge and approaches to pedagogy? There is no single answer, and at UWEC, we have sought both to strengthen access and engagement in quantifiable ways and to diversify honors faculty and curricula. As a whole, equity-minded strategies for honors reform should strategically mitigate historical patterns of exclusion in higher education and use data in planning and assessing strategies. The key move, it seems to me, is to look sequentially at admissions processes with help from colleagues on- and off-campus with experience in holistic admissions, course array, faculty resources, and co-curricular experiences to determine which potential intervention can best achieve more equitable outcomes.

To help guide reform efforts, a sizable body of interdisciplinary research has investigated the impact of diversity-related experiences on campus, providing language for rhetorical use and models to inspire innovation. According to J. Cherie Strachan and Chris Owens, diversity-related experiences, when designed effectively, help students develop "a willingness to consider the perspective of others, to engage in active citizenship, and to believe that other groups' values and beliefs are compatible with one's own" (467). A consensus in the research asserts that diversity-related programming should be embedded broadly in student life, should be visible among institutional and program missions, and should be embedded in student-learning outcomes. The AAC&U's models for liberal education reform and recent U.S. Supreme Court deliberations on admissions practices provide additional guidance. The AAC&U describes intercultural competence and civic engagement as essential learning outcomes to be "anchored through active involvement with diverse communities and real world challenges" ("Essential Learning Outcomes").

Adding to the consensus on the value of human diversity as a focus across educational practices, Derek Bok's expert testimony in the landmark 2003 *Grutter v. Bollinger* U.S. Supreme Court case lays out the "compelling case" for integrating diversity, including race and ethnic diversity, into admissions processes and day-to-day student experiences:

> A great deal of learning occurs informally. It occurs through interactions among students of both sexes; of different races, religions, and backgrounds; who come from cities and rural areas, from various states and countries; who have a wide variety of interests, talents, and perspectives; and who are able, directly or indirectly, to learn from their differences and to stimulate one another to re-examine even their most deeply held assumptions about themselves and their world. (Bok)

Bok's testimony calls for equity-minded and justice-minded practices across higher education, with both private and public colleges and universities being called on to enroll "academically qualified applicants who not only give promise of doing well academically, but who also can enlarge the understanding of other students and contribute after graduation to their professions and communities" (Bok).

Additional testimony in the *Grutter v. Bollinger* case calls for a broadly infused, transformational diversity in higher education, which includes racial diversity in campus experiences. Joining Bok in assessing the educational significance of racial diversity, Patricia Gurin observes:

> Complex thinking occurs when people encounter a novel situation for which, by definition, they have no script, or

when the environment demands more than their current scripts provide. Racial diversity in a college or university student body provides the very features that research has determined are central to producing the conscious mode of thought educators demand from their students. (Gurin)

The reasoning of Bok, Gurin, and others extends to the honors context; after all, a "compelling need for diversity in higher education" is as pronounced in honors as it is elsewhere on campus. The opinions of the full Supreme Court are more divided on the importance of numerical diversity, with Justice Kennedy's majority opinion in the Fischer v. the University of Texas case (2013) demonstrating deficit-mindedness in its claim that the University of Texas "admits minorities who otherwise would have attended less selective colleges where they would have been more easily matched" (Fischer v. the University of Texas). Of course, the value of the court testimony and deliberations does not stop there. The court debates clarify what is permitted for diversity-aware admissions strategies. It is worth noting that even under the restrictive language of the Fischer v. the University of Texas Supreme Court case, race-aware policies may still be instituted, although the court holds that "the educational benefits allegedly produced by diversity must rise to the level of a compelling state interest" (Fischer v. the University of Texas). Based on the recent legacies of the Fischer and Grutter cases, it is up to us as equity-minded educators to develop strategies on admissions, diversity, and student access that are ethically sound, that advance inclusive excellence in honors education, and that are consistent with U.S. Supreme Court findings.

Research on Diversity in Honors Programs: A Resource for Equity-Minded Honors Reform

A sizeable body of research on the philosophical relationship of diversity to honors education exists, and this research also highlights practical strategies for equity-minded program revision. The NCHC monograph *Setting the Table for Diversity* offers a review of individual program designs and examines philosophical orientations that might guide reform efforts (Coleman and Kotinek, 2010). The monograph includes perspectives on numerical (also described as compositional or structural) diversity in honors, as compared to transformational diversity. Transformational diversity enables a program or institution "to knowledgeably appreciate the manifold differences that set us apart and earnestly celebrate the remarkable variety of things that bring us together" (F. Coleman 245). Joining with Coleman's suggestions, I find that either/or thinking about diversity tends to be unproductive, and I agree with the suggestion that numerical diversity alone will not result in inclusive excellence. I urge us to remember, however, that unequal access to higher education is among our most systematic and intractable social problems, and while diversity is certainly not reducible to numeric formulas, it should be an end goal of all our work to serve and nurture human talent from all communities and to eliminate opportunity gaps that restrict the participation of any social group. These goals should be pursued consistently and collaboratively among honors and other campus programs.

Earlier, I mentioned a philosophical tension between the spirit of inclusion and the occasional charge of elitism that is directed at honors. As we pursue inclusive excellence in honors, it is particularly important to address the elitism charge, which can lead to skepticism about investments in honors, on the grounds that honors benefits a limited number of privileged students (see Dziesinski, Camarena, and Homrich-Knieling in this volume, pp. 81–106). In response to these opinions, published literature on diversity in honors is especially useful for identifying the common ground between the rigor and selectivity of honors traditions and the practices of inclusive excellence. Based on their work in engaging underserved Latino students in honors at a Nebraska university, Peter Longo and John Falconer assert that honors must have an answer when questioned about which populations our programs serve:

> If the social contract means that everyone can prosper through hard work and enhanced skills, then an educational system that does not serve specific groups would undermine

the contract and create disenfranchised peoples. Honors programs cannot be excluded from that contract. (58)

With limited resources being the norm, we in honors must be prepared to explain why our programs do not reinforce a system of privilege and elitism within our institutions. Additionally, we must explain why honors contributes to more equitable outcomes across campus. At UWEC, in addition to demonstrating through data the impact of our program on all student communities, we communicate to interested audiences that pedagogical innovations within our honors program can be piloted in a supportive context and adapted elsewhere on campus over time. These initiatives can include inclusive and culturally relevant pedagogy, as well as other pedagogical methods that foster student equity. Benjamin Moritz, for example, builds a convincing case that the "small class sizes, increased one-on-one interactions with instructors, and yes—elitism of honors programs" all tend to even the playing field between underserved college students and their peers (66). Maintaining strong relationships between honors administrators and other campus leaders of high-impact programs, such as undergraduate research and study abroad programs, is a practical way to work toward inclusive student participation in all signature programs.

With a working knowledge of the research on diversity in honors, equity-minded honors educators can challenge deficit-mindedness, a perception that can follow underserved students through multiple interactions on a single campus, even at Harvard, and can have a chilling effect on broader patterns of college enrollment. Contrary, in fact, to Justice Kennedy's fears that race-aware policies lead to placements at colleges where "underperfomance is all but inevitable because they are less academically prepared than the white and Asian students with whom they must compete," significant evidence indicates that as a cumulative result of deficit-mindedness, *undermatching* is occurring across diverse student populations seeking college opportunities (Fischer v. the University of Texas). As Caroline Hoxby and Christopher Avery suggest, "the vast majority of low-income high achievers do not apply to any selective college. This is despite the fact that selective institutions typically cost them *less*, owing to generous financial aid, than the two-year and nonselective four-year institutions to which they actually apply" (Hoxby and Avery 1). Arguably, honors programs may be less intentional in their recruitment of a diverse student population than selective colleges, and thus a similar on-campus undermatching may reinforce low enrollment patterns in honors programs among underrepresented students. Our implementation of holistic admissions at UWEC is guided by a hypothesis that our own honors program was being impacted by undermatching, leading some students to voluntarily opt out of program participation if they did not perceive themselves as being honors qualified, and we have sought to address this issue by emphasizing that the purpose of honors is to develop academic talent from all communities.

We are well aware of observations in the literature that honors pedagogy can help underrepresented students improve their social mobility, especially at public universities. The case for lower student-faculty ratios and other investments in high-impact honors pedagogy is grounded in an assumption of improved social mobility for public university students. In "Honors is Elitist and What's Wrong With That?" Norm Weiner references the early twentieth-century history of honors as an imitation of teaching methods favored by the Oxford and Cambridge university system in Great Britain, imported into the U.S. selective college context to serve the intellectual elite. Weiner remarks further, however, "no ivy-league school has a university-wide honors program today. Honors has moved from its upper-class, elite origins to a decidedly middle-class footing" (Weiner 21). As a result, many students enroll in honors programs because they are committed to social mobility and recognize opportunities to improve their credentials, and public universities, observes Weiner, are at the forefront in serving these needs:

> The Ivies don't have university-wide honors programs because they don't need them. Helping our students climb the class ladder is an important latent function of honors education. So is helping our students realize how smart and talented they are despite their society's assumption that the

more something costs the better it must be. So is encouraging them to develop their own ideas and explore means of living up to and benefiting from their full potential. (23)

At UWEC, where nearly 40% of the student body consists of first-generation students, the honors administrators follow Weiner in recognizing the importance of honors pedagogy in helping students participate in undergraduate research and prepare for high achievement in graduate schools, professions, and other life pursuits. Once again, though, we point out that for broader ranges of students to attain the benefits of honors, our program revisions must be driven by equity-minded, data-driven approaches in working with potential student populations.

The literature on diversity in honors provides a range of case studies documenting practical efforts to improve accessibility of honors programs to underserved student populations, including, according to Kristin Bagnato, community college students preparing to transfer to competitive four-year programs and urban high school students desiring a high-value college experience (5). One of the benefits of holistic admissions is to be able to look closely enough at student applications to account for opportunity gaps that can impact the scholastic records of incoming students. For instance, note Elizabeth Shaunessy and Patricia Alvarez McHatton, even the highest-achieving urban high school students may come in with fewer "marks of excellence" than their peers, and some urban students are not well served by "the impersonal nature of large classes, which didn't promote individualized assistance from teachers or relationships with educators" (497). In these ways, traditional measures of college preparation may not offer such students a sufficient case for honors admission in the first year. Further, while some honors students come into the university with a significant number of credits earned, underserved students may not have encountered such opportunities during their high school experience. Honors practitioners are well advised to keep these potential differences in mind as they prepare to work with first-year honors students.

Thinking Interculturally:
Community-Based Learning and Inclusive
Excellence in Honors

Building on established pedagogies in honors such as City as Text™ and Honors Semesters, honors at UWEC now features opportunities for community-based and intercultural learning that simultaneously serve the goals of intercultural competence, civic engagement, and inclusive excellence. Fortunately, our campus offers significant support for intercultural immersions in which a student-faculty team spends five or more consecutive days in a location that is outside of the immediate local environment. The pedagogy during this period emphasizes intercultural competence. Darla Deardorff describes intercultural competence as *"effective* and *appropriate* behavior and communication in intercultural situations" (66; emphasis in original). Community-based learning experiences such as intercultural immersions have significant potential to help students develop this competency, but ongoing, even lifelong interaction is required to sustain strong intercultural relationships.

UWEC was one of the first public colleges to require service learning for all students, providing a major precedent for community-based learning to build on as opportunities for intercultural immersions became available. In honors, several first efforts at immersion experiences included a service-learning component: an alternative spring break serving in nonprofit organizations in Milwaukee, WI; service learning in several southern cities during a Civil Rights Pilgrimage; and service learning in the school district of Fresno, CA, for a winterim immersion foregrounding Hmong American life and cultural history. We have tapped into literature on the effectiveness of immersion programs to guide our honors practice with the aim that intercultural pedagogy should be mutually beneficial for students and communities, should enable meaningful and sustained community interactions, should engage the whole identities of student participants, and should include experiences that are exciting and affirming as well as enigmatic. (See "Intercultural Pedagogical Principles" in Lee, Poch, Shaw, and

Williams 55–58.) We are committed to engaging as many students as possible in transformational intercultural learning, keeping in mind that equity-minded project outcomes are strengthened by the presence of a diverse range of participants, as highlighted by Strachan and Owens: "structural diversity in combination with curricular and interactional diversity yields cumulative effects" (470).

In scaling up the availability of intercultural experiences, one encounters the practical challenges of limited financial and time-related resources. It would be unfortunate to create an over-class of students who are able to access these experiences and an under-class of students who are not able to complete any immersions because of limited time, finances, and other resources. James Pfrehm and Robert Sullivan respond in part to this concern; they note that campus events, which are supported through existing resources and structures, can contribute to intercultural learning. Pfrehm and Sullivan embed these experiences into an honors seminar, during which students are intentional about choosing events that have different themes and purposes, and post-event reflections are guided by rubrics and shared publicly with other students. This "model of incorporating cultural encounters into the honors curriculum" adds to our array of options for regularizing the inclusion of intercultural experiences in our program practices, with the added benefit of strengthening the sense of community among students who plan, participate, and reflect on these experiences (Pfrehm and Sullivan 149).

PART V: AN HONORS COMMITMENT TO INCLUSIVE EXCELLENCE: OCCUPYING "BASIC CHARACTERISTICS"

This *Occupy Honors Education* chapter emphasizes the potentially vital role that honors programs can serve in the pursuit of inclusive excellence in higher education, from the wider adoption of holistic admissions to the greater infusion of diversity-related themes in curriculum, from equity-minded faculty development to increased availability of intercultural learning. To embed these commitments publicly within the honors mission, a highly visible starting point would be the NCHC "Basic Characteristics" document with which most of us in honors teaching and administration are familiar. Some useful grounding in the "Basic Characteristics" document already exists for a move towards inclusive excellence. Points 13 and 14 read as follows:

13. The program serves as a laboratory within which faculty feel welcome to experiment with new subjects, approaches, and pedagogies. When proven successful, such efforts in curriculum and pedagogical development can serve as prototypes for initiatives that can become institutionalized across the campus.

14. The program engages in continuous assessment and evaluation and is open to the need for change in order to maintain its distinctive position of offering exceptional and enhanced educational opportunities to honors students. ("Basic Characteristics," National Collegiate Honors Council)

These ideas support a re-envisioning of honors with inclusive excellence as a primary goal. Point 13 reminds us that curriculum and pedagogy in honors can lead the way towards campus transformation, engaging campuses in the formal articulation of new curricula and pedagogies in support of inclusive excellence, such as the following:

• exploring human creativity as expressed variously across cultural maps;

• investigating economic and ecological trends related to human diversity;

• examining the connectedness among equity, oppression, and privilege in social systems;

• examining constructs regarding human identity from both biological and social perspectives;

- piloting problem-based, solution-based, and community-based pedagogy in response to equity issues on and off campus.

Greater integration of these approaches into honors curricula will help students respond proactively and thoughtfully to related issues in their careers and personal lives.

Point 14 focuses on the need for assessment and evaluation to inform program revision. In honors, we can strengthen our collection and use of campus and community data to assess how well our programs can achieve equity-related outcomes. As I mentioned earlier, useful models are available for assessing equity and inclusion as institutional outcomes, such as the Equity Scorecard. Going beyond this particular tool, honors programs may review student data collected by institutional research offices on campus and by state and national agencies. Such data can contribute significantly to equity-minded program revision. A thorough review of internal program data to identify opportunity gaps can provide a foundation for thoughtful action.

To energize a national trend in which honors programs across the country engage in equity-minded reform, inclusive excellence requires a more prominent presence in the "Basic Characteristics" document. With that goal in mind and in the spirit of *Occupy Honors Education*, I propose two additions to this document, perhaps as Points 18 and 19:

18. Honors program leaders have an ethical responsibility to keep current on the professional literature and public debates surrounding diversity, equity, and educational access across all communities. Specific points of interest in this knowledge base include:

    - Familiarity with national debates on the predictive and exclusionary consequences of using standardized tests, class rank, and holistic approaches in admissions;

- Familiarity with U.S. Supreme Court decisions regarding race in admissions policies (including Fischer v. University of Texas, Gratz v. Bollinger/Grutter v. Bollinger, and the University of California Regents v. Bakke cases);

- Familiarity with literature that asserts the compelling case for diversity as a critical educational outcome;

- Familiarity with demographics in our feeder communities and enrollment trends on our own campuses, including underserved populations;

- Familiarity with admissions policies and goals at our own campuses and consortia.

19. Honors programs value both inclusion and excellence as attributes of high-impact student experiences. As a result, honors programs consistently collaborate with diverse organizations and people in the broader communities that surround their campuses and maintain effective working relationships with campus colleagues, including faculty and staff, whose teaching, research, and administrative interests are in the area of diversity.

The addition of these points to the "Basic Characteristics" document would clearly signal and inspire a renewed emphasis on inclusive excellence in honors.

HONORS AND INCLUSIVE EXCELLENCE: A FINAL WORD

The impact of our work at UWEC has been significant, positive, and widely felt across our honors student body and across our campus, even as the challenge remains of sustaining the improvements we have made and of helping to embed the practices of inclusive excellence within our program, across our campus, and in other post-secondary institutions.

My sincere hope is that this chapter is helpful for other honors educators, including those of us whose personal stories are inseparable from our journeys as educators. Bringing inclusive excellence to the forefront invites us to share our stories, as the Harvard students have done with the "I, Too" project. Thus, I have tried to convey some of the personal joys of honors work, even at a time of *occupation*. I am extremely grateful for the marvelous opportunities I have had to work closely with students, various communities, faculty, and fellow administrators during a first decade as an honors educator. My dream is for honors educators to partner with all equity-minded allies to build mutually beneficial connections among diverse student communities, honors programs, and whole institutions. Being a part of such work has been truly transformative and rewarding, and I encourage us all to see where a common commitment to inclusive excellence can take us.

ACKNOWLEDGMENTS

I wish to recognize and thank former UWEC Honors Director Dr. Jeff Vahlbusch for working so closely and earnestly with me in a multi-year professional collaboration, an experience that has been gratifying and enriching in numerous ways. I would also like to sincerely thank our honors student research team, an extremely dedicated and forward-thinking group of young scholars who have made essential contributions to this important work, including Demetrius Evans, Allison Fouks, Sammi Nelson, Tara Nichols, Nichole Peters, Anneli Williams, and Carolyn Wolff. Several academic staff at UWEC made important contributions to the long-term research project that made this chapter possible: Pam Golden, University Honors Program; Kari Herbison, Office of Institutional Research; and Andy Nelson, Director of the Office of Institutional Research. The former Assistant Director for Advising and Student Programs in honors, Dr. Ivy Gerbis, made it possible for a humanities professor to help facilitate the collection of over ten years of data about program performance and to use this data to improve operations. I am also deeply appreciative of Dr. Estela Bensimon and the Association of American Colleges and Universities for their wisdom and their vital contributions to the movement for inclusive excellence.

REFERENCES

"About CME." Center for Multicultural Excellence. Center for Multicultural Excellence Home Page. *University of Denver.* 29 Aug. 2013. Web. 18 June 2015.

Association of American Colleges and Universities. "Board Statement on Diversity, Equity, and Inclusive Excellence." *About AAC&U.* Association of American Colleges and Universities, 27 June 2013. Web. 29 Aug. 2013.

Bagnato, Kristin. "Honors Programs Draw Praise, Money and Students." *Community College Week* 18.26 (14 Aug. 2006): 5+. Print.

"Basic Characteristics of a Fully Developed Honors Program." National Collegiate Honors Council. NCHC Policy Document, 19 June 2014. Web. 22 June 2015.

Bok, Derek. "The Compelling Need for Diversity in Higher Education": Expert Report of Derek Bok." *Gratz, et al. v. Bollinger, et al., No. 97-75928.* Supreme Court Testimony. University of Michigan Admissions Lawsuits, 5 Sept. 2012. Web. 08 July, 2013.

Boyer, Ernest. *Scholarship Reconsidered: Priorities of the Professoriate.* Carnegie Foundation for the Advancement of Teaching: Princeton, New Jersey, 1990. Print.

Center for Urban Education. The CUE Equity Model: Frequently Asked Questions. Center for Urban Education. N.d. Web. 10 July 2017.

Coleman, Finnie D. "The Problem with Diversity: Moving Past the Numbers." *Setting the Table for Diversity.* Ed. Lisa L. Coleman and Jonathan D. Kotinek. Lincoln, NE: National Collegiate Honors Council, 2010. 239–49. NCHC Monograph Series. Print.

Coleman, Lisa L., and Jonathan D. Kotinek, ed. *Setting the Table for Diversity.* Lincoln, NE: National Collegiate Honors Council, 2010. NCHC Monograph Series. Print.

Deardorff, Darla. "Assessing Intercultural Competence." *New Directions for Institutional Research* 149 (2011): 65–79. Web. 18 June 2015.

DeLeon, Michael. "A Reflection on Serving Latina/o Honors Students in Texas." *Setting the Table for Diversity.* Ed. Lisa L. Coleman and Jonathan D. Kotinek. Lincoln, NE: National Collegiate Honors Council, 2010. 61–75. NCHC Monograph Series. Print.

Equity Scorecard Team. *Equity Scorecard Interim Report: Excellence.* Affirmative Action Office, University of Wisconsin at Eau Claire. 2009. Web. 28 May 2015.

"Essential Learning Outcomes. *About LEAP* (Liberal Education and America's Promise). Association for American Colleges and Universities, 23 Feb. 2014. Web. 18 June 2015.

Fischer v. the University of Texas, et al. Supreme Court of the United States. Court Opinions, 24 June 2013. Web. 06 Apr. 2015.

Gurin, Patricia. "Expert Report of Patricia Gurin." *Gratz, et al. v. Bollinger, et al.*, No. 97-75321. Supreme Court Testimony. University of Michigan Admissions Lawsuits, 05 Sept. 2012. Web. 04 Apr. 2015.

"Harvard University Endowment Earns 11.3% Return for Fiscal Year." *News Release.* Harvard University, 24 Sept. 2013. Web. 08 Mar. 2014.

Hoover, Eric. "Changing Times, Tough Choices." *Chronicle of Higher Education* 24 Jan. 2014: A26. Print.

Hoxby, Caroline, and Christopher Avery. "The Missing 'One-Offs': The Hidden Supply of High-Achieving, Low-Income Students." *Brookings Paper on Economic Activity.* Brookings Institution, Spring 2013. Web. 24 Feb. 2014.

"Inclusive Excellence." University of Wisconsin System. Wisconsin. edu. N.d. Web. 03 Apr. 2017.

Institutional Research Office. *Factbook 2013–4.* University of Wisconsin at Eau Claire Office of Institutional Research, n.d. Web. 08 Mar. 2014.

Lee, Amy, Robert Poch, Marta Shaw, and Rhiannon Williams. *Engaging Diversity in Undergraduate Classrooms: A Pedagogy for Developing Cultural Competence.* San Francisco: Jossey-Bass, 2012. McIntyre Library Search. Web. 18 June 2015.

Lipka, Sara. "Colleges, Here Is Your Future." *Chronicle of Higher Education* 24 Jan. 2014: A24, A26. Print.

Longo, Peter, and John Falconer. "Diversity Opportunities for Higher Education and Honors Programs: A View from Nebraska." *Journal of the National Collegiate Honors Council* 4.1 (2003): 53–60. Print.

Matsuda-Lawrence, Kimiko. *I, Too, Am Harvard.* Tumblr.com. 01 Mar. 2014. Web. 08 Mar. 2014. Photo Campaign.

Mettler, Suzanne. "College, the Great Unleveler." *New York Times* Editorial Page. Online Edition, 01 Mar. 2014. Web. 08 Mar. 2014.

Morello, Carol, and Ted Mellnik. "Census: Minority Babies Are Now Majority in United States." *Washington Post.* Online Edition, 17 May 2012. Web. 08 Mar. 2014.

Moritz, Benjamin. "Can the Elitism of Honors Help Students at Non-Elite Schools?" *Journal of the National Collegiate Honors Council* 12.2 (2011): 65–67. Print.

O'Shaughnessy, Lynn. "20 Biggest College Endowments." *CBS Moneywatch.* 04 Feb. 2013. Web. 22 June 2015.

Pfrehm, James, and Robert Sullivan. "The Cultural Encounters Model: Incorporating Campus Events into the Honors Curriculum." *Honors in Practice* 9 (2013): 141–53. Print.

Shaunessy, Elizabeth, and Patricia Alvarez McHatton. "Urban Students' Perceptions of Teachers: Views of Students in General, Special, and Honors Education." *Urban Review* 41 (2009): 486–503. Print.

Soares, Joseph. "The Future of College Admissions: Discussion." *Educational Psychologist* 47.1 (2012): 66–70. Print.

Steele, Bill. "Cornell's Endowment Gains, Pays Out More." *Cornell Chronicle*. Online Edition, 21 Oct. 2014. Web. 05 Apr. 2015.

Strachan, J. Cherie, and Chris Owens. "Learning Civic Identity Outside of the Classroom: Diversity and Campus Associational Life." *Journal of Political Science Education* 7 (2011): 464–82. Print.

U.S. Census Bureau. "State and County Quick Facts" (Wisconsin). Online Database, n.d. Web. 08 Mar. 2014.

U.S. News College Compass. University of Wisconsin at Eau Claire. *U.S. News and World Report*. Online Database, n.d. Web. 05 Apr. 2015.

Vaccaro, Adam. "Harvard's Endowment Is Bigger than Half the World's Economies." *Boston.com*. 25 Sept. 2014. Web. 05 Apr. 2015.

Weiner, Norm. "Honors is Elitist, and What's Wrong with That?" *Journal of the National Collegiate Honors Council* 10.1 (2009): 19–24. Print.

A Privilege for the Privileged?
Using Intersectionality to Reframe Honors
and Promote Social Responsibility

Amberly Dziesinski, Phame Camarena,
and Caitlin Homrich-Knieling
Central Michigan University

INTRODUCTION

Professionals in the greater honors community have already established a healthy dialogue about the significance of diversity and inequality within honors as reflected in the *Journal of the National Collegiate Honors Council* (*JNCHC*) special forum on social class (Long & Mullins, 2009) and the National Collegiate Honors Council monograph *Setting the Table for Diversity* (Coleman & Kotinek, 2010). A central theme emerging from these perspectives highlights the responsibility of honors programs to take an active stand against the kind of elitism that reinforces social inequalities and, instead, challenges honors to become a stronger force for social change. Much of this discussion addresses the importance of ensuring that a more diverse group of students from underrepresented

81

and marginalized backgrounds is able to find a home within honors. To further these ideas, this work directly challenges the honors community to use its resources and relative position of power to make honors a force for progressive social change both in the campus community and society at large.

Building from previous work in honors and drawing from concepts developed in feminist and sociological literature by Grzanka (2014), this chapter explores how honors culture and student identity can be shaped by an explicit attempt to reframe honors efforts in the context of diversity, inequality, and social responsibility rather than elitism and entitlement. Beginning with the argument that honors is in a position of privilege and has a responsibility to be an active agent for social justice, this chapter provides an honest reflection on the challenges of building a programmatic commitment to equity and social justice in the honors community within a public university. It also uses case studies to illustrate how this commitment has special significance for students from marginalized groups who are navigating a potentially uncomfortable intersection between experiences of inequality and honors privilege.

AN INTENTIONAL HONORS CULTURE—NAMING PRIVILEGE

Reframing honors as a force for social justice and equality begins with a call for enlightenment: to recognize that honors is almost always a place of privilege. This privilege is best exemplified in two interdependent processes. First, students are most often recruited into honors programs with the promise that they will receive extra opportunities for learning and enrichment. These privileges, available to a select few, may include priority registration, special housing options, smaller classes, select faculty, and extra scholarship options. Second, although criteria vary widely across programs, previous course grades, scores on standardized tests, and past records of academic-related achievement in and out of the classroom are all criteria often included in reviews for honors admission. Social science research, such as that done by Lipman (2004), has consistently documented that these factors are also shaped by more than personal work habits and intellectual potential.

Instead, background experiences made available in resource-rich families and schools give some students an advantage over competitors from families and schools unable to offer the same level of support and preparation for achievement. This disparity means that at least some portion of student achievement prior to entering honors is "unearned," according to Johnson (2006), because the same level of effort will not lead to the same level of achievement and preparation for honors admission on the part of all students (p. 23). Similarly, these class differences will most often mean that students enrolled in honors are more likely to come from backgrounds that are more privileged compared to students who were not admitted or who never considered applying *within* the same institution— even if those accepted to honors might be less privileged than peers who attended a more prestigious institution in the first place.

In that vein, part of what makes this process of recognizing and naming privilege in honors so difficult is that few honors programs are found in the most elite institutions. Most honors administrators and educators intentionally use their programs to reach out to students of high academic ability who might otherwise attend more prestigious and expensive institutions. As explained by Weiner (2009) in his essay on social class and elitism, honors programs attract top students to campuses with less elite reputations that these students might not otherwise attend and then help them "climb the class ladder" while fighting the assumption that "the more something costs the better it must be" (p. 23). In other words, because honors programs recruit students who come from relatively less privileged backgrounds compared to students who attend more elite schools, it is easy to forget that within the same institution, the honors students are still more likely to come from backgrounds of relative privilege compared to their non-honors peers. In his assessment of privilege and power, Johnson (2006) notes that "privilege is always in relation to others" (p. 8). In any given situation, who is privileged and who has power is relative. Naming this tendency toward privilege within honors is an essential first step in minimizing the negative impacts and increasing the opportunity for honors to be a force for positive social change rather than one that reproduces the social inequalities in our educational systems.

In contrast to the more traditional selective models focused on achievement indicators that are more likely to be shaped by early privilege, according to Mullins (2005), increasing numbers of honors programs are changing admissions procedures to enhance the recruitment of underrepresented students who demonstrate ambition, even if they have lower test scores or grades than other applicants (p. 22). (See also David M. Jones in this volume pp. 33–79.) This commitment to diversity is even explicitly addressed by some programs with a specific statement affirming the importance of diversity for their honors communities. (See Coleman & Kotinek, 2010, p. 253.) Similarly, as Klos, Eskine, & Pashkevich (2015) maintain, more programs are willing to make an explicit commitment to social justice as a valued goal and explicit learning outcome in order to take the emphasis off of individual achievement for the sake of self (p. 54).

Promoting these intertwined themes of diversity and social justice is important to honors in at least two key ways. First, it ensures that all students coming to the honors community will develop new tools to understand their identities and their place in society. This understanding prepares honors students to be advocates for social change and allies for their peers from more marginalized backgrounds. Second, students from underrepresented and marginalized groups would see honors as a welcoming community for them—a place where the intersection of honors privilege and other identities can be navigated in positive ways.

Programs that explicitly address privilege and power challenge hegemonic notions of society and the honors students' positions within it; these programs recognize that students are not "climbing the social ladder" apolitically but are instead embedded in broader dynamics of inequality, oppression, and privilege. Honors programs have an obligation to take a stand regarding social inequalities and are doing so whether they realize it or not. Programs that attempt to remain neutral, insisting that their curriculum and objectives are focused on helping all students achieve their highest academic potentials independent of any social bias or judgment, are missing the point. To the degree that programs do not actively challenge the social norms of privilege tied to honors, they are tacitly supporting the status quo that makes honors a privilege for the privileged.

Because of the challenges of recognizing embedded social inequality, intentional planning and strategic effort are necessary for honors programs to occupy the institution as a force for social change. Although the Central Michigan University (CMU) Honors Program does not claim to be a model of diversity or champion of social justice, we are able to offer practical examples that demonstrate how our commitment to social responsibility is strategically reflected in practical steps that reframe the meaning of honors privilege within the honors community.

MISSION AND VISION MATTER

Although this commitment to enlightenment and empowerment is an ongoing process, the effort of the honors program to formally redefine the program mission beyond traditional academic achievement and educational enrichment was an essential step. Like most honors programs and colleges, the previous honors vision and mission were focused on opportunities for enrichment that promised students unique learning experiences and advantages to entice them to apply and enroll. A revision to these statements placed a greater explicit emphasis on diversity and social responsibility as priorities over individual achievement. This sentiment is summarized with the program vision to "serve the University by fostering a diverse community of scholars committed to academic excellence, intellectual engagement, and social responsibility" ("Mission and Core Values"). In this model, academic achievement remains a priority, but it is in the context, as our mission states, of a commitment to using critical thought and scholarly inquiry to ensure that efforts are "for the greater good of our disciplines, our society, and our world" ("Mission and Core Values"). The importance of diversity initiatives specifically is reinforced by including "respect and appreciation for diverse peoples and ideas in a global society" as one of the four primary core program values ("Mission and Core Values"). Finally, to keep the emphasis on social change rather than personal achievement alone, the final two core program values juxtapose a call to high standards for personal achievement with an explicit expectation for "active citizenship and service for the greater good" ("Mission and Core Values"). As the formally approved mission of the program, both the specific wording of each core value and the spirit of these statements provide an institutionally approved guide for translating this mission into intentional action. (See Appendix A to read the full CMU Honors Program statements of vision, mission, and values.)

RECRUITMENT

Building off of the revised mission statement, recruitment messages highlight that the CMU Honors Program is not for all high academic ability students. Those who cannot see the significance of our core values will be more content in other campus programs. Our major recruitment programs include materials that explicitly target first-generation college students and address stereotypes about the students honors serves. Although our program has a competitive process and currently admits a limited number of students who are scholarship recipients, the evaluation process considers the degree to which students have overcome challenges in order to achieve. It is important to note that Michigan law limits the use of race and minority status as an admissions criterion. Our use of first-generation college status, however, as one indicator of educational resilience is not precluded by the law, and we are careful to examine high school backgrounds and the limits on opportunities for students from rural, urban, and low-income communities. Similarly, recognizing that institutional structures limit the degree to which we can recruit from underrepresented groups for our first-year class, our program has also developed a second track for honors admission that gives priority to students with high academic goals who are overcoming challenges to achievement once on campus. Referrals from both our faculty and our multicultural program office are useful tools for identifying students from diverse backgrounds who would specifically benefit from extra support and increased academic challenge. Admission to honors through this track has, in fact, increased student participation from underrepresented groups on campus, including students of color, first-generation college students, and international students.

CURRICULUM

Consistent with the honors program core values, the honors protocol requires six credits of diversity and global, culturally themed coursework along with 120 hours of documented service toward the greater good. The rationale for these requirements is introduced in recruitment, but it is then immediately reinforced in our required Orientation to Honors Seminar for new honors students. To reinforce diversity and social justice themes, this class includes:

1. a first-day discussion about honors privilege and responsibility;

2. an introduction to diversity in the campus community with an emphasis on the role of privilege, especially the difference between earned and unearned privilege, and inequality;

3. a discussion of active citizenship with a call to identify issues of personal passion; and

4. a requirement for students to participate in campus activities linked to both diversity and service, with a challenge to choose activities that stretch personal comfort zones (e.g., LGBTQ safe zone workshops, a field trip to a local Native American cultural center, serving as a conversation partner for an international student, participating in an alternative weekend service trip, etc.).

The opportunities listed above are not provided to suggest that students will be enlightened and empowered at the end of their first term; however, if our students clearly understand that diversity and service are priorities of the program, and if they are given the language of privilege and social justice theory, they are better prepared to engage in discourse around these issues and to reflect on how these concepts relate to their personal experiences. We conceptualize the educational process through which students come to recognize inequality in their daily lives as the development of critical consciousness—a central aspect of the critical pedagogy advocated by Freire (1970) that encourages action for progressive social change (p. 35).

As a follow-up to this introduction, various honors courses emphasize both diversity and social responsibility themes. Recent examples include a first-year seminar on inequality in American healthcare; a junior-level seminar on Latinos in the U.S., which included a spring break trip serving in a Miami cultural center; and a faculty-led international program focused on apartheid and the literature of South Africa. Additionally, the honors program has developed a service-learning designated course that brings faculty and students together to work on real-world service projects in the community while reinforcing active citizenship lessons.

ADVISING AND MENTORING

Although the honors program staff tries to develop personal relationships with all of our students, we are more intentional with students from underrepresented groups including students of color, first-generation college students, international students, students with disabilities, and others who have been identified as being at greater educational risk. These activities include annual targeted advising outreach from our Honors Academic Advisor and identification of informal staff mentors assigned to provide additional tracking and support. The honors program offers students both individual and group activities. For example, first-generation college students are invited to attend a dinner and movie night at the director's house to watch and discuss a film about educational achievement. Other students are encouraged to apply for the McNair Scholars Program, which promotes PhD achievement for underrepresented students, and are assigned an honors staff member who serves as a social mentor to support the scholar and promote collaboration across the two sets of program requirements.

PROGRAMMING

Both directly through our office and indirectly through supervision of our honors student organizations, we support programming that provides students with additional extracurricular opportunities to engage with diversity and social responsibility issues. For example, topics addressed by faculty at the monthly fireside chats in the honors residence hall include discussions of gender, religion, and the power of oppression. All honors students are also invited to join the honors program staff for our annual participation in the Martin Luther King, Jr., March. And first-generation college students enrolled in honors are invited to participate in a weekend retreat featuring first-generation mentors from the honors student body, faculty, and administration.

PARTNERSHIPS

Our success with these diversity and social justice efforts is significantly impacted by campus partnerships with the academic and student affairs programs that share similar goals. Academically, this process includes working with department chairs of general education programs with diversity-themed courses to offer honors sections for our students. In student affairs, we include a representative from the Office for Institutional Diversity on our advisory council and work with the Multicultural Office on programming and recruitment opportunities. Although the results of these partnerships are not equally successful, some, like our collaboration with the McNair Scholars Program, are a more natural fit and enable both units to fulfill their mission.

ASSESSMENT

Recognizing that our social responsibility to advocate for diversity and equity will never be complete, the honors program is committed to an ongoing assessment of our efforts to continually adjust and improve. (See also F. Coleman in this volume, p. 342.) The end-of-course evaluations for the first-year honors seminar

(HON 100) directly ask students to rate and comment on the degree to which experiences with this class impacted their appreciation for diversity and active citizenship. Similarly, while we recognize that not all honors coursework can or should have the same emphasis, the course evaluations used in all honors sections ask students to evaluate whether the course addressed honors diversity and citizenship themes. These evaluations remind both students and faculty of this important honors goal. Finally, as part of their senior exit surveys, graduating seniors are asked to review their honors experiences and to critique the effectiveness of our diversity and social responsibility efforts both in and out of the classroom.

CHALLENGES

Even with a clear set of initiatives and efforts, challenges to this mission are significant; they include policy decisions made by units outside of honors control, instability of staffing across partner offices, the strength of stereotypes about what honors is and the students it should serve, competing pressures from the academic and student service units of the university, and a general misunderstanding about the factual nature of inequality in U.S. higher education today. Although the opportunities and challenges the honors program faces are contextualized in the nature of our institution, some of these challenges are likely generalizable to other campuses.

By facilitating opportunities for students to wrestle with the meaning of their identities as they relate to power, privilege, and justice, the honors program seeks to enlighten students concerning their position within the social hierarchy. This strategy attempts to positively empower students to navigate their own identities and to share ownership for ensuring that honors is a force for positive social change. This emphasis has significance for all students within the program, but it has a special meaning for those coming into the program with backgrounds that might otherwise intersect negatively with the honors stereotype of elitism and privilege.

INTERSECTIONALITY AND HONORS PRIVILEGE

Regardless of the mission, curriculum, and approach of any particular honors community, integrating an honors identity into a coherent picture of self often creates some extra challenges for students from backgrounds underrepresented in higher education and those who identify with marginalized social groups. Integral to understanding this challenge of identity negotiation is the concept of intersectionality. In "Intersectionality as Buzzword," Kathy Davis (2008) explains that intersectionality "refers to the interaction between gender, race, and other categories of difference in individual lives, social practices, institutional arrangements, and cultural ideologies and the outcomes of these interactions in terms of power" (p. 68). Although this concept was originally introduced to encourage a more careful examination of the complex interaction of different forms of inequality and oppression in feminist research, intersectionality has also become a useful tool with broad practical applications. (See Grzanka, 2014.)

In the view of Davis (2008), the model of intersectionality has grown in popularity both because of the complexity of ideas implicated within it for scholars and because it helps generalists and practitioners conceptualize inequality and personal experience (p. 74). For honors professionals, at least two clear applications emerge from this research. First, intersectionality demands that any honors exploration of diversity be contextualized in terms of inequality and power and not simply as if differences between people and groups are natural and neutral. Second, as Davis (2008) notes, intersectionality provides a useful tool for "visualizing how differences intersect within a particular person's identity or in a specific social practice or location" (p. 75). This includes understanding how diverse groups of students make meaning of honors and how the specific social practices of any particular honors community might shape student experiences, including their own self-perceptions of privilege and social responsibility.

HONORS STUDENT IDENTITIES

During the application of intersectionality theory to honors, each student's identity is a unique composite of various social group memberships and personal identifications (e.g., racial, gender, religious), and these identities are charged with different implications related to power and oppression that vary by social context. Few honors students, however, come to their post-secondary education with a sophisticated understanding of how power and privilege are tied to honors and what this means for their personal identities. When they proceed through an honors program that acknowledges these inextricable linkages and explicitly states its priorities and practices related to social justice, students may undergo the complex process of identity renegotiation.

For students from majority groups, negotiating an honors identity may not be problematic in itself because honors likely coordinates well with other identities more associated with privilege. For these students, the challenge in navigating honors privilege comes from a call to self-reflect more critically on their privileged status in the social world and to use that awareness to become a force for positive social change, helping us fulfill the mission of our program. In contrast, for students coming from underrepresented or marginalized groups, becoming enlightened simultaneously to the privilege of honors and to the oppression related to their underrepresented or marginalized group status puts these students in a difficult position. To illustrate this process and its value to students and our mission, three narratives of CMU Honors Program students navigating identity in moments of conflicting power and oppression are presented and discussed in the subsequent sections.

To understand the student narratives that follow, it is important to first contextualize them within CMU, a White-majority university in a conservative, rural region of a state that is dominated by de facto racial divisions and urban-rural distinctions. Additionally, as part of a public, comprehensive university with favorable tuition rates, the CMU Honors Program is in a good position to recruit students of high academic ability who might not consider more expensive private liberal arts colleges or national research universities, even when they do qualify academically.

Within this context, we interviewed students about their process of navigating their personal identities and membership in the honors program. We sought honors participants who identified with at least one of three traditionally marginalized groups: first-generation college students (FGC); racial and ethnic minorities; and lesbian, gay, bisexual, transgender, and/or queer sexual orientation (LGBTQ). Our goal was both to learn more about the process of identity negotiation across these intersecting identities and to assess whether our programmatic efforts to reframe honors privilege and responsibility were reflected in these students' experiences. The narratives that follow draw from a more complete work that was conducted as part of an honors senior capstone project. (See Appendix B for research methodology.)

We have paired students' experiences with literature that highlights the generalized challenges students who identify with a specific identity group may face. We want to emphasize, however, that the experience of actual students may be very different from the generalized literature because other aspects of their identities intersect and influence their experience. In fact, most students interviewed described resentment toward this general identity categorization, acknowledging that, while there may be extra challenges from being first generation or a student of color, they do not want to be seen as at risk or only through the eyes of a deficit model (Pascarella, Pierson, Wolniak, & Terenzini, 2004). As honors students they know they are academically capable and expect to succeed at the university.

CASE STUDIES:
ENLIGHTENMENT AND EMPOWERMENT

Ray

Ray is a junior majoring in broadcasting and cinematic arts with a minor in political science. Through the support of the honors program, Ray defined his identity as a FGC, "Hispanic Caucasian" student: "I can say that honors certainly helped me in terms of finding my identity . . . [and] to look at it from an intellectual perspective."

Because Ray was a FGC student from a rural, lower socio-economic community, one of Ray's biggest challenges transitioning to honors was the perception that he was in an entitled position. Upon disclosing his honors status, he felt stereotyped by those who believed honors students were privileged and single-mindedly academic:

> I had to struggle with the whole concept of suddenly being entitled, because being in high school, I wasn't entitled at all . . . so to be told I'm entitled was something that I had to deal with in my freshman year. And I didn't like being entitled. . . . It made me feel guilty that I was in honors. It made me feel guilty that I was getting a full ride [scholarship] and maybe I'm not as smart as this other person.

Simultaneously, Ray is proud to serve as a role model for his entire family and intends to become the first grandchild to graduate from college. This dissonance is consistent with research by Frost (2009) that suggests FGC students conceptualize their college education as a means of climbing the social ladder and helping their families and communities do the same (p. 35). In opposition to this aspect of the FGC identity, honors status as a privileged position often leads others to perceive honors students as entitled or elitist, which demeans the humble beginnings of some FGC honors students. While research on FGC students in university honors programs is sparse, authors in the 2009 *JNCHC* "Forum on Social Class" demonstrate the necessity of attention to FGC students. (See Pressler, 2009, p. 39; Frost, 2009, p. 34.) Lisa Sanon-Jules (2010), in her chapter in *Setting the Table for Diversity*, also suggests that structured faculty and peer mentorship programs, extracurricular activities, and increased academic guidance benefit FGC students (p. 107). For example, FGC students in the honors program, like Ray, have the opportunity to participate in a variety of targeted programs including a first-generation retreat, which explores issues of equity in educational achievement and empowers students to take a strength-based approach to their joint status as first generation and honors.

Ray's experience in honors is further compounded by his identification as Hispanic Caucasian. In his predominantly White hometown, Ray was bullied for his racial minority status. Although he feels the "burden" of being one of the only Hispanic honors students in what he considers a very "whitewashed" system, Ray felt that his racial identity was welcomed in honors, and he took advantage of opportunities to study Latin American cultures through honors special topic course work:

> Before I got into the honors program, I was really unsure of myself in terms of what group I identify with. I didn't want to identify as Hispanic because I knew that I would be bullied for it and teased for it. . . . [On the standardized tests' race question] I had to put "I don't want to respond." And that killed me because it felt like I didn't know who I was. And obviously that brings about a lot of pain, a lot of questioning, a lot of doubts, a lot of misunderstanding, and so coming into the honors program and realizing that I can be alright in my own skin, that now that I'm away from a less accepting environment and can come here, I can identify as the thing that I want to identify as and present myself into that society as that.

Andrea

Andrea is a senior majoring in neuroscience. Although Andrea was born into an unstable environment, she was adopted and raised in a middle class, White suburban community. She entered college as a member of both honors and a program for multicultural students. As an academically oriented student in high school, transitioning to the academic rigor of honors was relatively seamless. Andrea's experience with the multicultural program, however, led her to further question her racial categorization, a process that she

95

now recognizes as a lifelong exploration: "I'm not really sure how I identify. I look like I'm half black and half white. I grew up in a White community." Most of her peers in the multicultural program grew up in inner-city environments, and Andrea perceived them to be less focused on academics or career pathways than she was. Because of different backgrounds and values, she does not feel that she always fits in with these students and was once told she could not hang out with a group of her peers because she "wasn't Black enough."

After discussing this conflict with honors faculty, Andrea came to understand marginalization as it relates to membership in seemingly contradictory groups. She subsequently mentored first-year honors students and helped her peers to navigate membership in both honors and multicultural organizations. Andrea is comfortable talking to other honors students about diversity but recognizes that the program does not necessarily represent diverse demographics. Andrea noted that identifying as honors has become a positive alternative that allows her to be accepted both for her academic orientation and for her unique racial background.

Despite trying to avoid identity categorizations all together, Andrea is often met with assumptions about her racial identity based on her physical appearance. As her experience illustrates, and the research of Harrell, Meyers, & Smedley (1993) supports, minority students in college may feel that they need to legitimize their competency while simultaneously proving their cultural identity to peers (p. 447). Consequently, as Pearson & Kohl (2010) report, minority students are less likely to self-select into honors, even when they have the academic credentials that meet or exceed admission requirements (p. 36). To encourage the participation of racial minority students and support their success, additional authors who contributed to *Setting the Table for Diversity* suggest staff training, peer-to-peer mentoring, and highlighting diversity in workshops, courses, and programming. (See Pearson & Kohl, 2010, p. 37; DeLeon, 2010, p. 70; Materon-Arum, 2010, p. 93.)

For students like Andrea, being evaluated through the lens of only one primary identity may invalidate their subjective experience. Literature on the subject, such as the research of KewalRamani,

Gilbertson, Fox, & Provasnik (2007), would suggest that students with her racial background are more likely to have attended high-poverty schools and be underprepared academically (p. 96). These challenges are not necessarily generalizable to Andrea's experience; she faces her own challenges as she wrestles with identity, which highlights the importance of an intersectional approach when addressing a student's unique situation.

Marshall

Marshall is a senior majoring in biology from a small rural community with few role models who had attended college. Marshall came to college as a FGC student without a preconception of honors students and only applied to honors at his mother's request. He has since grown to appreciate the program, which he feels kept him enrolled and involved in the university:

> I feel like if I wasn't in the honors program, I probably would have shut down really fast just because the college atmosphere in general doesn't push you to do many things. . . . The honors program just presented everything in an easy way, just to see everything and to an extent be a driving force to actually getting involved with things.

Smaller class sizes and honors professors who made an effort to get to know him taught Marshall how to interact with university faculty, a valuable skill that set him up for success in future courses.

The honors program has also helped Marshall accept his sexual orientation and affirm a positive gay identity. After a period of cautious "coming out" in the honors residential community, Marshall had the opportunity to participate in a diversity panel for first-year honors students and received positive feedback after sharing his story: "Identifying as gay, that took a lot of effort on my part. So it was really helpful just to be able to tell my story in front of the HON 100 students. I think the honors program helps just sort of being more open."

Among university students like Marshall, students who do not identify as heterosexual may exhibit greater mental health challenges. According to Oswalt & Wyatt (2011), these challenges may impact academic performance, thus jeopardizing continued membership in a grade-based honors program (p. 1270). Research on honors acknowledges the existence of LGBTQ students within honors communities and the need for inclusion, but it rarely addresses the unique challenges these students may face. Some honors programs, however, have implemented courses and lessons devoted to exploring sexual orientation that can heighten a sense of belonging for these students. (See Riek & Sheridan, 2010, p. 27; Newell & Baxter, 2010, p. 151.)

NAVIGATING IDENTITY

The interviews we conducted were not intended to provide a representative sample or data to be generalized to the honors community overall. Rather, we aimed to open a discussion concerning the unique challenges intersectionality of identity poses and to provide examples of students successfully undergoing identity navigation with the help of an honors community. In our research, even though we were conscious of intersectionality and identity formation theories, we were still often surprised when students whom we expected to identify with one categorization of identity disclosed that they identified with an entirely different group. Similarly, we were surprised to see that although the female majority gender demographics of our honors program is a regular topic of discussion among our own students, who also question what this pattern has to do with power and inequality, this issue was not something that the participants in our interviews spontaneously addressed.

The students we interviewed do not fit exactly into any category; rather, they exhibit a unique combination of personal and social identities that form their sense of self with honors as one key piece of intersection. We conceptualize intersectionality as this combination of identities associated with varying degrees of power and privilege. Some identities are in conflict while others are seamlessly combined, a process of constant and simultaneous identity negotiation. Although honors students may identify with the same race, class, or sexual orientation, their experiences can be vastly different from that of other students because their identities are also shaped by numerous additional factors such as religious affiliation, ethnicity, social class, and physical ability to create a unique combination owned solely by that individual. Ultimately, these students, like all individuals, are complex, and an intersectional approach necessitates seeing the totality of an individual based on the layers of groups and characteristics with which they identify.

Despite this complexity, for the sake of organization, students are often expected to "check a box" describing their race, gender, and other characteristics that are not as definitive as they appear on standardized questionnaires. For example, all of the students interviewed who identified with a racial minority noted, for various reasons, their frustration and confusion when they were asked to identify their race. Their cultural roots did not match their skin tone; they feared identifying with a racial minority would lead to marginalization and bullying; or they wanted to be seen for their personal definition of their race rather than for a perception plagued with stereotypes. Of course, identity is also shaped externally. For these students, automatic judgment can place them in a box before they get a chance to explain their story of identity navigation and chosen identity. While part of identity navigation involves processing external feedback, personal identities are ideally chosen with an awareness about the range and potential meaning of the identities available. An individual may choose to identify with a spectrum of genders and any combination of racial and ethnic groups. Similarly, students may also make choices about the meaning of their honors identity and how this will intersect with other valued dimensions of self.

The process of navigating identity can be an unproblematic transition, but it can also lead to personal crisis. For example, identifying as a gay member of the honors community was not an issue for the LGBTQ students we interviewed. In fact, Marshall seemed surprised when asked if his sexual orientation affected his perception of honors or vice versa. For Marshall, the transition was smooth, not because honors and sexuality never overlapped, but because

99

he felt honors was a community where openly identifying as gay was accepted by his peers. But not all identities mesh so easily. Ray struggled with notions of perceived entitlement. Andrea did not feel comfortable disclosing her honors status with her peers in the multicultural program. For these students, honors as a privileged identity produced conflict when it intersected with a marginalized identity. Rather than hindering their identity cohesion, these students embraced their honors identity as a means of understanding themselves socially and personally, which empowered them to embody and advocate for their marginalized identities. For example, Ray became comfortable with his racial identification by taking honors courses that focused on Hispanic heritage. He subsequently volunteered with the citizenship education of a Spanish-speaking population. Ray developed critical consciousness by making personal connections to social inequalities. He then applied his knowledge to work against oppressive systems. The development of Ray's consciousness demonstrates how critical-pedagogy can be implemented across an undergraduate curriculum.

While these underrepresented students may not be expected to embrace honors as smoothly as students from more privileged backgrounds, the enlightenment process and the effort of honors pedagogy to frame privilege in the context of social responsibility empowered them to take pride in their honors student designation. These students mentioned actively working against the honors stereotypes and fighting the automatic assumptions others might have of them based on their identification as honors and as a FGC, racial minority, or LGBTQ student. While they may not fit the traditional image of an honors student, by openly owning their honors identity and by taking an active stance for social justice consistent with our honors values, these students are reshaping perceptions of who honors students are and what the goals of honors should be.

CONCLUSION

This chapter began with the belief that honors has an obligation to be a social change agent and to intentionally fight the tendency for honors to become a privilege for the privileged. Although we do not claim that our program has all the answers, when it comes to creating and fostering critical consciousness, we are strongly committed to ensuring that the honors program occupies our campus responsibly. Our intent is that these efforts are a catalyst to encourage enlightenment and empowerment for all of our students to occupy honors as a force for both personal development and social change.

This intent led us to explore how our honors students are negotiating marginalized social identities as they intersect with honors privilege on our campus. In the end, our appreciation for the complexity of intersectionality and the challenge of navigating identities characterized by different manifestations of privilege and oppression has been enhanced. Furthermore, although we recognize that our own program has much work to do, we are encouraged by the fact that all of the students we interviewed found stronger voices in honors, at least in part, because of the efforts we made to directly address the links connecting diversity, inequality, and social responsibility as key elements of our honors community.

Finally, although overall program assessment was not a focus of this project and we did not explore intersectionality across all of the honors student body, our annual assessment work confirms that efforts to encourage a critical exploration of diversity, inequality, and social responsibility also have significance for students with social identities more characterized by privilege. Consistent with the principles of intersectionality, coursework and programming that promote enlightenment and empowerment around issues of inequality and privilege have the potential to shape the identities of all honors students, increasing the odds that they will begin to see themselves as advocates and allies for a more just society. Beyond the individual academic achievement and accolades that most honors students and programs seek, these paradigm shifts are outcomes that might be more difficult to document but are every bit as important to honors if we are to occupy our campuses and make honors a force for positive social change.

REFERENCES

Coleman, L. L., & Kotinek, J. D. (Eds.). (2010). *Setting the table for diversity*. Lincoln, NE: National Collegiate Honors Council. NCHC Monograph Series.

Davis, K. (2008). Intersectionality as buzzword: A sociology of science perspective on what makes a feminist theory successful. *Feminist Theory, 9*(1), 67–85. doi: 10.1177/1464700108086364

DeLeon, M. (2010). *Mira al espejo*: A reflection on serving Latina/o honors students in Texas. In L. L. Coleman & J. D. Kotinek (Eds.), *Setting the table for diversity* (pp. 61–76). Lincoln, NE: National Collegiate Honors Council. NCHC Monograph Series.

Dziesinski, A. (2014). Honors and identity: Navigating intersectionality. Unpublished manuscript—honors capstone project. Central Michigan University, Mt. Pleasant, MI.

Freire, P. (1970). *Pedagogy of the Oppressed*. (M. B. Ramos, Trans.). New York, NY: Continuum.

Frost, L. (2009). Class, honors, and Eastern Kentucky: Why we still need to try to change the world. *Journal of the National Collegiate Honors Council, 10*(1), 31–35. Retrieved from <http://digitalcommons.unl.edu/nchcjournal/249>

Grzanka, P. R. (2014). *Intersectionality: A foundations and frontiers reader*. Boulder, CO: Westview Press.

Harrell, S. P., Myers, H. F., & Smedley, B. D. (1993). Minority-status stresses and the college adjustment of ethnic minority freshmen. *Journal of Higher Education, 64*(4), 434–52. Retrieved from <http://go.galegroup.com/ps/i.do?id=GALE%7CA14444187&v=2.1&u= lom_cmichu&it=r&p=AONE&sw=w&asid=f290bd2908ac7ddbe639f6ff0be2330f>

Johnson, A. G. (2006). *Privilege, power, and difference*. Boston, MA: McGraw-Hill.

KewalRamani, A., Gilbertson, L., Fox, M., & Provasnik, S. (2007). Status and trends in the education of racial and ethnic minorities

(NCES 2007-039). National Center for Education Statistics, Institute of Education Sciences, U.S. Department of Education. Washington, D.C.: U.S. Government Printing Office.

Klos, N., Eskine, K., & Pashkevich, M. (2015). Assessing social justice as a learning outcome in honors. *Journal of the National Collegiate Honors Council, 16*(1), 53–70.

Lipman, P. (2004). *High stakes education: Inequality, globalization, and urban school reform.* New York, NY: Routledge-Falmer.

Long, A., & Mullins, D. (Eds.). (2009). Social class and honors. *Journal of the National Collegiate Honors Council, 10*(1).

Materon-Arum, E. (2010). African American males in honors programs: Suggestions and best practices for success. In L. L. Coleman & J. D. Kotinek (Eds.), *Setting the table for diversity* (pp. 91–98). Lincoln, NE: National Collegiate Honors Council. NCHC Monograph Series.

"Mission and Core Values." Honors Program. Central Michigan University. 16 November 2016. Web.

Mullins, D. W. (2005). What is honors? *Journal of the National Collegiate Honors Council, 6*(2). 19–22. Retrieved from <http://digitalcommons.unl.edu/nchcjournal/185>

Newell, B. M., & Baxter, B. K. (2010). A scientific perspective on diversity: An interdisciplinary approach to discussions of race, gender, sexual orientation, and class. In L. L. Coleman & J. D. Kotinek (Eds.), *Setting the table for diversity* (pp. 151–66). Lincoln, NE: National Collegiate Honors Council. NCHC Monograph Series.

Oswalt, S. B., & Wyatt, T. J. (2011). Sexual orientation and differences in mental health, stress, and academic performance in a national sample of U.S. college students. *Journal of Homosexuality, 58*(9), 1255–80. doi: 10.1080/00918369.2011.605738

Pascarella, E. T., Pierson, C. T., Wolniak, G. C., & Terenzini, P. T. (2004). First-generation college students: Additional evidence on college experiences and outcomes. *The Journal of Higher Education*, *75*(3), 249–84. doi: 10.1353/jhe.2004.0016

Pearson, B., & Kohl, D. (2010). African American males and honors programs: Why are enrollments so low? What can be done?. In L. L. Coleman & J. D. Kotinek (Eds.), *Setting the table for diversity* (pp. 31–40). Lincoln, NE: National Collegiate Honors Council. NCHC Monograph Series.

Pressler, C. (2009). The two-year college honors program and the forbidden topics of class and cultural capital. *Journal of the National Collegiate Honors Council*, *10*(1), 31–35. Retrieved from <http://digitalcommons.unl.edu/nchcjournal/249>

Riek, E., & Sheridan, K. (2010). Defining diversity in honors: Setting the table for diversity. In L. L. Coleman & J. D. Kotinek (Eds.), *Setting the table for diversity* (pp. 21–29). Lincoln, NE: National Collegiate Honors Council. NCHC Monograph Series.

Sanon-Jules, L. B. (2010). How honors programs can assist in the transition of gifted first-generation and African American college students. In L. L. Coleman, & J. D. Kotinek (Eds.), *Setting the table for diversity* (pp. 99–113). Lincoln, NE: National Collegiate Honors Council. NCHC Monograph Series.

Weiner, N. (2009). Honors is elitist, and what's wrong with that? *Journal of the National Collegiate Honors Council*, *10*(1), 19–24. Retrieved from <http://digitalcommons.unl.edu/nchc journal/258>

APPENDIX A

CMU Honors Program Statements of Vision, Mission, and Values

CMU Honors Vision Statement:
The CMU Honors Program will serve the University by fostering a diverse community of scholars committed to academic excellence, intellectual engagement, and social responsibility.

CMU Honors Mission Statement:
Providing high academic ability students with unique educational opportunities and experiences, the CMU Honors Program challenges students to aim higher and to achieve more academically, personally, and professionally for the greater good of our disciplines, our society, and our world.

CMU Honors Core Values:
The primary values that guide the implementation of the Honors Program mission include:

- Critical thought, scholarly inquiry, and creative expression
- Respect and appreciation for diverse peoples and ideas in a global society
- High standards for integrity and personal aspirations
- Active Citizenship and service for the greater good

("Mission and Core Values")

APPENDIX B

Research Methodology

The student case studies in this work were conducted as part of the honors senior capstone entitled "Honors and Identity: Navigating Intersectionality" (Dziesinski 2014), which sought to gain personal perspectives on student identity formation and honors involvement through qualitative research interviews. Students were recommended to participate by honors staff based on their good honors standing and public self-identification with a group underrepresented in the CMU Honors community, including a racial minority, LGBTQ sexuality, and/or low-income, first-generation status. After receiving IRB approval, we interviewed five students: four identified as a racial minority, two identified as gay, and two identified as first-generation college students. Participants were college juniors and seniors and therefore had more experience with the honors program and could assess changes over time.

Interviews were semi-structured to allow participants to share experiences unanticipated by the researchers, which produced a more comprehensive understanding of the individuals' experiences. The interviews, which took 30–60 minutes, were digitally recorded and subsequently transcribed. Personally identifiable information was removed, and names were changed for the purposes of this work.

Cosmopolitan Courtesy:
Preparing for Global Citizenry

STEPHANIE BROWN AND VIRGINIA COPE
OHIO STATE UNIVERSITY, NEWARK

As colleagues in the English Department and as a director of study abroad, service learning, and honors at a small regional campus of Ohio State University, we have recruited a range of students for experiential courses in which they encounter cultures very different from their own. We both led honors students to New Orleans in 2009 for a spring break course, and since then have separately taken students to New Orleans for service learning and to Berlin for study abroad, on trips from 10 to 30 days long. Our diverse student body includes many students who are financially strapped and inexperienced with travel, as well as a number who are nontraditional in age (Ohio State University Enrollment Services, "Newark . . . Pell," 2016). Accordingly, we have structured our programs to be affordable and flexible, and we have surveyed students about barriers to participation. We have also individually recruited students from underrepresented populations, who often are less likely to pursue study abroad opportunities. (See Soria and Troisi, 2014; Salisbury, 2011; Green, 2001.)

While these efforts have achieved our campus goal of expanding study abroad, service learning, and honors offerings and of attracting a range of students from diverse backgrounds, we realized early on that we also needed to innovate pedagogically to ensure that students, once enrolled in such courses, remained committed and engaged. We discovered that many students, no matter how academically well-prepared or well-traveled, struggle to adapt when faced with situations that defy their cultural expectations, whether in New Orleans or Berlin. Moreover, at times of stress they struggle to remain courteous and open to each other. To better prepare students, we developed a theory of cosmopolitan courtesy and accompanying classroom activities to provide students with a cognitive framework for processing and responding to the unexpected and unsettling. Cosmopolitan courtesy extends the familiar notion of courtesy to intercultural communication and situates it not simply as a form of politeness but as a mode of learning required for global citizenry. Understanding and practicing cosmopolitan courtesy has helped our students negotiate cultural barriers in the classroom and outside of it, improving dynamics among students as well as increasing their individual flexibility and openness to new experiences. Cosmopolitan courtesy has also broadened our own approach to travel, leading us to realize that it is a theory and a practice from which anyone can benefit, whether student or professor, young or old, world traveler or first-time passport holder.

Ultimately, we seek to empower students to view themselves not as mere observers of other cultures but as members of a global citizenry, motivated not simply by a desire to "study" or to "help" others, but by a recognition that they are inextricably part of a global community, representatives of one or more "others" among many. This shift from being a "good student" or a "good Samaritan" to a "good citizen," of course, informs much of the theory behind the concept of global citizenship, both in cosmopolitan and post-cosmopolitan contexts. (See Beck, 2000; Dobson, 2003; Westheimer and Kahne, 2004; and Noddings, 2005.) Regardless of whether our goal is to move students beyond a preconception of study abroad as one long note-taking exercise or to extricate them from the limitations of what Lilie Chouliaraki (2014) calls the "inadequacy of the discourse of pity" in volunteerism (p. 109), what we seek is to increase our students' (and our own) ability to see, as David Killick (2012) has put it, "their *self-in-the world*, which shapes inclinations and the will to *act-in-the-world*" (p. 373).

BARRIERS TO PARTICIPATION

As Kinghorn and Smith (2013) note, increasing numbers of college students nationwide fit the profile of "nontraditional"; thus, new approaches will be crucial to ensuring that experiential-learning programs succeed and that students get the most out of an increasingly costly college experience (p. 15). Studies have shown students who are first generation, low-income, or, like those studied by Soria and Troisi (2014), from underrepresented populations, are less likely than their peers to engage in courses that take them outside of the classroom (p. 262). We have certainly found this pattern to hold true for our campus population, in which more than a third are the first generation of their family to attend college (Ohio State University Enrollment Services, "Newark . . . First Generation," 2016). A similar share of students struggle financially, as evidenced by their receipt of Pell grants, while many of our students work full-time or nearly so (Ohio State University Enrollment Services, "Newark . . . Pell," 2016). In recent years, increasing numbers of our students have been military veterans, more than 30% are non-White, and some are non-native speakers of English (Ohio State University Enrollment Services, "Newark . . . Ethnicity," 2016). Not surprisingly, these students face obstacles, psychological as well as financial and logistical, to participating in experiential-learning programs that require greater commitments of time and money.

Some of our most capable, high-achieving students have dismissed our suggestions that they study in Berlin or join an honors class that includes travel to New Orleans, even when we have clarified that the program fees are low and the trips short-term. When one of us encouraged a 31-year-old woman, a strong student who was the first in her family to attend college, to apply for a Berlin course, she immediately waved her hand dismissively and said,

"That's not for me." When pressed, she cited work and family obligations, but also her sense that those kinds of programs would be filled with the smiling, carefree young adults pictured in glossy brochures—not an overscheduled woman in her 30s, struggling to make ends meet. Incoming students who responded to our survey in the fall of 2013 made similar comments; others said the application process sounded bewildering. More worrisome, a fair number said they did not know what we meant by "study abroad."

In our estimation, all college students need access to these opportunities. Study abroad and service learning classes not only enrich the college experience but are among the high-impact practices that improve retention, academic achievement, and employment opportunities. (See Kuh, 2008; see also Braid and Long, 2000; Green, 2001; Kronholz & Osborn, 2016; Machonis, 2008; Pelco, Ball, & Lockeman, 2014; Salisbury, 2011; and Sutton & Rubin, 2010.) Sutton and Rubin, for example, find improved grade point averages among students who study abroad and a greater likelihood of graduating in four years. Kronholz finds that study abroad experiences increased participants' self-knowledge and therefore their ability to choose careers and employability (p. 770); Pelco, Ball, & Lockeman find that service learning courses result in "significant academic and professional development" for first-generation students (p. 49). According to Astin, Vogelgesang, Ikeda, & Yee (2000), service learning has also been shown to increase students' sense of values, self-efficacy, and leadership, among other variables (ii). Indeed, we contend, engaging in opportunities for learning outside the classroom and in the community offers the best hope for taking advantage of students' increasing interest in improving their understanding of other cultures and countries, a goal that has steadily moved up the list of priorities since it was added to the *American Freshman* survey in 2002 (Eagan et al., 2016, pp. 84–85).

With these study abroad and service learning offerings, we hope to shape students into citizens of the community and of the world. In keeping with this goal, we have responded to student concerns about cost and time away from jobs and family by providing generous subsidies, scheduling carefully, and attentively promoting

110

our programs in order to attract students with limited resources or experience. For example, we limit most trips to 7–10 days because students had difficulty leaving behind work and family obligations for longer periods, and we carefully controlled costs, opting for no-frills accommodation choices, public transportation, and local tour guides with reasonable rates. Our campus offered generous scholarships to make the courses possible and subsidized passport expenses. We held multiple orientations providing information on matters ranging from carry-on baggage restrictions to questions about the availability of church services. Students confided that even with the cost of the courses largely covered, the time away from work would be a financial hardship, and that they had budgeted strictly in preparation. Because we anticipated this problem, we arranged for lodging that provided ample breakfasts and rooms with refrigerators for storing leftovers.

To our surprise, however, during travel a significant number of students failed to embrace the very opportunity they had worked hard to achieve. It became apparent that many students come to international education and even domestic travel with expectations that do not line up with the reality of the experience, and frequently they lack the resources to usefully process the difference. This cognitive dissonance means that some students retreat emotionally or physically, or they behave in ways that initially appear rude. They laugh or make inappropriate comments; they refuse to speak or make eye contact with individuals; they take refuge in an electronic device; or they reject novel experiences. In one memorable moment in New Orleans, as a talented sous chef at a John Besh restaurant explained the history and technique behind the cup of crab bisque being served, several students recoiled and began fishing out the crab claw garnish, too self-absorbed to note the look of dismay on the chef's face. In Berlin, students on a tour of a local mosque made audible, nervous comments about the desirability of "blowing up" the structure, while others complained to the instructor, a Berlin resident deeply involved in work with refugee and immigrant communities in the city, that they considered such a tour "inappropriate," given that they were not also touring a Christian church, forgetting that they had visited the Church of Saint Michael in the Kreuzberg neighborhood on their first day.

It was obvious that, having assiduously addressed pragmatic travel issues, we now needed to think more holistically about the obstacles to student learning in unfamiliar environments. The problem, we came to realize, is not one of manners; rather, the issue is that in the moment of confrontation with the unfamiliar, students suspend their understanding, often with less than optimal results. Students are not revealing character flaws but responding predictably to what Mezirow (1991) describes as a "disorienting dilemma" (p. xvi). For Mezirow, a disorienting dilemma is an opportunity for growth; it can lead to transformative learning if it causes a student to reassess his or her naturalized assumptions. For this to happen, however, Mezirow (1997) argues, the dilemma must permanently disrupt the "frame of reference" or "the structures of assumptions through which we understand our experiences . . . [that] selectively shape and delimit expectations, perceptions, cognition, and feelings" (p. 5). Such disruptions can be uncomfortable, even painful—and, if unprepared for, can lead students to behave reflexively in unproductive ways that prevent them from doing more than cursorily acknowledging other cultures.

It is important to note that the reactions in Berlin and New Orleans came from smart and decent people and from students who were relatively sophisticated as well as from those who were inexperienced travelers. Moreover, because our campus is small, we knew these students well and had every reason to be confident in their potential for success. They had written essays expressing their desire to travel and interviewed successfully with us. Several were stars in their departments. For these participants, something clearly happened between formulating their desire to have intercultural experiences and the moment in which they were actually having them. They were not ready to go off road, and, most importantly, we had not prepared them to do so. We had failed to anticipate that the primary reaction some students might feel upon encountering newness would be anxiety and that they might cope with this feeling by retreating into what looked like boorishness. Instead of smoothly crossing intercultural boundaries, they fortified their isolationist positions. It was our Mezirowian epiphany—that the students were undergoing a disorienting dilemma, not simply suffering an unexpected lapse in judgment—that led us to recognize that without better preparation, many students would return from their cross-cultural encounters baffled and unenlightened, not emboldened and better educated.

The scene at the John Besh restaurant helped us recognize where we had gone wrong. We had done little to prepare students for what was supposed to be one of the great treats of the week: sampling classic New Orleans cuisine with a charismatic, native-born sous chef who could eloquently describe the multicultural history of the dishes and the restaurant's take on them. In our planning, we had anticipated that the experience would give students a sensory lesson in the distinctiveness of New Orleans culture and the city's blend of French, Spanish, and Caribbean influences. In our own enthusiasm, we had not considered the potential for discomfort inherent in the outing. When handed soup with an unusual name and a surprising garnish, the students regressed, preferring to perform their lack of engagement by exchanging glances with their peers, raising their eyebrows, and fishing out the offending crab claw. Their disorientation at the restaurant created responses that were not conducive to learning: passivity (eating nothing) and rejection (wrinkled noses).

Similarly, in Berlin, we realized that their discomfort in the mosque, not the desire to offend, inspired their retreating to each other's company to mutter asides rather than attending to the guide. We had made the assumption, given students' general knowledge of the history of Jews and synagogues in Germany during the Nazi era, that students would easily recognize the crucial role that non-Christian places of worship play in an international, multiethnic city and would embrace the opportunity to consider the position of Muslims in Germany. (Indeed, several students expressed strong interest in learning more about the Jewish community in Berlin.) Our mistake lay in not attending more closely to the enormous differences between the discourses students used to situate their reassuringly historicized understanding of the Holocaust and those they used to situate their uncomfortably contemporary and open-ended understanding of the depiction of Islam by the media.

The same discomfort was likely the inspiration for a range of negative reactions to trivial matters, often related to food. Because we consider openness to new culinary experiences (barring health concerns) as a leading indicator of students' receptiveness to cultural difference, we took their often comical observations seriously. One student was unhappy that creamy salad dressings in Germany "look but don't taste like ranch dressing" and a surprising number described the prevalent carbonated water as "nasty." In Berlin as well as in New Orleans, students retreated by seeking out American fast food outlets to patronize on the sly; others ate as little as possible. One student in Berlin was within hours of being hospitalized for dehydration because she not only avoided the hotel's tap water but the free bottled water and ample breakfast buffet.

We should note that our courses are not designed to teach our students how to use a dinner napkin or select the proper fork: the term "courtesy" in our theory invokes something larger than etiquette. Table manners, like all etiquette, are situational and culture-specific. Yet we provide these examples because we consider engagement with food a crucial vector for transformative learning. And almost all of the students we accompanied on our early trips to New Orleans (in 2009) and Berlin (in 2011) had not only rejected these opportunities but seemed to bond over doing so, finding in each other a welcome relief, perhaps, from the disorienting dilemmas with which we had unwittingly presented them.

GETTING PAST THE DISORIENTING DILEMMA

Clearly, in these encounters in Berlin and New Orleans, students had been presented with disorienting dilemmas (do I drink the water? admire the mosque?) but not achieved a transformative learning experience as envisioned by Mezirow: confronting their limits, expanding their frames of reference, changing their expectations of themselves or others, and engaging in what Mezirow (1990) describes as "critical self-reflection, which results in the reformulation of a meaning perspective to allow a more inclusive, discriminating and integrative understanding of [their] experience" (p. xvi). Of course, we should not have been surprised that in these short-term study tours, students had not negotiated the six stages delineated by Bennett (1986) in his Developmental Model of Intercultural Sensitivity, in which he argues that the path from "ethnocentrism" to what he terms "ethnorelativism" (p. 182) is marked by the successful movement from denial of, and defense against, cultural difference, through a stage of minimization leading to acceptance of difference, to adaptation and, ultimately, to integration of difference into one's own identity (pp. 181–86). Nevertheless, we continue to believe, as Ritz recently put it, that "a short term, faculty-led study abroad program, as a course component, can be pedagogically designed to provide significant learning experiences [and] promote transformative learning" (pp. 164–65). Toward this end, we developed cosmopolitan courtesy to help students develop the cognitive and emotional resources to respond to and learn from intercultural encounters on campus, while working with the community, or when traveling. Our set of exercises and discussion prompts encourage students to articulate and practice strategies in the classroom that help them cope with unfamiliar and potentially disturbing experiences in distant locales.

COSMOPOLITAN COURTESY FOR THE GLOBAL CITIZEN

The concept of cosmopolitan courtesy builds on recent work in philosophy and sociology concerning the pragmatic uses of theories of cosmopolitanism. These notions are based on Immanuel Kant's notion of "universal hospitality," broadly defined here as "the right of an alien not to be treated as an enemy" but rather to be shown respect (1983, p. 118). Cosmopolitan courtesy encourages people to see every encounter with another as a "visit," to use Kant's term, and thus to treat all such others as "visitors," even when, as in study abroad, students might reasonably consider themselves to be the ones visiting (1983, p. 118). In preparing students to travel to Berlin in 2013, we assigned readings that ranged from Kant's "To Perpetual Peace" (1795) to philosopher Kwame Anthony Appiah's

Cosmopolitanism: Ethics in a World of Strangers (2006) and sociologist Elijah Anderson's *The Cosmopolitan Canopy: Race and Civility in Everyday Life* (2011), and we scheduled in-class discussions and activities to allow students to process the ideas contained in the readings and to model "courteous" behaviors and reactions.

The first exercise, for example, asks students to speculate on the etymologies of the words "cosmopolite" and "polite." Upon being told that the word "cosmopolitan" derives from the Greek words *cosmos* and *polites* and means "citizen of the world," students typically guess that the root of the English word "polite" is "citizen" and suggest an etymological connection, perhaps that city-dwellers need to have good manners to get along with one another. Even when they are informed that the root of polite is actually the Latin *polire* (to polish), suggesting that polite individuals are those without rough edges, students make a valuable association between notions of courtesy and world citizenship. In this nonthreatening discussion, they begin to recognize the possibility of "rough edges" in their interactions and their need to acquire a nuanced manner. One student drew the attention of the others to metaphorical language in Robert Walser's essay "Friedrichstrasse" (written in 1907) that had caused her to think about the idea of a stream of pedestrians on a city street and the constant jostling among them that would cause them to smooth, not soften, their surfaces, like pebbles, to avoid friction. This observation led other students to talk about the importance to cosmopolitanism of physical proximity to others who are unlike you and to speculate on the role played, for example, by public transportation in maintaining what Walser himself describes as a "concept of neighbor [that] takes on a genuinely practical, comprehensible and swiftly grasped meaning" (p. 10). All agreed that using the subway system, an experience none of them had had, would be a crucial part of their learning experience in Berlin.

Given that students at our open-admission campus range from academically underprepared to high-achieving students and include students from diverse cultures and experiences, we also sought to provide students with an opportunity to bridge gaps in their understanding of each other. We created ways for students to practice teamwork and professionalism among themselves before they encountered unsettling situations in another city or country. An emphasis on cosmopolitanism has obvious implications for cooperative efforts in all educational settings, since, as philosopher Appiah (2006) writes, two strands intertwine in the concept:

> One is the idea that we have obligations to others, obligations that stretch beyond those to whom we are related by the ties of kith and kind, or even the more formal ties of a shared citizenship. The other is that we take seriously the value not just of human life but of particular human lives, which means taking an interest in the practices and beliefs that lend them significance. [. . .] There's a sense in which cosmopolitanism is the name not of the solution but of the challenge. (p. xv)

These two elements of the cosmopolitan consciousness come together in the notion of courtesy, making the two ideas a natural fit. It is simple enough to tell students that they should be interested in the practices and beliefs of others, but a curriculum that foregrounds the importance of diversity, such as that at our university, makes this clear. Yet it is much more effective to demonstrate to students the power of cosmopolitan courtesy as a model for their interactions with others generally—with other students in their classes, for example, whose backgrounds and identities may be very different from their own; with their instructors; with the authors of the texts they are reading; and even with knowledge itself. Declaring one's self "open" is fine as far as it goes; the next step is determining how to maintain one's openness in the face of a difficult or unexpected situation. As Appiah writes, "practices and not principles are what enable us to live in peace" (p. 85). Our goal, then, is to offer our students the tools to join in what he has described as "conversations across boundaries of identity" that are "a metaphor for engagement with the experience and the ideas of others" (p. 85).

PREPARING FOR BERLIN:
LITERARY STUDY, ORAL PRESENTATIONS

One way to accomplish this goal, as Appiah has suggested, is to begin with "imaginative" engagement with fiction (p. 85). We implemented this strand in 2013 in the literature-based course that precedes the Berlin study tour. Students found a multitude of ways to use the concept of cosmopolitan courtesy to better understand the unfamiliar worlds described in texts ranging from Walser's essays on Berlin at the turn of the twentieth century to films like *Die Fremde (When We Leave)*, set in the Turkish community in twenty-first-century Berlin. For example, one class discussion centered on a passage, in Hans Fallada's 1947 novel *Jeder stirbt für sich allein* (*Every Man Dies Alone*), in which a retired judge, choosing to shelter his elderly Jewish neighbor when she is pursued by the Nazis, refers to his act as hospitality. Drawing on their previous knowledge of Kant's notion of "universal hospitality," developed in discussions of "To Perpetual Peace," students worked together to develop a reading of the novel that helped them better understand how Fallada's work illustrates the mechanisms of fascism, whose primary goal is the creation of a group identity that necessarily entails exclusionary principles, which deny basic human dignity, as well as the categorical imperative, generally understood as the prescription that people should act only in ways that they would have others act, regardless of circumstances.

After introducing the idea of cosmopolitan courtesy and "universal hospitality" into the classroom, we encourage students to recall how they responded to situations such as receiving an important guest (a relative who has traveled far, for example) at their family home or welcoming a new member into a club or activity. We also have asked them to consider times when they have been guests in unfamiliar places or have met people for the first time who are of a different generation or background (even, for example, visiting a friend's elderly grandparent). With these recollections in mind, students then suggest ways in which one indicates a willingness to show hospitality to another. Their suggestions typically include positive actions that communicate a desire to bridge the gap between self and other, at least for the duration of the visit. For example, most recognize that the grandparent might expect more formal behavior and that they would indicate respect by not slouching or using slang. Students have suggested, as indications of hospitality, that one "refuse nothing that is offered" (with exceptions, of course, for health concerns). They typically list physical manifestations of close attention, such as looking directly in the eyes of an interlocutor or nodding. They also have suggested that the best way to show interest in another person's words is to ask a minimum of one question about whatever is said, even if the answer to the question seems obvious, since the purpose of the question may be to indicate attentiveness rather than to gather information. Students in the 2013 Berlin course also suggested learning a minimum of three polite phrases in German for social situations, such as "please," "thank you," and "you're welcome."

These steps seem obvious to most instructors, and indeed, once articulated, they often seem self-evident to students. Yet using the markers of cosmopolitan courtesy takes effort, as the students discover in the classroom when they begin to practice these activities in pursuit of what Anderson (2011) calls "cosmopolitan canopies" or safe "pluralistic spaces where people engage one another in a spirit of civility, or even comity and goodwill" (p. xiv). (See also Nancy West in this volume, pp. 199–213.) Anderson's work describes urban spaces in which "people of diverse backgrounds feel they have an equal right to be there" and in which "they can observe and be observed by others, modeling comity unwittingly" (p. 281). Anderson's use of "comity" here, not unlike our use of the term "courtesy," carries resonances that go well beyond the dictionary definition of the term. For Anderson, "comity" encompasses not merely civility and tolerance but the true recognition of the value of others' contributions to a community. In such spaces, everyone becomes a Kantian "alien" and a "hospitable" resident simultaneously (p. 118). In a classroom setting, when students agree to "model comity" as a group as they articulate their own differences, they can accustom themselves to what Kiely (2005) identifies as "low-intensity dissonance" (p. 11).

This practice allows them to develop and perfect strategies for recognizing and making sense of the higher intensity dissonance they may feel when they travel, dissonance that Kiely says "creates permanent markers in students' frames of reference" (p. 12).

Before leaving the classroom for experiential learning, we now ask students repeatedly to present themselves both as individuals and as students to the other members of the class. Introductions preceding teamwork exercises can provide opportunities for students to describe themselves to their fellow classmates in ways that foreground differences among members of the group even as they build bonds as a team. They may be asked to explain "one obstacle to my participation in this program that I had to overcome" or "one fear that I have about this experience" or even "one reason I never thought I would study abroad." We encourage them to identify a set of behaviors that they can use to perform cosmopolitan courtesy, such as maintaining eye contact or asking follow-up questions, and then motivate them to use those behaviors. This exercise allows students to show one another hospitality and positions them to really listen to one another. Such exercises can reassure students that their honest contributions will be met with honest attempts at comprehension, and they can assist in bridging gaps between traditional and nontraditional students, who may entertain stereotypical views of one another. They also accustom them to extending their attention as a matter of course, and not merely because they have been told that "there will be a quiz," a skill that will attune them to their surroundings and, once they reach their destination, to potential opportunities for transformative learning. Henry James (1884) famously advised would-be writers: "Try to be one of the people on whom nothing is lost!" (p. 510). This maxim could also be usefully adopted by educators preparing students for intercultural encounters.

Another practice we often use is asking students to present research projects based on their own personal or professional interests to the rest of the class. The working assumption is that these presentations will be organized around information not already presented in the course and that they may be only tangentially connected to the emphases of the course. Oral presentations are often unsuccessful in a variety of courses because of the lack of a courteous connection between the presenter and the audience. Students frequently feel that such presentations are directed at the professor and not at the class and that they are merely bystanders with no obligation to do more than be physically present. The principles of cosmopolitan courtesy, however, can elucidate the process by which the oral presentation becomes a model for interaction with the unfamiliar, especially when students choose topics that are provocative in some way. In the 2013 Berlin course, students agreed that every presentation would be met with a minimum of two follow-up questions, both of which had to require that the speaker provide additional information rather than merely repeat something already said. Following this rule led to an atmosphere in which cosmopolitan courtesy was the norm: students gave presenters their full attention and devised questions on subjects about which they knew little beforehand, ranging from the development of ersatz versions of unavailable consumer products during World War II to gay subculture in Berlin.

This exercise proved invaluable when we arrived in Berlin in December 2013 for our ten-day program. On a city tour at the beginning of the program, the students saw a vocal group of protesters near the Brandenburg Gate, shouting what was to them the incomprehensible slogan "Free Water!" While one or two students responded unhelpfully, making jokes about how they too felt like taking to the streets because German restaurants do not customarily offer diners free glasses of drinking water, one student approached a protester to ask for more information. He was rewarded with a detailed explanation of the group's objections to corporate control of natural resources. After thanking the group for the information and for their commitment to their cause, he shared what he had learned with the rest of his cohort. Over lunch, recounting this story led to his question about why he had never seen such a protest in the United States and a lengthy and spirited conversation, in which most of the group took part, about the obligations of governments, the rights of citizens, and the proper role of corporations.

121

APPLYING OUR FINDINGS TO A SERVICE-LEARNING COURSE IN "FOREIGN" NEW ORLEANS

To our Midwest students, New Orleans can seem as foreign as Berlin, and two trips in 2012–13 included an ambitious service-learning component. With students facing the dual challenge of traveling to an unfamiliar city and working closely with community members, preparing them well for interacting with people with cultural expectations often quite different from their own was imperative. Students would be immersed in a culture that was both familiar (i.e., American) and largely unfamiliar (New Orleans subcultures and immigrant groups), and they would be performing what many of them initially considered charity work. Based on their preferences, we divided the 15 students into three teams that would work with different local organizations with which the students were initially unfamiliar. One non-profit organization, Coastal Community Consulting, provided services to the fishing community, primarily comprised of Vietnamese and Cambodian refugees; another, the Mardi Gras Indian Council, was an association composed of participants in the Mardi Gras Indian parading tradition; and the third was the Backstreet Cultural Museum, which exhibits memorabilia from the Mardi Gras Indian culture, including the elaborate suits hand-sewn by the leaders, known as chiefs, of these groups.

When putting together this two-semester service-learning course, we gave much thought to how to prepare the students for this cultural encounter, eventually deciding to provide two trips to the city, one at the end of each semester, with the on-campus time being used to prepare them intellectually and psychologically. In December 2012, after a semester of reading, discussion, and exercises, students spent four days in New Orleans, learning the city and the work of the organizations with which they would be serving. In the spring semester, they studied website development and film editing to prepare for creating websites and promotional videos for their respective organizations. In May 2013, students returned for another week of service.

In the fall semester, students were introduced to the organizations and the social issues in which they were embedded. They watched films and documentaries to learn about New Orleans history and culture, including the legendary African American neighborhood of Tremé, the history of the Mardi Gras Indians, and the devastation that the fishing industry as well as the city suffered after Hurricane Katrina and the failed levees. They met with New Orleans native Lolis Elie and watched the films and TV shows to which he has contributed (HBO's *Tremé* and the documentary *Faubourg Tremé: The Untold Story of Black New Orleans*). They read articles on the city's geographical, political, and cultural history, and they sampled red beans and rice. But we knew these steps were not enough to prepare students to engage with the most unusual of American cities and its combination of Southern hospitality, urban sophistication, and unique cultural traditions, including *beignets*, *lagniappe*, and Mardi Gras.

To familiarize them with the idea of culture as both observed and unobserved actions and beliefs, we distributed a version of Edward T. Hall's visual representation of culture as an iceberg. We encouraged them to recognize that even so small a choice as a pair of socks reflected a cultural stake and a performance of identity. We asked them to reflect upon their own peculiar cultures, whether by neighborhood, family, class, gender, or ethnicity, and share any unique traditions that would not be understood by those outside that culture. We also asked them to "consider an example of deep culture that has been a topic of debate between groups with differing ideologies—in the news or in your experience." They readily found examples from recent news stories and their own lives. These questions situated the students in an analytical framework for exploring cultural conflicts, moving from ones that were unthreatening to more divisive issues. Finally, after these reflection sessions, we asked the class, in groups of three, to take turns explaining a tradition or perception from their own experience with which others in the group might be unfamiliar, listening and responding to that explanation, or observing that interaction and reflecting on the rewards and challenges of the discussion. After lively discussions in small groups, several spoke of holiday traditions or described generational differences. Vy Do, a student whose parents were raised in Vietnam, charmed the class by bursting out with, "Well, my grandfather has seven wives and I can NEVER explain that very well to my friends!" She then explained quite well how she herself "made sense" of this tradition in visits to her grandfather and his wives, which opened up a discussion of the ways in which we all "make sense" of our own cultures.

In another session in preparation for our New Orleans service-learning trip, we asked students, in groups of three, to brainstorm expressions of hospitality, spoken and unspoken, and then to perform a short skit for the rest of the class, displaying hospitality and disrespect, whether subtly or dramatically. The rest of the class was asked to recognize and explain the various expressions displayed. This exercise created some giggling as well as a quite animated discussion about the necessity of maintaining eye contact and silencing phones. We also asked them to write down (anonymously) basic questions that they probably felt reluctant to ask but certainly wanted answered: Why are we doing this project? What advantages do traveling to another city and working with these organizations offer us? We also asked them to write in their journals about their fears, concerns, anxieties, and dislikes related to the trip and New Orleans culture, recognizing that for some the city's distinctive culture might not be appealing. In class and in their journals, several admitted that they were quite fearful of appearing ignorant or rude to the formidable Mardi Gras Indian chiefs or to Sylvester Francis, the elderly founder of the Backstreet Cultural Museum, and some expressed naïve hopes, such as that they would solve racism. Early in the first semester, few mentioned the potential for their own emotional and intellectual growth in providing service to these organizations, as evidenced by the fact that many cited their mission as being one of service ("to help them") rather than of learning.

SERVICE LEARNING ON THE GROUND IN NEW ORLEANS:
PROJECTS AND RESULTS

When we traveled with students to New Orleans in December and again in May, we were gratified to see the personal and intellectual growth the students demonstrated. In four days of immersion in a city many found astounding and unnerving, not one student engaged in the kind of discourteous or inattentive behavior we had witnessed in 2009, and all were deeply attentive to the cultural negotiations. Continuing the practice of journaling that we had begun in class, each day we offered prompts to inspire reflection, such as "what situations have you encountered today that were unsettling or unexpected and how did you respond?" In their later journal entries and in a post-travel discussion, students no longer presented themselves as privileged outsiders offering to help, but as visitors eager to learn and be part of a community whose hospitality they much appreciated. One student, Max Moore, who had been assigned to work with Coastal Communities Consulting (CCC), the nonprofit organization serving the Vietnamese fishing community, admitted that he was initially not particularly interested in the work, designing a website for the group, with which we had been tasked. He changed his mind after taking a driving tour of Lower Plaquemines Parish with Sandy Nguyen, executive director of CCC, and hearing her describe the devastation from both the failed levees after Hurricane Katrina and the BP oil spill. She first introduced the team to Vietnamese and Cambodian fishing families by taking the students to their homes. She then took them to the docks to watch freshly caught shrimp being unloaded. Nguyen advised the owners on their status in the BP oil spill claim and then dashed off to sauté the fresh shrimp for us.

In the spring, students in the group reviewed film footage, photos, and their notes to create a Coastal Communities Consulting site to attract donors, inform the community of its services, and present the compelling story of a community first devastated by Hurricane Katrina and the BP oil spill but now fighting back. Moore, who had taken on the visual aspects of the site, worked tirelessly to edit

125

photographs in Photoshop to create a professional site that offered compelling images of the people we had met; the other members of the team wrote and edited the website, even continuing work long after the course ended. Moore recalled what Nguyen had told him as she drove him down the long stretch of highway in the parish, the southernmost point in Louisiana: "Sandy said that when she had a website, she got lots of donations. Without a website, nothing. This place would fall apart without her. Listening to her compelled me to want to help. And that doesn't usually happen with me." Similarly, Vy Do said she had never considered the impact on the fishing community when prices went down: "Now I'm not happy when I see that the shrimp in the store is cheap."

The students learned to model comity not only to the community but to each other. One student, Chelsea Hinshaw, participated in two trips to Berlin as well as the 2012–13 service-learning course in New Orleans. After returning to Ohio, she posted a note on the group Facebook page, thanking her peers for the support and reflecting on the transformative experiences of her immersion in these two very different cultures. "When I was in Berlin, I learned about myself, and in New Orleans I reinforced what I learned and gained so much confidence," she wrote, referring both to her fellow students and the people she met in the city. "Over and over again I saw how kind and generous people can be, and it was a really pleasant surprise. I've found myself just asking people I don't know random things to still attempt to have this connection." The experiences transformed her academic life as well. After her return from Berlin, Hinshaw revised her coursework to include her new interests: instead of majoring in anthropology, she decided to minor in that field while pursuing a double major in English and German. She also received grants from our campus to conduct research in New Orleans on a forgotten graveyard called Odd Fellows Rest. She presented that research in the student poster section of the 2014 National Collegiate Honors Council conference.

Students who were assigned to conduct filmed interviews with the Mardi Gras Indian chiefs had a moment to demonstrate their cosmopolitan courtesy. The Mardi Gras Indians are groups of

African Americans from different neighborhoods in New Orleans who design and hand-sew elaborately beaded costumes each year. In a tradition dating back to the nineteenth century, they parade on Mardi Gras and other festival days in these extraordinary costumes; although the origins of the tradition are unclear, one legend is that the costumes are a tribute to the Native Americans who helped Africans escape slavery. The Mardi Gras Indian Council had asked the students to build a website and interview the chiefs to document this rich and often misrepresented history. After the group set up elaborate film equipment at the home of one of the chiefs, Vikas Pulluru, a student of Indian descent, nervously began the interview. The chief, Larry Bannock, leaned in to listen, then burst out with, "I can't hear a word you're saying!" The student may have been speaking too softly, or perhaps Chief Bannock assumed that Pulluru's English would have an accent he would find difficult to understand. Whatever the reason, Bannock expressed impatience. Rather than questioning the chief, Pulluru simply stepped aside and let another student, Tiffany O'Connor, take over the interview.

It is possible that the chief was not behaving with "cosmopolitan courtesy," but Pulluru in that split second decided to set aside any embarrassment or offense he might have felt for the good of the group's project, which in this instance was capturing this chief's story on videotape for posterity. O'Connor demonstrated her attentiveness by stepping in without hesitation, and the students left with forty-five minutes of videotape in which Bannock discussed his thirty-eight-year history as an Indian, beginning with the very first suit he sewed, on the sly, in his Gert Town (17th Ward) neighborhood back in 1972. He spoke memorably about the thrill of participating in the parade-day rituals: "From a little boy to a man, I always wanted to be an Indian." Back at the hotel that night, the students had an animated discussion about the awkwardness of the moment and the skill with which it was handled. Pulluru admitted his initial confusion at the chief's response but also the privilege he felt in listening to his rich story. The footage gained greater poignance after Chief Larry Bannock died unexpectedly in May 2014. We provided the unedited video to the Chief's family and, with their permission, to the *New Orleans Times-Picayune*, which included it in their tribute to the legendary man (Fensterstock, May 8, 2014). The two documentaries created from the interviews aired on New Orleans' PBS affiliate (WYES) in 2016, and one was nominated for an Emmy by the Suncoast chapter of the National Academy of Television Arts & Sciences.

In our debriefing and reflection session a month after our return, several other students made comments suggesting that they had come far since their early journal entries in which they imagined themselves as charity workers. Cecilia Feick, a student whose team worked with Sylvester Francis, the creator of the Backstreet Cultural Museum, to catalog his collection and create a video for this website, said simply, "I feel really privileged to work with Mr. Francis, and to hear his stories personally and in depth." (The video is on the Backstreet Cultural Museum's homepage.) Amanda Ruth, who worked with the fishing community, spoke of her pleasure in "seeing inside the lives and learning about what means so much to them," while also admitting she almost did not enroll in the course, despite an attached scholarship, because of her disappointment in high school service-learning projects. "This was real service learning," she said, unlike her previous experiences with tasks like gardening at a nursing home that involved little interaction with the population being served.

The most moving example of cross-cultural sensitivity came after our return from New Orleans and in response to a frightening event. On Mother's Day 2013, our last day in New Orleans, four students joined a second-line parade, a traditional New Orleans event in which a brass band, the "first line," leads dancing followers, the "second line," through the neighborhood. While twelve students were booked on a flight back to Ohio that afternoon, two of the students who attended the parade planned to stay another week to conduct additional research on the parading tradition. Equipped with video cameras, the students joined the parade on that sunny Mother's Day, enjoying the lively music, the traditional dance, and the bright yellow outfits of the sponsors, the Big 7 Social Aid and Sponsor Club. Half an hour into the parade, gunshots rang out; the students, following closely behind the musicians, fell to the ground with the crowd, then ran for cover. Nineteen people were wounded, one seriously. (Within days two brothers would be charged with attempted murder for shooting into the crowd.) The students, shaken but unharmed, contacted the program leaders and were taken back to the hotel. We offered counseling and immediate flights home for Chelsea Hinshaw and Michael Lee, the two students who had plans to stay in the city. After some thought, they chose to stay and complete their work. Even more remarkably, a month later, when back in Ohio, they posted an announcement on Facebook: They were holding a yard sale to raise funds to help the most seriously wounded of the victims, Deborah "Big Red" Cotton. Hinshaw and Lee, financially strapped themselves, gathered items ranging from DVDs to shoes for the sale, raising $300, every dime of which they sent to the Gofundme site set up for Cotton, with "warm wishes for a quick recovery." Clearly they saw themselves not as natives of a city or a state but of the nation and, potentially, the world.

CONCLUSIONS, THUS FAR

Engaging in a thoughtful, philosophically grounded discussion of the ramifications of cosmopolitan courtesy can transform how students, and indeed anyone interacting cross-culturally, respond to the inevitable unsettling moments. We initially designed this approach to help nontraditional students, who often expressed concerns about fitting in with participants from traditional student populations, and to help students facing challenges in processing the disorienting dilemmas that precede transformative learning. Yet we have discovered that preparing students for the unknown through a carefully designed, praxis-based approach like cosmopolitan courtesy pays outstanding dividends. Several participants in the 2013 Berlin program observed in anonymous course evaluations that they found the classroom activities good preparation for their research in Berlin and in particular for their interactions with their fellow students, especially those who had initially seemed, in the words of one student, like "people . . . I wouldn't have hung out with before." "While on the trip we were able to communicate with the other students . . . in more depth," wrote another. In fact, they requested that the summer travel be reconfigured into a spring break trip so that they would have the opportunity to continue to work together after returning from Berlin.

Understanding courteous interaction with unfamiliar people and experiences as not just good manners, but as an ethical imperative, and identifying and practicing a set of practical actions that allow participants to model comity offer students an active role in extending Kantian hospitality to those unlike themselves. The effects of these transformative learning experiences are immeasurable, ranging from changing students' life goals (over 80% of the students who responded to our most recent survey reported that they had "reassessed their personal and professional goals" as a result of study abroad) to making them keen to participate again in international education (roughly a third of the students in our study abroad programs go on to apply to another). Perhaps more important still is the fact that they are also eager to encourage their fellow students to study abroad, volunteering to address information sessions on opportunities in international education and providing invaluable word-of-mouth advertising for future programs via social media. Cosmopolitan courtesy, then, does not just show students the world: it makes them active citizens of it.

REFERENCES

Anderson, E. (2011). *The cosmopolitan canopy: Race and civility in everyday life*. New York: Norton.

Appiah, K. A. (2006). *Cosmopolitanism: Ethics in a world of strangers*. New York: Norton.

Astin, A. W., & Antonio, A. L. (2012). *Assessment for excellence: The philosophy and practice of assessment and evaluation in higher education*. Plymouth: Rowman & Littlefield.

Astin, A. W., Vogelgesang, L. J., Ikeda, E. K., & Yee, J. A. (2000). *How service learning affects students*. Los Angeles: Higher Education Research Institute, UCLA.

Astin, A. W., Astin, H. S., & Lindholm, J. A. (2011). *Cultivating the spirit: How college can enhance students' inner lives.* San Francisco: Jossey-Bass.

Beck, U. (2000). The cosmopolitan perspective: Sociology of the second age of modernity. *British Journal of Sociology, 51*(1), 79–105.

Bennett. M. (1986). A developmental approach to training for intercultural sensitivity. *International Journal of Intercultural Relations 10*(2), 179–96.

Braid, B., & Long, A. (2000). *Place as text: Approaches to active learning.* Lincoln: National Collegiate Honors Council. NCHC Monograph Series.

Chouliaraki, L. (2010). Post-Humanitarianism: Humanitarian communication beyond a politics of pity. *International Journal of Cultural Studies 13*(2), 107–26.

Dobson, A. (2003). *Citizenship and the environment.* Oxford, UK: Oxford University Press.

Eagan, K., Stolzenberg, E. B., Ramirez, J. J., Aragon, M. C., Suchard, M. R., & Rios-Aguilar, C. (2016). *The American freshman: Fifty-year trends, 1966–2015.* Los Angeles: The Higher Education Research Institute.

Fallada, H. (2009). *Every Man Dies Alone.* (Trans. Michael Hofmann.) Brooklyn: Melville House. (Original work published in 1947).

Fensterstock, A. (2014, May 8). Watch: Golden Star hunters Big Chief Larry Bannock and others discuss the Mardi Gras Indian tradition. *The New Orleans Times-Picayune.* Retrieved October 4, 2014 from <http://www.nola.com/music/index.ssf/2014/05/watch_golden_star_hunters_big.html>

Green, A. (2001). "But you aren't white": Racial perceptions and service-learning. *Michigan Journal of Community Service Learning, 8*(1), 18–26.

Hall, E. T. (1976). *Beyond culture.* Oxford, UK: Anchor Books.

James, H. (1884). The art of fiction. *Longman's Magazine, 4*(23) 502–21.

Kant, I. (1983). To perpetual peace: A philosophical sketch. In *Perpetual peace and other essays.* (Trans. Ted Humphrey). Indianapolis: Hackett Publishing. (Original work published in 1795).

Kiely, R. (2005). A transformative learning model for service-learning: A longitudinal case study. *Michigan Journal of Community Service Learning, 12*(1), 5–22.

Killick, D. (2012). Seeing-ourselves-in-the-world: Developing global citizenship through international mobility and campus community. *Journal of Studies in International Education, 16*(4), 372–89.

Kinghorn, J. R., & Smith, W. W. (2013). Nontraditional honors. *Journal of the National Collegiate Honors Council, 14*(1), 15–21.

Kronholz, J. F., & Osborn, D. S. (2016). The impact of study abroad experiences on vocational identity among college students. *Frontiers: The Interdisciplinary Journal of Study Abroad, 2,* 770–84.

Kuh, G. (2008). High-impact educational practices: What they are, who has access to them, and why they matter. Washington, D.C.: American Association of Colleges & Universities.

Machonis, P. (Ed.) (2008). *Shatter the glassy stare: Implementing experiential learning in higher education.* Lincoln: National Collegiate Honors Council. NCHC Monograph Series.

Mezirow, J. (1990). *Fostering critical reflections in adulthood: A guide to transformative and emancipatory learning.* San Francisco: Jossey-Bass.

—. (1991). *Transformative dimensions of adult learning.* San Francisco: Jossey-Bass.

—. (1997). Transformative learning: Theory to practice. In P. Cranton (Ed.), *Transformative learning in action: Insights from practice—New directions for adult and continuing education: No. 74.* (pp. 5–12). San Francisco: Jossey-Bass.

Noddings, N. (2005). Global citizenship: Promises and problems. In N. Noddings (Ed.) *Educating citizens for global awareness.* (pp. 1–21). New York: Teachers College Press.

Ohio State University Enrollment Services Analysis and Reporting. (2016). Newark retention and graduation rates for new first year students, Autumn 2015.

—. (2016). Newark retention and graduation rates for new first year students, Pell, Autumn 2015.

—. (2016). Newark retention and graduation rates for new first year students, first generation students, Autumn 2015.

—. (2016). Newark retention and graduation rates for new first year students, ethnicity, Autumn 2015.

Pelco, L. E., Ball, C. T., & Lockeman, K. S. (2014). Student growth from service-learning: A comparison of first-generation and non-first-generation college students. *Journal of Higher Education Outreach and Engagement, 18*(2), 49–66.

Ritz, A. A. (2011). The educational value of short-term study abroad programs as course components. *Journal of Teaching and Tourism, 11*(2), 164–78.

Salisbury, M. H. (2011). Why do all the study abroad students look alike? Applying an integrated student choice model to explore differences in the factors that influence white and minority students' intent to study abroad. *Research in Higher Education, 52*(2), 123–50.

Soria, K. M., and Troisi, J. (2014, July). Internationalization at home alternatives to study abroad: Implications for students' development of global, international, and intercultural competencies. *Journal of Studies in International Education, 18*(3), 261–80.

Sutton, R. C., & Rubin, D. L. (2010). Documenting the academic impact of study abroad: Final report of the GLOSSARI project. Paper presented at the NAFSA Annual Conference, Kansas City, Missouri. Retrieved from <http://glossari.uga.edu/datasets/pdfs/FINAL.pdf>

Tallant, M. (2010). A conceptual framework for exploring the role of studies abroad in nurturing global citizenship. *Journal of Studies in International Education, 14*(5), 433–51. doi:10.1177/1028315309348737

Walser, R. (2012). *Berlin Stories*. New York: New York Review of Books Classics.

Westheimer, J., and Kahne, J. (2004). Educating the "good" citizen: Political choices and pedagogical goals. *Political Science & Politics, 38*(2), 241-47.

Cosmopolitanism and New Racial Formations in a Post-9/11 Honors Curriculum on Diversity

Lopamudra Basu
University of Wisconsin-Stout

INTRODUCTION

This chapter examines the challenges encountered in designing and offering thought-provoking honors courses on topics of racial and ethnic diversity, given the traditional separation of domestic and international racial and ethnic studies. Although new university initiatives at my home institution, the University of Wisconsin-Stout (UWS), focus on inclusive excellence, as does the policy statement from the Association of American Colleges and Universities (AAC&U) on "Making Excellence Inclusive," the domestic/international divide dominates curricular models.[1] While such initiatives and policy statements emphasize the many aspects of diversity, like race, gender, national origin, and sexuality, and focus on the interconnected nature of the global and the national, these curricular requirements and policy statements for diversity

135

are often not in sync. Curricular models tend to have distinctive requirements for global perspectives and United States diversity content. This paper envisions a curriculum that keeps pace with inclusive excellence policy initiatives.

Diversity is an agreed-upon ideal enshrined in the mission and vision statements of most institutions of higher education. There is consensus among honors educators that the honors curriculum should produce greater awareness of the nuances of cultural difference and prepare students for global citizenship. Institutionally, however, the modes of understanding and responding to the complex realities of diverse societies remain mired in rigid and somewhat outmoded pedagogical models that emphasize the domestic/international divide. Unless these models are checked, the experience of diversity education can turn into a bureaucratic hurdle that professors and students have to negotiate strategically, instead of allowing for an encounter that could lead to a transformational life experience.

Using examples from my own experience of designing a course on 9/11 literature for the Honors College at UW-Stout, I reflect on the challenges in current models of diversity education. Drawing from theories of cosmopolitanism, I examine ways in which diversity education has to negotiate between and among universal ideals in particular historical contexts. In a post-9/11 world, issues of racial identity are complex, often encompassing various facets of identity like religion, citizenship, and ethnicity. The purpose of this chapter, then, is to explore pedagogies that can keep pace with the complex realities on the ground and reinvigorate diversity education, making it responsive to new racial and ethnic formations.

"AFTER 9/11:
AMERICAN LITERATURE OF TRAUMA AND PUBLIC CRISIS"

My scholarly training in postcolonial literature and transnational studies and my own life experience as a New York resident encouraged me to develop the course titled "After 9/11: American Literature of Trauma and Public Crisis." I had lived in New York

City as a graduate student from India at the City University of New York at the time of the 9/11 tragedy. I moved away in 2002 and have made Wisconsin my home since 2005. Thus, after a hiatus of more than ten years, this course was an attempt, in part, to revisit my past and re-examine lessons of identity and racial formation. Having been an international student in New York City shortly after the tragedy, I wanted to understand my own experiences and their implications for my own racial identity, which I had never fully unpacked. In the aftermath of the event, I remember suddenly feeling vulnerable, not only as a resident of a city that had faced an unprecedented attack, but because I was being viewed as a brown-skinned foreigner expected to carry my passport at all times to prove my legitimacy. Suddenly, the comforting ambience of graduate school could no longer protect me from being perceived as a racial other. That my family was not Muslim did not matter. There was very little to distinguish my body from those of young Muslim or Arab women.

In the decade since, I have felt the effects of a system of surveillance that 9/11 ushered in on many occasions, and this course has become my attempt to understand, and to help my students understand, the arbitrary and constructed nature of racial formation. In order to arrive at this understanding, the course focuses on the new racial formations in a post-9/11 era in which religion, particularly Islam, and ethnicity (South Asian/Arab) have become the new axes of othering in the contemporary United States. Arab Americans are not part of the four designated minorities, African American, Hispanic/Latino Americans, Asian Americans, and American Indian, that belong to the list of federally designated, under-represented minorities to be studied in diversity courses.[2] Yet, in the past decade, on the domestic front, South Asians and Arabs have faced the brunt of racial surveillance, profiling, and even incarceration without trial. Junaid Rana's *Terrifying Muslims* examines reports by the American Civil Liberties Union and the Office of the Inspector General on the conditions of detained U.S. immigrants after 9/11. Rana concludes: "The reports' accounts of violations of civil liberties and human rights verify immigrants' claims of procedural malfeasance and abuse" (161).

Diversity requirements have become mandatory in most undergraduate degree programs. A cursory search on the internet for undergraduate general education curricula reveals that most universities have a three-credit diversity requirement. Some like the University of Washington added this into their curriculum as recently as 2013; however, most program plans do not specify that the four designated federal minorities must be studied. While I appreciate the original desire of University of Wisconsin System diversity plans to make the underrepresented minorities a curricular priority, this vision has not accommodated changes brought upon racial and ethnic categories following 9/11.

In fall 2014, I taught "After 9/11: American Literature of Trauma and Public Crisis" for the first time after a year in development. The lengthy process of creating the course was eye opening. It expanded my own knowledge of new racial formations in the United States and the world as well as my understanding of the place of religion as a fault line along which identities and differences are increasingly constituted. As I explain below, in my preparation for the course and in the class itself, I explored the intellectual tradition of cosmopolitanism as a possible path towards bridging the increasingly fragmented and polarized post-9/11 world by asking, "How can the ideals of cosmopolitanism and religious and ethnic differences be reconciled?" The course, then, attempted to bring the local and the global to a productive synthesis by studying the racialization of Arab and Muslim populations in the United States within the larger context of wars abroad and the global growth of varied religious fundamentalisms. Honors students were encouraged to bring these issues to productive juxtapositions within the context of their own observations and experiences and think of ways in which paths towards dialogue and peace could emerge. In the first offering of the course, the process of learning, for many students, not only about the details of the traumatic event but about its ongoing repercussions was a profoundly moving experience.

PATRIOTISM VERSUS COSMOPOLITANISM

This section investigates the philosophical tradition of cosmopolitanism as a possible path toward reconciliation of religious and cultural differences in a fragmented and divisive world. In order to posit cosmopolitanism as a desirable ideal for honors education on diversity, I will define this term, which is not without its share of controversy, and examine its evolution, its resurgence in contemporary studies on diversity, and its relevance as an educational ideal.

One of the most relevant definitions of cosmopolitanism emerges from Martha C. Nussbaum's, "Patriotism and Cosmopolitanism," the lead essay in her anthology, *For Love of Country?* Here she defines the two terms in her essay title as antithetical to each other. Nussbaum is highly critical of the excesses fostered by patriotic nationalism and advocates for allegiance to the world as a whole instead of allegiance solely to the nation of one's birth. She traces the intellectual lineage of cosmopolitanism from the Greek philosopher Diogenes the Cynic and his idea of *kosmou polites* or "world citizen" to the Stoics, whom she considers to be Diogenes's philosophical descendants. The cosmopolitan is one whose allegiance is to a worldwide community of human beings rather than to human beings belonging to one particular nation. Nussbaum posits these ideas as an antidote to the excesses fostered by patriotism when she asserts, "I believe . . . this emphasis on patriotic pride is both morally dangerous and, ultimately, subversive of some of the worthy goals patriotism sets out to serve—for example, the goal of national unity in devotion to worthy moral ideals of justice and equality" (4).

To support her claim, Nussbaum draws upon the novel *The Home and the World,* written by Bengali Nobel laureate Rabindranath Tagore. In her analysis of the two main male characters, Sandip and Nikhil, Sandip represents the ideal of patriotism, whereas Nikhil represents the contrasting ideal of allegiance to cosmopolitanism. Sandip, the flamboyant nationalist, inspires Bimala, the female protagonist of the novel and wife of Nikhil, to give up the upper-class Hindu practice of *purdah* or veiling and to embark on a personal quest of liberation that parallels

139

India's demand for *Swadeshi* or self-rule.[3] As the novel progresses, Sandip has no qualms in using religious demagoguery to propel his nationalist cause, leading to tragic consequences. Nikhil, Bimala's husband, is far more circumspect about the rhetoric of nationalism, particularly the kind that is charged with religious overtones. His first duty as a landowner is toward the protection of his peasantry, and, in the communal violence that erupts, Nikhil risks his life for the sake of quelling the carnage. Nussbaum interprets Nikhil's tragic fate as a demise of cosmopolitan values but sees the author, Tagore, as prophetic in predicting the dangers of the Hindu Right in pushing forth a political agenda that does not take into account the multiplicity of ethnic and religious identities in India.[4] Nussbaum reads *The Home and the World* as Tagore's endorsement of Nikhil's ideal of cosmopolitanism, a fellowship and empathy with people of diverse religious persuasions, as well as a cautionary tale against the singular pursuit of self-determination by one dominant religious group. Amartya Sen, India's noted Nobel laureate economist and philosopher, in his reading of the same novel in *The Argumentative Indian,* contrasts Tagore's cosmopolitan sensibility to the nationalist commitment of Mahatma Gandhi.[5]

After Nussbaum provides a historical tracing of cosmopolitanism from a Greek ideal of world citizenship and a literary analysis of the term through her reading of Tagore's novel, she discusses cosmopolitanism as a desired educational practice: "By looking at ourselves through the lens of the other, we come to see what in our practices is local and nonessential, what is more broadly or deeply shared" (11). Nussbaum goes on to argue, "If we really do believe that all human beings are created equal and endowed with certain inalienable rights, we are morally required to think about what that conception requires us to do with and for the rest of the world" (Nussbaum 13). In invoking the rest of the world, Nussbaum alludes to thinkers in the cosmopolitan tradition, like Immanuel Kant, particularly to Kant's notion of co-existence and hospitality, explored in his treatise *Perpetual Peace* (*For Love of Country?* 134).

In this treatise, Kant defines cosmopolitanism as a condition of universal hospitality, a right of all world citizens:

> Hospitality means the right of a stranger not to be treated as an enemy when he arrives in the land of another. One may refuse to receive him when this can be done without causing his destruction; but so long as he peacefully occupies his place, one may not treat him with hostility. It is not the right to be a permanent visitor that one may demand. A special beneficent agreement would be needed in order to give an outsider a right to become a fellow inhabitant for a certain length of time. It is only a right of temporary sojourn, a right to associate which all men have. . . .

> Originally no one had more right than another to a particular part of the earth. Uninhabitable parts of the earth—the sea and the deserts—divide this community of all men, but the ship and the camel (the desert ship) enable them to approach each other across these unruled regions and to establish communication by using the common right to the face of the earth, which belongs to human beings generally. (*Perpetual Peace* 20–21)

According to Kant's definition, as co-inhabitants of the world and fellow travelers on this planet, every human being is entitled to hospitality and tolerance. Kant's ideas of hospitality and tolerance are imbued with a sense of idealism and offer a manifesto for world peace and co-existence. It would appear that these ideas could generate agreement; however, this vision of a common shared destiny entitling all human beings to hospitality has been criticized by detractors of cosmopolitanism.

CRITIQUES (AND DEFENSES) OF COSMOPOLITANISM:

In response to Nussbaum's advocacy of cosmopolitanism over patriotism, various scholars have offered critiques of cosmopolitanism. These debates are included in Nussbaum's *For Love of Country?*. Michael Walzer, for instance, points out that cosmopolitanism, or an allegiance to a trans-national ideology, has not been a guarantee against the excesses of violence and bloodshed. Communism, for example, an ideology of the twentieth-century ostensibly committed to universalist ideals, did not have any specific allegiance to territory, but that still did not stop it from exacting its toll of lives. Walzer asks the provocative question, "Isn't this repressive communism a child of universalizing enlightenment?" (127). His question emphasizes the fact that both patriotism and cosmopolitanism, carried to the extreme in the form of ideologies like fascism and communism, respectively, can have devastating consequences.

Another trend of criticism against cosmopolitanism, voiced by Judith Butler in "Universality in Culture" and also included in Nussbaum's collection, is directed at the universalizing tendencies of this discourse. Butler writes, "The problem emerges, however, when the meaning of the term, 'the universal,' proves to be culturally variable, and the specific cultural articulations of the universal work against its claim to a transcultural status" (45). Here Butler alludes to the contested nature of the universal: obtaining consensus on our definition of universal human rights is difficult, and what has passed as universal, if analyzed, will reveal itself to be the product of a specific time, place, and tradition that has become dominant or hegemonic.

In his contribution to a different collection on cosmopolitanism, Daniel Chernilo discusses the critique of universalism based on its original locale. Universalism's historical roots lie in the particular geographical and socio-cultural context of ancient Greece, and this western origin is something that neither cosmopolitanism nor universalism can transcend. Chernilo opines that cosmopolitanism is intimately tied to universalism, and the cosmopolitan project consists of the refinement of universalism rather than the abandonment of it. In Chernilo's view, cosmopolitanism inherits many of the critiques directed at the primacy of western civilization and culture.

In spite of the critiques leveled at cosmopolitanism as a philosophical discourse, several scholars from non-western backgrounds have articulated strong arguments in defense of it. For example, Amartya Sen in *The Argumentative Indian* and in essays like "Humanity and Citizenship" deconstructs the notion that democracy, citizenship, justice, and rights are uniquely western concepts or that they originate purely from Greek civilization. Sen offers examples of proto-democracy in ancient India by citing the goals of pacifism and justice pursued by Ashoka, the Buddhist emperor of ancient India, and by referencing the ideas of religious and cultural pluralism that flourished in the reign of the Mughal emperor Akbar.[6] Sen disputes the notion that some societies, like those in ancient Greece, have had a greater affinity for freedom and democracy while others, like societies in China, have shown more of a propensity for authoritarianism. Sen is more invested in locating seeds of democracy and freedom in a variety of cultural contexts even if these examples are not those of a fully developed democracy (*The Argumentative Indian* 15–21). Sen cites Aristotle as an example of a Greek philosopher who is considered pivotal in the development of democratic thought even though he was unabashedly supportive of slavery in some of his treatises (Sen "Humanity and Citizenship" 118).

In *Cosmopolitanism: Ethics in a World of Strangers,* Kwame Anthony Appiah attempts to provide a nuanced defense of cosmopolitanism by subtly distinguishing it from universalism. Appiah argues, "Cosmopolitans suppose that all cultures have enough overlap in their vocabulary of values to begin a conversation. But they don't assume like some universalists that we could all come to agreement if only we had the same vocabulary" (57). Appiah concedes: "conversation doesn't have to lead to consensus about anything, especially not values; it's enough that it helps people get used to one another" (85).

In the realm of culture and co-existence, cosmopolitanism celebrates hybridity, mélange, and inter-mingling of traditions rather than myths of cultural purity. With regard to the growth of radical Islam and other radical religions in the contemporary period, Appiah draws on the work of Olivier Roy to build his analysis. In *Globalized Islam: The Search for a New Ummah*, Roy argues that the growth of radical Islam is peculiarly a phenomenon that has developed from Muslims living as minorities in the metropolitan centers of the first world. The longing in the radical Islamic movements to establish an *Ummah* or universal community is, according to Appiah, an expression of a universalism without tolerance (140). Roy sees a link between radical Islam and radical Christianity in the quest for a universal community unmediated by local or cultural differences, and he posits, in both cases, "a move towards the individualization of religions" (149). Unlike the universalisms of radical religious movements in Islam and Christianity that substitute allegiance to a nation for that of allegiance to a religious community, cosmopolitanism is committed to pluralism rather than exclusivity. According to Appiah, cosmopolitanism is also committed to fallibilism, the belief that errors can be made and corrected in philosophical positions. This is quite different from religious radicalisms that are convinced of their infallibility. Cosmopolitanism is based, according to Appiah, on the principle that knowledge is provisional and subject to revision (144). This contrast between the ideologies of cosmopolitanism and religious radicalisms is crucial as a foundation to a course on 9/11 literature in order to understand why the traumatic event happened and how such events might be prevented in the future.

CHALLENGES RELATED TO DESIGNING THE 9/11 COURSE AND EMBEDDING COSMOPOLITANISM INTO ITS CONTENT

The tensions between the allegiances to a national as opposed to a global affiliation were fully evident as I worked to create the new course on 9/11 literature. I offer the following narrative detailing the difficulties of this process as a guide to any professor who wishes to take on the challenge.

This course was a response to curricular needs that arose in UW-Stout because of the revision of the General Education (GE) program that resulted in the creation of two new GE categories,

"Contemporary Issues" and "Social Responsibility and Ethical Reasoning." As director of the UW-Stout Honors College and a faculty member in English, I was interested in offering an honors course in these new categories. Along with revisions in GE, the university also changed its requirements for racial and ethnic studies and global perspectives, graduation requirements mandated by the University of Wisconsin System.

According to the UW-Stout website, the content of a racial and ethnic studies course has to focus on the four federally designated racial minorities in the U.S. As mentioned earlier, these include "African American, Hispanic/Latino, Asian American (with an emphasis on Southeast Asian American) and American Indian" ("Racial and Ethnic Studies Requirement"). The Racial and Ethnic Studies committee and the Curriculum and Instruction committee of UW-Stout, which are standing committees of the Faculty Senate, mandated that racial and ethnic studies courses must draw on the following subject topics, according to the same website: "historical and ideological construction of race, racial/ethnic identity formation, racial impact on public policy, stratification of differences and exploration of students' cultural and racial/ethnic experience" ("Racial and Ethnic Studies Requirement").

UW-Stout also has a global perspectives requirement for graduation. UW-Stout's mission makes it desirable that students appreciate cultural, economic, political, environmental, and social differences. Learning a second language at the college level and developing an understanding of another culture provide students with skills they will use in international situations. To earn a bachelor's degree, students who started Fall 2010 or later must fulfill a global perspective requirement by "completing a program of university-approved work or study abroad, or completing six credits of courses approved as fulfilling the global perspective requirement" ("Racial and Ethnic Studies Requirement").

Thus the two components of diversity—racial and ethnic studies and global perspectives—are seen as separate parts of the student's experience, and courses are generally divided into

145

global perspectives or race and ethnic studies, determined by whether the content focuses on domestic or international topics. This split in curriculum echoes in a strange way the debate between patriotism and cosmopolitanism outlined earlier. I would also surmise that this split in curriculum is not unique to UW-Stout. The fact of the matter, however, is that a course on 9/11 literature cannot be neatly compartmentalized in either category and exemplifies the imbrication of the national with the global in the events of 9/11 and the responses that ensued.

When I started conceptualizing the 9/11 literature course, I had no doubt that the course content would focus heavily on racial and ethnic identity formation as well as on the impact of public policy on race and ethnicity. September 11, 2001, marks a watershed moment in American history and national life. It is the most dramatic encounter with public trauma for most Americans. For the present generation of college-going students, it is a memory of a public event forever etched in childhood memories even if it was experienced indirectly on the television screen. Although memorialized as the iconic image of the burning towers, this historic event marks a crisis of American racial and ethnic identity formations. It is the moment that brings to crisis the traditionally designated ethnic identities and transposes old hostilities with new sets of stereotypes. The African American male, as a stereotypical figure associated with violent crime, is quickly joined by the Arab American or South Asian Muslim, now typecast as a terrorist. The costs of public trauma are registered disproportionately on minorities. The retaliatory U.S. wars in Afghanistan and Iraq as well as Patriot Act legislation add new complexities to questions of American citizenship, freedom, and democratic engagement in a post-catastrophe world.

Another important teaching point in the class is the Patriot Act, signed by President George W. Bush six weeks after the attacks of September 11, 2001. This law vastly expanded the government's ability to monitor its citizens and eliminated many checks and balances to prevent the misuse of the state's sovereign power over its citizens, which had previously been in place. The law was passed quickly, without the opportunity for many legislators to become fully aware of its far-reaching ramifications. In particular, the Patriot Act vastly expanded the government's power to conduct secret searches and seize records without having to inform citizens of such actions. Provisions of the Patriot Act violate protections of free speech in the First Amendment and protections from illegal searches in the Fourth Amendment of the U.S. Constitution. While the ostensible reason for the passage of this law was to help law enforcement be efficient in capturing terrorists, in reality, it was used to target Arab Americans, Muslims, and South Asians as terror suspects and to detain them indefinitely, without any trial. Henry A. Giroux, a leading Canadian scholar and public intellectual, in analyzing this phenomenon has written in the online publication *Truthout*, "The war on terrorism has morphed into a new form of authoritarianism and its real enemy is no longer limited to potential terrorists, but includes democracy itself" (Giroux). Giroux is not questioning the efforts of the U.S. in protecting itself from its potential enemies, but he is deeply critical of the ways in which this desire was carried out, resulting in the transformation of the U.S. from a democracy to a surveillance state in which all citizens are only a step away from becoming detainees with no civil rights. Like the Japanese Internment Act[7] and the Chinese Exclusion Act[8] that preceded it, the Patriot Act passed in the aftermath of terrorist attacks by Arabs and led to the construction of a new racialized enemy of the U.S.: the Arab/Muslim terrorist.

In the last decade, a rich tapestry of works has emerged that grapple with these political and personal consequences of the aftermath of 9/11 in genres as varied as lyric poetry, graphic memoirs, films, and novels. I wanted this course to examine these literary expressions of American identity in a time of crisis and study them in conjunction with emerging theories of American nationalism and political policy. There existed a need for a systematic study of American literature produced in this decade that memorializes this traumatic event. Such a course did not exist in the catalog of literature courses at my university although 9/11 literature courses have been taught in other universities.

The first difficulty that the course ran into occurred when I applied for curricular incubation grant funding to develop it. The committee awarding grants for the development of new courses pointed out that this course focusing on Arab and Muslim Americans did not deal with content on the four designated racial and ethnic minorities of the U.S. This obstacle was solved by a justification document explaining that the course was dealing with racial and ethnic identity formation, and, in a post-9/11 era, religion has become a new axis for racial "othering." I argued that 9/11 marks a change in racial discourse in the U.S. and presents a unique opportunity to study contemporary racial politics. My course uses the immediate and continuing effects of 9/11 in the racial stigmatization of West Asian (Arab) Americans, South Asians from the Indian sub-continent, and Muslims from Southeast Asia as an entry point to grapple with the complex history of racism in the U.S. and its ubiquitous presence. It is this ubiquitous presence of racism that structures contemporary social and political formations within domestic and global contexts. That date marks the culmination of long-existing prejudice against immigrants from the Arab/Muslim world and the escalation of this prejudice under the aegis of an official "War on Terror" and public policy like the Patriot Act.

After the initial approval of funding, the nebulous status of Arab Americans was brought up again at the College Council meeting. Arab Americans are regarded as Caucasians by the U.S. Census. In the 1920s, however, South Asians, particularly those like the Sikh immigrant Bhagat Singh Thind, who tried to make a similar legal claim to citizenship, were denied this claim of Caucasian ancestry.[9] South Asians, particularly Southeast Asians, are regarded as a U.S. ethnic minority, but Arab Americans, who faced racial hostility and prejudice in the aftermath of 9/11, are not regarded as official minorities. These facts reveal the difficulties in racial classification and the problems that arise when new indices of identity like religion deconstruct earlier classifications. I must emphasize that the committees were broadly supportive of the course and enthusiastic that it be offered under the "Racial and Ethnic Studies A" classification, but they were constrained by the rules established by UW-System guidelines. The committees also encouraged me to seek a "Global Perspectives" designation for the course, in addition to its "Racial and Ethnic Studies" designation, something I had not initially planned to pursue. Committee members understood the limitations of these categories and worked to make it visible to students that this course would cover national and international topics.

The other cumbersome aspect of the course approval process was the emphasis on the specific quantification of racial and ethnic studies content. While I fully empathize with the intentions of the curriculum committee to measure the amount of racial and ethnic content, I am not sure if topics in the humanities can be quantified in this manner. Even if a course comes up with a strong quantification of content, that, in itself, is not an indicator of whether the course content will be able to have a transformative impact in the lives of students in terms of making them think of the contested and diffi-cult topics of race and ethnicity in a more productive and powerful way. The other serious limitation is that this kind of rigid adherence to UW-System rules and regulations restricts ways in which diver-sity can be thought of as a multi-faceted issue. Questions of race and ethnicity cannot be separated from other vectors of identity like class, gender, sexual orientation, religion, and nationality (see Dziesinski, Camarena, and Homrich-Knieling on intersectional-ity in this volume, pp. 81–106). All these components of identity have an impact on determining our response to diversity. Instead of each of these elements being in competition with each other, it is most important to investigate ways in which multiple components of identity can be studied together and introduced into the curricu-lum to promote ongoing critical thinking on diversity.

In my course rationale, I illustrated the many aspects of race and ethnicity on which the course would concentrate. I touched on aspects of racial formation, racial impacts of public policy, stratifica-tion of difference, and students' own experiences of race. I outlined the specific ways in which these topics interfaced with events of 9/11 and the literary works that were produced in its wake.

Historically, immigrants of color have been viewed as the racial other in the U.S. This widespread prejudice has deep historical roots as in the examples of the Chinese Exclusion Act of 1882 and the Japanese internment legislation enforced in 1942. Immigrants of color from Latin America have continued to face many more barriers to integration and acceptance in American society. Muslims, South Asians, and Arab Americans have been doubly marginalized and "othered" because of their racial and religious difference. With the declaration of a War on Terror, Muslims living in the U.S. are often collapsed in the popular imagination with terrorists and are now under fresh waves of scrutiny and suspicion that deeply impact their ability to lead normal lives. Through the reading of many memoirs and creative works by Muslim Americans, my course examines how 9/11 and the events that follow led to the racialization of Arab and Muslim Americans.

The focus of the course on Muslim Americans offers a unique opportunity to examine the complexities of various racial identities in contemporary American society. On the one hand, the election of an African American president may be celebrated as a case for progress; however, one of the greatest challenges faced during his election campaign was the inability of many Americans to accept his Muslim middle name of Hussein. This has led Ali A. Mazrui, an eminent scholar of African political studies and Islam and holder of numerous appointments in Kenya, the U.S., and Britain during his distinguished scholarly career, to argue that religion has emerged as a powerful component of racial formation. On the other hand, the marginalization of traditionally underprivileged racial minorities like African Americans continues unabated. In the memorialization of 9/11 heroes, particularly firefighters, for example, acknowledgement of the twelve African American New York City firefighters who died saving lives has been absent. In today's news African American youth continue to suffer from alleged cases of police brutality, leading to public outrage and confrontations in cities like Ferguson, Missouri.[10]

Through an exploration of post-9/11 literature and film, students examine the origins of prejudice against Muslim and other Asian Americans as a consequence of 9/11. Continuing effects of prejudice and ignorance of specific histories lead to violence, like that against Sikh Americans at the Sikh temple in Oak Creek, Wisconsin, in 2012.[11]

The two most significant public policy events and laws studied in this course are the War on Terror and the Patriot Act. The course examines how the draining of fiscal resources to finance two massive wars have had deleterious effects on racial minorities, who are often most vulnerable economically. Economists have linked the recession of 2008 to the War on Terror, and the recession has affected minorities[12] and the economically disadvantaged populations the most.[13] Soldiers recruited for the war tend to also come from minority and economically depressed communities. The War on Terror has resulted in massive profits for companies, like Halliburton, while extracting tremendous costs from the countries attacked as well as domestic minority populations. The Patriot Act, as I have outlined above, has radically affected American civil liberties, rapidly shrinking public discourse on the war and causing Muslim minorities to live under constant surveillance and profiling. Moustafa Bayoumi's American Book Award winning work, *How Does It Feel to be a Problem?: Being Young and Arab in America*, contends that in post-9/11 America, Arab and Muslim communities are facing active discrimination and the erosion of hard-won gains of the civil rights struggles. Bayoumi writes: "Bias crimes against Arabs, Muslims and those assumed to be Arab or Muslim spiked 1,700 percent in the first six months after September 11 and have never since returned to their pre-2001 levels" (3). Bayoumi also argues that government policies exacerbated these hostilities when President George W. Bush allowed for the selective use of racial profiling to combat potential terrorist threats (4). Bayoumi concludes that while profiling of other groups was "officially and legally un-American, profiling Arabs and Muslims made good national-security sense" (4).

South Asians and West Asian Muslims have traditionally embodied the "model minority" myth, embodying economic success, as opposed to Hispanic and African Americans, who have been cast as "problem minorities" in mainstream discourse. The history of 9/11 deconstructs the mythology inherent in this stratification by recasting Muslims as the problem minority and often incarcerating Muslims who are profiled as terrorists. Scholars like Vijay Prashad and Amitava Kumar document the targeting of Arabs and South Asians in the global war on terror launched in the aftermath of 9/11. South Asian and Arab men incarcerated and tortured in Guantanamo Bay share a kinship of suffering with ever-increasing numbers of incarcerated black men.

The course challenges students to engage in these ethical debates about stereotyping, racial profiling, and incarceration without trial for many American racial and ethnic minority groups. While being attentive to racial and ethnic differences, the course attempts to identify parallels in the embattled situations of different minority groups, emphasizing a cosmopolitan approach to understanding the commonalities of experience.

MUSLIM WOMEN IN POST-9/11 NOVELS AND THEIR HISTORICAL AND RELIGIOUS CONTEXTS

In this final section of this chapter, I examine the liminal presence of South Asian Muslim women in post-9/11 literary works featured in my course. The condition of women in Islam brings debates about cosmopolitanism and patriotism to an interesting juxtaposition. Western feminists see Islamic women as suffering from many limitations to their individual rights and freedoms. This perceived lack of freedom is often used as a rationale for imperial war, ostensibly to secure freedom and democracy for populations deprived of these conditions. In teaching post-9/11 novels centered on Muslim women, I ask honors students to explore the question of freedom and agency within a cosmopolitan as well as a culturally specific context and how the two might be reconciled with regard to issues facing Muslim women. I work to avoid the easy position of cultural relativism, a passive acceptance of difference, because it is occurring in a different cultural context. Instead, I encourage students to develop their skills of ethical judgment in order to come to informed judgments about different issues affecting Muslim women. Since the course fulfills "Social Responsibility and Ethical

Reasoning" and "Contemporary Issues" categories, as well as the "Literature" category at UW-Stout, the course objectives emphasizing diversity education readily align with those promoting ethical reasoning.

Because students are introduced to these issues through the discipline of literature, I teach works like Amy Waldman's *The Submission* and Ayad Akhtar's *Disgraced,* with a focus on the aesthetics of tragedy and the power of literary works to evoke empathy for characters and enable engagement with the issues from a variety of perspectives. This focus on empathy emanates from my commitment to the ideal of cosmopolitanism as a desirable goal in honors education. The study of these texts serves a number of purposes:

1. to examine debates about the status of women in Islam;

2. to review unexamined circulating images and preconceptions;

3. to analyze specific examples of conflicts emerging as an ideological impasse between cosmopolitan and Islamic ideals; and

4. to enable students to explore ways in which Islamic women negotiate the impasse.

The goal of these studies is to see Islamic women as dynamic actors in their destinies rather than as passive recipients of traditional strictures on their lives. The historical context of the emerging debates on women in Islam needs to be provided for students to grapple with these literary texts. Thus, as a background to these novels, students are introduced to scholarship by Islamic women and others on questions of women's agency, on their personal acts of piety, and on their participation in public life. I summarize some broad currents in this scholarship in the section that follows.

I focus here on texts that investigate the embattled situation of Muslim women as they experience the forces of a neoliberal globalization (see Stoller in this volume, pp. 3–32) that facilitates the flow of goods and ideas over real and cyber-space, on the one hand, and the contradictory but not unrelated movement that re-inscribes religion in the quotidian lives of women. This dialectic of modernity and spirituality gets accentuated in the aftermath of

9/11 and its ensuing debates on U.S. nationalism and belonging. These texts engage in rethinking questions of Islam and democracy, with particular emphasis on female agency. They also investigate the possibilities of female agency and emancipation against the background of a rising wave of religious extremism and constraints placed on women's lives by newly emerging patriarchies. These texts, however, also coalesce their representations of the tragic consequences of female agency thematically. The emotional responses produced by the aesthetics of tragedy enable not just a classical Aristotelian catharsis but an affective response of empathy and recognition of a common humanity with these women at a time when the dominant trope of representation of Islam in the West has been through the lens of the "Other."

Even before the cataclysmic events of 9/11, for much of the second half of the twentieth-century, Islam has been represented as the "Other" of secular modernity. The most visible symbol of its recalcitrant anti-modern ethos has been crystalized in the image of the veiled Muslim woman. Students in the honors "After 9/11" course are introduced to debates surrounding the veil in Muslim societies, which has been read in the West as a sign of female oppression. This debate about the veil emerged during anti-colonial struggles when the passage of a woman from a state of being covered to being unveiled became a symbol of a nation moving from the colonized past to a liberated modernity, a movement often instigated by the anti-colonial male elite without any consultation with women about how they felt about this intimate violence forced on their bodies. The veil was a feature of both Hindu and Muslim South Asian women's lives, as expressed in novels like Rabindranath Tagore's *The Home and the World* and studied by Inderpal Grewal in her book *Home and Harem*. Grewal argues that the colonialist imperative to abolish this custom is a project based on the impulse to discipline the colonized female bodies. Thus, "to 'civilize' 'Eastern' women functioned to make them less opaque, to strip them of their veils, and to remove them from harems where they lived lives hidden from the European male" (49). For Muslim women, the veil has been a recurrent issue that has come back as recently as this decade in controversies about French authorities banning the Islamic dress code for girls in French public schools.

In the mainstream media, journalists like Nicholas D. Kristoff writing with Sheryl Wudunn have asked the question, "Is Islam Misogynistic?"(149). Kristoff has argued in *Half the Sky,* a journalistic account of gender injustice in many parts of the world, that early Islam had in fact enshrined more rights for women than the other Abrahamic religions, but in recent times Christianity has a better record of ensuring the rights of women than Islam. Kristoff has focused mostly on the repressive regimes in Afghanistan, in which women who commit adultery can be stoned to death under *Sharia,* the Islamic legal system derived from the *Koran* and the reported collections of teachings by Prophet Mohammed. In this system, a woman's testimony is considered to be of half the value of a man's (Kristoff and Wudunn 150–51).

Students are offered a selection of mainstream liberal opinion on women in Islam by a journalist like Kristoff, in conjunction with the scholarly perspectives on Islam by feminist historians of Islam. Feminist scholars of Islam, like Leila Ahmed and Fatima Mernissi who insist on the principles of ethical egalitarianism embedded in Islam, seek scriptural and historical examples of female agency in early Islam. Both Mernissi and Ahmed agree that in spite of Islam's egalitarian principles, the institution of veiling got used by the male elite to restrict women from claiming their rights within Islam, such as the right to own property and to remarry after the death of a husband or divorce. According to Ahmed, the authoritarian imposition of the *hijab,* or veiling, was a function of the Umayad, and, particularly, the Abbasid periods of Islamic history.[14]

Instead of viewing Islam and Christianity as polar opposites of each other, separated by geography and ideology, students are exposed to works by scholars like Anouar Majid, Talal Asad, and Saba Mahmood, all of whom investigate common threads in the intellectual currents within each religious tradition. Majid's *A Call for Heresy* grapples with the question of how to reconcile modernity with the spiritual precepts of Islam. Instead of casting the West and particularly the U.S. and Islam as polar opposites in a post-9/11 world, Majid tries to establish similarities in the foundational texts of both. Citing early Puritan thinkers like John Winthrop, William Bradford, and Jonathan Edwards, Majid points out that the early Puritan leaders had a vision of establishing an ideal, egalitarian community, a vision not very different from that embodied in early Islam. While the writers of documents like the U.S. Constitution and the Declaration of Independence consciously chose to separate religious life from that of the nation, this separation of the church and the state is not as clear in the present-day U.S. as it was originally intended to be. With the rise in evangelical Christianity, there has been a resurgence of the kind of early Puritanical rhetoric that was prevalent in the writings of Winthrop and Edwards. Having established a basic similarity between the U.S. and Islam, Majid argues that the return to religious fundamentalism, worldwide, is a corollary to globalization and the uneven distribution of the spoils of global capitalism.

Saba Mahmood's *Politics of Piety*, her ethnographic study of the mosque (or piety) movement in Cairo, Egypt, questions the biases of western feminism, which assume patriarchy and female agency to be in sharp opposition to each other.[15] In her study of the mosque movement, she finds that women in Islamic societies do not operate under the strict binary of support for patriarchy or defiant opposition. While apparently supporting conservative practices like *hijab*, prayer, and varied practices of traditional Muslim life, these women work on subtly changing the structures of religious orthodoxy while inhabiting and interacting with these structures. For example, Mahmood argues that many mosques have female discussion leaders, and women engage in lively debates with their leaders about various aspects of their lives with regard to dress, prayer, and family responsibilities. In an interview published online, Mahmood argues that mosques were traditionally male spaces, but with the start of the piety movement, five hundred women started showing up at a mosque twice a week ("The Light"). She considers this to be transformative because although they were using the same religious text, they were reading it differently. Mahmood also cites the example of a woman, who, due to her more extensive scriptural knowledge, was able to challenge the imam or official leader of the mosque and assert her right to lead her female companions in prayer ("The Light"). Mahmood explores the movements of ethical reform like the piety movement in Egypt to study ways in which they "unsettle key assumptions of the secular-liberal imagination even when they do not aim to transform the state" (78). In exploring the imbrication of religion in the structures of the Egyptian state, Mahmood, like Majid, blurs the boundaries of the secular and the religious in western liberal democracies, calling attention to Puritanism in America. Thus, both Majid and Mahmood trace commonalities between western and Islamic polities rather than view them in the light of Samuel Huntington's theory of a "clash of civilizations." The "clash of civilizations theory," in brief, is the argument presented by Huntington that after the end of the Cold War, religion, rather than political ideology, becomes the fault line along which political conflicts emerge.

Judith Butler is most widely known as a scholar/theorist of gender studies and as a scholar of non-normative sexualities. Her work, however, defies such pigeonholing. From early works like *Gender Trouble* and *Bodies That Matter*, Butler's subsequent works like *Precarious Life* and *Antigone's Claim* seek to draw parallels between the marginality of the lives of gay and lesbian subjects with respect to the state with other marginalized people not recognized by the state, like illegal immigrants and those detained in the War Against Terror. Drawing on such classical works as Sophocles' *Antigone*, Butler painstakingly points to parallels between the lack of recognition of queer families within the heteronormative structures of the state and the lack of accommodation of detainees and illegal immigrants to the obligation to meet basic human rights, like the right to humane treatment, fair trial, and mourning and memorialization, among others. It is only with the recent June 26, 2015, U.S. Supreme Court ruling that same sex marriage can no longer be banned by individual states. This is the greatest legal victory for gay rights advocates in recent times.

In texts written prior to this ruling, Butler is sharply critical of hierarchies that present capitalist modernity and states following this system as better preservers of human rights. She also criticizes the tendency of such states to consider the rest of the world, particularly those following Islam, as primitive and barbarous. In a recent essay, "Bodies in Alliance and the Politics of the Street," Butler points out how countries like the Netherlands subject immigrants from Islamic countries to tests to assess their openness to progressive movements like gay and lesbian marriage equality. Since homosexuality is a taboo in Islam, immigrants from these countries will be unable to establish themselves as appropriately progressive. In the same vein, Butler is also highly critical of French feminists who advocate for transgender rights and the rights of transgendered people to dress of their own volition in public spaces while ironically opposing Islamic religious dress like the veil or *hijab* in public schools for undermining the secular identity of the French nation. She wonders why the rights of religious minorities are being diminished or negated while the rights of sexual minorities are accommodated? Moreover, why does accommodation of the rights of sexual minorities in western European nations become a sign of progressivism and freedom when those pursuing religions like Islam are faced with more obstacles in the cultural expression of their religious identities? Butler opines:

> Hence, we are left to fathom the many universalist French feminists who call upon the police to arrest, detain, fine, and sometimes deport women wearing the Niqab or the Burka in the public sphere in France. What sort of politics is this that recruits the police function of the state to monitor and restrict women from religious minorities in the public sphere? Why would the same universalists (Elisabeth Badinter) openly affirm the rights of transgendered people to freely appear in public while restricting that very right to women who happen to wear religious clothing that offends the sensibilities of die-hard secularists? If the right to appear is to be honored "universally" it would not be able to survive such an obvious and insupportable contradiction. (Butler, "Bodies in Alliance")

Butler adamantly insists on the equality of human claims and refuses to see one kind of identity struggle as more legitimate than the other. Even though she is an American, first-world feminist, queer theorist, and Jewish, she does not privilege any of these aspects of her identity and these struggles as more legitimate than others. On the contrary, she explores ways in which one can oppose the Israeli state from a Jewish standpoint and refuse the label of being a self-hating anti-Semite. Butler's refusal to privilege any one kind of component of identity as more deserving of accommodation than another and her insistence on the shared struggle for human rights in diverse areas provide a theoretical space to rethink how inclusive excellence, defined by UW-Stout as "fostering inspiration through diversity, equity, inclusion, and excellence," can be approached and taught in the honors curriculum.

How can we translate some of these theoretical ideas derived from Butler into specific strategies for the honors curriculum on diversity? For one, honors courses on diversity should focus on multiple and ongoing struggles for equity and justice. The old model of having a course on U.S. race and ethnic studies and another on global perspectives is unproductive. Race, religion, gender, sexuality, and other components of diversity have to be studied in a comparative framework. The discourse of gender is integrally linked to post-9/11 racial formations as the chief arsenal in vilifying Islam since the charge of misogyny is easily leveled against it. Butler's formulations and warnings against an easy shorthand of equating Islam to a pre-modern time frame, backwardness and misogyny, while championing Christianity and the secular West as avatars of progressivism and women's rights can be interrogated fruitfully in this course.

In what follows, I examine a few print and film texts I have taught in the course thus far and the methods I have used to train honors students against the pitfalls of these easily received and unexamined binaristic assumptions about cultures. Studying a novel like Amy Waldman's *The Submission* helps them examine notions of women's rights in Islamic and secular western societies and obliges students to rethink their assumptions vis-à-vis greater freedom and autonomy for women in the U.S. and oppression for women in Islamic societies. This novel also leads them to question the received division of the world into the secular West, which includes the U.S., and the pre-modern religious East, which includes the nations following Islam.

In Waldman's *The Submission*, readers encounter a very different vision of a Muslim woman's agency. The novel is a fictional representation of the 9/11 memorial controversy through which students are introduced to the debates that ensued over the proposal of building an inter-faith religious center close to ground zero. The novel re-imagines the 9/11 memorial controversy as a design contest in which the winning design, submitted anonymously, turns out to be the work of Mohammad Khan, a Muslim architect, with the proposal including a garden resembling an Islamic paradise. This win results in a polarization between victims' families, who view this as an insensitive insult, and defenders of freedom of religion, who want to honor the civic process but eventually succumb to popular sentiment and then pressure Mohammad Khan to withdraw his design. In the midst of this controversy, at the public hearing, Asma, a Bangladeshi widow of an undocumented worker who died in the Twin Towers, makes a passionate speech in Bengali about her loss as a Muslim woman, blurring the categories of Muslims as perpetrators and non-Muslims as the victims of the tragedy. Later in the novel, Asma becomes the target of a random act of violence and dies because of this tragic attack.

Waldman's *The Submission* raises two critical issues pertaining to Muslim identity in the U.S. The first issue concerns the separation of religion from American public life. The author suggests that the eighteenth-century, post-Enlightenment ideology that shaped the foundational documents of the American nation and defined the ethos of the country have become compromised after the trauma of 9/11. Waldman's novel invokes the resurgence of America as a Christian community, invoking Majid's study, which analyzes the re-emergence of the idea of a religious and specifically Christian national identity for the U.S.

The second controversy the novel touches on is the more complicated issue of what is a publicly grievable death and whose deaths deserve and receive memorialization after a traumatic event like 9/11. These issues are raised by Butler in *Precarious Life* and are echoed in the sentiments of Asma, the widow of the undocumented Bangladeshi victim of 9/11.Writing under a climate of *de facto* censorship in the immediate aftermath of 9/11 and the passage of Patriot Act legislation by President George W. Bush, Butler makes an ardent plea for mourning, especially mourning for those whose deaths are not recognized as human losses. She includes in this group the countless dead who are unmourned because they have been victims of HIV or are the dehumanized inmates of Guantanamo Bay, who have been denied indefinitely universal human rights to legal trial, or Palestinian civilians and children whose deaths seldom receive any mention in U.S. news media. For Butler, grief and mourning represent "the transformative effect of loss" (*Precarious* 21). Butler also notes that feminism has been co-opted historically for imperial designs, and she references Gayatri Chakravorty Spivak's classic essay "Can the Subaltern Speak?" to re-invoke the use of feminism to liberate brown women from brown men. Butler does not want to align herself to a feminism that sets up first-world and third-world hierarchies among women and uses Islam and its restrictions on women as a rationale for imperial war. Butler is positing a very different kind of feminism than the stereotypical nineteenth-century missionary/savior posture. Instead, Butler draws attention to "the precariousness of those lives that we destroyed," admitting American responsibility for the destruction of civilian life in Afghanistan as well as the drone strikes that are still continuing (*Precarious* 150). She thinks it is from this recognition of the precariousness of the life of the other that a broad consensus against the war can be generated.

In Waldman's *The Submission,* Asma makes a plea to mourn the life of a victim who is, generally speaking, unmournable. Because her husband has no legal status as a citizen or legal alien, his death, like those of HIV victims, Guantanamo residents, and other such categories of individuals, is denied recognition as a human death.

Asma does not accept this situation in a spirit of religious resignation. In fact, her faith gives her the courage to insert herself in a secular space, a public hearing about the memorial. In her speech, which she gives in Bengali, she decimates the notion that Muslims were perpetrators and not victims of 9/11 and speaks in support of the chosen design. This speech pushes her into the limelight. Later in the novel, however, when she is randomly stabbed by a stranger, this tragic event helps to bring the Bangladeshi community closer together and enables them to express their feelings more openly rather than be forced into the role of a silent minority. For Asma, the act of mourning is recognition of her humanity and her agency.

After reading this text, students are invited to ask questions about Muslim women's lives. Some possible questions might include the following:

1. Are these women able to claim agency and autonomy by reclaiming traditional religious practices like reading the *Koran* and praying?

2. How can we rethink ideas of freedom and agency in the light of these differences?

3. Can we conceptualize freedom for women more broadly than just freedom of dress or movement into the public sphere?

Another text studied in the course is Valarie Kaur's documentary *Divided We Fall,* which examines hate crimes and rampant prejudice against Sikhs in the wake of 9/11. In a section of this documentary, the new racialization of Arabs, South Asians, and Sikhs is traced in the long background of hate crimes and racial prejudice. The killing of Balbir Singh Sodhi in Mesa, Arizona, on September 15, 2001, marks one of the first fatalities of anti-Muslim/South Asian prejudice. This murder is compared to other hate crimes such as the killings of James Byrd, an African American man murdered by white supremacists in Jasper, Texas, in 1998, and Matthew Shepard, a student at the University of Wyoming who was tortured and left to die in Laramie, also in 1998, because of his homosexual identity. The documentary deliberately forces audiences to see commonalities in varied expressions of hate. Although the speaker in the documentary laments the lack of sufficient public outrage at the death of the Sikh victims, she sees these deaths in a continuum and asks the audience to reflect on what inspires mourning and remembrance and who is consigned to oblivion. The death of African American James Byrd and the murder of Matthew Shephard, the gay student in Laramie, garner far greater outrage and protest. By exposing the common links of bigotry and hatred, the film is calling for strategic alliances.

Divided We Fall also makes the important connection between the detention and interrogation of suspected Muslims and Arabs to the earlier historic internment experiences of Japanese Americans during the Second World War. Seeing these actions as part of a continuum helps students to recognize the excesses of paranoia and national security, the demonization and scapegoating of innocents. Present-day Islamophobia is seen as a parallel to xenophobia against Japanese after the attack on Pearl Harbor.

The theme of racial profiling and backlash against Muslims in post-9/11 America is also examined in the Bollywood film *My Name is Khan,* which is also part of the course curriculum. This film is in the genre of the Bollywood musical romance, but despite its sentimental presentation it tackles many components of inclusive excellence. The protagonist, Rizwan Khan, is a South Asian Muslim immigrant who also has Asperger's Syndrome. Students are presented with several aspects of his marginality, which include religion, skin color, and disability, and his difficulty fitting into mainstream America. Rizwan's adopted son, Sam, becomes a victim of a hate crime. The film veers toward tragedy after the murder of Sam by a group of teenage bullies, but in fact it charts a process of recuperation and racial integration and forgiveness after trauma. The film depicts Khan's ability to identify with the struggles of rural African Americans facing hurricanes in the South and empathize with their losses. The film also highlights ethnic and religious tensions between Hindus and Muslims in the South Asian immigrant community. Through Rizwan's long and frustrating attempt to meet the president to tell him his name is Khan and that he is not a terrorist, the viewer is taken on a journey into the complex, diverse cultural landscape of the post-9/11 U.S.

CREATING A CONTEXT IN WHICH PRESENT-DAY STUDENTS MAY STUDY THE AFTER-EFFECTS OF 9/11

Students often understand these concepts of racial inequities, profiling, and injustice at a theoretical level but feel disconnected, given their context as students at a small Midwestern university town when they try to relate to a national and global event like 9/11. Moreover, a generational distance from this event already exists for traditional-age honors students taking this course. Many of these students were between the ages of five and seven in 2001 and have limited personal experience or memory of the national trauma from which to draw. To negotiate this problem of geographical and generational distance from the history being studied, I designed a specific assignment that asked students to use materials in the library archives in order to answer these questions: "How did the community in the Chippewa Valley in western Wisconsin, where UW-Stout is located, experience and respond to 9/11, and how do the local experiences connect with course materials, fiction, films, and memoirs of the traumatic event?" I found that by having an introductory session in the library archives and drawing on the dedicated support from the archives staff, students discovered some startling glimpses of the past. For example, student research in the archives of the local newspapers and the student weekly newspaper, *Stoutonia,* revealed that there were students at UW-Stout who had relatives in the Pentagon and who, for several hours, did not know their whereabouts. Through archival research sources, students found out the existence of a still surviving 9/11 memorial on campus near the Applied Arts building. Students also found it very interesting to research the recurrent scares of domestic terrorism and the examples of the pipe bomber and the arsonist, who emerged in the small, mostly white, university community of Menomonie, WI, shortly after the 9/11 attacks. The perpetrators of these crimes were discovered. Luke Helder, a UW-Stout student, was found, in 2002, to be the infamous Midwest pipe bomber who was attempting to make a smiley face across the map of the U.S. by planting pipe bombs in mailboxes across the country. The best papers the students wrote not only found interesting primary source materials about the impact of 9/11 in the local community but extended class discussions about racial profiling to ask if there indeed was a single profile of a terrorist and if it was justifiable to profile Muslims and Sikhs, when so-called normal, Midwestern students and residents were capable of criminal behavior resembling that of terrorists.

The archival research allowed students to bring this tragedy closer to home by enabling them to feel a personal sense of ownership and discovery in relation to the material. For a final project, I designed an assignment that asked students to think about ways in which they could promote a peaceful and diverse world and inculcate this message among youth. What could be done to promote narratives of peaceful co-existence instead of ideologies of intolerance and racial exclusivism? Students were invited to supplement the research paper with creative projects that could include art work, videos, comics, songs, and other materials that spread a message of peace and tolerance and rejected hatred in a language and style that could make an impact on youth. I received some inspiring final projects, including a series of digital paintings of torture by a graphic design major, followed by a research paper that traced the visual representations of torture from the past to Abu Ghraib, advocating against these methods of interrogation. Another project included a fictional diary of a Guantanamo Bay inmate, advocating against indefinite detention without trial. The end of the semester evaluations clearly demonstrated that students had been exposed to challenging ideas that obliged them to reconfigure earlier received knowledge of 9/11. The process of encountering some of the course material certainly proved to be difficult and emotionally challenging to some students. Others found that their old certitude about patriotism had been shaken, and they were still trying to reconcile love for their country with the knowledge of its fallibilities. I hoped that leaving my students with some theoretical concepts of cosmopolitanism would help them in the work of resolving their dilemmas.

The process of creating and teaching "After 9/11" has helped me understand the complexities of racial identity in the contemporary U.S. and become more attentive to them as I teach racial and ethnic diversity content in honors courses. This process has also helped me rethink my own research agenda as well as investigate ways in which students and faculty can collaborate in undergraduate humanities research projects. In the next iteration of the course, I will work on developing some of these elements. For example, the series of digital paintings created by a student in this course has sparked my own interest in the visual archive of post-9/11 violence and torture. I am also thinking of offering this course over the winterm, with a Study Away component in New York City.

The questions that originally inspired me to create a course on 9/11 literature have become even more urgent in the time since I first taught the course. Even though 2016 marked the fifteen-year anniversary of 9/11, radical Islam has morphed from its 9/11 incarnation of Al Qaeda to the even more violent and dangerous shape of the armed forces of the Islamic State. Acts of terror continue to be enacted by ISIS sympathizers in European countries and the U.S. Meanwhile, prejudice and violence against Muslim Americans continue to escalate. There is a greater need than ever to study the interconnected nature of these events and to strive even harder for a cosmopolitan sensibility that promotes peace and understanding as a basic expectation of honors education.

ACKNOWLEDGMENTS

I would like to thank the faculty and administrators at the University of Wisconsin-Stout for the help I received while developing my "After 9/11" course. These include my friend and mentor, the late Dr. Michael Levy; Glendali Roderiguez, Associate Vice Chancellor; Dr. Maria Alm, Dean of the College of Arts, Communications, Humanities and Social Sciences; Dr. Robert Horan, Founding Director of the Honors College; Dr. Chris Ferguson, Director of Honors; Dr. Kevin Drzakowski, Chair of English and Philosophy; Dr. Jerry

Kapus; Dr. Terri Karis; and the many honors students at Stout who made the work so rewarding. Finally, I am deeply grateful to the UW-Stout library, particularly, Josh Steans and Heather Stecklein.

NOTES

[1]Inclusive excellence, which focuses on increasing diversity in the composition of the university and producing the best learning environments so that students from diverse backgrounds can succeed, is a planning priority in many institutions. As noted, inclusive excellence has been a major initiative of the Association of American Colleges and Universities (AAC&U). On its website on diversity, titled "Making Excellence Inclusive," appears the following:

> AAC&U calls for higher education to address diversity, inclusion, and equity as critical to the wellbeing of democratic culture. Making excellence inclusive is thus an active process through which colleges and universities achieve excellence in learning, teaching, student development, institutional functioning, and engagement in local and global communities (AAC&U website, "Making Excellence Inclusive").

The following passage is excerpted from the University of Wisconsin-Stout website, "Inclusive Excellence":

> *Inclusive Excellence* is a UW System planning process aimed at creating a set of initiatives to achieve an integrated set of goals surrounding diversity. In particular, Inclusive Excellence
>
> - Employs a dual focus in diversity efforts, concentrating on both increasing compositional diversity and creating learning environments in which students of all backgrounds can thrive;
> - Requires a more comprehensive, widespread level of engagement and commitment ensuring that every student fulfills their educational potential;

- Places the mission of diversity at the center of institutional life so that it becomes a core organizing principle around which institutional decisions are made;

- Calls for a close attentiveness to the student experience itself including the impact of race and ethnicity, and the influence of physical ability, sexual orientation, gender expression, socioeconomic background, and first-generation status on their learning experiences; and

- Demands that the ideals of diversity and excellence be pursued as the interconnected and interdependent goals they are.

UW-Stout is a community committed to this process, whose aim is to cultivate an environment fostering and promoting diversity, equity, inclusion, and accountability at every level of university life. We value the diversity intrinsically and for the benefits it brings to our community. We are engaged in creating learning environments in which students, faculty, and staff of all backgrounds can thrive and fulfill their academic, personal, and professional potential in an increasingly diverse global environment.

The UW System and UW-Stout are inclusive of diversity in the areas including, but not limited to, the following:

- Age
- Ancestry
- Arrest or conviction record
- Color
- Gender identity or expression
- Genetic testing
- Marital status

- Sexual orientation

- Veterans' status or military membership

- Mental disability

- National origin

- Physical disability

- Political affiliation

- Pregnancy

- Race

- Religion or creed

- Use or nonuse of lawful products off the employer's premises during nonworking hours (UW-Stout website "Inclusive Excellence")

[2]The study of four designated U.S. minorities is mandated by the UW-System. It originated in the UW System Design for Diversity Plan that existed from 1988–98. In 1998, when Plan 2008 succeeded the Design for Diversity initiative, the three-credit graduation requirement to study the four federally designated minorities remained unchanged. Also, different universities within the UW-System have interpreted and applied the requirements differently. Based on a look at the online undergraduate catalogs of UW schools, many differences appear. For example, UW-Whitewater and UW-Stevens Point both require a three-credit U.S. diversity course. Stevens Point does not specify the study of four U.S. minorities in its undergraduate requirements while Whitewater does. UW-Stout, my own school, requires six credits of race and ethnicity content.

[3]*Swadeshi* in Indian languages like Bengali and Hindi translates to the rule of a country by its own people. It was a basic principle structuring the Indian independence movement, which led to the successful end of British colonial rule and political independence for India in 1947.

[4]Although India declares itself to be secular, unlike its neighbor Pakistan, Hindu nationalism has been a strong current in the independence movement. Gandhi was assassinated by a Hindu religious extremist. In recent times, the political party representing this brand of exclusive religious nationalism has gained ascendancy, with the right wing Hindu party currently holding the political majority and power at the national level.

[5]Amartya Sen notes that Gandhi and Tagore, who were both committed to Indian independence, clashed on many aspects of the independence movement. Although Tagore was deeply critical of British rule and publicly protested against many colonial policies, he did not ever reject western civilization in rejecting western colonialism. Tagore, according to Sen, "rebelled against the strongly nationalist form that the independence movement took" and was critical of Gandhi's reliance on Hinduism in mobilizing the mass movement against colonialism (*Argumentative Indian* 107). Tagore was committed to post-Enlightenment scientific rationality and did not agree with Gandhi's valorization of Hindu spirituality over this discourse.

[6]The Mughal dynasty, originally invaders from central Asia, ruled in India from the sixteenth to the eighteenth centuries. This dynasty was able to unify most of India, set up an effective administration, promote harmony among Hindus and Muslims, and promote arts and learning.

[7]Following the Japanese attack on Pearl Harbor, President Franklin D. Roosevelt signed Executive Order 9066 in February 1942, which authorized the forceful removal or internment of people of Japanese origin. More than 100,000 U.S. citizens of Japanese origin were sent to internment camps. In 1980, under mounting pressure, President Jimmy Carter opened an investigation on the justification of these governmental actions. The Commission did not find evidence of Japanese disloyalty. This finding led to the passage of the 1988 Civil Liberties Act, signed by President Reagan, which offered reparations to survivors of these camps.

[8]The Chinese Exclusion Act of 1882 was the first major law in U.S. history that restricted immigration; it was enacted as a result of growing fears on the west coast that the unemployment and declining wages of the native population were due to the arrival of Chinese workers, who were viewed as racially inferior.

[9]In the 1920s, U.S. law allowed naturalization only for "free white people." In 1923, Bhagat Singh Thind, a South Asian immigrant, petitioned for U.S. citizenship on the grounds that Asian Indians belonged to the Caucasian race. His case was denied by the Supreme Court, which ruled that even though Thind was Caucasian, as defined by anthropologists, he was not white. This decision marked a shift in a case three months previous to Thind's, when a Japanese native, Takao Ozawa, tried to petition for U.S. citizenship on the basis of the fact that his skin was white. His petition was denied on the grounds that he was not of the Caucasian race. In Thind's case, even though his Caucasian race was not disputed, he was not granted citizenship because he was not white according to the common understanding of "whiteness." These early examples reveal the shifting and constructed nature of whiteness and American belonging, which is exacerbated in post-9/11 America, with a redrawing of borders for Americans and enemy races. For further elaboration of the shifting nature of racial construction, see Jennifer Lee and Frank D. Bean's "Re-inventing the Color Line."

[10]On August 9, 2014, Michael Brown, an African American youth, was shot by police officer Darren Wilson, in Ferguson, Missouri, which led to widespread protests that turned violent. The officer was not indicted for the death of Michael Brown.

[11]Sikhs were attacked immediately after 9/11. Their religiously mandated attire of turbans made them visually similar to Al Qaeda and other Islamic extremists responsible for the 9/11 attacks. In spite of a vigorous campaign by the Sikh community to educate American people about their religion, on August 5, 2012, a Sikh temple known as "gurdwara" in Oak Creek, WI, was attacked by a white supremacist gunman who claimed the lives of six Sikh followers.

[12]See Loretta Napoleoni's *Terrorism and the Economy* for an analysis of 9/11 and the retaliatory wars that led to the credit crunch and eventually to the Great Recession of 2008. Napoleoni is critical of Alan Greenspan's policy of lowering interest rates, which began in the 1990s and started the sub-prime mortgage crisis. The staggering cost of the wars in Afghanistan and Iraq broke the artificially created real estate bubble, plunging the world into global recession. Napoleoni argues further that the cost of the wars "sucks money and lives from the state and taxpayer, without contributing anything to peace and to the economy" (71).

[13]Amy Lutz's "Who Joins the Military?" analyzed many demographic factors; she concludes: "In sum, the economic elite are very unlikely to serve in the military" (178). In 2000, African Americans were over-represented in the military as compared to military age African Americans who were not in the military.

[14]Umayad is the first great dynasty to rule over the Muslim Empire from 651 to 750 AD, following the first civil war over succession. The Umayad dynasty was followed by the Abbasid dynasty, which ruled from 750–1258 AD, when they were overthrown by the Mongols.

[15]The mosque movement, also known as the piety movement, refers to the movement in recent decades in many Islamic countries, like Egypt, in which women are becoming actively engaged in studying Islam. This study often takes place within mosques, which have traditionally been male spaces. Unlike within Islamic fundamentalism, women engaged in the mosque movement are interested in exploring how to lead more spiritually meaningful lives without rejecting education, employment, and other institutions of modernity.

REFERENCES

Ahmed, Leila. *Women and Gender in Islam: Historical Roots of a Modern Debate*. New Haven: Yale University Press, 1992. Print.

Akhtar, Ayad. *Disgraced*. New York: Back Bay Books, 2013. Print.

Appiah, Kwame Anthony. *Cosmopolitanism: Ethics in a World of Strangers*. New York: Norton, 2007. Print.

Asad, Talal. *Genealogies of Religion: Discipline and Reasons of Power in Christianity and Islam*. Baltimore: Johns Hopkins University Press, 1993. Print.

Bayoumi, Moustafa. *How Does it Feel to be a Problem?: Being Young and Arab in America*. New York: Penguin, 2008. Print.

Butler, Judith. *Antigone's Claim: Kinship Between Life and Death*. New York: Columbia University Press, 2000.Print.

—. "Bodies in Alliance and the Politics of the Street." *European Institute for Progressive Cultural Politics Journal*. Sept. 2009. Web. 02 Oct. 2014.

—. *Bodies That Matter: On the Discursive Limits of Sex*. New York: Routledge, 1993. Print.

—. *Gender Trouble: Feminism and the Subversion of Identity*. New York: Routledge, 1990, Print

—. *Precarious Life: The Powers of Mourning and Violence*. New York: Verso, 2004. Print.

—. "Universality in Culture." *For Love of Country?* Martha C. Nussbaum. Ed. Joshua Cohen 45–52. Print.

Chernilo. Daniel. "Cosmopolitanism and the Question of Universalism." *Routledge Handbook of Cosmopolitanism Studies*. Ed. Gerard Delanty. New York: Routledge, 2012. 47–59.

Divided We Fall. Dir. Sharat Raju. Perf. Valarie Kaur. New Moon Productions, 2008. DVD.

Giroux, Henry A. "The War on Terrorism Targets Democracy Itself." *Truthout*. Web. 06 Aug. 2015.

Grewal, Inderpal. *Home and Harem: Nation, Gender, Empire and the Cultures of Travel*. Durham: Duke University Press, 1996. Print.

Huntington, Samuel. *The Clash of Civilizations and the Remaking of World Order*. New York: Simon and Schuster, 1998. Print.

"Inclusive Excellence" *University of Wisconsin-Stout*. Web. 12 Dec. 2015.

Kant, Immanuel. *Perpetual Peace*. Ed. Lewis White Beck. New York: Liberal Arts Press, 1957. Print.

Kristoff, Nicholas D., and Sheryl Wudunn. *Half the Sky: Turning Oppression into Opportunity for Women Worldwide*. New York: Vintage, 2010. Print.

Kumar, Amitava. *A Foreigner Carrying in the Crook of His Arm a Tiny Bomb*. Durham: Duke University Press, 2010. Print.

Lee, Jennifer, and Frank D. Bean. "Re-inventing the Color Line: Immigration and America's New Racial/Ethnic Divide." *Social Forces* 86.2 (2007): 561–86. *JStor*. Web. 12 June 2015.

Lutz, Amy. "Who Joins the Military?: A Look at Race, Class and Immigration Status." *Journal of Political and Military Sociology* 36.2 (2008): 167–88 Web. 05 Aug. 2015.

Mahmood, Saba. "The Light in Her Eyes: Interview: Saba Mahmood." 03 Aug. 2017. Web.

—. *Politics of Piety: The Islamic Revival and the Feminist Subject*. Princeton: Princeton University Press, 2005. Print.

"Making Excellence Inclusive." *Association of American Colleges and Universities*. Web. 15 Dec. 2015.

Majid, Anouar. *A Call for Heresy: Why Dissent is Vital to Islam and America*. Minneapolis: University of Minnesota Press, 2007. Print.

Mazrui. Ali A. "Is this the Dawn of a Post-racial Age? From Othello to Obama." Andrew Young Lecture Series. The Africa Society of the National Summit of Africa. 29 Jan. 2009. Web. 05 Jan. 2015.

Mernissi, Fatima. *Islam and Democracy: Fear of the Modern World*. New York: Basic Books, 1992. Print.

My Name is Khan. Dir. Karan Johar. Perf. Shah Rukh Khan and Kajol. Twentieth Century Fox, 2010. DVD.

Napoleoni, Loretta. *Terrorism and the Economy: How the War on Terror is Bankrupting the World*. New York: Seven Stories Press, 2010. Print.

Nussbaum, Martha C. *For Love of Country?* Martha C. Nussbaum. Ed. Joshua Cohen. Boston: Beacon, 2002. Print.

—. "Patriotism and Cosmopolitanism." *For Love of Country?* Martha C. Nussbaum. Ed. Joshua Cohen. Boston: Beacon, 2002. 3–17. Print.

Prashad, Vijay. *Uncle Swami: South Asians in America Today*. New York: New Press, 2012, Print.

"Racial and Ethnic Studies Requirement." *University of Wisconsin-Stout*. Web. Dec. 2012. 05 Jan. 2015.

Rana, Junaid. *Terrifying Muslims: Race and Labor in the South Asian Diaspora*. Durham: Duke University Press, 2011. Print.

Roy, Olivier. *Globalized Islam: The Search for a New Ummah*. New York: Columbia University Press, 2004. Print.

Sen, Amartya. *The Argumentative Indian: Writings on Indian History, Culture and Identity*. New York: Farrar, Strauss and Giroux, 2005. Print.

—. "Civilizational Imprisonments: How to Misunderstand Everybody in the World." *The New Republic* 10 June 2002. 28–33. Print.

—. "Humanity and Citizenship." *For Love of Country?* Martha C. Nussbaum. Ed. Joshua Cohen. Boston: Beacon, 2002. 111–18. Print.

Spivak, Gayatri Chakravorty. "Can the Subaltern Speak?" *Colonial Discourse and Postcolonial Theory: A Reader*. Ed. Patrick Williams and Laura Chrisman. New York: Columbia University Press, 1994. 66–111. Print.

175

Tagore, Rabindranath. *The Home and the World.* Trans. Surendranath Tagore. New York: Penguin, 2005. Print.

Waldman, Amy. *The Submission.* New York: Farrar, Strauss and Giroux, 2011. Print.

Walzer, Michael. "Spheres of Affection." *For Love of Country?* Martha C. Nussbaum. Ed. Joshua Cohen 125–27. Print.

Family Issues of Diversity and Education for Asian American Immigrants: How Universities, Colleges, and Honors Programs Can Understand and Support the 1.5 and Second Generation

Alan Y. Oda, Ye Eun (Grace) Oh,
and Hyun Seo (Hannah) Lee
Azusa Pacific University

Asian Americans were once labeled the so-called "Model Minority," which implied this subpopulation—in contrast to other ethnic minority Americans—experienced few dilemmas or difficulties adapting to the mainstream culture, instead demonstrating exceptional performance in school without presenting the distresses experienced by other immigrant Americans. Suzuki (2002) discussed the inaccuracy and the hazards associated with this stereotype, yet found the "Model Minority" label continues to be pervasive in spite of the shortcomings of this label (pp. 22–23). As a corollary to our research on Asian Americans, with specific attentiveness to multigenerational ethnic Koreans, we recognized the importance of education and academic achievement for this American minority group but also documented this achievement was hardly without challenges or complications for many. Moreover, we conjecture that honors colleges and programs need to be attentive to a student's family dynamics to provide better and more effective support for students who identify with collectivist cultures such as Korean and Asian American.

With the exception of those who identify as Native Americans or as African Americans whose ancestors did not choose to come to the Americas of their own free will, the United States is composed of a heterogeneity of different immigrant populations. Today's American colleges and universities reflect this heterogeneity, each of the subgroups having their own histories, particularly as they pertain to the heritage of current and past generations.

Traditional models of American immigrants use the term "first generation" to describe the original migrants, with their children and grandchildren referred to as "second generation," "third generation," and beyond. Colleges use this term in a similar manner, with programming offered to assist "first-generation" college students in particular.

Ethnic Koreans and some other Asian immigrants to the United States add a different categorization. Between the traditional first- and second-generation distinctions, immigrants who entered the United States before the age of twelve are referred to as *il chom-o-se*, the "one-point-five (1.5) generation," as noted in Hurh (1990, p. 21), whose article, "The 1.5 Generation: A Paragon of Korean-American Pluralism," employs that designation in its title (see Hurh pp. 21–31). A similar definition is suggested by Rumbault and Ima (1988) about Southeast Asian refugees (pp. 1–2).

As noted above, the concept of the 1.5 generation is not necessarily unique to Koreans (see Zhou, Lee, Vallejo, Tafoya-Estrada, and Xiong, 2008, p. 44), but it is most frequently associated with this subpopulation. This in-between generation, situated between the traditionally defined first generation and their second-generation children, offers insights into the adaptation process of an American ethnic group, which can be generalized to other minorities. Of particular interest to this study is what enhances and attenuates academic achievement and success because of generational antecedents and practices.

GENERATIONAL DESIGNATIONS OF JAPANESE AND KOREAN IMMIGRANTS TO THE U.S.

Previous studies of Asian American subgroups consider intergenerational differences based on distinct demographic categories. For example, as Kitano (1981) notes, Japanese Americans have been classified by the terms "*Issei, Nisei, Sansei*, and *Yonsei*" indicating a multigenerational presence in the United States defined by distinct, separate generations (p. 131).

Although there were earlier immigrants from Korea, it was not until a third wave of immigration, beginning in the 1960's, that the exponential growth of Koreans in America has taken place. As Yu, Choe, and Han (2002) explain, the first wave of immigrants during the early twentieth century were workers for the Hawaiian sugar plantations and comprised approximately 7,000 predominantly male immigrants. The Gentlemen's Agreement of 1907 between the United States and Japan (and thus Korea, which was then a Japanese territory) as well as the 1924 Immigration Act imposed stringent limits on Korean immigration until the 1950s. During the 1950s a second wave of Koreans arrived in America as a consequence of the Korean War (pp. 73–74).

According to Kim (2014), a milestone for Asian immigration occurred with the passing of the 1965 Immigration Act, which ended the quotas based on national origin (p. 157). Since then, the third wave of Korean immigration to the United States has been rapidly growing. The U.S. Census reported there were 354,529 ethnic Koreans in America in 1980. By 2010, the Census reported that 1,463,474 people self-identified as Koreans, an increase of 33 percent from the previous Census in 2000, as noted by Hurh and Kim (1990) (p. 19; see also U.S. Census Bureau, 2015). Economic opportunities, better education for children, and reuniting family members were among the reasons for Korean immigration.

INTERGENERATIONAL DIFFERENCES AND PSYCHOSOCIAL CHARACTERISTICS OF ASIAN IMMIGRANTS

The reasons for immigration are not particularly unique, but the significant number of the 1.5 generation who are immigrating is a notable distinction, with this cohort continuing to enter the United States to the present day. What is not well documented, however, are the psychosocial characteristics that distinguish this group and the implications these psychosocial characteristics have for education.

One facet to highlight includes the intergenerational differences between the 1.5 generation, and the first and second generation, and the ramifications of those differences. Identity and social conflicts between different generations have long been discussed, particularly between first- and second-generation ethnic Asian populations, as Masuda, Matsumoto, and Meredith (1970) note (pp. 199–207). Sue and Sue (1971) offered the first theory of Asian American personality types considering intergenerational themes. Specifically, the authors described different personality types negotiating acculturation issues, stating there is a transitional sequence for Chinese (and, by extension, other Asian subgroups) progressing through generations, from tenaciously upholding traditional beliefs and values to full acceptance of a bicultural identity (pp. 36–49). It should be noted that Tong (1971) strongly dissented from this view of acculturation (pp. 1–31), which assumes adaptation to a mainstream culture does not preclude one's heritage culture.

STRESS AND THE ACCULTURATION PROCESS: A FRAUGHT TOPIC

There is conflicting information about stress and the acculturation process. Mui and Kang (2006) found an interrelationship between acculturative stress and depression among Korean and other Asian American groups (pp. 249–54). Similar findings were reported by Bernstein, Park, Shin, Cho, and Park (2011) in their study of Korean immigrants in New York City; they reported that depression was almost twice the rate for this immigrant population as compared to the general U.S. population, taking into account both acculturative stress and discrimination (pp. 31–33).

It is worth noting there is criticism of acculturation theory, which may be defined as the adaptation of an immigrant group to the dominant mainstream population. Uba (2002) is one of several scholars who question the assumed goals of acculturation for American minority populations. She argued that acculturation theory reflects the bias of Westernized psychology, minimizing the value of ethnic minorities. She questioned why minorities can only be considered successful American immigrants if the group continues to replace long-held cultural traditions for more mainstream behaviors and practices (pp. 103–05). Arguably, Uba is defining customary acculturation theory based on a deficit model (also referred to as a cultural deficit model). Solorzano and Yosso (2001) considered the model in terms of education, stating that specific minority cultural values are dysfunctional compared to mainstream values, resulting in educational and social deficits in achievement (p. 6).

Generational differences in attitudes toward education provide several intriguing questions. Asian cultures place great value on education, particularly parental expectations of their children's achievements. Kao (1995) compared Asian versus White parents in describing the role of parents: "systemic group differences in parental behavior exist between Asians and whites [sic]. It may be, on average, Asian parents not only have higher expectations of their children *but are also unwilling to negotiate these terms*" (p. 125, emphasis added).

The acculturation process may attenuate, but does not mitigate, parental involvement in children's education. Portes and MacLeod (1999) noted students of Chinese and Korean parents succeeded in school regardless of whether they attended high-status or poorer schools, particularly compared to students of other ethnic subgroups (p. 391).

CULTURE AND CONTEXTUALISM

In explaining the prioritizing of education within Asian culture, Hirschman and Wong (1986) stated the roots of this value

181

originate from the context of collectivism and its ethical principles, especially that the group (such as one's family) status is as important if not more important than individual achievement (pp. 3–4). Chen and Uttal (1988) noted that another important antecedent is the Confucian view of education, where education is a key component of self-improvement, regardless of class (p. 353). Although this account is common, Rumbaut and Ima (1988) stated other Asian subgroups influenced by Confucianism—specifically Southeast Asians—are less successful in school compared to their Korean, Chinese, and Japanese counterparts (p. 119). Portes and MacLeod (1999) also noted many of Chinese and Korean ethnicity are Christians (p. 391), yet as Park and Cho (1995) point out, the values of Confucianism pervade Korean culture despite the heterogeneity of religious beliefs (p. 118–20).

As to the prevalence of parental influence, filial piety is a frequent theme in the writings about Asian American families. Hwang (1999) emphasized the Confucian roots of this theme: "the Confucian idea of filial piety is constructed on the simple fact that one's body exists solely because of one's parents" (p. 169). A more corporeal view of filial piety offered by Mehta and Ko (2004), includes the belief that one must pay attention to parents' wishes and obey their preferences, while pleasing one's parents and bringing them honor (p. S77). The practical implication of filial piety is that a student is not attending school only for her or his individual achievement or advancement, but that the success of the student reflects favorably on parents and the family. Another application of filial piety is parents are expected to have an active role in the decisions about their child's education.

Szapocznik and Kurtines (1993) illustrate the interrelationship between the individual, family, and culture by considering the concept of contextualism. Figure 1 illustrates the traditional view of the influence of culture and family in the development of the individual. The traditional view is that family and culture are just two of perhaps numerous variables important in perceiving the individual. Szapocznik and Kurtines illustrate a different perspective, where the individual is embedded in her or his family, while the family itself is embedded in a culture. This perspective implies that an individual cannot be fully understood without acknowledging the importance of family and that family cannot be fully understood without acknowledging their culture. Further, an individual's understanding of culture is mediated by family (1993, p. 402).

FIGURE 1. OLD AND NEW CONTEXTUALIST PARADIGMS
            (SZAPOCZNIK AND KURTINES, 1993, P. 402)

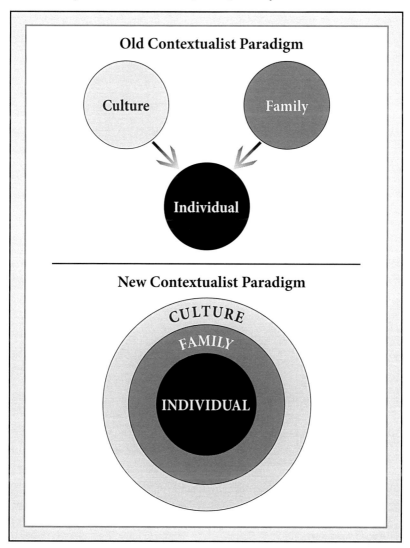

A recent image associated with Korean and Asian Americans is the "Tiger Mom," first described in *Battle Hymn of the Tiger Mother* (2011), a popular book written by author Amy Chua. As Juang, Qin, and Park (2013) note, the book details the parenting practices of a Chinese mother who is highly controlling, authoritarian, and strongly limiting of children's extracurricular activities to drive her children to succeed educationally (p. 2). Although the authors disagree with the general stereotype, there is affirmation about the uniqueness of parental involvement within Chinese, Korean, Japanese, and other Asian American families. Disagreeing with the description of "authoritarian" to describe Chinese and Asian parenting, Chao (1994) reframed such parenting practices as being more accurately described as "training" of children via the authority of the parent (pp. 1111–19). Nonetheless, what remains consistent is the observation that traditional Asian parents are integral to the education of their children. Indeed, Mordkowitz and Ginsburg (1986) note that authoritative Asian parents are involved with and support their children's education efforts by having high expectations, monitoring their children's time for studying, and arranging for tutors (pp. 85–91).

A major contrast should be acknowledged about mainstream American culture. Triandis (1988) stated: "Perhaps the most important dimension of cultural difference in social behaviour, across the diverse cultures of the world, is the relative emphasis on individualism v. collectivism" (p. 60). Arguably most of our colleges assume the importance of developing and nurturing the success of the individual to foster a student who can make independent decisions via self-reflection based on critical thinking and engagement. In contrast, Asian as well as many non-Western cultures emphasize interdependence and collectivism (see Chao and Tseng, 2002, p. 64; see also Singelis, 1994, p. 580). Students of Asian heritage can sustain a personal belief that beyond individual success, their achievement is also important for family repute. Accordingly, decisions about academics may be facilitated in a collective manner rather than considered as independent decisions to be made by the child.

The model offered by Szapocznik and Kurtines (1993) provides a further insight, that family—and by extension, parent-child relationships—are embedded in cultural practices and traditions such as filial piety and parental training of children. The influence of culture, then, cannot be ignored as an important variable in supporting and encouraging students in education. This influence thus presents the question as to whether or not family diversity and ethnic diversity in general are adequately considered in the development and execution of educational programs like honors. An additional and important distinction concerns the aforesaid parental participation with the Korean college students compared to their non-Asian counterparts. Conceivably, the counseling, intervention, and support for Korean and other Asian students would be more complex because of the origin of their family.

To reiterate, aside from the typical concerns of being in college and the additional load of being an honors student, Korean and other Asian students can face significant challenges because of their culturally based family expectations. For example, the collegiate may have selected her or his major because of parental directives. Song and Glick (2004) stated that little difference existed between White and Asian men on choice of college major, but that Asian women were more likely to select more lucrative college majors than their White counterparts (p. 1401). Arguably, parental influence affected the academic choices of these students. If students find their studies as a pre-medical or pre-law student personally unrewarding or overly difficult, they may need to answer to their parents as well as their professors about their academic progress or lack thereof. As a result, students can experience additional stress and strain beyond the usual burdens of succeeding in their studies and the self-imposed angst of succeeding in school. Further, as Liem (1997) notes, although referring to the parent-child relationship in Asian families as "shame-based parenting" is overly simplistic, using shame as well as anger is still a common theme in understanding the parent-child relationship (p. 365–66). In their study of Asian Indian families, Farver, Xu, Bhandha, Narang, and Lieber (2007) identified parental use of shame, guilt, and moral obligation to control their adolescents' behavior (p. 190).

185

Much of the literature about parenting and academics addresses generalized issues of different ethnic groups, generally White, Latino/Hispanic, Black, and Asian. What is less evident is discussion of generational differences and the effects of acculturation. Vartanian, Karen, Buck, and Cadge (2007) asserted that once individual and family factors are controlled—including generational status—parental expectations and family structure are generally weaker for Asian Americans compared to non-Asians while parent immigrant status is stronger (p. 165). Tran and Birman (2010) believe that Asian Americans of any generation generally work hard and have high educational expectations: "So Asian culture may have impacted Asian Americans' work ethics, but their high educational expectations may be a product of American acculturation and/or their desire to overcome perceived oppression" (p. 111). Chung (2001) argued that acculturation processes lessen the differences between Asian Americans of later generations and their non-Asian counterparts (p. 384), but also cited the work of Sue and Zane (1987), who observed that intergenerational issues and conflict are important themes for many ethnic clients, including clients of multiple ethnic generations (p. 37–45).

A plethora of theories exist about the implications of intergenerational differences on the achievement and psychosocial health of Asian American college students. Still, claiming that intergenerational differences have only negligible effects on this subpopulation would be erroneous. Hwang and Ting (2008) observed that ethnic Asian students exhibit higher levels of stress than their White (European) counterparts: "acculturative stress is a more proximal risk factor for psychological maladjustment than level of acculturation, even after accounting for the effects of general perceived stress" (p. 152). In other words, a student who is the child of second- or third- or even subsequent-generation parents can still experience acculturative stress, with ethnic Asian students being particularly vulnerable to this occurrence. This finding suggests that even students whose cohort is some distance from the original immigrant families can have issues because of their ethnicity.

THE 1.5 GENERATION

Our current research is looking at a particular feature of one Asian American group, specifically Korean Americans. We previously described the characteristics of the 1.5 generation, which are observed in other Asian American populations but arguably most applicable to ethnic Koreans. The 1.5 generation offers numerous issues unique to this cohort. For Hurh (1990), individuals classified as part of the 1.5 generation are a hybrid of two different cohorts, an "in-between" position of individuals who do not fit traditional definitions and models (p. 22). Rumbault and Ima (1988) specified 1.5-generation individuals as foreign-born youths immigrating to the United States before the age of twelve (p. 1–2). Park (1999) noted that the Asian American community uses a more inclusive definition for the 1.5 generation, ranging from immigrants who have completed grade school to those individuals who have finished junior high or high school (p. 140). Shih (1999) viewed the 1.5 generation as neither "Korean," "American," nor "Korean American," but all three. Park (1999) argued that this position is ambiguous and antagonistic in relationship with first- and second-generation Koreans (p. 142). Instead of using chronology, Chang and Kim (2010) differentiated 1.5- and second-generation Korean Americans based on language proficiency, with 1.5-generation individuals fully bilingual while second-generation members have limited, if any, aptitude with Korean (p. 44). Similarly, Kim, Brenner, Liang, and Asay (2003) stated 1.5-generation subjects of different Asian ethnicities report English aptitude as being significant in adjusting to American culture (p. 163). Anecdotally, there are Korean Americans who may fit the descriptions for 1.5 generation, but they may instead refer to themselves as second generation, and vice versa.

Limited studies comparing 1.5- and second-generation Koreans reflect some attitudinal and experiential differences. Lee, Juon, Martinez, Hsu, Robinson, Bawa, and Ma (2009) considered mental health issues based on focus groups consisting of members of eight different ethnic Asian groups. Their findings note the pressure to meet parental expectations of academic achievement, concerns with dealing with family obligations, and the challenge of balancing

187

two different cultures. In particular, many of the participants stated being "1.5 or second generation immigrants" was a significant source of stress (p. 147). Nonetheless, there are few, if any, studies of differences in parent-child relations, particularly as they relate to support for and influence on education.

Our studies of Korean Americans found an intertwined relationship between educational achievement and parental expectations that is similar to that of other Asian American sub-populations. In considering ethnic Korean families, we suspect unique generational differences exist between 1.5- versus second-generation ethnic Koreans although the empirical research on this topic of Koreans in America is scarce. Our current research efforts are focused on gathering information from these different cohorts to find similarities and contrasts, with a particular interest in the parent-child relationship and how it affects educational achievement, particularly since the 1.5 generation offers a distinctive acculturation experience compared to the more traditional first-/second-/third-generation pattern.

Often 1.5- and second-generation cohorts are acknowledged in research, yet the groups are not distinguished in the analysis of the data. For example, prioritizing education facilitated by parental influence is a dominant theme with Korean students, as was previously described with Asian students as a generalized belief. A more subtle but also significant theme is the distinction between 1.5- and second-generation Korean Americans in attitudes toward education. In the previous study by Lee et al. (2009), data from the 1.5- and second-generation subjects were aggregated so distinctions could not be ascertained. Similarly, other studies, such as Kibria (1999), also studied 1.5- and second-generation subjects together in the same cohort.

ACADEMIC ENCOURAGEMENT AND SUPPORT IN HIGHER EDUCATION AND HONORS EDUCATION

Substantial information already exists regarding the encouragement and support of Korean American students in higher education.

Successful students are not necessarily students who are adjusting adequately to the college environment. Stated more simply, we may be erroneously assuming that optimal academic performance by Korean American students, as well as other ethnic Asian students, implies optimal adjustment to college life.

As a general observation, much of the literature is applicable and relevant to honors. Students of Asian heritage are a significant subpopulation in honors colleges and programs. Henfield, Woo, Lin, and Raucsh (2014) stated students identified as Asian American/Pacific Islander (AAPI) start off as being overrepresented in gifted programs in K–12 schools. This observation, they note, has been cited in reinforcing the stereotype of AAPIs as the "Model Minority," a high-achieving American subgroup, as noted above, which is otherwise nonprovocative and well-adjusted (p. 137). As a consequence, "society has begun to expect excellence from all Asian American students," yet this "imposes pressure to achieve social expectations and generates negative experiences related to racial bias" (p. 137). Further, the authors stated, "the stereotypical image of gifted students as socially awkward, physically inferior, and effortlessly high achieving is historically proliferated in public discourse," although this is admittedly a stereotype with little empirical support (p. 138). The question is whether or not such pressures continue in post-secondary education.

Henfield et al. (2014) studied four female students of Asian heritage enrolled in a large, predominantly White Midwestern American institution who participated in the university's honors program. Their structured interviews revealed that self-imposed high standards within competitive advanced courses caused emotional distress and emotional dissatisfaction. As for family, Henfield et al. stated: "parents' support and high academic expectations influenced participants' learning attitudes, coping strategies, and career plans, which is consistent with previous findings," with parents having a prominent role in choosing a career, generally more prestigious, and/or lucrative occupations (p. 145). An interesting observation was that these Asian women did utilize academic advisors and university counselors, which contrasts with the findings from the well-known Terman longitudinal study of giftedness, which stated advanced students do not need help from others (cited in Henfield et al. p. 145).

Admittedly, Henfield et al. provided information from a very small sample, yet the findings support many of the aforementioned observations and theories about the Asian family and their involvement in their children's education. Their study provides specific examples applicable to both the college experience of Asian students and the context of honors education.

Discussions about honors generally center on curriculum, programming, and recruitment. Perhaps less examined are the personal challenges experienced by honors students. Stress associated with perfectionism and social disconnections associated with high achievement were documented in a short-term study of honors students by Rice, Leever, Christopher, and Porter (2006). The study suggested implications for counseling and intervention for these students; however, the authors acknowledged their sample was primarily White (approximately 80 percent) (p. 532).

The research of Henfield et al. (2014) suggests that the perceived high achievement of ethnic students should be considered within the context of psychosocial health. Stereotypes about the "Model Minority," such as disproportionate parental involvement and expectations, among other factors, are not helpful in the adjustment of college students. For honors colleges and programs, the question is whether the academic challenges inherent in honors education exacerbate the already demanding expectations of simply being an ethnic Asian student in college.

In 2017, the National Collegiate Honors Council adopted the theme "Just Honors" for the annual conference. Part of the description of the theme stated: "it is a challenge that many honors programs and colleges, even at diverse institutions, are not very diverse" (Fifty-Second NCHC). Although Asian students may be more greatly represented in honors than some of their ethnic American colleagues, the need still exists for honors programs and colleges to recruit and support more Asian students as well as other students from different cultures and with different heritages.

Therein, a major challenge is apparent. Increasing diversity in education also requires acknowledgement of an increasing need to offer a greater variety of resources and support. The case has been made that Asian American students of different generations constitute a qualitatively different cohort than the majority European (White) student body.

To reiterate, Szcapocznik and Kurtines (1993) argued that family and culture are not merely two separate variables among many in defining the psychology of the individual: individuals are embedded within their family and culture. In other words, understanding an individual's family and culture is imperative to fully understanding that individual. The model also suggests that an individual's understanding of her or his culture is mediated and facilitated by family (p. 401–02). By extension, to fully appreciate the challenges of Asian and other ethnic minority students, honors colleges and programs need to understand family and cultural dynamics. This paradigm does not mean parents should be contacted before a student makes a decision because that act would violate student confidentiality, but awareness of family on the part of professional mentors can be an indispensable resource for a student.

CONCLUSION

There are clear diversity issues in providing appropriate resources for honors students. The diversity of a campus can be overwhelming, yet this diversity cannot be ignored and dismissed as not being vital. Family and culture are antecedents to student success for all students. As we have reported here, this situation is particularly true for Asian students and the various immigrant generations with which they identify. The challenge for honors colleges and programs and their various administrative, faculty, and staff leaders is to acknowledge the diversity of their campus and address such diversity. While knowing the idiosyncratic characteristics of each minority group on the campus may be challenging, making the effort is important. But what is even more crucial, especially as first steps, is accepting and acknowledging their presence and the particularity of their diversity.

Instead of viewing diversity from a deficit perspective, in which each group seems to be making demands on limited resources, honors programs and colleges should take advantage of the situation by recognizing and acknowledging that these groups offer their own unique contributions to campus diversity. Cultural contextualization, where the unique heritage of a student is acknowledged, accepted, and addressed, provides the foundation for a better education for all students, not just for one individual. A quotation describing the 2017 NCHC Conference expresses this succinctly: "Honors is also the place where high-ability, highly engaged students can get the customized education that best serves them, regardless of socio-economic status or parental education levels" (Fifty-Second NCHC). Particularly because of the primacy of education for so many Asian students and their families, honors colleges and programs can help students not only endure but thrive in the challenging environment of America's colleges and universities.

NOTES

[1]The survey used by the authors, the National Education Longitudinal Study of 1988, was recently updated in 2012 in their longitudinal study of 2002 high school sophomores ten years later (National Center for Education Statistics, 2012). There was no breakdown of major based on ethnicity in the report, although it noted that over 50 percent of students who identified as Asian attained a Bachelor's degree or higher, while the percentage for White students was 39.8 percent, 19.8 percent for Black students, and 18.7 percent for Hispanic or Latino (p. 8).

REFERENCES

Abe-Kim, J., Okazaki, S., & Goto, S. G. (2001). Unidimensional versus multidimensional approaches to the assessment of acculturation for Asian American populations. *Cultural Diversity and Ethnic Minority Psychology, 7*(3), 232–46.

Bernstein, K. S., Park, S., Shin, J., Cho, S., & Park, Y. (2011). Acculturation, discrimination, and depressive symptoms among Korean immigrants in New York City. *Community Mental Health Journal, 41*(1), 24–34.

Chang, E., & Kim, B. (2010). Korean Americans. In E. Wen-Chu & G. J. Yoo (Eds.), *Encyclopedia of Asian American issues today.* Santa Barbara, California: Greenwood Press. 41–46.

Chao, R. K. (1994). Beyond parental control and authoritarian parenting style: Understanding Chinese parenting through the cultural notion of training. *Child Development, 65*(4), 1111–19.

Chao, R. & Tseng, V. (2002). Parenting of Asians. In M. H. Bornstein (Ed.), *Handbook of parenting, volume 4: Social conditions and applied parenting,* (2nd ed.) pp. 59–93. Mahwah, New Jersey: Lawrence Erlbaum Associates.

Chen, C., & Uttal, D. H. (1988). Cultural values, parents' beliefs, and children's achievement in the United States and China. *Human Development, 31,* 351–58.

Chua, A. (2011). *Battle hymn of the Tiger Mother.* New York, New York: Penguin Press.

Chung, R. H. G. (2001). Gender, ethnicity, and acculturation in intergenerational conflict of Asian American college students. *Cultural Diversity and Ethnic Minority Psychology, 7*(4), 376–86.

Farver, J. M., Xu, Y., Bhandha, B. R., Narang, S., & Lieber, E. (2007). Ethnic identity, acculturation, parenting beliefs, and adolescent adjustment: A comparison of Asian Indian and European American Families. *Merrill-Palmer Quarterly, 53*(2), 184–215.

Fifty-Second NCHC Annual Conference, National Collegiate Honors Council. (2017, March 27). Retrieved from <https://www.nchchonors.org/events/2017-conference/about>

Gans, H. J. (1997). Toward a reconciliation of "assimilation" and "pluralism": The interplay of acculturation and ethnic retention. *International Migration Review, 31*(4), 875–92.

Gibson, M. A. & Ogbu, G. (Eds.), (1991). Minority status and schooling: A comparative study of immigrant and involuntary minorities. New York, New York: Garland.

Gordon, M. M. (1964). *Assimilation in American life: The role of race, religion, and national origins.* Ithaca, New York: Cornell University Press.

Henfield, M. S., Woo, H., Lin, Y., & Rausch, M. A. (2014). Too smart to fail: Perceptions of Asian American students' experiences in a collegiate Honors program. *Gifted Child Quarterly, 58*(2), 137–48.

Hirschman, C., & Wong, M. G. (1986). The extraordinary educational attainment of Asian Americans: A search for historical evidence and explanations. *Social Forces, 65,* 1–27.

Hurh, W. M. (1990). The 1.5 generation: A paragon of Korean-American pluralism. *Korean Culture, 11*(1), 21–31.

Hurh, W. M., & Kim, K. C. (1990). Religious participation of Korean immigrants in the United States. *Journal for the Scientific Study of Religion, 29*(1), 19–34.

Hwang, K. K. (1999). Filial piety and loyalty: Two types of social identification in Confucianism. *Asian Journal of Social Psychology, 2*(1), 163–83.

Hwang, W., & Ting, J. Y. (2008). Disaggregating the effects of acculturation and acculturative stress on the mental health of Asian Americans. *Cultural Diversity and Ethnic Minority Psychology, 14*(2), 147–54.

Juang, L. P., Qin, D. B., & Park, I. J. K. (2013). Deconstructing the myth of the "Tiger Mother": An introduction to the special issue on Tiger Parenting, Asian-heritage families, and child/adolescent well-being. *Asian American Journal of Psychology, 4*(1), 1–6.

Kao, G. (1995). Asian Americans as model minorities? A look at their academic performance. *American Journal of Education, 103*(2), 121–59.

Kibria, N. (1999) College and notions of "Asian American": Second-generation Chinese and Korean Americans negotiate race and identity. *Amerasia Journal, 25*(1), 29–51.

Kim, B. S. K., Brenner, B. R., Liang, C. T. H., & Asay, P. A. (2003). A qualitative study of adaptation experiences of 1.5-generation Asian Americans. *Cultural Diversity and Ethnic Minority Psychology, 9*(2), 156–70.

Kim, I. (2014). *New urban immigrants: The Korean community in New York*. Princeton: Princeton University Press.

Kitano, H. H. L. (1981). Asian-Americans: The Chinese, Japanese, Koreans, Pilipinos, and Southeast Asians. *The Annals of the American Academy of Political and Social Science, 454*, 125–38. Retrieved from <http://www.jstor.org.patris.apu.edu/stable/1044250>

Lee, M. K., & Landreth, G. L. (2003). Filial therapy with immigrant Korean parents in the United States. *International Journal of Play Therapy, 12*(2), 67.

Lee, S., Juon, H. S., Martinez, G., Hsu, C. E., Robinson, E. S., Bawa, J., & Ma, G. X. (2009). Model minority at risk: Expressed needs of mental health by Asian American young adults. *Journal of Community Health, 34*(2), 144–52.

Liem, R. (1997). Shame and guilt among first- and second-generation Asian Americans and European Americans. *Journal of Cross Cultural Psychology, 28*(4), 365–92.

Marin, G., & Gamba, R. J. (1996). A new measurement of acculturation for Hispanics: The bidimensional acculturation scale for Hispanics (BAS). *Hispanic Journal of Behavioral Sciences, 18*(3), 297–316.

Masuda, M., Matsumoto, G. H., & Meredith, G. M. (1970). Ethnic identity in three generations of Japanese Americans. *The Journal of Social Psychology, 81*, 199–207.

Mehta, K. K., & Ko, H. (2004). Filial piety revisited in the context of modernizing Asian societies. *Geriatrics and Gerontology International, 4,* S77–78.

Mordkowitz, E. R., & Ginsburg, H. P. (1986). Early academic socialization of successful Asian-American college students. *Quarterly Newsletter of the Laboratories of Comparative Human Cognition, 9,* 85–91.

Mui, A., & Kang S. (2006). Acculturation stress and depression among Asian immigrant elders. *Social Work 51*(3): 243–55. DOI: <https://doi.org/10.1093/sw/51.3.243>

National Center for Education Statistics (2012). Education longitudinal study of 2002 (ELS: 2002): A first look at 2002 high school sophomores 10 years later. Washington, D.C.: U.S. Department of Education.

Park, I. H., & Cho, L. (1995). Confucianism and the Korean family. *Journal of Comparative Family Studies, 26*(1), 117–34.

Park, K. (1999). "I really do feel I'm 1.5!": The construction of self and community by young Korean Americans. *Amerasia Journal, 21*(1), 139–63.

Portes, A., & MacLeod, D. (1999). Educating the second generation: Determinants of academic achievement among children of immigrants in the United States. *Journal of Ethnic and Migration Studies, 25*(3), 373–96.

Rhee, S. (1996). Effective social work practice with Korean immigrant families. *Journal of Multicultural Social Work. 56,* 49–61.

Rice, K. G., Leever, B. A., Christopher, J., & Porter, J. D. (2006). Perfectionism, stress, and social (dis)connection: A short-term study of hopelessness, depression, and academic adjustment among honors students. *Journal of Counseling Psychology, 53*(4), 524–34.

Rumbaut, R. G., & Ima, K. (1988). The adaptation of Southeast Asian refugee youth: A comparative study. Final report to the U.S. Department of Health and Human Services, Office of Refugee Resettlement, Washington, D.C.

Shih, S. (1995). Feminist diaspora and the nation: Theresa Hak-Kyung Cha's *Dictee* and Myung Mi Kim's *Under flag*. Paper presented at the conference on "Traditional Korea: division and diaspora." University of Southern California, Los Angeles, California.

Singelis, T. M. (1994). The measurement of independent and interdependent self-construals. *Personality and Social Psychology Bulletin, 20*(5), 580–91.

Singh, G. K., & Siahpush, M. (2001). All-cause and cause-specific mortality of immigrants and native born in the United States. *American Journal of Public Health, 91*(3), 392.

Solorzano, D. G., & Yosso, T. J. (2001). From racial stereotyping and deficit discourse. *Multicultural Education, 9*(1), 2–7.

Song, C., & Glick, J. E. (2004). College attendance and choice of college majors among Asian American students. *Social Science Quarterly, 85*(5), 1401–21.

Sue, S., (1974). Personality and Mental Health: A Clarification. *Amerasia Journal, 2*(2), 173–77.

Sue, S., & Sue, D. W. (1971). Chinese-American personality and mental health. *Amerasia Journal, 1*(2), 36–49.

Sue, S., & Zane, N. (1987). The role of culture and cultural techniques in psychotherapy. *American Psychologist, 42*(1), 37–45.

Suzuki, B. H. (2002). Revisiting the model minority stereotype: Implications for student affairs practice and higher education. *New Directions for Student Services, 97*, 21–32.

Szapocznik, J., & Kurtines, W. M. (1993). Family psychology and cultural diversity: Opportunities for theory, research, and application. *American Psychologist, 48*(4), 400–07.

Tran N., & Birman, D. (2010). Questioning the model minority: Studies of Asian American academic performance. *Asian American Journal of Psychology, 1*(2), 106–18.

Tong, B. R. (1971). The ghetto of the mind: Notes on the historical psychology of Chinese America. *Amerasia journal, 1*(3), 1–31.

Triandis, H. (1988). Collectivism v. individualism: A reconceptualisation of a basic concept in cross-cultural social psychology. In C. Bagley and G. K. Verma (Eds.), *Cross-cultural studies of personality, attitudes, and cognition.* London: Macmillan. 60–95.

Uba, L. (2002). *A post-modern psychology of Asian Americans: Creating knowledge of a racial minority.* Albany, New York: State University of New York Press.

U.S. Census Bureau. (2015, November 7) *The Asian Population: 2010 Census briefs.* Retrieved from <https://www.census.gov/prod/cen2010/briefs/c2010br- 11.pdf>

Vartanian, T. P., Karen, D., Buck, P. W., and Cadge, W. (2007). Early factors leading to college graduation for Asians and non-Asians in the United States. *The Sociological Quarterly, 48*(2), 165–97.

Yoo, S., and Skovholt, T. M. Cross-cultural examination of depression expression and help-seeking behavior: A comparative study of American and Korean college students. *Journal of College Counseling, 4,* 10–19.

Yu, E. Y., Choe, P., & Han, S. I. (2002). Korean population in the United States, 2000. *International Journal, 71,* 7–107.

Zhou, M., Lee, J., Vallejo, J. A., Tafoya-Estrada, R., & Xiong, Y. S. (2008). Success attained, deterred, and denied: Divergent pathways to social mobility in Los Angeles's new second generation. *The Annals of the American Academy of Political and Social Science, 620,* 37–61.

Inclusivity Versus Exclusivity: Re-Imagining the Honors College as a Third Place

NANCY M. WEST

UNIVERSITY OF MISSOURI

DREAMS AND REALITIES OF SPACE IN HONORS

In 2013, I visited a certain honors college during the Southern Regional Honors Council Conference. Housed in a newly renovated Georgian-style building, this particular college has a spacious lounge that includes leather sofas and club chairs, Oriental-style rugs, Kravet upholstery (readers of *House Beautiful* will know what I mean), and two fireplaces. The building is replete with oak-paneled conference rooms, insuring that the seminar-style courses honors promotes so heavily have just the right setting. The dean's office may be the stateliest one I have ever seen; it commands a magnificent prospect of rose bushes and an estuary. As we toured the facilities, I watched the faces of my comrades. A few looked savage with envy. Others looked deflated. "Feeling like a poor relative?" someone whispered to me. His college occupies the third floor of a former infirmary.

When I became director of the Honors College at the University of Missouri (MU) in 2010, I dreamed of the day when we would get such a building ourselves. I fantasized about a miniature Oxford right in the heart of Missouri where I would preside as an Americanized don, a cross between Natalie Portman and Glenn Close, walking the halls in long linen dresses.

Not willing to wait around for an endowed building, I have worked hard to move us from our present location, which is a cluster of administrative offices and a conference room we share with another unit, to a building on campus that could be renovated to suit our needs. But given how much competition exists on our campus for space these days, I have made little progress on that front. Relocation may happen, or it may be we have to wait for that endowed building after all. Either way, we are not moving anytime soon.

In the long meanwhile, I have had plenty of time to think about space.[1] I now realize that an opulent building is not what I want for MU's honors students. No doubt, buildings like the one I described above impress many prospective students and their parents, but perhaps other students would be intimidated by such surroundings. I have tried to imagine my eighteen-year-old self, a first-generation honors student raised in Newark, NJ, feeling at home in such an environment. The trouble with these buildings, which have sprung up around the country as honors colleges become an increasingly attractive target for donorship, is that they reinforce what Kevin Knudson describes as a widespread perception of honors as "flying in first class" ("'Honors'"). Such a view sees honors as a reward for high ACT scores or GPAs rather than as a challenge. (How can you feel challenged while sitting in a Kravet-upholstered chair, after all?) Worse still, the particular opulence of these buildings flagrantly aligns honors with white affluence, even as, ironically, much effort goes into diversifying the population of honors colleges.

This is not to say that space does not matter. It matters deeply. As Winston Churchill says, "We shape our buildings; thereafter they shape us" (Churchill qtd. in O'Toole 161). What kind of space should an honors college occupy, then? Answering this question, I have discovered, requires more than just considering square footage and architectural features. It means probing deeply into what an honors education should be and what kind of role an honors college should occupy on its campus.

WHY AND HOW SPACE MATTERS

As I considered the kind of building best suited for MU's Honors College, I consulted the work of several sociologists who have written on space. The first of these is the German sociologist Georg Simmel, whose two-volume book, *Sociology: Inquiries into the Construction of Social Forms*, was published in 1908. In chapter nine of the first volume of the book, "Space and the Social Ordering of Society," Simmel explores how the external spaces people inhabit influence their internal experiences. He identifies several key characteristics that transform empty space into meaningful space. Meaningful space, he observes, must have:

1. a sense of uniqueness;

2. spatial divisions and boundaries;

3. fixedness of content; and

4. a sense of its own changeability as a location. (543–620)

For Simmel, the uniqueness of a space includes not only its physical characteristics but also the distinctiveness of its inhabitants. That is, humans and their activities define space as much as inanimate objects and architectural features do. The building that houses an honors college thus gains its meaning partly from the high caliber of the students who inhabit it. Conversely, the condition and nature of a physical space—its splendor, modesty, funkiness, or dilapidation—contribute to the social identity of the group who uses it, which suggests that the more imposing the building, the more honors students can become linked with elitism, even snobbery. I have wondered if it would not be better to house honors students in a physical space that embodies some of the qualities we

201

hope to see in them, such as a spirit of innovation, creativity, and openness.

Simmel's second characteristic, spatial divisions and boundaries, alerts us to how social groups gain their sense of identity partly through constructing their difference from other groups. "The boundary," writes Simmel, is "not a spatial fact that has sociological consequences but a sociological fact that forms itself spatially" (119). In other words, we construct physical boundaries to symbolize social ones. This observation underscores why our Vice Provost for Undergraduate Studies was right when he maintained that housing MU's Honors College within a residence hall, occupied mainly by honors freshmen, would have been a bad idea. I was all for the idea at first, considering that it would have allowed my staff and me to interact closely with at least one group of honors students. But symbolically, it would have sent the wrong message. An honors college needs to serve all of its students, and its space must reflect this fact.

Boundaries mark a space as socially different from other spaces. The physical space it occupies can thus establish the social difference of an honors college from other colleges on campus. It can suggest that an honors college offers its students more resources, support, and attention than other students receive on campus, which is an age-old promise of honors. But this promise may not be one we want to keep making. Perhaps it is time to rethink that promise by locating our colleges within spaces that assert the collaboration of honors with other colleges/units on campus rather than its separation from them. One model currently being considered by our Vice Provost, for example, is locating honors within a center dedicated to academic excellence. This would mean pairing the honors college with the Office of Fellowships and the Office of Undergraduate Research, both of which serve all students on campus.

Simmel's "fixedness of content" refers to how a physical space localizes and fixes social interaction. Simmel emphasizes that individuals within social groups require a physical space in order to connect with each other and bolster their common identity; without such spaces, they remain isolated from one another, never possessing more than a vague sense of attachment to their social group. Space enables different individuals in a social group to encounter each other—and for Simmel, human encounters, no matter how brief, are profoundly important. They enable us to change through direct contact with one another; as the encounter unfolds, we move toward each other, forgetting ourselves, perhaps even getting carried away in the spontaneity of interaction. Encounters also shape our memories. Space, rather than time, is thus paramount to memory because it is where pleasurable, important, or eventful encounters occur. In the absence of physical space, Simmel writes, memories form much less readily. And so without a space where students can meet and interact, they are unlikely to form lasting memories around their honors education. Just as important, the possibility that diverse social groups within honors, such as first-generation, ethnically underrepresented, working-class, and affluent students, will spend time together becomes less and less likely.

Simmel's final characteristic, "changeability as a location" suggests that meaningful space must anticipate its own outmodedness for a specific social group (121). This observation stands at odds with the current trend of courting wealthy donors to fund buildings for honors colleges. If an honors college, such as the one I visited in 2014 acquires its building from a donor wishing to leave a permanent and visible legacy, it must remain within that building even if the honors operation outgrows it. For example, members of an honors college and a donor might specify the possibility of future additions or changes to the building, as needed, leaving funds in reserve to effect such developments.

Another sociologist whose work I consulted is Henri Lefebvre. For Lefebvre, physical, mental, and social space are distinct from one another, yet they always exist together as different aspects of space (5–6). He famously argued that social relations both produce space and are shaped by it and that space and society are mutually constituted (26). Space, then, is not merely a container but an *agent*; as such, it has the potential to exert tremendous cultural influence. As we think about physical space for an honors college, then, we might think about how space has a certain kind of social or cultural power. A college located centrally on campus, for example, can exert a certain kind of social or political power, and that power may be different from the power that might be generated by an honors college located on the periphery of campus.

Lastly, I considered the work of cultural geographer Doreen Massey, who argues that in an age marked by the twin forces of globalization and digital communication, we need to adopt a "progressive sense of place" (11). Such a sense requires what she calls an "extroverted" notion of community, which is outward-looking, dynamic, and open, rather than an "introverted" one, which is inward-looking, static, and bounded (11). Place, she writes, should be seen as one point, one location, in a vast network of "social relations and understandings . . . that are constructed on a far larger scale than what we happen to define for that moment as the place itself . . ." (14). Massey was among the first to argue that the twenty-first century demands a "global sense of place" that has a consciousness of its links with the wider world. This observation is apt for an honors college, whose students will number among the future leaders of that wider world. But housing them within a building such as the one I described at the beginning of this essay—with the sense it conveys that everything an honors student could need or want is within its walls—subverts this idea.

METAPHORS FOR HONORS

As we think about space and honors, we should also pause for a moment on the subject of metaphors. Metaphors take abstract concepts and give them specific meaning. They also allow us to feel things directly and to let us know something differently. As poet Jane Hirschfield puts it, they are "handles on the door of what we can imagine." All of which is why metaphors are so important to our sense of space and why they have played such a profound role in architectural planning and design.

Since their origin in the early twentieth-century, honors colleges have been described as small private colleges within large universities. Although this description is not strictly metaphoric, it does, in effect, describe an honors college by what it is not. The idea is to sell an honors experience to prospective students, their parents, and even the faculty we wish to recruit as the rough equivalent of an Oberlin or Swarthmore. This description positions it as other from the large, public university that houses it. An honors college thus emerges as an exclusive, protected, and self-contained world, free from the taints of its parent institution.

Quite frankly, we can no longer afford this description. For one thing, the current academic climate in which deans and directors need to find creative and collaborative ways to make the best use of limited resources makes such uppity thinking downright foolish. Rather than view honors in terms of exclusivity, we need to reinvent it in terms of inclusiveness. Such a reinvention has been decades in coming; for ever since honors colleges came into being, they have occupied an uncertain and contested place in their universities. This dilemma exists largely because the association of honors with elitism rankles many Americans. As Americans, we understand that talent should be nurtured and groomed. But we are also uncomfortable with the anti-democratic nature of that belief. And at a land-grant university such as the University of Missouri, such ambivalence is trebly felt.

Honors colleges need a fitting metaphor as much as they need a stronger sense of their own spatial identity. Let us turn now to a concept that provides them with both.

THE THIRD PLACE

Back in the early 1990s, in *The Great Good Place*, sociologist Ray Oldenburg coined the term "third place" to refer to environments, separate from work and home, that people attend frequently, voluntarily, happily. Examples include coffeehouses, cafes, the nineteenth-century salon, the corner bar, the barbershop, the beer garden, and, according to some, the Internet. Third spaces are anchors of a community, fostering broad and creative kinds of interactions among people, which are often and not surprisingly fueled by a cup of coffee or glass of wine. They nurture good conversation. They foster new friendships. They inspire different kinds of thinking and different kinds of identity. They create a community of the curious.

The classic example of a "third place" is the London coffeehouse, which had its beginning in the mid-seventeenth century. The idea caught on quickly, and coffeehouses flourished throughout the eighteenth century when, among others, Samuel Pepys and Isaac Newton developed their ideas over cups of very black and gritty coffee. One could visit a coffeehouse, or several of them, either daily as part of a regularized routine or spontaneously without much forethought or effort. The coffeehouse became a social institution in Britain, a place where individuals, no matter what their social status, could go. Indeed, early coffeehouses were enthusiastically democratic in the composition and conduct of their habitués. They were places where people discovered one another apart from the ranks and classes that had earlier divided them. The coffeehouse thus allowed for the kind of spontaneous encounters among different social groups that Simmel describes. "Unlike the formal social interactions prescribed by a visit to the 'great house' of an aristocrat," Brian Cowan observes, "coffeehouse visits were more spontaneous and less rigidly ritualized. The protocols of recognizing rank and precedence were abandoned . . . " in an attempt to reject the excessive and stifling formalities of the past (102).

London coffeehouses were boisterous places where conversation reached lively heights daily. Indeed, conversation was the cardinal and sustaining activity of coffeehouses, as it is of *all* third places. Conversation in a coffeehouse was a kind of sport, enacting what Henry Sedgwick, in his wonderful book *The Art of Happiness*, describes as "the game of conversation," where good talk "exercises the intelligence and the heart . . . calls on memory and the imagination . . . and has all the interest derived from uncertainty and unexpectedness" (31). Much of the conversation in eighteenth-century coffeehouses revolved around politics. Good political talk, argues David Matthew, creates and reflects an enlarged mentality (qtd. in Oldenburg 71–72). It is where we develop the capacity to understand the structure and functioning of the whole social body, which is the capacity to govern ourselves democratically. It is also where we discover "what is common amidst our differences" (Sedgwick 27).

Third places have long flourished in countries like France, England, Italy, and Germany, where one cannot throw a stone without hitting a cafe. In stark contrast, America has never been big on third places. Yes, we have Starbucks, which promotes itself in these terms: "There's work. There's home. And there's Starbucks." But given the overloaded, hurried nature of American culture, most people who visit Starbucks simply grab their cups of coffee and head to work. They don't linger. Compared to the citizens of other countries, Americans fail miserably at the art of conversation; they also fail at the art of relaxation, which good conversation requires. As ironic evidence of this fact, certain Starbucks in America have recently changed their décor, visibly shaving down their comforts, to ensure that their customers do not linger. The tables are smaller, the seats harder, and fluorescent lighting has replaced softer lighting. The message is clear: Starbucks is not a place to sit for very long.

Even more sadly, our universities lack third places. Granted, freshmen and sophomores have third places in the form of lounge areas in their residence halls, and most universities have some sort of center where all students can congregate. Some universities even have lounges for their faculty and staff. But with these exceptions, universities typically organize their physical space around the discrete populations and activities of faculty, administration, and students. Faculty members typically work in buildings that house their departments or academic units exclusively. Upper administration usually occupies its own building. Students reside in residence halls on the periphery of campus. Moreover, those areas on campus intended to be third places, such as faculty lounges or student centers, do not truly operate as such; over the years, as the schedules of faculty and students have grown more demanding, they have become places to grab a quick coffee or bite to eat while checking one's iPhone. That this situation will change radically in the years ahead is almost inconceivable. And certainly it limits how we think and work and teach and interact.

Just as the concept of a dream house has replaced the concept of creating an ideal city in America, we now have individual units clamoring for their own fancy spaces rather than participating in a collective effort to create an ideal university community. Americans act as though a house can substitute for a community if only it is spacious and comfortable enough. The effect of this mindset, writes Oldenberg, is that "the essential group experience is being replaced by the exaggerated self-consciousness of individuals" (13). Similarly, the overall concept of a university has been overrun by the increasing emphasis placed on individual units. For all the push these days toward interdisciplinary thinking and collaborative research, this dream house mentality leaves us within our own spaces, forcing us to move from home to work, or residence hall to classroom, again and again. Meanwhile, the social function of a university becomes less and less clear.

HONORS COLLEGES AS THIRD PLACES

Thinking about an honors college as a university's third place might shift our ideas about the role of honors education and our ideas about the role of the university. Honors as a third place would emphasize conversation as a component of one's college education. As part of their assessment, honors students would be expected to converse well with both their peers and their professors, and in the process they would help our universities restore a moribund skill. Honors colleges could have freshmen seminars on "The Art of Conversation." These courses would require students not only to learn the principles of good conversation but also to keep up with the news, cultural events, and the latest books to read. This focus would also require them to become more informed citizens and provide a way for them to question what they read and hear on the news and in the classroom. As Brian Cowan explains, coffeehouse conversation and debate offered an important face-to-face complement to the unruly world of print publication and the formal meetings of the Royal Society in the social world of the virtuosi (27). It allowed Londoners the opportunity to make sense of a wild media and a chance to explore what was omitted from the narrow curriculum of specific institutions. And so it should be today. The best counter to the pernicious and alien influence that the media often exert is face-to-face groups in which people participate in discussions of what is important to them and how to preserve it. Such conversations rarely happen on our campuses. Conversations have too often become witless and trite, self-centered and unreflective, even among faculty, and yet it is the first step to building a true community of thinkers.

Re-imagining honors colleges as third places would also foster a spirit of creativity, which is so vital to a university. Much attention is now being given to creative studies, it is true, but this is motivated by job market conditions. Creativity should be fostered for its own sake, for the health of a university and its citizens, and honors colleges are one place where this can happen. Because honors colleges can offer a much more fluid curriculum than departments, this spirit is essential to the distinction of an honors college from other units. This spirit often emerges, for example, in conversations with a faculty member about courses; this spirit of play comes alive. I will never forget the time an agricultural journalist on campus burst into my office with his idea for a course on chocolate, or when one of my good friends, an English professor who had recently become a marathon runner, suddenly realized she could offer an honors course that combined writing with running.

With a new emphasis on conversation and creativity, honors colleges might create a new kind of virtuoso community similar to the one Cowan portrays. "The virtuosi," writes Cowen, "held an almost limitless curiosity about the wider worlds around them" (11). This curiosity was "an attitude of mind involving a fascination for the rare, novel, surprising and outstanding in all spheres of life" (11). Cowan defines the virtuoso sensibility as an "insatiable appetite for the strange and ingenious in all things, from works of art to natural wonders and mechanical inventions" (11). It was part of the very character of a virtuoso to be learned and wise without becoming a pedant or effete scholar. With this vision in mind, an honors college could create a curriculum that fosters curiosity about the rare, the novel, the surprising and persuade students to willingly explore subjects other than the specialized material they need to know for their careers.

The third advantage to re-imagining honors colleges as third places is the new opportunities it would create for interdisciplinary teaching and research. Interdisciplinarity is third-place thinking. It is, as I tell my students, the "space in between." Honors colleges are uniquely positioned to house an interdisciplinary curriculum, given that their job is to bring faculty and students from different disciplines together. Like all third places, honors colleges are neutral ground, separate from departments and yet in the business of serving them all; as such, they provide an ideal space for the kind of in between collaboration required by interdisciplinary work. Honors colleges are where team-teaching—that activity we all say we should do more of but cannot because of departmental restrictions—really can happen.

Perhaps the greatest benefit to repositioning honors colleges as third places is that it would divorce them from their exclusionary, elitist associations. The best third places are social levelers. They welcome anyone who has the creativity, curiosity, and sense of adventure to be there. And while thinking of honors colleges as levelers seems radically counterintuitive, doing so will allow us to put much more emphasis on a person' s intellectual curiosity than his or her resumé or transcript. As third places, honors colleges can openly welcome as part of their community students who do not have a perfect 4.0 GPA. The key to coming into an honors college would, instead, be a catholicity of interest and a fierce desire for breadth of knowledge.

The same welcome attitude should also be applied to the faculty who teach for honors. One of the troubling aspects about honors colleges is the common boast that only regular, tenure-track faculty doing cutting-edge research teach honors courses. Having such star faculty teach in honors colleges is certainly beneficial since honors students especially need to be introduced to the inside world of research. But let us be honest: these faculty have huge demands on their time and often cannot teach undergraduate courses or, worse, have little desire to do so.

But this last point is secondary to my real one, which is that honors colleges should welcome and celebrate a variety of faculty. This variety would include emeritus professors, who have both the experience and the time to teach well; graduate students, whose youthful passion for their discipline would be infectious and who would model for our honors students what they could be in several years; and non-regular faculty, whose less-demanding research agendas could allow them to provide honors students with the mentoring they need. As in all third places, a strong network would unite these different generations of faculty in a viable community dedicated to honors education. Oldenberg notes that one of the key aspects of a third place is the presence of a "hard core of regular patrons" (174). "It is the regulars, whatever their number on any given occasion, who feel at home in a place and set the tone of conviviality. It is the regulars whose mood and manner provide the infectious and contagious style of interaction and whose acceptance of new faces is crucial" (34). Having retirees and non-regular faculty, rather than feeling marginalized as they often do, assume a leadership role in honors colleges in which they welcomed and mentored new faculty to bring them into the honors community as regulars would be wonderful.

CONCLUSION

In one of the many instances of the book's idealism, Oldenberg remarks:

> The third place is largely a world of its own making, fashioned by talk and quite independent of the institutional order of the larger society. If the world of the third place is far less consequential than the larger one, its regulars find abundant compensation in the fact that it is a more decent one, more in love with people for their own sake, and, hour for hour, a great deal more fun. (48)

If universities are becoming ever more corporatized, plagued by the pressures of the economy, honors colleges can be an antidote to that, a place to go where phrases like "game-changer," "leverage," "best practice," and "buy-in" are never to be heard.

Oldenberg writes that the actual physical space of a third place should not be too impressive or too grand. "Third places are unimpressive looking for the most part," he writes, "because they need to have a characteristic homeliness" (36). With this in mind, my new vision of an honors college is a space quite different from the building I described earlier. It is an open and inviting space, with many comfortable seats (not upholstered by Kravet) and areas for talking. It is filled with newspapers and magazines, including those from other countries. Several rooms are painted orange to inspire creativity. It is filled with whiteboards and walls that can be marked and painted and repainted by students. Retired faculty members have offices in them, and they meet with students all the time, the young and the old coming together. And yes, it has a coffeehouse within it, open to midnight or beyond.

NOTES

[1]For a rich and extensive discussion of honors space from grand grounds and buildings to functional to transitory and aspirational, see *Housing Honors*, which, like this volume, is part of the NCHC Monograph Series. Edited by Linda Frost, Lisa W. Kay, and Rachael Poe, this text includes survey information about honors space from over 400 institutions and offers a range of perspectives on a variety of spaces, including offices, classrooms, lounges, and residence halls, and the impact they have on programs and students.

REFERENCES

Cowan, Brian. *The Social Life of Coffee: The Emergence of the British Coffeehouse*. New Haven: Yale University Press, 2005. Print.

Hirschfield, Jane. "The Art of Metaphor." TED Ed: Lessons Worth Sharing. Voice recording. July 2014.

Housing Honors. Ed. Linda Frost, Lisa W. Kay, and Rachael Poe. Lincoln: National Collegiate Honors Council, 2015, NCHC Monograph Series. Print.

Knudson, Kevin. "'Honors' Should Mean a Challenge, Not an Upgrade to First Class." *The Chronicle of Higher Education.* Commentary Section. 14 July 2011. Print.

Lefebvre, Henri. *The Production of Space.* London: Wiley-Blackwell Press, 1992. Print.

Massey, Doreen. *Space, Place, and Gender.* Minneapolis: University of Minnesota Press, 1994. Print.

Oldenburg, Ray. *The Great Good Place: Cafes, Coffee Shops, Bookstores, Bars, Hair Salons and other Hangouts at the Heart of a Community.* Philadelphia: Da Capo Press, 1997. Print.

O'Toole, Randal. *The Best-Laid Plans: How Government Planning Harms Your Quality of Life, Your Pocketbook, and Your Future.* Washington, D.C.: Cato Institute, 2007. Print.

Sedgwick, Henry. *The Art of Happiness.* New York: Bobbs-Merrill, 1940. Print.

Simmel, Georg. *Sociology: Inquiries into the Construction of Social Forms.* Vol. 1. Trans. and Ed. Anthony J. Blasi. Ed. Anton K. Jacobs and Mathew Kanjirathinkal. Boston: Brill, 2009. Print.

Engaging the Bard:
Honors, Engagement, and a
New Chautauqua

SHAWN ALFREY
UNIVERSITY OF DENVER

INTRODUCTION

Early in the twentieth century, education philosopher John Dewey explored the process of reflective thinking, describing what we would today consider the key components of critical thinking, one of the main values of honors education. This chapter explores how such reflective thinking results from the "situatedness" of service or community-engaged learning and suggests that honors courses can involve both academic rigor and community engagement as they continue the project of liberal education.

As a case study, I follow my own community-engaged seminar that puts honors students together as instructors and mentors for a Denver Public Schools Shakespeare Club and a Festival performance. From January until the day of the Festival, my students navigate the sometimes difficult situatedness at the heart of community engagement and support what I would argue constitutes a contemporary expression of the twenty-first century public sphere—a new-style Chautauqua—that brings academics and civic work together to create a balanced honors experience.

HONORS, EXPERIENTIAL LEARNING, "NEGATIVE CAPABILITY," AND CRITICAL THINKING

Since the pioneering days of the American honors movement in the early 1920s when Frank Aydelotte established the honors program at Swarthmore College, experimentation and innovation have been the essence of honors education.[1] Indeed, honors education, according to Julianna K. Chaszar, has been a leader in "experimentation and reform, challenging notions about appropriate curricula, instructional formats, and the timing of course work, and more broadly about the nature of a democratic educational system" (189). With support from the National Collegiate Honors Council (NCHC), numerous experiments have been launched, and many NCHC monographs and journal essays have championed their methods and results. As William W. Daniel explains, back in 1976 the first Honors Semester exploring "Place as Text" set out with the goals of

1. "active learning";

2. "an expanded concept of text";

3. "an integrated and collaborative approach to learning"; and

4. "complementary values of autonomy and community" (8).

More recently but in a similar vein, Kevin Knudson, Director of the University Honors Program at the University of Florida, states that the job of today's honors programs is to develop coursework that leads students "from a culture of achievement to a culture of engagement" (Knudson).

The early twentieth-century American educator and philosopher John Dewey is embraced for his progressive theories on education and the experimental classrooms he created at the University of Chicago that led to all sorts of innovations in K–12 pedagogy. His anti-hierarchical attitudes toward the content of coursework, as well as his focus on the value of experiential education itself, became touchstones more than fifty years later when, in the 80s and 90s, a new generation of scholars sought to infuse higher education with the personal relevance and civic values Dewey saw as the goals of education. For contemporary champions of service learning and community engagement in higher education, especially, that old philosopher of democracy and education has become something like a patron saint.

David D. Cooper, an advocate for Dewey's positions, has been active in service learning and community-engaged scholarship and pedagogy since the 1990s. For Cooper, Dewey's thinking has enriched the practice and theory of service learning, and it has helped him explore both its academic value and the academy's ability to value it. Besides linking service learning with a particularly lively, democratic view of the purpose of education, Cooper builds on Dewey's insights, as revealed in his 1910 publication *How We Think*, to explore the potential of service learning to foster reflective thinking and transformative learning. Although it is not Cooper's focus, many of the statements Cooper quotes from Dewey's text seem to echo John Keats's description of negative capability. Transformative education, Dewey claims, originates with "the strife of alternative interpretations" (qtd. in Cooper 50). The process involves "a state of doubt, hesitation, perplexity, mental difficulty . . . and a concomitant act of searching, hunting, inquiring, to find material that will resolve the doubt and settle and dispose of the perplexity" (Dewey qtd. in Cooper 53). Indeed, Dewey's *Art as Experience*, published a year after *How We Think*, cites Keats's theory as "more of the psychology of productive thought than many treatises" (33–34).

"Negative capability" is Keats's term for a special creative faculty. In a famous 1817 letter to his brothers, the poet first articulated this ability: "at once it struck me, what quality went to form a Man of Achievement, especially in Literature, & which Shakespeare possessed so enormously—I mean *Negative Capability*, that is when a man is capable of being in uncertainties, Mysteries, doubts, without any irritable reaching after fact & reason . . ." (Keats). Keats considered this ability to entertain irrational or contradictory possibilities a necessity for the creative writer; more generally, the phrase describes a state of openness to different, competing contexts and claims. One website glosses it thus: "The word 'doubt' is from the Latin, 'dubitare' and comes from 'two' as in two minds. In most conflicts, two minds oppose each other. Yet instead of fighting the other, Keats finds the situation to be one that is open for creativity. In this sense, Negative Capability is a[n] . . . expression of supreme empathy" ("Keats' Kingdom"). This ideal state may be hard to sustain when faced with an academic calendar or a catalog of requirements, but it is relevant to my discussion here. Keats's example is William Shakespeare, a writer who might supply material for any self-respecting honors program.

Dewey's belief in transformative education aligns him with both practical and philosophical values, the schoolhouse and the ivory tower. Not only does Dewey articulate a value similar to the creativity of Keats's "negative capability"; the process Dewey describes as reflective thinking is related to other lofty aesthetic experiences. One is reminded of William Wordsworth's claim that poetic speech requires extreme emotion recollected in tranquility; or, on a grander scale, the struggle to comprehend the incommensurable known as the Kantian sublime: "the mere capacity of thinking which evidences a faculty of mind transcending every standard of sense" (Kant 98). Dewey's view of the purpose of reflective thought in fact sounds very much like the experience of the sublime. To critic Thomas Weiskel, the sublime's usual trajectory moves from a sort of disturbing, threatening encounter through a delicate phase of mutuality to a new state, a meta moment of gravitas and conceptual understanding (see Weiskel 23–24). Likewise, for Dewey, reflective thought is a process that "transform[s] a situation in which there is experienced . . . conflict [or] disturbance of some sort, into a situation that is clear, coherent, settled, harmonious. . . . Genuine thinking winds up, in short, with an appreciation of new values" (Dewey, *How* 101; qtd. in Cooper 50).

"Genuine thinking" is the naturally vague prerequisite linking aesthetic transport with down and dirty experience. It is also the elegant heart of the scientific method and the noisy engine of the democratic process. Dewey thus describes the process of transformational learning in terms we would recognize at the center of the tradition of liberal education and, more particularly, honors education. As a participant in the summer 2010 Honors Assessment Institute, I worked with my colleagues to boil down the *je ne sais quoi* of honors education. Despite all of the differences in our programs' sizes and requirements, everyone agreed that at its core honors education values effective communication, research, interdisciplinarity, and, above all, critical thinking, which Dewey in essence describes as "active, persistent and careful consideration of any belief or supposed form of knowledge in the light of the grounds that support it and the further conclusions to which it tends" (Dewey, *How*; qtd. in Ash and Clayton 137). Such a practice, claim Sarah Ash and Patti Clayton, supports such academic values as "deeper understanding and better application of subject matter and increased complexity of problem and solution analysis . . . [as well as] openness to new ideas" (140).

SITUATING CRITICAL THINKING AND COMMUNITY-ENGAGED COURSES

Reflective thinking involves what Donald A. Schön describes as a "continual interweaving of thinking and doing" (Schön qtd. in Ash and Clayton 137). For Dewey, it thus requires "the provision of a real situation that arouses inquiry" (Dewey, *How*; qtd. in Ash and Clayton 151). This engagement is the source of what Dewey calls "the *situatedness* of reflective thinking. . . . Follow the stuff of knowledge far enough and you will find some situation that is directly experienced, something undergone, done, enjoyed, or suffered, and not just thought of" (Dewey, *How* 99; qtd. in Cooper 51–52). Such "situatedness" can be discovered in every discipline; indeed, the Place as Text concept developed by Bernice Braid and Ada Long is a wonderful example of transformative learning

219

through involvement in a real, particular situation. Service and community-based learning by their very nature can provide the situatedness that occasions the transformative educational experience (see Braid 20).

In the community-engaged courses I have taught in the honors program, especially the honors seminar called "Engaging the Bard: DU Students and the Denver Public Schools Shakespeare Festival," transformative experiential education is the point. Meeting once a week from January through May, the class brings University of Denver students of various majors together with elementary school students to work on and learn about Shakespeare's plays in an after-school Shakespeare Club. The occasion for this club is the annual Denver Public Schools Shakespeare Festival, which takes place every year in late April or early May. Housed typically in the auditorium, library, foyer, or art room of Carson Elementary School, the course is replete with the situatedness that Dewey highlights, and it generates the reflective thinking such situatedness makes possible.

When I began teaching in the University of Denver Honors Program, I realized that work with the Shakespeare Festival would provide a compelling context for a community-engaged honors course, one in which the literary and civic value of the Bard could be explored. The class has two main components. The first or most obvious is the work the University of Denver students do with the fourth- and fifth-graders at Carson, teaching them about Shakespeare and helping them learn scenes from his plays. This situation provides a context for the work done by the honors students, but it also complicates, supports, and sometimes confounds the other component of the class: the readings and discussions the honors students have regarding both the Bard and the school. What both enriches and frustrates their experience is the occasion for the class itself: the situation the DU students find themselves in each year when faced with a group of 24–34 fourth- and fifth-graders hoping to perform their scene in front of family, friends, and other audience members at the annual Shakespeare Festival.

What is a class project for the honors students is an after-school club for the Carson students who meet every week so that they can learn and practice a scene from one of Shakespeare's plays. In the process, they also learn about Shakespeare's work, aspects of Elizabethan culture and history, and the genres and traditions of theatre. At the start of each of the club meetings, the participants throw their backpacks into squeaky auditorium seats, settle down in a circle on the stage, and eat whatever afternoon snack they brought from home, even as their University of Denver colleagues engage them in what we call "Shakespeare Moments" about witchcraft or monarchy, Elizabethan clothing or disease.

This situation requires that the honors students be both creative and pragmatic; they must be flexible and able to think on their feet. Acting as teachers themselves, they develop a curriculum, their Shakespeare Moments, based on whichever play they are doing that year. They also must handle the issues that arise as the elementary students learn the play, including addressing the combined needs and interests of the two vastly different groups of students. Besides these lessons, each meeting includes work on the scenes themselves. Here the honors students become both mentors and scholars, forced to know the text in more ways than they might as students alone. They must call upon a variety of skills and approaches as they collaborate with the Carson students on a shared vision. On their way to performing a scene from a growing list of plays including *King Lear, Love's Labour's Lost, As You Like It, The Merchant of Venice, Romeo and Juliet, Hamlet,* and *Macbeth,* the Carson students take ownership of Shakespeare and his texts. Not incidentally, so, too, do the honors students. At the same time they are students, they are also teachers.

The honors students contextualize their experiences at Carson by reading articles regarding the history and philosophy of public education and the place of Shakespeare in it.[2] Their readings address questions of how and why to teach Shakespeare to children. They discuss the history of Shakespeare's adaptations and their political, ideological, and aesthetic implications. The academic focus is thus both magnified and splintered by the community and service learning context of the course, which generates new and unexpected academic concerns. How should one teach Shakespeare to young people? Should the focus be on story or language, on supposedly universal issues or character or imagery, narrative or drama? And why should these literary and philosophical concepts even be taught at all? Why is this festival focused on Shakespeare, for instance, and not Ibsen? These abstract questions are activated through the readings and discussions as well as through the concrete situation with the elementary students.

The class's situatedness also concerns the pacing of the coursework because the syllabus must accommodate two different school calendars. DU is on the quarter system; DPS is on the semester. Holidays and spring breaks differ, and, importantly, it takes two quarters, with a mix of continuing and new students, to take the Carson Players from their first day to their last. Each year the academic components of the course, the reading, writing, and discussion required of the DU students, must be aligned with the DPS calendar. Beginning in 2011, for instance, the Shakespeare Festival that is the culmination of the club members' effort was almost three weeks earlier than in years past. This meant that, for the DU students, all the theory had to follow the practice. This reversal caused some in the class to feel that they had endured an initiation by fire, but it had the salutary effect of adding a shared body of experiential knowledge to the course materials.

Another important aspect of this situatedness is the variety of people involved: two groups of students, various teachers and parents, the principal, secretary, and custodial staff. Generally, what could have devolved into teaching disasters has resulted in actual teaching and teachable moments because of the real partnership that my course has created and upon which it relies. Key to any meaningful community engagement, the partnership began before the class, and the class was developed with the needs and expectations of that partner in mind. While I have been teaching the course for nine years, I have been working with the Carson Players for thirteen. I began my work there as a parent volunteer when the school was trying to develop an after-school program to allow its students to participate in the Shakespeare Festival. I helped launch the enterprise, and I proudly watched my second-grade son, acting as Kent, upbraid a prideful King Lear. When I started working in the honors program, I realized that both groups of students could learn from each other and that in this way I, too, could continue to support both communities. My own children have moved on; so, too, have two principals and several drama teachers. Nevertheless, this well-established relationship continues, having weathered each of these changes.

OUTCOMES

Ultimately, because of the secure yet flexible partnership between the DU Honors Program and Carson Elementary School, the most important relationship, the one between the Carson students and their DU colleagues, has been able to develop. Central to this relationship has been the anti-hierarchical structure of the class. I ceded almost all authority as artistic and creative director to the DU students, who now develop the audition scenes and rubrics, edit the scenes, determine the topics to be covered in the Shakespeare Moments, and work with the Carson Players as they block their scenes and learn their lines and their characters. The result has been a creative collaboration in which both groups learn from each other, often in surprising ways. The elementary students add Shakespeare to their known universe and lexicon; the honors students learn not to fear and actually to like his work. Indeed, I have been surprised by how often my honors students, even an occasional English major, have confessed to not really understanding, getting bored by, or questioning the value of Shakespeare's work. Through the example of the young children still being playful with language and, perhaps—á la Dewey or Keats—more comfortable with perplexity and doubt, the elder college students seem to gain enthusiasm for Shakespeare and meaningfully experience his text.

In fact, the students are able to share gifts that were not envisioned in the syllabus. One, a member of the DU choir, found the music Thomas Arne wrote for the song in *Love's Labour's Lost* and helped everyone learn it. Another serendipitously discovered an old mandolin in a storage closet and taught the play's little Boyet how to play it. Another DU student came to class each week with a clip-on tie and a funny hat, providing much fun and some emotional succor. After his two quarters were up, he became my Service Learning Associate, himself teaching and collaborating with both groups of students. Based in part on his experience with the Carson Players, he went on to pursue a Masters in Social Work with an emphasis on child welfare.

At its most mundane, the situatedness of the course involves a number of logistical issues: coordinating academic calendars, transporting honors students to and from Carson Elementary School, and aligning the number of honors students who register for the course with the number of fourth- and fifth-graders. And before the class begins, in order to volunteer at all, students must submit to the Colorado Bureau of Investigation background check, a reminder that even they are subject to scrutiny. These logistical factors have a powerful effect on the class. Over the years, as the school population and demands have grown and changed, the classroom, of necessity, has varied from the faculty lounge to the office foyer to, this year, a classroom for Early Childhood Education hearing-disabled students. Every year the number of honors students is limited, not because there are not enough elementary students wanting to participate, but because—with after-school homework support, child care, and enrichment classes—Carson does not have the space to accommodate more students.

These circumstances and the location have opened my students' eyes, even as they are planning their Shakespeare Moment, for example, on education in Shakespeare's day, to the community and societal context of today's public schools. In a concrete way, the limits on their working space have taught the honors students to think about public resources and those areas where society does and does not invest. In terms of the academic public sphere, something interesting happens when college seniors sit in teeny plastic chairs at desks with hand-printed name tags and empty juice boxes to discuss editing and history. So, too, in choosing their Shakespeare Moments, the honors students become aware that they are developing a curriculum. Recognizing their choices as such, they are forced to ask how curriculum is developed, how syllabi are devised. They thus become aware of the tautology they may have accepted since they started school. Why is it important for children to learn what they do? Is it simply because that is what we teach?

A CONTEMPORARY CHAUTAUQUA

The Denver Public Schools Shakespeare Festival was begun in 1984 by its Gifted and Talented Office in order to provide enrichment and to support literacy instruction throughout the district.[3] Now entering its 34th year, it has become the oldest and largest student Shakespeare festival in the United States. Its supporters include the world-renowned Folger Shakespeare Library in Washington, D.C. ("Welcome to DPS Shakespeare Festival"). Even the famous Shakespearean Ian McKellan has *Liked* it on Facebook. After a semester or more of preparation, on one Friday every spring, students from neighborhood schools, charter schools, and magnet programs pile into buses and go downtown, traipse in costume to the grounds of the Denver Center for the Performing Arts (DCPA), and spend the day performing scenes from Shakespeare's plays and reciting his sonnets. Parents and community members as well as students and teachers descend on the grounds of the DCPA to see 5,000 students from kindergarten through high school perform on one of fifteen or so stages, set up indoors and out, all day long.

I consider the Festival an instructive site where the humanities and civil society connect. In fact, I would describe the DPS Shakespeare Festival and much of the work surrounding it as a contemporary expression of the idealized, ultra-American public sphere known as the Chautauqua. The Chautauqua Movement began in the early nineteenth century, the broadest and most lasting expression of a fervor in American society for mass enlightenment witnessed earlier in both the lyceum movement and the more torpid Protestant Revivals that swept nineteenth-century popular culture. As Eldon Snyder points out, the lyceum movement encouraged self-education through public lectures as well as the establishment of museums, libraries, and schools; the Revival movement sought Christian rebirth through camp meetings with mass attendance and excitement (80). In effect, the Chautauqua Movement joined the two. It borrowed the fervor of the Revival Movement's belief in human perfectibility but focused on mass education, not on grace. The archive, housed on the University of Iowa's website, with its linked essay "What Was Chautauqua?" describes its development. Originally meant as support to Protestant Sunday School teachers, the movement became more secular and more diverse in its subject matter, gradually adding languages, literature, science, and, ultimately, all types of entertainment.

It spread geographically, too. Permanent homes of the Chautauqua meetings were established first in Michigan, and then, famously, near New York's Chautauqua Lake, and, later, as far west as Boulder, Colorado, where Chautauqua Park still contains the cottages and auditorium meant to welcome working adults, and later families, to enriching lectures, music, and entertainment. The Circuit Chautauqua began in 1904 and by the 1910s could be found almost everywhere, presenting its message of self and civic improvement to millions of Americans. At its peak "in the mid-1920s, circuit Chautauqua performers and lecturers appeared in more than 10,000 communities in 45 states to audiences totaling 45 million people" ("What Was Chautauqua?").

The Chautauqua Movement responded to a felt need throughout the United States to provide the increasing and increasingly diverse middle class a shared set of cultural knowledge. "As a sort of diverting, wholesome and morally respectable vaudeville the Circuit Chautauqua was an early form of mass culture," which one manager described as "the essence of . . . Americanism in days gone by" ("What Was Chautauqua?"). As a support to middle class values and mores, it was alternately embraced and reviled:

> Theodore Roosevelt called it "the most American thing in America," Woodrow Wilson described it during World War I as an "integral part of the national defense," and William Jennings Bryan deemed it a "potent human factor in molding the mind of the nation." Conversely, Sinclair Lewis derided it as "nothing but wind and chaff and . . . the laughter of yokels," William James found it "depressing from its mediocrity," and critic Gregory Mason dismissed

it as "infinitely easier than trying to think." ("What Was Chautauqua?")

Despite some educated elites ridiculing the Chautauqua Movement as being hopelessly middlebrow, there can be no question it furthered the cause of helping Americans share in discussions of the issues of the day and the great books meant to inform an American canon. As one spectator claimed, it "'broadened our lives in many ways'" (qtd. in "What Was Chautauqua?"). Not surprisingly, frequent on this culture-building circuit were spare productions of Shakespeare's work. Bringing these performances "first seen at Harvard University and Theodore Roosevelt's White House" to the Circuit at first raised suspicion and made managers nervous, but they proved a great hit ("What Was Chautauqua?"). As one actor put it, "'These people are God-fearing, God-living, and know their Bible and their Shakespeare'" (qtd. in "What Was Chautauqua?").

Understanding the significance and consequences of this particular aspect of the Chautauqua Movement provides some of the context for the more theoretical and critical readings and discussions of the DU students. Certainly, the measure of the audience is no longer that they be "God-fearing" and "God-living," but students, for example, find it interesting to consider what values the Bard, a cultural lightning rod, represents to an American public and its educational system. Still, the architects of the Denver Public Schools Shakespeare Festival in their dream of forging a common language seem to be involved in a similar goal: to bring "people together to improve their minds and renew their ties to one another" ("What Was Chautauqua?"). For one day at least, the public school is itself on parade, demanding the attention of downtown businesses and traffic cops and news reporters. And the students, too, are on parade as themselves and as characters from a variety of very different worlds.

Certainly, the Shakespeare Festival comes out of a particular social context and reflects one moment in our evolving American "Chautauqua" to understand and explore our cultural heritage and the desire to forge a shared knowledge that socializes students and shapes us as citizens.

A CLOSING REFLECTION

For a long time, honors programs and honors colleges have included service learning and civic engagement as core elements in their teaching. As the University of Denver's participation in the Denver Public Schools Shakespeare Festival and partnership with the Carson Elementary School through my honors course, "Engaging the Bard: DU Students and the Denver Public Schools Shakespeare Festival," indicate, the scholarship, service, leadership, and community engagement described here signify that the DU Honors Program and its students are occupying honors in a rich sense. Honors is promoting an activist agenda of educating and being socially engaged and inclusive. Courses such as the one at DU are happening across the honors landscape, and they are promoting the values that must be at the core of honors education and our obligations as individuals, scholars, and students in the academy and in the public sphere. In this course the honors students both confront and contribute to the teaching of Shakespeare. Acknowledging the Bard's role as *The* Man—avatar of culture—and The *Man*—enforcer of ideological hegemony—our students begin to recognize that no curriculum is disinterested, and that we should always ask why as well as how something should be taught.

NOTES

[1]For rich discussions of the history of honors education in America, see Guzy, Rinn, and Andrews.

[2]Class readings include articles by education historian Diane Ravitch, chapters in Frey and Bristol, and a variety of essays on teaching Shakespeare to children—from third grade pedagogy to a critic in the mode of Russian Formalism—in Miller.

[3]After the 1973 *Keyes* decision that required the Denver Public Schools to integrate its schools and the concomitant *Poundstone* amendment that made further annexation of the suburbs illegal, the commonly termed "white flight" drained the schools of many

resources, including much of its tax base and many families with academic resources. The Shakespeare Festival began in 1984 as a way to provide enrichment to all the district's schools in the wake of these demographic changes. See "Study Documents the Resegregation of Denver Public Schools" discussion in the Piton Foundation's *Term Paper* on Denver's de- and re-segregation and its academic implications.

REFERENCES

Andrews, Larry. "The Wisdom of Our Elders: Honors Council Discussions in *The Superior Student*, 1958–65." *Journal of the National Collegiate Honors Council* 12.2 (2011): 17–46. Print.

Ash, Sarah L., and Patti H. Clayton. "The Articulated Learning: An Approach to Guided Reflection and Assessment." *Innovative Higher Education* 29.2 (Winter 2004): 137–54. Web. 01 July 2012.

Braid, Bernice. "Honors Semesters: An Architecture of Active Learning." Braid and Long 19–27.

Braid, Bernice, and Ada Long, ed. *Place as Text: Approaches to Active Learning.* 2nd ed. Lincoln: National Collegiate Honors Council, 2010. NCHC Monograph Series. Web. 06 Dec. 2013.

Bristol, Michael D. *Shakespeare's America, America's Shakespeare.* New York: Routledge, 1990. Print.

Chaszar, Julianna K. "The Reinvention of Honors Programs in American Higher Education: 1955–1965." Diss. Pennsylvania State University Graduate School College of Education. University Park, PA: 2008. Web. 15 Dec. 2012.

Cooper, David D. "Reading, Writing, and Reflection." *New Directions for Teaching and Learning* 73 (Spring 1998): 47–56. Web 20 June 2012.

Daniel, William W. "Honors Semesters: An Anatomy of Active Learning." Braid and Long 7–13.

Dewey, John. *Art as Experience*. New York: Penguin/Putnam, Inc. 1934. Print.

—. *How We Think*. Boston: D. C. Heath and Company, 1910. Print.

Frey, Charles H. *Experiencing Shakespeare: Essays on Text, Classroom, and Performance*. Columbia: University of Missouri Press, 1988. Print.

Guzy, Annmarie. *Honors Composition: Historical Perspectives and Contemporary Practices*. Lincoln: National Collegiate Honors Council, 2003. NCHC Monograph Series. Print.

Kant, Immanuel. *Critique of Judgment*. Trans. James Creed Meredith. Oxford: The Clarendon Press, 1952. Print.

Keats, John. *Selections from Keats's Letters* ["On Negative Capability: Letter to George and Tom Keats, 21, ?27 December 1817"]. Poetry Foundation. n.d. Web. 24 Jan. 2014.

Keats' Kingdom. "Negative Capability." 2004–17. Web. 22 Aug. 2017.

Knudson, Kevin. "Honors Should Mean A Challenge, Not An Upgrade To First Class." *Chronicle of Higher Education*. Commentary. 11 July 2013. n. pag. Web. 13 July 2013.

Miller, Naomi J., ed. *Reimagining Shakespeare for Children and Young Adults*. New York: Routledge, 2003. Print.

Ravitch, Diane. "Education and Democracy." *Making Good Citizens: Education and Civil Society*. Ed. Diane Ravitch and Joseph P. Viteritti. New Haven: Yale University Press, 2001. Print.

Rinn, Anne. "Major Forerunners to Honors Education at the Collegiate Level." *Journal of the National Collegiate Honors Council-Online Archive* (Fall/Winter 2006): 63–84. Web. 03 Jan. 2014.

Schön, Donald A. *The Reflective Practitioner: How Professionals Think in Action*. New York: Basic Books, 1983.

Snyder, Eldon. "The Chautauqua Movement in Popular Culture: A Sociological Analysis." *Journal of American Culture* 8.3 (1985): 79–90. Print.

"Study Documents the Resegregation of Denver Public Schools." *The Term Paper* 5.1 (2006): 1–11. Denver, CO: The Piton Foundation. Web. 24 Jan. 2014.

Weiskel, Thomas. *The Romantic Sublime: Studies in the Structure and Psychology of Transcendence.* Baltimore: Johns Hopkins University Press, 1976.

"Welcome to DPS Shakespeare Festival." Denver Public Schools 2017. Web. 22 Aug. 2017.

"What Was Chautauqua?" *Traveling Literature: Circuit Chautauqua in the Twentieth-Century.* The University of Iowa Libraries: Special Collections and University Archives. n. d. Web 20 Apr. 2013.

Occupying Native America

Lisa L. Coleman, Rachel Childers, Samantha Faudree,
and Jake Martin
Southeastern Oklahoma State University

We gather up these strands broken from the web of life.
They shiver with our love, as we call them the names of
our relatives and carry them to our home made of the four
directions. . . .
>—Joy Harjo, "Reconciliation: A Prayer," (xvi, 4.1–3)
>*The Woman Who Fell from the Sky: Poems*

The interpenetration of place and time is a marker of
Oklahoma culture, one that can probably be traced to the
influence of Native American philosophies.
>—Jeanetta Calhoun Mish, *Oklahomeland* (28)

WHAT IS NATIVE AMERICA?

Philosopher, cultural analyst, and early founder of the field of
sociology, Georg Simmel (1858–1918), is fundamentally concerned with the interaction between people and their places.[1] In
this interaction, he notes, a relationship is formed (*Simmel on
Culture* 142–43). As Jeanetta Calhoun Mish presciently cautions

in *Oklahomeland*, however, "Relationships are rarely uncompli-
cated" (60). This chapter, "Occupying Native America," speaks of
the relationship between people and their places and the challenge
involved when we desire to learn not just *about* Native cultures but
from them and the places they have historically occupied. Yet, as my
student co-authors, Rachel Childers, Samantha Faudree, and Jake
Martin, and I discovered, by following the City as Text™ approach
to experiential learning in walkabouts in our own state as well as in
Chicago, Illinois, and even in Ireland, Wales, and London, England,
we were able to cultivate relationships between us and the places we
visited that helped shed light on the abstract concepts of diversity,
equity, and inclusion and the importance of cultural education.[2] We
also became aware of the engaged thinking and rethinking such
education requires in understanding these concepts as goals.[3]

Further, despite the historically rural location of the city of
Durant that has been home to Southeastern Oklahoma State
University (SE) for over 100 years, we were also able to draw conclusions on the value of developing a cosmopolitan perspective and
attitude toward learning about the culture of Durant in particular
and Native America in general that is at the same time *global* and
yet *rooted* in the places one calls "one's own."[4]

In fact, one of the most counterintuitive conclusions of our
research is that the Choctaw and Chickasaw tribes on whom the
course is focused, members of what came to be called the five civilized tribes (Choctaw, Chickasaw, Cherokee, Seminole, and Creek
[or Muscogee]), presented what we think of today as a cosmopolitan perspective and attitude, even in first contact with European
explorers.[5] As each of us will explain, to develop our hypotheses
and conclusions, we draw on the words of Native thinkers from
many tribes, inside and outside Oklahoma, as well as upon a number of non-Native philosophers, thinkers, writers, and theorists
whose work we put in conversation with one another here, a conversation we see as one among equals.

This chapter thus chronicles the development and implementation of my course "Native America: What Does It Mean to Live,
Learn, and Work Here?" It is the first honors course in the history

of the modern iteration of the Honors Program at SE to address Native America, even in the face of the fact that 30% of the student body as well as 30% of the approximately 120 honors program students claim a Native American ethnic identity.

To explain the long overdue development of such a course requires that I begin by backing up to see Native America from the widest possible vantage point; thus I suggest that to see Native America as it deserves to be seen is analogous to the view of the Earth from space. Only this view and the alteration in perspective it provides properly situate our university, our state, and our country in relation to our Native populations. [6] In particular, this chapter will highlight the resistance of this country and its people—including me and my students—to telling, hearing, and understanding the stories of Native America and its inhabitants. To that end, each of us will also speak in varying measures about our own relationships with Native America, the material of the course, and the fact that resistance to the course and its contents was palpable on the part of teacher and students the first time the course was taught in spring 2015 and, perhaps to lesser degrees in spring 2016, during the second iteration of the class.

"Native America" is a slogan for the state of Oklahoma and the tag line on the citizens' license plates.[7] The history of the place, Native America, however, is a long one that begins before the first Europeans arrived here and ostensibly includes North and South America; moreover this story is only now being told by the Natives of this country in their own time and in their own words.[8] As my student co-authors and other student contributors will explain, what they took from and contributed to the course was affected and effected by the history lessons they had previously learned in school, by their own Native ancestry or lack thereof, and by the content of the course. The course included a number of assigned readings as well as walkabouts in the city of Durant, Oklahoma; an interview with a professional in the city; a walkabout in the Choctaw Casino and Resort in Durant; and a field trip, tour, and, most tellingly and described here, a walkabout in the Chickasaw Cultural Center in Sulphur, OK, a little more than an hour's bus ride away.

We draw our conclusions about what it means to occupy Native America by looking locally and focusing on the Choctaws and Chickasaws, currently the largest tribes in Oklahoma in and near Durant, where the Choctaws keep their tribal headquarters.[9] The tribes have been historically intertwined, and, in pre-historic times, the two tribes are believed to have been one.[10] As Arrell M. Gibson explains in *The Chickasaws* (1972), Blue Clark chronicles in *Indian Tribes of Oklahoma: A Guide* (2009), and Rennard Strickland relates in *The Indians in Oklahoma* (1980), various groups of Indians have occupied Oklahoma for a very long period, perhaps as long as "30,000 years" (Clark 3). But the large populations of Choctaw and Chickasaw Indians who currently occupy central and southeastern portions of the state were not its original inhabitants.

The Choctaws and Chickasaws arrived prior to statehood, when Oklahoma was already called Indian Territory and occupied by other Indian tribes. The Choctaws were the first of the civilized tribes to be removed from their homes in the east, primarily Mississippi, and brought to Indian Territory over a period of four years as the result of the 1830 Treaty of Dancing Rabbit Creek (Clark 113). The Chickasaws were the last civilized tribe to be removed and, "through the Treaty of Doaksville in 1837 . . . agreed to settle amid the Choctaws in Indian Territory and to pay $530,000 to the Choctaws for a portion of the new land" (Clark 99). By virtue of being removed last, the journey to Indian Territory for the Chickasaws was somewhat better planned with less loss of life, but their safety was in question because the land they occupied west of the Choctaws was subject to raids by "bands of Kickapoos and Shawnees" as well as "fierce Kiowas and Comanches" (Gibson 191).

MAKING DIVERSITY A LOCAL AND GLOBAL HAPPENING IN NATIVE AMERICA

This chapter is the result of a long intellectual and physical journey taken by me and my students over the course of several years, beginning in 2013 when I wrote a faculty development grant to attend the National Collegiate Honors Council (NCHC) Institute,

"The *New* Old England: Manor, Market, and Mosque," which took place during the summer of 2014. As the institute's title suggests, its goal was to study how the inhabitants of the United Kingdom (UK), whether calling themselves British, English, or immigrants to that country, are changing the face of the nation in terms of age, religion, and ethnicity. In addition to the tiny village of Harlaxton, in Lincolnshire, England, where the manor in which we stayed was located, institute participants also visited three other locations: nearby market town, Grantham, birthplace of Margaret Thatcher and home to The King's School, attended by Isaac Newton; the market town Melton Mowbray, inhabited by an aging white population (based on observations from my one-time visit); and the much larger and multicultural city of Peterborough, which housed a mosque and required a train ride and a rather long walk to reach. The manor in question, an eighteenth-century estate called The Gregory, which served as our home base, was built as a Jacobethan manor (mix of Jacobean and Elizabethan styles), by Gregory Gregory. Each of these locations served as places where we were trained in the Place/City as Text™ (PAT or CAT) teaching methodology; the institute was designed to provide such experiences as well as teach the participants how to devise a Place/City as Text experience for their students or colleagues. The PAT or CAT experience asks that participants read and study about a place or city to get a sense of what it is about, then go out into the field in teams and become ethnographers, observing, mapping. listening, and reflecting on the experience by writing papers about their walkabouts in conjunction with their readings, their note taking, and numerous group conversations.[11]

While several of the Institute attendees were professors who had plans to take honors students on international trips, for my purposes at the time, the Institute would help me determine how to create a PAT or CAT course for the first-year experience in the SE Honors Program. Like many honors programs nationally and internationally, the SE Honors Program curriculum had for years been tied to general education classes, a curricular plan no longer feasible due to the large numbers of students who had already taken or placed out of their basic core requirements. The PAT/CAT curriculum promised a welcome alternative that could inform the three-hour honors humanities course that the honors program requires for first-year students during their spring semester.

After the Institute, I determined that the only way I could create a Place as Text experience for my students would be by attending to where we live, learn, and work—Native America. My experience visiting the towns and places that made England both "old" and "new" made it increasingly clear to me that I had to occupy the space we dwelled in and learned from, the city of Durant, Oklahoma, and the greater community around Durant for the sites of our City/Place as Text studies. I made this decision not so much because I wanted to, because for a number of reasons that I will explore below I did not, but, in the end, because of monetary and logistical constraints, I decided we had to do so in order to justify the Place as Text-style first-year course and do justice to everyone who would be taking part in it, including me. By doing justice, I mean that in addition to describing the course and its contents, which we do below, we also have to describe the context, the place, in which the course came to be. This description of our place was required to be just to the land in which many of my students were born as well as do justice to the ongoing cultural education of each of us, before, during, and after the class (see Faudree, Childers, and Martin below).

Situated in Durant, Oklahoma, a small town with a population of approximately 16,000, SE, which began as a normal school for teachers, has an undergraduate student population of approximately 3,500. When I first arrived at SE, from Arlington, Texas, in 1994, Larry Williams, then president of the university, often referred to Durant and its environs as "Little Dixie;" a statue commemorating a Confederate soldier is on the courthouse lawn. The legacy of the South historically extended to the Native population as well; both the Chickasaw and Choctaw tribes owned slaves before the Civil War and fought in that war on the side of the Confederacy.

Study of the town and inhabitants of Durant was key to our course, as was the Choctaw Casino Resort in Durant, which began as Choctaw Bingo over twenty years ago and is now the largest employer in southeastern Oklahoma. In my estimation and in that of my students, the Chickasaw Cultural Center proved to be one of the most influential institutions in the area in terms of sharing stories of Chickasaw Indian heritage and culture and providing a learning experience in which all visitors are asked to participate.

This story of the "Native America" class we tell here and its effect on teacher and students alike developed out of two iterations of the course. My co-authors, Faudree, Childers, and Martin, were part of the first iteration in spring 2015. They also took the class that preceded it, a required honors "College Success" course that contained a Place as Text feature as well. In that course the students first practiced their observing, mapping, listening, and reflecting skills on the SE campus in the fall before venturing further afield during the spring semester's "Native America" class into the city of Durant and the greater Oklahoma community. While these two courses ultimately became the SE Honors Program's first-year experience, the process, as I have noted, was not without its resistances and reservations.

"OCCUPATIONAL" CHALLENGES MITIGATED BY OUR RELATIONSHIP TO "WORLD"

I was leery of undertaking this course for a number of reasons, including being unprepared to take on the subject matter of a course with "Native America" in its title. As a college professor from Texas, with a PhD in rhetoric/composition and critical theory, who wrote a dissertation linking the writer Virginia Woolf to rhetoric and composition studies, I resisted this subject matter because in 2014, despite teaching in Oklahoma for twenty years, I had little knowledge of the state or of its Native cultures. While I had enthusiastically attended and moderated sessions at the Native American Symposium, held on our campus annually from 1996–97 and biennially from 1999 forward, and, perhaps even more importantly, had married an Oklahoma man in 2000, who identifies as Native American but claims Choctaw, Chickasaw, and Caucasian ancestry,

I was by no means a scholar on the subject.[12] To mitigate these facts, I did not ascribe to the course a Native American designation but rather focused in on *Native America* as a place to which each of my students and myself had a certain *relationship*, as Simmel notes (Embrée et al. 641; emphasis added).[13]

The course was thus designed to help each of us figure out what our particular relationship was to the place where we either lived, learned, or worked and why we had it. It was also designed to help us take note of and try to understand both our predilections for this place as well as our aversions, even what Thomas Rickert calls, in *Ambient Rhetoric: The Attunements of Rhetorical Being* (2013), our "attunement." Tracing one history of attunement to place, Rickert goes all the way back to the early peoples who interacted with prehistoric caves discovered in Lascaux, France, and the newly recognized ambient nature of those caves. This discovery has sparked scientific and aesthetic interest in the means through which ancient cave artists paired and attuned their art with the various sound qualities enabled by the composition of the caves themselves (3–6). In a similar fashion, I wanted to explore our attunement to the place Native America and the attunement of Native America to us.

In addition to engaging prehistoric cultures and the Greeks and Romans in his history of ambience and attunement, Rickert also draws on the work of German philosopher, Martin Heidegger (9), a modern thinker with a postmodern philosophy that works to account for what the philosophies of Plato and Aristotle forgot about "the Question of Being" (Heidegger, *Being and Time* 21).[14] For Heidegger, attunement to world involves practicing a state of mind that is open and receptive and that lets the world come to us or appear (or sound) in its own way rather than across our *a priori* expectations. Rickert describes this relationship: "we can glimpse here an idea of a fundamental reciprocity between world and person, one that suggests that the subject/object dichotomy characteristic of modern thought has not always held such sway" (6–7). The Native perspective of a modern writer like Linda Hogan speaks similar words on the relationship between world and person in *Dwellings: A Spiritual History of the Living World* (1995).

Although my students did not study Heidegger or Hogan *per se*, in the "Native America" class, Heidegger's philosophy of teaching, described in *What is Called Thinking?* as "to let learn" (15), underscores my approach (see Coleman, "Psyche as Text" 215–19).[15] For her part, Hogan, whose book title also speaks of dwelling and relationship, works, as does Rickert, to put aboriginal ways of knowing and being into conversation with "Western traditions of consciousness" that derive from them (51).

Indeed, the very title of this chapter, "Occupying Native America," follows from Heidegger's "Building Dwelling Thinking," wherein he "calls into," or phenomenologically explores, each word of his title (145–46); it is also the result of Hogan's reflections in *Dwellings* on her "exploration of the human place within this world" (12). While the original impetus of the *Occupy Honors Education* monograph was the Occupy Movement of 2011 and the pay and resources inequity promulgated by Wall Street and the 1%, in the time that has passed since the initial call for papers in 2012 by the editors of this monograph, my relationship with the words "occupy" and "occupying" has deepened and broadened.

In addition to my interest in the activist side of the word "occupy," with the suggestion of resistance to the powers that be and the taking over of a place that the Occupy Movement implies (writ large in 2016–17 by the Standing Rock movement), I also wanted to think about occupying from a phenomenological or relational perspective, as being taken over by something, taken in by something, concerned with it.[16] In the same fashion, just as Hogan is concerned with "the world . . . as seen by native people" and "the world . . . as seen by those who are new and young on this continent" (11), so is this chapter concerned with the possible meaning of the words "Native America" as well as with resistance to those meanings.

While the word "resistance" does not appear in our chapter title *per se*, resistance is a force that runs throughout Native studies. As psychical denial, resistance can be felt as an undercurrent in the way in which our ongoing occupation of Native America takes place because white Americans have yet to come to terms with the treatment of the Native populations of this country. Of course, resistance also makes itself apparent as a tool in political activism. Finally, resistance makes itself felt as part and parcel of the learning experience itself.

EARTH, SKY, DIVINITIES, AND MORTALS:
CREATING A CONTEXT FOR NATIVE AMERICA

When I was choosing texts for my course, I looked to ones that would narrow our focus and inspire us to learn. I wanted the texts to inspire and clarify some preliminary responses to the question the course sub-title asks: "What Does It Mean to Live, Learn, and Work Here?" This subtitle resonates with connections to Rickert's *Ambient Rhetoric,* Heidegger's "Building Dwelling Thinking," and Hogan's *Dwellings.* Rickert's book, informed by and taking issue in some measure with Heidegger, investigates the way in which human beings, called "Dasein" by Heidegger and translated as "being there" (Heidegger, *Being and Time* 27), are by their very nature, first and foremost, dwellers who necessarily dwell in world. World, then, is not separate from humans but always already surrounds humans as the place in which they find themselves—their dwelling. World is not a backdrop against which human beings move; rather, to be human is to be "situated in a world" (Rickert, *Ambient* 13).

For example, in "Building Dwelling Thinking," Heidegger describes the relationship of a bridge with the land it sits on, the bank that opposes it, the water it spans, and the human beings who pass over it. Heidegger uses the bridge, *as thing,* to set up the importance and value of human beings' relationship to things, to show how things and human beings create their places and *thus their world,* and to demonstrate how humans dwell with things, thereby conditioning those places. For Heidegger, a thing means a "gathering or assembly" ("Building" 153); thus, "The bridge *gathers* to itself *in its own* way earth and sky, divinities and mortals" (153, his emphasis). This "gathering" Heidegger calls "the four fold" (153).[17]

Heidegger's work, which in large measure obviates the subject/object dichotomy of Western thought since Descartes, has much in common with Native approaches to "world." The example mentioned earlier of backing up to look at our world as the moon does is instructive here. "Building Dwelling Thinking" converses brilliantly with Hogan's *Dwellings* and with the idea of Native America as a space that becomes a place á la Bernice Braid, the creator of City as Text, (Foreword 9) because of the relationship between that space and the human beings who dwell there:

> Participants [in PAT] are invited to see themselves as explorers—that is, to move and to simultaneously watch themselves moving through uncharted territory. The mapping they undertake is, therefore, of a space, of themselves moving through that space, of themselves transforming that space into a place that has taken on the tangible familiarity of what they, the mappers, have measured by their alert movement through it. (Braid, "Honors Semesters" 19)

Braid's words also illustrate what the students' walkabouts may make possible for them—a way of seeing and experiencing a familiar place as they never saw it before or a way of coming closer to the roots of a new place than a more superficial walk through could provide.

While my concentration on the local was resonating strongly with my choice of walkabout locations and my early vision for the class, I also wanted the students to be able to see themselves and their state in a global context—that took some doing and resulted in an international trip I did not foresee as possible when I first devised the course. As I co-edited the *Occupy Honors Education* monograph and read the chapter submissions of Basu and Brown and Cope, I was reminded of my interest in Immmanuel Kant and his work on cosmopolitanism. Thus I included the study of cosmopolitanism in the course with readings from Kant, Kwame Anthony Appiah's *Cosmopolitanism: Ethics in a World of Strangers,* and Martha Nussbaum's *For Love of Country?*, a text that contains an essay by Appiah, "Cosmopolitan Patriots," in which Appiah describes his notion of "rooted cosmopolitanism" (22), a state of being he learned from his African father and his white, British mother. For Appiah, a rooted cosmopolitan is one who is a citizen of both his or her hometown "with its own cultural particularities" (22) and the world as a whole.

With this context of the local and the global in mind and the caveat so important to Basu's work that there is no real separation between the two (138), for the second iteration of the class in 2016, I added two texts that would provide some local flavor, *Listening to our Grandmothers' Stories,* by Chickasaw and Oklahoma native Amanda J. Cobb [-Greetham], Director of Native American Studies at the University of Oklahoma, and *Oklahomeland* by Oklahoma native Jeannette Calhoun Mish. Both of these texts, like those of Appiah and Nussbaum, make apparent the lenses through which one looks at the world, a prime directive in the reflection portion of the PAT/CAT experience, but also model listening to the world differently (think of the caves of Lascaux, here). To that end I included as well Peggy McIntosh's "White Privilege: Unpacking the Invisible Knapsack," an excellent text that encourages readers to consider their perceptual and conceptual cultural assumptions.

In a further effort to develop awareness of our cultural biases, the classes read from Clifford Geertz's *Local Knowledge: Further Essays in Interpretive Anthropology* to investigate what he calls the "understanding of understanding" (5). An excerpt chosen from Kant's "Perpetual Peace" helped the class see the results of cultural assumptions and how hard it is to avoid then.[18] As Sam Faudree and Jake Martin note below, at the time of the discovery of Africa and what came to be called the Americas, the cultural lenses of the discoverers did not encourage them to see the humanity of those they discovered. To that end, we also study a review of George Steiner's *The Kingdom of Appearances,* the opening line of which is, "The eye is never naked" ("Books" 132). Our class assignments and conversation underscored the difficulty of negotiating the cultural binds to become attuned to our cultural biases; nevertheless, as time and a trip to Ireland, Wales, and London demonstrated to us, it is not impossible (see Faudree and Childers below).

Finally, after I had considered, read, and rejected many possible works of fiction to include on the syllabus, a Dirty Santa book exchange at a Sigma Tau Delta Christmas party in December 2014 put Harper Lee's *To Kill a Mockingbird* in my hands. I had seen the movie but never read the book, and I was newly amazed by the story and awed by the craft of the writer. But what really drew me to the narrative and the story it told was the frame it provided for my course. The unexpected lines on the first page are these: "If General Jackson hadn't run the Creeks up the creek, Simon Finch would never have paddled up the Alabama, and where would we be if he hadn't?" (Lee 3).[19]

CHICAGO AND BEYOND

I was able to incorporate travel and further underscore the cosmopolitan underpinnings of the class when three of my students from the first iteration of the course (my three co-writers) agreed to send a proposal to the Diversity Forum of the 2015 NCHC conference. Our proposal, titled "No Little Plans: Making Diversity a Local and Global Happening in Native America," was accepted, and we journeyed to the conference site in Chicago, where our panel was a roaring success. After Jake Martin delivered the final segment of our presentation, a paper he has enhanced for this monograph, people actually cheered.

To bring this experience full circle, Rachel Childers and Sam Faudree had earlier committed to the EF Tour to Ireland, Wales, and London I was co-sponsoring over spring break in 2016, thus creating the condition for the possibility that our occupation of Native America could lead to a global happening. The tour stopped in Bailic Park in Midleton, Ireland, County Cork, where "Kindred Spirits," a sculpture linking the Irish and the Choctaw people, had only just been installed. The sculpture, consisting of nine enormous yet delicate, stainless steel eagle feathers shaped around an empty space, commemorates the gift of $170 collected by a group of Choctaws in Scullyville, OK, and donated to the Irish people during the Great Potato Famine in 1847. Some sixteen years earlier, the Choctaws had undergone the Trail of Tears, and they strongly identified with their starving Irish counterparts. For sculptor Alex Pentek, his work represents "this great moment of compassion, strength, and unity" (Choctaw Nation).

As I have noted, I was unprepared in many ways for this course, one of which was the students' relationship to our topics and their very real and visceral engagement with Native America. My co-authors present three different perspectives and emotional responses to the experience of taking the class and attending the NCHC conference in Chicago. Sam Faudree and Rachel Childers will also comment on our tour to Ireland, Wales, and London.

CULTURAL EDUCATION

Samantha Faudree

Education affects every part of our lives. It is what gives us sight of the world and how we interact within it. Education should be available to everybody, but sometimes what we get is not exactly what we need. In several cases, education has been used as a weapon to undermine someone's heritage and way of life. According to Bryan H. Wildenthal, the Indian tribes of North America were faced with this problem when Europeans tried making them civilized. The Europeans considered themselves superior to the Indians, and the majority of them had no desire to learn and educate themselves about the Indian's culture and knowledge. Only after we open our minds, however, to accept others as they are and learn about their way of life will we truly become educated. Embracing cosmopolitanism provides insight into and understanding of the people around us so that we are not blinded by our own judgments and culture.

When Europeans first encountered Native Americans, the Europeans believed them to be uncivilized. The Native Americans spoke a different language, ate different foods, worshipped differently, and lacked the common household structure to which the Europeans were accustomed. As Wildenthal explains, the Europeans could not begin to understand how another group of people could live in such a way, and the thing is, the Europeans did not even try to understand. Over time, many conflicts arose between these two groups, but it is easy to see why. What was the solution to these conflicts? Education. The Europeans believed that giving the Native Americans a proper education would help them assimilate into white culture. The attempt by Europeans to understand the Native Americans amounted to fashioning them into something similar to what they already knew. The education that they received was clearly flawed. The Native Americans were forbidden to speak their own language while at these schools (Wildenthal 26). Fearful of the threats that were made if they did speak it, some gave it up completely. Because of this "education," many Native American languages face extinction today.

Europeans discovered the Americas by accident. Once discovered, however, there was a great demand as well as desire to explore and conquer this new land. Before that, Europeans did not know that the Americas existed or that people inhabited them. Everything these explorers encountered was new to them and for the taking. As Immanuel Kant noted, "America, the negro [sic] countries, the Spice Islands, the Cape, etc. were looked upon at the time of their discovery as ownerless territories; for the native inhabitants were counted as nothing" (106). This attitude occurs many times throughout history. Native Americans, tribes in Africa, and various other groups around the world have been treated with such cruelty to the point that they are not even recognized as people anymore. That this behavior and way of thinking gets passed down to future generations has caused problems we still face today.

Education is not just what students learn in schools. Education also includes the beliefs and ideals that are passed down from generation to generation. It is not uncommon for children to hold the same beliefs that their parents do. This practice contributes to the racism we are still facing today even though it has been many years since equality laws have been passed. People are sometimes unwilling to see things from a different perspective, or they simply do not know how to do so. Education can be the solution to broadening our perception of others; however, a problem occurs because of the quality and type of education different people are receiving. Elaine Scarry writes: "The way we act towards 'others' is shaped by the way we imagine them" (98). How we see people is not the way they actually are but rather how we expect them to be. More often than not, people will take other people or things at face value rather than dig deeper and discover their true worth for themselves. "The eye is never naked," suggests a reviewer of George Steiner's *The Kingdom of Appearances* ("Books" 132). Although we see many things going on around us in the world, we are typically blind to the reality and depth of those things until they directly affect us.

Education is also gained from experience. One of the best ways to learn about the world is for students to go out in it and see it for themselves. Living in Native America, our class already had our perceptions and knowledge of the area. Traveling outside this area of the country revealed that such knowledge is not universal. Visiting Chicago, a city not known for its Native culture but rather for its sports teams—the Blackhawks, the Cubs, and the Bears—provides a different experience in regards to how Native American culture was represented. Native Americans did not visibly seem to populate that area; thus the general population only gained their perspective based on the media and what, if anything, was taught to them in school. Most of the world's knowledge of Native Americans hearkens back to Christopher Columbus and other European explorers' accounts of them. Thus, we get the happy story of Thanksgiving in memory of all the kind and generous things the Natives and the Europeans did for each other.

When our travels continued to Ireland, we wanted to see a sculpture created by one of the locals to commemorate the generous donation made by the Choctaw tribe to Ireland during its tragic potato famine. On March 23, 1847, the Choctaws gathered money from each family of the tribe, and altogether they raised $170 to support a starving country in need of help an ocean away. The Choctaws were all too familiar with these circumstances because they had just made the 500-mile trek known as "The Trail of Tears." The Native Americans were able to relate to these complete strangers and help them in a time of need. The Irish never forgot after all those years.

More often than not, most people base their opinions and knowledge on what they are exposed to and see. Learning about Native American history and seeing not just how it has impacted this area but also the rest of our country and the world is great. But seeing places with my own eyes and consciously experiencing the town I live in, Chicago, or even Ireland, revealed how these places are different but also how they are alike.

Education is an important factor in advancing the state of our world, but in the past it has been used as a way to take away precious characteristics that make a person or culture unique. Today, Native American tribes are desperately trying to hold on to the remnants of their original culture that they were once forced to leave behind. How we are raised has an impact on how we view and interact with the world. Once we educate ourselves about other cultures and peoples and realize that we do not need to change everyone to be the same as us, we can then begin to understand ourselves and others and where we fit in in this world.

COSMOPOLITANISM:
THE INDIVIDUAL AND THE COMMUNITY

Rachel Childers

Almost an entire year has passed since I was enrolled in Dr. Coleman's class "Native America." Thus, I have had plenty of time to reflect on the class as a whole now that I find myself outside of it. It is often difficult for students to pinpoint the theme of a class when they are being required to do papers for it. That alone tends to cloud their judgment. Setting the workload aside, so far aside that I never have to think about it again, I can address what the class taught me and what it did for my experience within the SE Honors Program. The first components that I would like to address are the lessons learned. I thought I knew them when I finished the class. That was not the case. I thought I understood when I had finished my time in Chicago. I was wrong once again. (For an honors student I spend a majority of time in the wrong I have discovered.) My new version of right, which I believe is more complete, has only come to me after contemplating my experience in Ireland, Wales, and England.

In Dr. Coleman's class, the name of the game is cosmopolitanism. Cosmopolitanism in general is a hard concept when one's experience is based on a small area like Southeastern Oklahoma. Especially if that area is in the rural south, which has never been known for its all-inclusive nature. The quest becomes even harder when other members of the class itself are added to the mix. For the most part, the class was comprised of locals. If not locals, they were Oklahomans, and if they were not Oklahomans, then they were Derek from Arkansas. Understanding the main point of the class with that group of students and this location was rough going. We had come to accept the parts of Native America we saw as everyday life and did not see how cosmopolitanism came into play. We struggled to look past the familiarity. Finding Native America in Oklahoma is like finding a piece of hay in a haystack. This situation made me assume cosmopolitanism was a community-driven idea, and it was the community's job to extend it.

The only way for me to comprehend how Oklahoma was impacted by the Native Americans was to travel outside of Oklahoma. The first journey was travelling to Chicago for the National Collegiate Honors Council conference. The difference in culture surrounding Native Americans was astounding, but Jake will touch on that further. What it showed me were the differences in who actually practiced cosmopolitanism. In the area where we stayed, Chicago was accepting; its accepting nature, however, seemed to be extended in correlation to a person's educational level. It challenged my idea that a community extended cosmopolitanism by calling into question the nature of the community itself. Those attending the NCHC conference were one community, and those who were not on their level were perceived as other.

The answers finally came to me when my travels took me to another continent. We were not in Chicago anymore. We were in a small town in Ireland, in the mom-and-pop ice cream shop that had been around since the eighties. Everyone who walked through the door was welcomed with open arms. Then, we were in the streets of London. Busy and chaotic, the welcoming nature changed from person to person. At that moment I realized that it was not the community that practiced cosmopolitanism but the individual. And I believe that is what Dr. Coleman was trying to tell us all along.

The direct impact of the class within honors furthered this idea. At the end, the class simply created a community by means of the individual's perceptions. It raised awareness of surroundings. The class created a common ground among the honors students. Each one of us had to form our own understanding of what cosmopolitanism was and extend it to another. Forming those perceptions created a level of knowledge in which communication could happen. It created colleagues and established a freshman honors class of students who were close and familiar with each other beyond what past systems in the program achieved. And it finally answered how cosmopolitanism worked, even if it took a year of reflection. The individual informed cosmopolitanism, and it, in turn, created the community.

WHAT DO YOU THINK OF WHEN YOU HEAR THE TERM "NATIVE AMERICAN"?

Jake Martin

Being a part of an Indian Nation, a citizen of Oklahoma, and an opinionated, relatively intelligent college student, I have my own personal view on Native Americans. I live in a community with a considerable Native population, have good friends who are Native, and have learned the ins-and-outs of the sophisticated, sovereign Indian Nations and the cultures that they are attempting to preserve through a class taught by Professor Chris Wesberry (then Director of the Native American Institute at SE), and the City as Text curriculum taught in Dr. Coleman's "Native America" course I was a part of during my freshman year.

With that background, I feel I am moderately qualified to discuss the disgusting, disrespectful tragedy that is the blatant misrepresentation and disrespect of Native Americans in mainstream American culture.

I will start with two questions. What do you think of when you hear the term "Native American"? Do you think of an irrelevant, extinct race of people that was eradicated after European arrival on their homeland? Perhaps you picture people with tan skin and broad facial features adorned in leathers, turquoise jewelry, and feathers in their long, braided hair and possessing a name such as "Soaring Eagle" or "Running Bear," people who are part of a novelty culture and living on a reservation. Or perhaps, more realistically, you do not think of anything at all, for you were never taught anything worth knowing about the tens of millions of indigenous people who inhabited the landmass of the Western hemisphere of the earth tens of thousands of years before Europeans arrived.

Sure, you know the fairytale of the first Thanksgiving, in which the Natives were instrumental in teaching the clueless English pilgrims how to properly plant and harvest corn and were repaid with devastating disease and westward expansion, but that is usually all that is provided by the American public education system concerning Native Americans. Most people remain clueless about the full extent of the plight brought to the Natives by European arrival. Utter genocide, forced boarding schools that attempted to eradicate their traditional languages and culture, exploitation, and a withholding of the right to citizenship until 1924 or 1956, depending on your perception, are historical facts you rarely hear about, especially in a classroom.

I find this gap interesting. In the turbulent American society we live in, rife with social unrest and racial tensions, most people have never mentioned Natives or even thought of them. With movements like Black Lives Matter and the unrest surrounding the deaths of Michael Brown and Trayvon Martin, American focus on police and government oppression of minorities has rarely been stronger, and it should be, for there is no excuse for racial profiling by Americans in positions of authority. But, interestingly enough, with all of this focus on race and political correctness, little attention is given to the countless sports teams, businesses, and schools using some of the most undeniably racist, offensive Native American imagery imaginable to represent themselves.

Teams like the Washington Redskins and the Savages, the mascot of my own high school, Broken Bow High School in Broken

Bow, Oklahoma, continue to carry on. Think of that. The Red-skins, featuring a logo of a dark-skinned Indian with feathers in his hair and fans that literally paint themselves brown and wear headdresses. The Cleveland Indians' mascot is nothing more than a blatantly racist cartoon Native. Nonetheless, examples like these persist. How long would a mascot of the Blackskins or the Brown-skins with similarly racist imagery last? It would be gone before anyone could bat an eye at it. Why? Because people can relate to African Americans, Mexican Americans, and other minorities and understand the racism and oppression they have received because they are taught about it and see examples constantly.

Some people are never given the opportunity to see or meet an actual Native American, so Indians are simply swept under the rug as some sort of mystical, extinct people, when they are very much still around and have experienced just as much and arguably more racism and mistreatment due to race and culture. Everyone knows when the Emancipation Proclamation occurred, but do they know when Natives gained their independence? Of course not. Why would we? They are all extinct, right?

If they are not extinct, they probably still live in tepees and hunt buffalo to survive, right? Native Americans have become the cruel butt of a joke in American society, simple imagery to form sports clubs around, or names to call military vehicles. The people who inhabited this land long before anyone else have had their numbers drastically reduced through disease and genocide, but they are still very much around and enjoying monumental economic success through their business ventures like casinos and legal marijuana growth. Nonetheless, American culture and perception reduce them to savages and demi-humans.

The city of Chicago has even provided me with a brilliant exam-ple of this. On the Chicago River, prominently displayed, there is a stone carving of European explorer, Robert de la Salle. This carv-ing places "fearless explorer" La Salle, who was the first European to travel through Illinois, in the very center in a godly stance, with an angel directly above his head, a monk grasping his arm, and nearly naked Natives literally bowing at his feet as if he were some sort of demi-god. Of course, they are nearly naked in an attempt to dehumanize them and make the superior whiteness of La Salle even more evident.

I understand that this carving was commissioned in the painfully racist decade of the 1920s and may be a part of the city's identity, but it is nearly a hundred years later, and if every other ethnicity is finally gaining the justice and respect that they deserve, it is time for Natives to receive the same treatment. Tear down the carvings, change the teams, and recognize Natives for who they are: a beautiful race with a beautiful culture that deserves to be preserved and cherished.

SHERMAN ALEXIE AND THE INVISIBLE INDIAN

While Martin's observations focus in particular on stereotypical and racist representations of Native cultures, he also notes that such representations render actual Natives and their accomplishments invisible to other Americans, including what is now the considerable economic wherewithal garnered by various tribes through casinos and other ongoing economic ventures.

Sherman Alexie, Jr., underscores Martin's points in an interview with Trevor Noah, host of *The Daily Show*, on May 9, 2016. Alexie, a Spokane and Coeur d'Alene Native and writer of novels, poetry, and short stories as well as a filmmaker, visited the show to tout *Thunderboy, Jr.*, a children's book aimed at explaining Alexie's own feelings when his father and namesake died. A discussion of naming and the "existential weight" (Alexie) of naming ensues, wherein Alexie corroborates the point Martin makes above that reducing any culture to a set of ethnic features renders a false and misleading representation. While a considerable amount of laughter is elicited by the remarks of Noah and Alexie, the underlying message is worth pondering. Excerpts from the interview include the following:

Noah—How do you feel about naming of things? For instance, the Redskins; that's a discussion I always see on TV and people on Twitter fighting about, and the honest truth is I've never actually seen Native Americans be part of the discussion.

Alexie—Well, we're never a part of the discussion about our lives, ever. We're colonized.

But the thing is, I know that "Redskins" is a racial slur because it's never been said in a positive way to me. I have never heard . . . "Hey, way to do well on your SAT, Redskin."

Noah—I know I . . . come from a different world [South Africa], but it seems to me . . . that Native Americans are just not part of the conversations or the discussions. . . . Where's the people of the place?

Alexie—Well, the strangest thing is that we're everywhere in pop culture. . . . I mean . . . don't turn the channel, but if you turned the channel right now, there's probably 17 channels with some Native American imagery going on. There's always something going on featuring this ancient idea of us, but nobody ever thinks of us in a contemporary sense, and we disappear as well. I mean I come to New York, and I become so ambiguously ethnic I get spoken to in 178 different languages. I mean, everybody thinks I'm half of whatever they are. (Alexie)

NARRATIVE AND THE IMPORTANCE OF CONTEXT (OR WORLD)

This interview between Noah and Alexie, with its discussion of identity and mistaken identity, and the essay-narratives by Faudree, Childers, and Martin, which reflect on identity, stereotypes, and cultural education, take us to the importance of storytelling and context (or World) best commented on by Kameron Dunn, a student from the 2016 spring semester. In his paper, "Water, Narrative, and Native America," Dunn speaks of the "importance of context . . . and the human experience as it pertains to narrative" (Dunn), but his paper also underscores my earlier point about the deficit model inherent in positivist, subject/object thinking and the fact that humans are dwellers, always already bound up with world.

Dunn's opening gambit is a quotation from the commencement speech David Foster Wallace delivered at Kenyon College in 2005: "the most obvious, important realities are often the ones that are hardest to see and talk about" (Wallace qtd. in Dunn). Dunn notes this line rings true "specifically in regards to Native American culture" and comments further, "Whether reading *To Kill a Mockingbird*, a section of Appiah's *Cosmopolitanism*, Cobb's *Listening to Our Grandmothers' Stories*, or hearing a personal story from Jeanette Calhoun Mish [in *Oklahomeland* and in her visit to SE], the truths we gleaned in this class came from others' narratives" (Dunn). Noting that "the source of narrative is important," Dunn references Cobb's interviews with Chickasaw women who had attended several iterations of the Chickasaw boarding school, Bloomfield Academy (Dunn). When Cobb states, for example, "'[t]he term "literacy" is complicated' [Cobb 12, qtd. in Dunn], she attaches the greater narrative of Chickasaw women to her own personal narrative [herself the granddaughter of a Bloomfield graduate] as a method of sharing history" (Dunn).

Dunn then retells the story Wallace relates in his speech on the difficulty of recognizing something that is always around us. As Dunn puts it, "The anecdote goes like this: A wise, old fish swims past two younger fish and says in passing to them, 'Hey there! How's the water?' A little later, one of the younger fish looks at his friend and says, 'What the hell is water?'" (Wallace qtd. in Dunn). Reiterating Dunn's point through Wallace, to tell the story of the history of Native populations in Oklahoma (and, I would add, in America, or even the Americas for that matter) is to be inundated by water, by moonlight, by the fourfold, by what is around us at all times, so much so that without this awareness we are oblivious to their influence or their import.

Our readings taught us that even before removal, the Choctaws and Chickasaws were "civilized"; they had adopted western clothes, been Christianized, and taught English by missionaries. Before and after removal, they valued education and created schools in their new land even before removal was completed (DeRosier 166). They prospered almost as soon as they arrived in Indian Territory, but westward expansion and the encroachment of the white European settlers did not abate. After the civil war, the Curtis Act gave the federal government the power to allot previously reserved lands to the Indians individually, anathema for a culture that had always held land in common (Gibson 304); the loss of many Indian properties ensued because of unscrupulous business dealings (Clark 14). Children were taken from the tribes and put in boarding schools (Clark 14; see also Cobb), and, upon statehood in 1907, all of what had been Indian Territory was "incorporated . . . into the state of Oklahoma" (Clark 15).

During the twentieth-century, Indians were declared United States citizens, and the Choctaw and Chickasaw tribes suffered "severe setbacks" because of "[tribal] termination policies" in the 1950s (Clark 15). Yet the tribes benefited from a resurgence in the activist 60s (Clark 16), realized "self-governance" with the Indian Self-Determination and Education Assistance Act in 1975 (Clark 16), and in the 90s, when I took my job at SE, created bingo games centers as revenue sources. In 2004, when gambling was approved by Oklahoma voters, the Choctaw and Chickasaw Indians became major players, landholders, and investors in the economic scene of Oklahoma and beyond.[20]

NARRATIVE AND PERSPECTIVE

The value of story and story telling, as Dunn notes above, and as Faudree, Childers, Martin, and Alexie demonstrate, is central to the telling of the history of Native cultures. This history is preserved in stories passed down through the generations. It is also imaged in Native art and traditional dance moves and made audible through songs and their accompaniment on drums and flutes, mounted deer toes, and tortoise shell (or aluminum can) shakers.

My students and I learned firsthand the value of oral story-telling when we traveled to the Chickasaw Cultural Center in Sulphur, Oklahoma, in both iterations of my "Native America" class. While numerous tribal histories have been written down as well, as Rennard Strickland notes in *The Indians of Oklahoma*, "white Oklahomans know little about the history and the life of the state's Indian citizens" (xiii). After our research, the writers of this chapter broaden Strickland's claim about white Oklahomans to posit that many of the state's Native citizens and, more broadly, Americans in general, know little of the history of the original cultures that inhabited all of America.

One of the reasons for this lack of knowledge of Indian culture, as my co-writers and other student contributors maintain, is that Indian ways of being, doing, knowing, and dwelling do not necessarily lend themselves to positivistic, post-enlightenment, dualistic, and Western-style analyses. This truth is put forward brilliantly by Simon J. Ortiz in "Song, Poetry, and Language—Expression and Perception." (Ortiz is discussed below.) Further, as Sherman Alexie notes in his interview with Trevor Noah, Indians today are not recognizable to others or even often to themselves. As Alexie proclaims. "We're colonized" (Alexie).

In the closing pages of his book, Strickland, of the Osage and Cherokee tribes, notes, "The story of the Indian is the literature of America. It is not trite to say that the Indian sings the songs of our forests, of our birds, of our souls. His world is our world. He is of America. And he is America" (120). Strickland also offers his readers a line from Thoreau, "The Indian has property in the moon" (qtd. in Strickland 120), indicating the close connection between Native cultures and the one planetary body that appears to change daily as it orbits our planet. As my students and I learned from our class texts, goods and land were held in common by the Choctaws and Chickasaws, and land ownership did not originally have a place in their culture, but their investment in nature and in the moon with its nightly and seasonal guidance was deep.

Thus, like Strickland, like Childers, I suggest once again that to gain insight into Native cultures and their relationship to Earth, one can surely benefit from an alternative perspective, a perspective garnered by the view from another state or another continent, or by literally and figuratively backing up to stand in a place from which few people have viewed the Earth, the place made possible

258

for humans by the United States' space program and evoked by the famous photograph called "Earthrise," originally taken by astronaut William A. Anders from *Apollo 8*, on December 24, 1968 (Zimmerman). This photograph, which pictures our blue and white planet hanging against the blackness of space, puts the inhabitants of this world into a new relation with the Earth that holds us up and with the planet that all the peoples of Earth, in their turn, hold in common. (For a more recent Earthrise image, see the cover of this monograph.)

In *Dwellings*, Chickasaw native, Linda Hogan, also comments on the view of the Earth from the moon, stating that pictures of the Earth taken from space were at first classified by the government: "It was thought, and rightfully so, that the image of our small blue planet would forever change how we see ourselves in context with the world we inhabit" (126–27).[21] Corroborating this unease described by Hogan, rhetorician and cultural theorist Thomas Rickert, notes in *Ambient Rhetoric* that, Heidegger, another philosopher of spaces and places, was "alarmed" by the *Apollo 8* pictures. For Heidegger, the pictures indicated "the uprooting of humans has already taken place. We only have purely technological relationships anymore" (Heidegger, *Heidegger Reader* 325; qtd. in Rickert, *Ambient*, Note 11, 306).

For his part, however, Rickert reads the "Earthrise" picture differently, in a way that resonates with the views expressed by Strickland above:

> This photographic image of the earth differs from all other images so much that it cradles and makes available to us a new sense of world and our belongingness to it. The earth is now an ecological world, including not just humans but animals, plants, stones, water, soil, clouds and more, *all of which need and are affected by one another* and are rendered unique and precarious against the dark depths. (215)

I would add that while it is challenging to do so, developing a planetary perspective of the Earth coincides with the insightful perspective of Kant. In the eighteenth century, he posited that the finite nature of our round planet means that we have to share this world with others. Kant's perspective shapes the beginning of what Brown and Cope describe as "cosmopolitan courtesy" (see 108 in this volume) and what Hogan describes as "a reciprocal and balanced exchange with life" (44), one like that practiced by Native cultures.

As Hogan further notes, those like the Spaniard Hernando de Soto, who colonized the Americas, had no planetary perspective and instead practiced a grave "disregard for life" (44). Even later in America's history, in the 1930s, Hogan tells us, when the Spiro burial mounds were discovered in Oklahoma, looters were denied their artifacts. In retaliation, they dynamited two of the mounds as if to spite the land and the people who came from it (44).

A similar story, one about de Soto's disregard for planetary humanity, was told by Jesse Lindsey, the Chickasaw Cultural Center storyteller, who invited all of us to dance with him. He told how the Chickasaws treated de Soto well upon first contact in December 1540. But when the Spaniards took advantage, war ensued, and many Spaniards were killed. For the next 150 years there was no European contact.

Matt Slaten, a student in the second iteration of the "Native America" class, underscores Lindsey's observation in his paper, "A Recent Trip to the Past," which describes our trip to the Center. Drawing on Gibson's *The Chickasaws*, Slaten notes the "cordial" nature of the early relations of the Indians with Hernando de Soto (Slaten). After repeatedly trying their patience, however, "The Spaniards soon found the warrior side of the Chickasaw Nation" (Slaten; see Gibson 31–32). Hogan describes this first contact in *Dwellings*:

> [the conquerors] were unable to receive the best gifts of land, not gold or pearls or ownership, but a welcome acceptance of what was offered. They did not understand that the earth is generous and that encounters with the land might have been sustaining, or that their meetings with other humans could have led to an enriched confluence of ways. (44)

Hogan continues:

> there are laws beyond our human laws, and ways above
> ours. We [speakers of English] have no words for this in our
> language, or even for our experience of being there [at one
> with earth]. Ours is a language of commerce and trade, of
> laws that can be bent in order that treaties might be broken,
> land wounded beyond healing. (45–46)

EXPRESSION AND PERCEPTION:
WHY NATIVE LANGUAGES MATTER

In "Song, Poetry, and Language—Expression and Perception,"
Ortiz, an Acoma Pueblo Indian, offers more on the difference
between his native language and that of English, explaining how
his knowledge and study of English caused him to believe language
could be broken apart. His father, an Acoma Pueblo elder, assures
him that in their language, *Aacqu*, each word is complete in itself.
It does not "break down into anything" (107). What this assurance
means is that while a language can be broken down linguistically,
that breaking down concerns the "expression" of the language
(Ortiz 107). Ortiz says his father is referring to the "experience" or
"perception" of language (109). Ortiz likens this "experience" to a
child singing a song and "the sensations he is feeling at the moment
with his body and mind" (109).

Ortiz also relates how his father sang songs to tell about a friend
he sang and danced with: "This old man used to like to sing, and
he danced like this" (117). By showing how the man danced and by
singing this song, Ortiz's father shared his relationship with the old
man as well as the good feeling the old man invoked in him. Ortiz
explains: "the song was the road from outside himself to inside—
which is perception—and from inside himself to outside—which
is expression. That's the process and the product of the song, the
experience and the vision that a song gives you" (118).

Like Ortiz, Hogan also ponders the importance of nature and
song for tribal and aboriginal cultures, as well as the value of myth

for all peoples. For Hogan, myth returns us to the beginning of creation and "allows us to hear the world new again" (51). Drawing on Octavio Paz to address the difference between current day English and tribal languages, she notes that Paz "has written that in older oral traditions an object and its name were not separated. One equaled the other. To speak of corn, for instance, was to place the corn before a person's very eyes and ears. It was in mythic time that there was no abyss between the word and the thing it named" (Hogan 51–52), but he (Paz) adds "'as soon as man acquired consciousness of himself, he broke away from the natural world and made himself another world inside himself'" (Hogan 51; Paz qtd. in Hogan 52).

Like Strickland and Rickert, Hogan observes: "there is a separation that has taken place between us and nature" (52). She also notes psychologist C. A. Meier, whose research suggests "as the wilderness has disappeared outside of us, it has gone to live inside the human mind[;] thus, the threat to life which once existed in the world around us has now moved within" (Hogan 52).

THE THINGS OF NATURE ARE ALREADY WORLD:
THE FOURFOLD

Perception, expression, and our relationship with nature are highlighted by Matt Slaten as well, who offers another perspective on our trip to the Chickasaw Cultural Center. Addressing a quotation from Picasso, "I do not seek I only find" ("Books" 132), Slaten, a young man who is already running his own landscaping business, recounts his experience on the trip:

> our eyes have lenses. These lenses are formed by social and cultural customs. I tried to take off my southern lenses and allow myself to find. The southern lenses are lenses that keep me from truly seeing the story of an amazing group of people because of prejudices or racism in general. (Slaten)

When he visits the Cultural Center in spring 2016, he endeavors to see the Chickasaws anew:

With these lenses off I glanced from one part of the campus to another: I began to think to myself how far the Chickasaw Nation has gone to reach this point. It's amazing that they have gone from a tribe . . . people were afraid of, to a tribe that people come to visit and learn about their culture. (Slaten)

In the introduction to his paper, he reiterates a point that Faudree, Childers, Martin, and Alexie make above: "Whether people realize it or not, regardless of what part of Oklahoma or surrounding areas they inhabit, they are directly or indirectly affected by Native American culture" (Slaten).

As a landscaper, Slaten has a keen awareness of nature; he is struck by the grounds of the Center and by the plants they have placed there:

As you walk through the campus, they made the landscaping supplement to the tone they were trying to set. They were trying to inspire people. They were trying to evoke thought. Each plant was strategically placed and paired with a complementary plant to tell a story, a story of a past landscape that we will never experience. (Slaten)

Slaten's horticultural expertise causes the plants on the campus to show up for him as "things" that condition the "tone" or ambience of the place and help to tell the Chickasaw story of earth, sky, divinities, and mortals, a story that predates the theories of Heidegger by millennia.

Slaten concludes by noting, the Center "gave me insight into my own life by looking into the past of others." He quotes a line from Peggy McIntosh's "White Privilege: Unpacking the Invisible Knapsack": "[W]hites are carefully taught not to recognize white privilege" and further allows that he did not really agree with McIntosh when he first read her piece, giving voice to resistance expressed by others. After going through the exhibits at the Center, however, he gains a heightened awareness of the lenses though which he was looking. Paraphrasing and adding to McIntosh's litany of benefits for whites, Slaten states: "I found that there is a benefit to being white. Whites were not judged and passed over for land. Whites received fair court trials. Whites were generally accepted among the local citizens."

OKLAHOMA AND NATIVE AMERICA, YESTERDAY AND TODAY

Oklahoma has been a state that the educated have often left, as Lt. Governor Todd Lamb intimated in his extemporaneous commencement address at SE on Saturday, May 7, 2016. He repeatedly asked the graduating students not to leave the state of Oklahoma upon graduation, taking their hard-won learning and intellectual abilities with them. Truly, as Jeanetta Calhoun Mish notes about her home state in *Oklahomeland*, "there exists in the state a long standing dismissal of intellectual work" (24). As Lamb also remarked, Oklahoma is a land that was originally occupied by Native populations, then by tribes who were removed there, and then by waves of settlers from various ethnic backgrounds who came for the promise of the land. Lamb concluded with pride and poignancy that Oklahoma "is a state unlike all the others."

In the early days of my teaching at SE, twenty-three years ago, one of my nontraditional students wrote a paper that contained the line "N---ers and Indians enter by the back door." I cannot remember the student's name, but I have never forgotten that line from her paper.

When I began writing about my past and my relationships with issues of Native American ethnicity, I failed early on to think of ways to integrate my interests in ethnic identity with my concomitant interests in feminism and Virginia Woolf. Similarly, one of my points of resistance to learning and teaching about Native America was my belief that I could not connect that theme to my other professional interests. And yet when I gave my students the article by Peggy McIntosh, she had laid out a blueprint for a connection: through her work in feminist studies and the idea that men do not understand the privilege that they hold in the world, she realized that neither do white people. A connection from feminism to Native studies was forged for me always already.

RECLAIMING RESISTANCE

Rickert claims that resistance is not necessarily a bad thing (*Acts* 151–59). He concludes in *Acts of Enjoyment* that if our students resist us and our teaching agendas or if we resist ourselves and what may or may not be a clear path to teaching something important, the very fact that resistance exists offers "hope" (*Acts* 159). (Remember the Chickasaws and the Choctaws.) The very fact that all people can and do resist the powers that be and their power networks means that change can happen (see F. Coleman in this volume, pp. 311–52). Resistance is of a piece with learning. We resist even as we learn and change. There is an all-at-onceness to this resistance and the concomitant learning that can arise from it, although, as Rachel Childers reflects, the time and space involved may be longer and greater than we anticipate. This resistance also means, as Rickert maintains, that the power networks in which we are all entangled are not total. We have a chance to make our way through them (*Acts* 159). As another SE student, Emilie Cox, notes below, cultures can join other cultures; people can see and hear and respond differently.

PERSPECTIVE, AGAIN

In "Culture Integration: The Good, the Bad, and How to Be Better," Cox, also from the second iteration of the "Native America" class," offers two quotations. After Arthur (Boo) Radley saves the Finch children from Bob Ewell's attack in *To Kill a Mockingbird*, Scout walks Arthur home, and seeing the view from his porch for the very first time, she recalls her father's words: "'you never really know a man until you stand in his shoes and walk around in them'" (Lee 374, qtd. in Cox). Cox then compares this quotation to one from Appiah that revises the Golden Rule: "'The idea behind the Golden Rule is that we should take other people's interests seriously, take them into account. We should learn about other people's situations, and then use our imaginations to walk a while in their moccasins'" (Appiah, *Cosmopolitanism* 63, qtd. in Cox).

265

Joy Harjo, poet and musician of the Muscogee (Creek) tribe, offers a case in point that shows how differently she and other Natives feel about Washington, D.C., than other Americans might. For America's Bicentennial in 1976, for example, what Honors Semesters saw as an opportunity to experience "'Americana'" "in its showplace capital city" (Braid, "Honors Semesters" 9), Harjo experiences as a nightmare when she visits our nation's capital: "I suffered from vertigo and panic attacks. I saw rivers of blood flowing under the beautiful white marble monuments that announced power in the landscape. I knew of the history embedded in the city. All tribes in this country have sharp memories located there" (*The Woman* 47).

The Woman Who Fell from the Sky: Poems was published in 1994, the year I moved to Durant, Oklahoma. In it Harjo remembers sending a friend off to D.C. "to argue a tribe's right to water" (47). She also notes her "great-great grandfather Monahwee went here with other tribal members to conduct business on behalf of the tribe. Those concerns have never been settled" (47). While Harjo, Martin, and Alexie are certainly correct that we have far to go in terms of Native American rights to equity and respectful inclusion in the U.S., from the perspective of 2017, some degree of justice is being addressed. In an online report, the Chickasaw Nation states that on Tuesday, October 6, 2016, U.S. Secretary of Interior Sally Jewell, Chickasaw Nation Governor Bill Anoatubby, and Choctaw Chief Gary Batton met "to sign a historic $186 million settlement of a lawsuit involving federal management . . . and disposition of more than a million acres of Chickasaw and Choctaw tribal lands that the U.S. government took control of on the eve of Oklahoma statehood" (Chickasaw Nation).

In her 2016 *New Yorker* article, "Holy Rage: Lessons from Standing Rock," Louise Erdrich, of the Chippewa tribe, recounts how the group, who called themselves "water protectors" rather than "pipeline protesters," used respect, prayer, and kindness to others—including offering drinking water to police—to prevent the Dakota Access Pipeline (DAK) from laying an oil pipeline under the Missouri River. "On the afternoon of December 4th," Erdrich states, "the Army Corps of Engineers made the stunning announcement that it had denied Energy Transfer Partners [DAK owners] an easement to cross under the Missouri River" (Erdrich).[22]

CONCLUSION

> Oh sun, moon, stars, our other relatives peering at us from the inside of god's house walk with us as we climb into the next century naked but for the stories we have of each other. Keep us from giving up in this land of nightmares which is also the land of miracles.
>
> We sing our song which we've been promised has no beginning or end.
> —Joy Harjo, "Reconciliation: A Prayer" (xv, 2.1–6)

Perhaps no people who read this chapter will actually see the Earth from space with their own eyes; it is still possible, however, to view the image captured by astronaut Anders and figuratively understand the importance of our relationship to all the others who inhabit this planet, including those who for various historical and political reasons have been constituted by the powers that be as "others." The Choctaws demonstrated this understanding when they sent money to Ireland to alleviate in some small way the suffering of a people who, like them, were considered less than, dispensable, not worthy of the food it would take to keep them from starving. The sculptor Alex Pentak demonstrated this understanding when he created "Kindred Spirits," his sculpture in honor and remembrance of the Choctaw's gift to his people. The "water protectors" in Dakota demonstrated this understanding when they offered water to police on the other side of the protector's line (Erdrich). My co-authors and other student contributors demonstrated this understanding when they joined me in writing this chapter. "All acts of kindness," as Harjo notes, "are lights in the war for justice" ("Reconciliation" xvi, 3.1).

For reasons such as these, the class called "Native America" encourages a global citizenry and a cosmopolitan perspective,

267

suggesting that even if educational efforts to "let learn" do not lead where we think they will and resistance to thinking some thoughts persists, that somehow, in the course of striving, resisting, and doing what is needed, things can get better, positive change can take place, justice may be done.

Harjo's poem of place, of the north, south, east, and west, meditates on "our home made of the four directions" and speaks a prayer of reconciliation ("Reconciliation" xvi, 4.3). Perhaps Standing Rock's work of activist resistance and protection, in which a large and disparate group of people have taken part, is also the beginning of the breakdown of psychical resistance in terms of our collective relationship to Native America, Native Americans, and the Earth we all inhabit; for the truth is, all of us live, learn, and work here.

NOTES

[1]In *Simmel on Culture*, editors David Frisby and Mike Featherstone comment on the difficulty of confining the work, the thought, or the man, Simmel, to one category only (2). Indeed, "Simmel's own practice of placing sections of essays and thematic issues in a variety of different contexts within his own work . . . is a practice which, in part, creates the impression of developing a conscious perspectivism—a viewing of themes from a variety of standpoints" (1).

[2]"Diversity," "equity," and "inclusion" (F. Coleman, "The Problem" 243) are key words I borrow from Finnie D. Coleman and his chapter from *Setting the Table for Diversity*, "The Problem with Diversity: Moving Past the Numbers." Two of these words, coupled with "social justice," appear in the title of his chapter in this monograph as well, "A Blueprint for Occupying Honors: Activism in Institutional Diversity, Equity, Social Justice, and Academic Excellence."

[3]"Thinking and rethinking" is a watch phrase repeated by James Herbert in his essay "Thinking and Rethinking: The Practical Value of an Honors Education." It refers to the process of working through an idea on one's own and in conversation with others, which is

commonly practiced in honors education. For the idea of engagement, I am grateful to Shawn Alfrey and her chapter in this volume, "Engaging the Bard: Honors, Engagement, and a New Chautauqua" (215–31).

[4]On the first page of *A Room of One's Own*, Virginia Woolf explores what might be meant by the words "Women" and "Fiction" (3), calling in to those words much as Heidegger "calls in" to the words "building," "dwelling," and thinking," in his essay with that title. In the same fashion, the rest of Woolf's book is an effort to explain what the words "Women" and "Fiction" have to do with "money" (4) and "a room of one's own" (3).

[5]The "civilized tribes" designation was given to the Chickasaws, Choctaws, Seminoles, and Creeks (also called Muscogees) by Europeans during the colonial and federal periods of the United States because these tribes took on some of the European behaviors and values. As the *Wikipedia* entry notes, the term "civilized" refers to the European perspective of what that term should mean (*Wikipedia* Contributors, "Five Civilized Tribes."; see also Frank).

[6]In *Listening to our Grandmothers' Stories*, Amanda J. Cobb states the following in a "Note to Readers": "When referring to American Indian tribes and people more generally, I have used the terms *American Indian, Native American, Native,* and *Indian* interchangeably, although I tend to prefer the terms *American Indian* and *Indian*" ("Front matter," italics in the original). I have tried to follow Cobb's example in this chapter, but my preference has been for the terms Native, Native American, and Indian to underscore the idea that the Western landmass described as the Americas could once have been referred to as Native America. See note 8 below.

[7]When I moved to Oklahoma in 1994, the state license plate featured the motto "Native America" with the shield of the Osage Nation, which is an emblem also on the state flag. In 2000, the motto stayed the same, but the image changed to an Apache warrior shooting an arrow into the sky. The 2017 license plate features an image of the state bird, the scissor-tailed flycatcher, with the directive "Explore Oklahoma" at the top of the plate and the subtitle

"Travelok.com" as a helpful website at the bottom. According to the *Tulsa World* website, the new plate is expected to raise 11 million dollars for the state after expenses (Hoberock).

[8]In the course of contributing to the writing of this chapter, which included creating the frame for my student co-writers' contributions, I came to the conclusion that all the Americas were originally "Native America" and could be accurately so designated, although such a designation does not correlate to the historic treatment of these Western landmasses.

[9]According to Blue Clark's *Indian Tribes of Oklahoma: A Guide*, the "Choctaw Nation" has its tribal headquarters in Durant, Oklahoma, "ninety miles north of Dallas," even though their capital is in Tuskahoma (107), while the "Chickasaw Nation" has its headquarters in Ada, Oklahoma. "(Before 1997, it was in Sulphur, Oklahoma)" (93). The Chickasaw Cultural Center is located in Sulphur, Olahoma.

[10]According to Angie Debo, the stories of the Choctaw and Chickasaw tribes of Oklahoma, for example, explain that they were once one tribe who traveled east from lands in the West (2). The land they traversed is part of the Western hemisphere landmass that Blue Clark points to as "America," so named by "a European mapmaker [who] borrowed the name of another explorer" (Clark xi).

As the genesis of the Chickasaw and Choctaw tribes goes, as told by Clark, on the eastward journey of their proto-tribe, each night they planted a pole in the ground; the next day, the planted pole always leaned east and the two brothers leading the tribe, Chahta and Chickasah, took their people in that direction. After crossing a great river, the brothers disagreed on whether their planted pole was still leaning or erect. One brother, Chahta, stayed where he was "on the banks of the Yazoo River" (Clark 109), while the other, "Chicasah" [sic], took his followers "north to [what became] northern Mississippi and western Tennessee" (Clark 109). Thus the two tribes were formed.

[11]For the Place as Text experience that is practiced at all NCHC conferences, basic readings are provided electronically beforehand

to prepare participants for what they may experience emotionally and intellectually when they go out in a city or other location and explore it. In addition to developing the skills of mapping, listening, observing, and reflecting, perhaps most importantly, participants gain practice in learning to recognize the culturally inspired lenses or filters that literally constrain what they see, hear, and are even able to experience through their interactions with the places they move through and the people they encounter who find their dwelling there.

For the "Native America" class, I followed the example of the NCHC PAT experience in terms of readings appropriate to our walkabouts. We also practiced a phenomenological approach to our walkabouts in terms of observing, mapping, listening to, and reflecting on what we encountered out in the field—and how who and what we encountered concomitantly encountered us. (See Childer's section below.)

[12]I credit Kathy A. Lyon, one of the facilitators of the England NCHC Institute, for her reminder that she had taken on any number of subjects "outside of [her] discipline" for honors, learning and growing in the process (99).

[13]Before editing Nancy M. West's chapter for this monograph, "Inclusivity vs. Exclusivity: Re-Imagining the Honors College as a Third Place," I was unfamiliar with Georg Simmel (199–213). As someone who has previously studied the work of the philosophers Immanuel Kant and Martin Heidegger, the former who influenced Simmel and the latter who was influenced by him, I was encouraged by West's text to read more about this cultural theorist who became one of the founders of sociology.

In the "Georg Simmel" entry in the *Encyclopedia of Phenomenology*, for example, the editors claim that while Simmel's interests were wide and his essays address an array of cultural phenomena, in all his writing he had one overarching question: "What is the precise nature of the relationship between subjective experiential life and the objective cultural forms that it engenders and encounters?" (Embrèe et al. 641). My thought is that moving from the philosophy of Kant to that of Simmel and then to that of Heidegger demonstrates a progression in Western philosophy toward a relationship with "world" that calls into question the subject/object duality posited between self and world. Discussions by Native writers Simon J. Ortiz and Linda Hogan, recounted in this chapter, call the post-enlightenment Western will to duality into question (see also Rickert, *Ambient* xii–xvi).

[14]Rickert and I were privileged to study Heidegger under Dr. Luanne T. Frank at the University of Texas at Arlington in the 80s and 90s. Rickert's *Ambient Rhetoric: The Attunements of Rhetorical Being* (2013) reflects the considerable study and scholarship on Heidegger he has done since, including on Heidegger's philosophy of attunement. Attunement to the world "indicates one's disposition to the world, how one finds oneself embedded in a situation" (Rickert 9). Attunement, as Rickert's research reveals, is practiced by ancient cultures (3–8). I discuss this term as well in my chapter "Psyche as Text" in *Setting the Table for Diversity* (205).

[15]Letting learn is an approach to teaching called for by Heidegger's *What is Called Thinking?* "Teaching is more difficult than learning because what teaching calls for is this: to let learn. The teacher must be capable of being more teachable than the apprentices. . . . [T]here is never a place in it for the authority of the know-it-all or the authoritative sway of the official" (15).

[16]Louise Erdrich's article in the *New Yorker* describes the effort of the Sioux tribe of Standing Rock (joined by many others) to stop the Dakota Access Pipeline from going under the Missouri River and through Sioux tribal lands, thus protecting the river water. The phenomenological definition of "occupying" provided in this chapter (as "concerned with," etc.), does not exclude the Sioux champions, who call themselves "water protectors" rather than "pipeline protestors" (Erdrich).

[17]The bridge presented by Heidegger in "Building Dwelling Thinking" as illustrative of a "thing" is part and parcel of World. As a "thing" the bridge is something that "gathers" (Heidegger, "Building" 153). What does it gather? "As this thing it gathers the fourfold" (Heidegger, "Building" 153). What is the fourfold? "The

bridge *gathers* to itself in *its own* way earth and sky, divinities and mortals" (Heidegger, "Building" 153). (For more on "the fourfold," see Rickert *Ambient*).

[18]In 1795 Kant is able to discern that at the time of the discovery of Africa, America, and their people, the cultural lenses of the discoverers did not encourage them to see the humanity of those they discovered, counting them as "nothing" (Kant 106). Nevertheless, Kant also reveals his own bias with the following quotation and the employment of the term "savages": "Thus warlike courage, with the American savages, as with their European counterparts in medieval times, is held to be of great and immediate value—and not just *in times of* war (as might be expected), but also *in order that* there may be war" (Kant 111; emphasis in original). While "savage" is employed by Kant in the context of war, it is, nevertheless, a dehumanizing term.

[19]When I consider this question posed by Harper Lee's character Scout from the distance of the year 2017, it resonates with one posed by the American populist movement that just elected Donald Trump: "What will 'we' (the culture in power) do with immigrants to 'our' country?" That question and the one asked by Scout render this novel, as well as Lee's newly published *Go Set a Watchman* in which Scout figures centrally, relevant to the twenty-first century.

[20]Casino-style gaming was voted on and approved by the state of Oklahoma in 2004 (Mason). Choctaw Casino and Resort, on Interstate 75, north of Dallas, Texas, was Choctaw Bingo when I moved to Oklahoma in 1994. Twenty-three years later, the Choctaws and Chickasaws are major players in the economic scene of southeastern Oklahoma and beyond. Indeed, according to the Winstar World Casino website, the Winstar Casino, owned by the Chickasaws and situated north of Fort Worth, Texas, on Interstate 35, is the largest casino in the world, and their profits (like those at Choctaw), are used to assist their people.

[21]Although I was not able to corroborate this statement, it could be that Hogan is thinking of the images of the moon that were taken from space before U.S. manned space missions.

[22]With the advent of the Trump presidency, on January 24, 2017, Trump issued an executive order reviving the Dakota Access Pipeline project. The pipeline was completed in April 2017 and opened for commercial use on June 01, 2017 (see *Wikipedia* contributors, "Dakota Access Pipeline").

REFERENCES

Alexie, Sherman. *The Daily Show with Trevor Noah*. Comedy Central. Interview. 09 May 2016.

Appiah, Kwame Anthony. "Cosmopolitan Patriots." Nussbaum 21–29.

—. *Cosmopolitanism: Ethics in a World of Strangers*. New York: Norton, 2006. Print.

Basu, Lopamudra. "Cosmopolitanism and New Racial Formations in a Post-9/11 Honors Curriculum on Diversity." Coleman, Kotinek, and Oda 135–76.

"Books." Review of *The Kingdom of Appearances* by George Steiner. *The New Yorker* 04 Apr. 1977: 132–40. Print.

Braid, Bernice. "Honors Semesters: An Architecture of Active Learning." Braid and Long 19–28.

—. Foreword. *Shatter the Glassy Stare*. Machonis 9–11.

Braid, Bernice, and Ada Long, ed. *Place as Text: Approaches to Active Learning*. 2nd ed. Lincoln: National Collegiate Honors Council, 2010. NCHC Monograph Series. Print.

Brown, Stephanie, and Virginia Cope. "Cosmopolitan Courtesy: Preparing for Global Citizenry." Coleman, Kotinek, and Oda 107–34.

Chickasaw Nation. "Chickasaw Nation News Release." 07 October 2016. Web. 07 October 2016.

Choctaw Nation. "The Choctaw-Irish Bond Lives On." 30 March 2016. Web. 04 January 2017.

Clark, Blue. *Indian Tribes of Oklahoma: A Guide*. Norman: University of Oklahoma Press, 2009. Print.

Cobb, Amanda J. *Listening to Our Grandmothers' Stories: The Bloomfield Academy for Chickasaw Females, 1852–1949*. Lincoln: University of Nebraska Press, 2000. Print.

Coleman, Finnie D. "A Blueprint for Occupying Honors: Activism in Institutional Diversity, Equity, Inclusion, Social Justice, and Academic Excellence." Coleman, Kotinek, and Oda 311–52.

—. "The Problem with Diversity: Moving Past the Numbers." Coleman and Kotinek 239–49.

Coleman, Lisa L. "Psyche as Text: Diversity Issues and First-Year Honors Composition." Coleman and Kotinek 201–28.

Coleman, Lisa L., and Jonathan D. Kotinek, ed. *Setting the Table for Diversity*. Lincoln: National Collegiate Honors Council, 2010. NCHC Monograph Series. Print.

Coleman, Lisa L., Jonathan D. Kotinek, and Alan Y. Oda, ed. *Occupy Honors Education*. Lincoln: National Collegiate Honors Council, 2017. Print.

Cox, Emilie. "Culture Integration: The Good, the Bad, and How to Be Better." Unpublished Paper. Southeastern Oklahoma State University. 19 April 2016. Typescript.

Debo, Angie. *The Rise and Fall of the Choctaw Republic*. 1934. Second Edition. Norman: University of Oklahoma Press, 1975. Print.

DeRosier, Arthur H. *The Removal of the Choctaw Indians*. Knoxville: Tennessee Press, 1970. Print.

Dunn, Kameron. "Water, Narrative, and Native America." Southeastern Oklahoma State University. Unpublished paper. 25 April 2016. Typescript.

Embrée, Lester, et al., ed. "Georg Simmel." *Encyclopedia of Phenomenology*. Dordrecht, Netherlands: Springer Science + Business Media BV, 1997. Print.

Erdrich, Louise. "Holy Rage: Lessons from Standing Rock." *New Yorker*. 22 December 2016. Web. 04 January 2017.

"Five Civilized Tribes." *Wikipedia, the Free Encyclopedia*. 19 December 2016. Web.

Frank, Andrew K. "Five Civilized Tribes." *The Encyclopedia of Oklahoma History and Culture*. 21 December 2016. Web.

Geertz, Clifford. (1983) *Local Knowledge: Further Essays in Interpretive Anthropology*. 3rd Edition. New York: Basic Books, 2000. Print.

Gibson, Arrell M. *The Chickasaws*. Norman: University of Oklahoma Press, 1972. Print.

Harjo, Joy. "Reconciliation: A Prayer." *The Woman Who Fell from the Sky*, xv–xvi.

—. "Wolf Warrior: For All the Warriors." *The Woman Who Fell from the Sky*, 44–47.

—. *The Woman Who Fell from the Sky: Poems*. New York: Norton, 1994. Print.

Heidegger, Martin. *Being and Time*. Trans. John Macquarrie and Edward Robinson. New York: Harper and Row, 1962. Print.

—. "Building Dwelling Thinking." *Poetry, Language, Thought*. Trans. and Intro. Albert Hofstadter. New York: Harper and Row, 1971. 145–61. Print.

—. *The Heidegger Reader*. Ed. Günter Figal. Trans. Jerome Veith. Bloomington: Indiana University Press, 2009. Print.

—. *What Is Called Thinking?* 1968. Trans. J. Glenn Gray. New York: Harper Perennial Reprint, 2004. Print.

Herbert, James. "Thinking and Rethinking: The Practical Value of an Honors Education." Reprinted in "Forum on the Value of Honors." *Journal of the National Collegiate Honors Council: 50th Anniversary Issue*. Vol. 16, No. 2, Fall/Winter 2015. Web. 29 Dec. 2016.

Hoberock, Barbara. "Officials Unveil New Oklahoma License Plate with State Bird Design." *Tulsa World*. 24 Aug. 2016. Web. 15 Jan. 2017.

Hogan, Linda. *Dwellings: A Spiritual History of the Living World*. New York: Norton, 1995. Print.

Kant, Immanuel. "Perpetual Peace." *Kant: Political Writings*. 2nd Edition. Ed. Hans Reiss. Trans. H. B. Nisbett. Cambridge: Cambridge University Press, 1991. 93–130. Print.

Lamb, Todd. Southeastern Oklahoma State University, Durant, Oklahoma. 07 May 2016. Commencement Address.

Lee, Harper. *To Kill a Mockingbird*. New York: Grand Central Publishing, 1960. Print.

Lyon, Kathy A. "Crete Faculty Institute: A Change in Pedagogical Style." Machonis 99–104.

Machonis, Peter A., ed. *Shatter the Glassy Stare: Implementing Experiential Learning in Higher Education*. Lincoln: National Collegiate Honors Council, 2008. NCHC Monograph Series. Print.

Mason, W. Dale. "Indian Gaming." *The Encyclopedia of Oklahoma History and Culture*. Web. 11 Jan. 2012.

McCoy, Marcella L. "A Place for Diversity: Experiential Projects in Honors Curricula." Coleman and Kotinek 135–50.

McIntosh, Peggy. *The National Seed Project*. "Peggy McIntosh's White Privilege Papers." "White Privilege: Unpacking the Invisible Knapsack" (1989) (Excerpt). "White Privilege and Male Privilege: A Personal Account of Coming to See Correspondences Through Work in Women's Studies." (1988). Working paper 189. Wellesley, MA: Wellesley Centers for Women. Web. 18 Jan. 2017.

Mish, Jeanetta Calhoun. *Oklahomeland*. Beaumont, TX: Lamar University Press, 2015. Print

Nussbaum, Martha C. *For Love of Country?* Ed. Joshua Cohen. Boston: Beacon Press, 2002. Print.

Ortiz, Simon J. "Song, Poetry, and Language—Expression and Perception." *Genocide of the Mind.* Ed. Marijo Moore. New York: Nation Books, 2003. 105–18. Print.

Rickert, Thomas. *Acts of Enjoyment: Rhetoric, Žižek, and the Return of the Subject.* Pittsburgh: The University of Pittsburgh Press, 2007. Print.

—. *Ambient Rhetoric: The Attunements of Rhetorical Being.* Pittsburgh: University of Pittsburgh Press, 2013. Print.

Scarry, Elaine. "The Difficulty of Imagining Other People." Nussbaum 98–110.

Simmel, Georg. *Simmel on Culture.* Ed. David Frisby and Mike Featherstone. London: Sage Publications, 1997. Print.

Slaten, Matt. "A Recent Trip to the Past." Unpublished Paper. Southeastern Oklahoma State University. 26 April 2016. Typescript.

Strickland, Rennard. *The Indians in Oklahoma.* Norman: University of Oklahoma Press, 1980. Print.

Wallace, David Foster. "This is Water." Kenyon College, Gambier, Ohio. 21 May, 2005. *YouTube.* YouTube, 19 May 2013. Web. 09 August 2017. Commencement Address.

West, Nancy M. "Inclusivity Versus Exclusivity: Re-Imagining the Honors College as a Third Place." Coleman, Kotinek, and Oda 199–213.

Wikipedia contributors. "Dakota Access Pipeline." *Wikipedia, The Free Encyclopedia*, 05 Aug. 2017. Web. 08 Aug. 2017.

—. "Five Civilized Tribes." *Wikipedia, The Free Encyclopedia*, 02 June 2017. Web. 08 Aug. 2017.

Wildenthal, Bryan H. *Native American Sovereignty on Trial.* Santa Barbara: ABC-CLIO, 2003. Print.

Winstar World Casino and Resort. "Winstar World Casino and Resort: About Us." Web. 10 Jan. 2017.

Woolf, Virginia. *A Room of One's Own.* 1925. Annot. and Intro. by Susan Gubar. Mark Hussey, Gen. Ed. Orlando: Harcourt, 2005. Print.

Zimmerman, Robert. *Genesis: The Story of Apollo 8.* Mountain Lake Park, MD: Mountain Lake Press, 2012. E-book.

What is Truth?
Teaching the Constructivist Perspective for Diversity in Honors

Jonathan D. Kotinek
Texas A&M University

INTRODUCTION

This chapter addresses the question "Why is diversity important to honors education?" by illustrating the central role of
critical thinking to honors education and the need for a diversity of
perspectives to make critical thinking more effective. The chapter
also reflects on the concept of truth and how truth is transmitted
in post-enlightenment Western culture. The chapter centers on the
philosophical concept of constructivism in contrast with positivism
and makes a case for the more inclusive constructivist perspective.
The thesis of this chapter maintains that teaching and learning constructivist thought contribute to the mission of diversity, equity,
and inclusion in honors, as well as in higher education in general, because constructivism provides both teachers and learners
a framework for recognizing their own biases and teaches an ethic

of seeking alternative perspectives and valuing those in decision making. This methodology is imagined in the honors educational context as teaching honors students to be curators of the particular and encouraging them to seek out and rely on one another's expertise as a strategy to equip them to engage difference productively as tomorrow's leaders.

EXCURSUS

I am in a prolonged battle of wills with my oldest son about his shoes. These are fairly new shoes that are in good condition, and they are neither too big nor too small for him. Every time I ask him to put on the shoes, however, he gets frustrated, claiming that they do not feel good. I have checked the amount of toe-space he has with the shoes on; run my fingers through the inside of the shoes, feeling for irritating protrusions; and tried loosening the laces—all to no avail. When I cannot stand the fight any longer, he often wears an old, ratty pair that were getting too small when we bought the offending ones. He does not complain about the old pair. I see two options: I can believe that my son is lying or that he truly finds the shoes uncomfortable. Since I am actively trying to cultivate trust in my children, I choose the latter. This option leaves me with a difficult situation: whatever is causing my son's discomfort is something I cannot apprehend.

I am also engaged in an ongoing discussion with a high school friend about White privilege. This friend and I come from similar family backgrounds, have similar educational accomplishments, and share many of the same values. Yet we have very different views about the nature and extent of the privilege that we enjoy. I find myself frustrated at trying to present an argument to him for a phenomenon that seems so patently obvious to me. Comparing my feelings about this impasse with my friend to what my son might feel about my inability to understand his discomfort with his shoes, I am struck by how absurd my child must find the situation in which his experience of reality is not shared by so close a relation. Is it any wonder, then, that when this kind of dissonance is experienced by people who feel themselves at odds, the frustration may turn to resentment, anger, or even violence?

The discussion of diversity, equity, and inclusion that follows takes place in the challenging light of these two scenarios.

WHY IS DIVERSITY IMPORTANT TO HONORS EDUCATION?

In the introduction to *Setting the Table for Diversity*, co-editor Lisa L. Coleman (2010) posits that teaching in honors must "now include an ethical responsibility" to welcome students and faculty who have been excluded in a structural approach to diversity (p. 17). Later in the same volume, Ellen Riek and Kathryn Sheridan (2010) suggest that one way to live up to this responsibility includes constructing learning experiences that foster an "engaged, interactive, and transactional" environment (p. 28). The groundwork laid by this first National Collegiate Honors Council (NCHC) monograph on diversity identifies honors education as a space that can be used productively to further the cause of diversity, access, and inclusion, not just for honors students but ultimately for all students and anyone involved in the educational mission of the university, as I argue below.

In the *Journal of the National Collegiate Honors Council* (*JNCHC*) commemorating the 50th anniversary of the organization, editor Ada Long (2015) summarizes the reflections on the value of honors education from the university presidents represented in the volume. Topping the list is the teaching of critical thinking, which Long identifies as a characteristic approach in honors education that shapes the experience of students, faculty, and staff alike (p. xv). This understanding of honors education as thoughtful, intellectual exchange might characterize the ideal for anyone engaged in the enterprise of liberal education, so how does honors differ?

A definition of honors education has proven elusive.[1] NCHC's recent publication of a definition of honors education on its website as a "learner-directed" enterprise that features "measurably broader, deeper, or more complex" activities, however, provides a starting point for considering what honors education is in the abstract (Lanier, Reubel, Scott, Torda, and Kotinek, 2013).[2] In the elaborating document, NCHC further emphasizes five different "modes of learning":

1. research and creative scholarship;

2. breadth and enduring questions;

3. service learning and leadership;

4. experiential learning; and

5. learning communities.

These learning modes map very well to the "high-impact practices" advocated by the American Association of Colleges & Universities (AAC&U), and laid out by George Kuh (2008) in his seminal book, *High Impact Educational Practices: What They are, Who has Access to Them, and Why They* Matter. These practices include:

> First-year Seminars and Experiences; Common Intellectual Experiences; Learning Communities; Writing Intensive Courses; Collaborative Assignments and Projects; Under-graduate Research; Diversity/Global Learning; Service/Community-Based Learning; Internships; and Capstone Projects (Kuh, 2008; see also Rice, 2015; Kelly, 2013).

The necessity for these "high-impact practices" can be traced to a statement released in January 2002 by Carol Geary Schneider, AAC&U president. Her statement, reprinted in the spring/summer edition of the 2002 issue of *JNCHC* and quoted from here, declares that a liberal education should prepare students to answer "questions about the wider world, about our own values, and about difficult choices we must make as both human beings and citizens" (p. 33). This statement, also named the President's Campaign for the Advancement of Liberal Learning, or CALL, served as the origin of the AAC&U "LEAP Initiative" (with LEAP standing for Liberal Education and America's Promise), "a public advocacy and campus action initiative designed to engage students and the public with what really matters in a college education for the twenty-first century" (AAC&U, 2017). Today that initiative has been developed into what Schneider (2015) calls "The Leap Challenge." In an AAC&U article in which Kuh's high-impact practices are also listed, Schneider (2015) argues that all students in higher education should engage in "Signature Work" of import to the student and society at large over the course of more than one semester in their college careers.

The issue of *JNCHC* in which Schneider's 2002 AAC&U essay was reprinted followed the "Forum on Liberal Learning," organized by Sam Schuman and Anne Ponder in conjunction with the NCHC annual conference in Chicago in 2001 (see Long, Mullins & Rushton, 2002, p. 13). Presciently, the editorial note introducing Schneider's contribution to the volume states that the "AAC&U is urging, in effect, an 'honors' education for all students" (p. 33) Given the history of the current AAC&U LEAP challenge, the answer to the question I posed earlier as to how honors education differs from the ideal liberal education may be that it does not, or *should* not, except insofar as the dedicated and motivated students and faculty in honors can serve as trailblazers for new and exciting pedagogies that foster the five different "modes of learning" noted by the NCHC definition of honors education and employ Kuh's "high-impact practices."

These modes of learning and high-impact practices return us to the concept of critical thinking, mentioned above, that serves as the heart of the honors educational enterprise. In its turn, as the research of Hubert, Pickavance, and Hyberger (2015) bears out, reflective thought lies at the heart of critical thinking. Hubert, Pickavance, and Hyberger's work with eportfolios, for example, suggests that the connections students make in the reflective process required by these eportfolios are central to what makes the experiences described by Kuh (2015) "high-impact." Further, according to Stein, Haynes, and Redding (2016), the process of critical thinking (as evaluated by Tennessee Tech's Critical Thinking Assessment Test) must also include evaluating information, finding creative or innovative solutions, learning and problem-solving, and communication (p. 5).

In order to engage the high-impact activities these researchers champion, it is helpful (if not imperative) to also have a sense of one's own biases, a sense of how those biases are interacting with the way information is perceived, and the will/desire to figure out where gaps exist between one's own and others' interpretation of the same information. In short, to function effectively, critical thinking requires a diversity of perspectives. Accordingly, if critical and creative thinking are at the heart of an honors education, then exposure to, appreciation of, and equal opportunity for diverse perspectives must also serve as core elements of honors education. In this manner, the critical thinking that shapes the experience of honors education also calls for (and may help to create) a culture that can foster diversity, equity, and inclusion.

The conditions necessary to foster equity and inclusion, however, require more than just a diversity of perspectives. These additional conditions speak to power dynamics and an appreciation that more than one perspective may be valid.

CULTURE, TRUTH, AND PARADIGMATIC THINKING

Pilate saith unto him, What is truth?
—Gospel of St. John 18:38

What is truth? How each person answers this question provides insight into the unique intersection of what a person counts as knowledge and where that knowledge comes from (epistemology), the source of reality (ontology), and what values are prioritized (axiology). These overlapping lenses inform people's perceptions of reality differently because they are each enculturated differently.

One of my favorite metaphors for culture comes from the biological sciences, where a culture is the medium in which something grows. Thinking about culture in this manner provides a way to understand how the environment plays a role in feeding and shaping what is seen as normal and acceptable. March and Olsen (1995) describe how cultural identity is shaped by what is deemed "appropriate": those things that are considered "normal, natural, right, [and] good" (p. 31). They claim that enculturation leads people to "act, think, feel, and organize themselves on the basis of exemplary or authoritative (and sometimes competing or conflicting) rules derived from socially constructed identities and roles" (p. 30). Culture, then, plays a role in filtering those truths that are appropriate for consumption and promulgation.

In lecture slides prepared for a class on hip hop culture, Finnie D. Coleman (2016) describes a cycle of how truth is reified according to this perspective. Culture, which Coleman glosses as "values, norms, and artifacts," determines the myths that let us know who we are and where we come from. These origin myths determine our epistemology, or what is considered knowledge. Knowledge, which includes facts, justified beliefs, and opinions, determines our hermeneutics, or how we interpret that knowledge into meaning about the world around us. Hermeneutics determines hegemony, or the ideas that shape and control power. Hegemony determines ideology, and those ideologies, in turn, determine the values, norms, and artifacts that make up culture and the myths we tell to explain who we are and where we come from (F. D. Coleman). Within this cycle, we can understand the relationship between truth and quantifiable reality, or facts, as being just one of several ways of understanding the world. Knowledge also includes opinions (personal interpretations of phenomena) and justified belief (beliefs borne out by subjective experience). In both of these other ways of knowing, culture plays a role in providing the context for and determining what will be accepted as truth.

In an essay titled "Myth Became Fact," C.S. Lewis (2002) explains how myth functions to give the necessary critical distance to understand how belief is a framework for subjective experience: "in the enjoyment of a great myth we come nearest to experiencing as a concrete what can otherwise be understood only as an abstraction" (p. 140). Mircea Eliade (1963) further explains what might seem an anachronistic understanding of the word "myth." For Eliade, "'myth' means a 'true story' and, beyond that, a story that is most precious in possession because it is sacred, exemplary, [and] significant" (p. 1). In discussing how myth and history operate to inform the lives of archaic and modern persons, respectively, Eliade declares:

> modern man, though regarding himself as the result of the course of Universal History, does not feel obliged to know the whole of it, [while] the man of the archaic societies is not only obliged to remember mythical history but also to re-enact a large part of it periodically. It is here that we find the greatest difference between the man of the archaic societies and modern man: the irreversibility of events, which is the characteristic trait of History for the latter, is not a fact for the former. (p. 13)

Knowing the origin of ideas and ways of thinking in the archaic societies Eliade describes gives the knower a power to "abolish the past, to begin his life anew, and to re-create his World" (p. 140). This paradigmatic understanding of reality is at odds with the syntagmatic or linear perspective that Eliade attributes to modern man, who sees history as a one-way chain of cause-and-effect.

"Paradigmatic" and "syntagmatic" are terms offered by semiotics, a structural approach to understanding language conceived by Ferdinand de Saussure. According to Kaja Silverman (1983), semiotics identifies constituent units in a system, such as values, social practices, or texts, and describes the relationships between them as one of three types: "between a signifier and a signified; . . . between a sign and all of the other elements of its system; and . . . between a sign and the elements which surround it" (p. 10). As Saussure (1983) explains, a sign consists of a signifier and that which is signified (p. 12). For example, a signifier such as the word "truth" has a signified concept that could be defined as a "fact or belief that is accepted as being in accord with reality" (Saussure, 1983, p. 12). Paradigms and syntagms are related but different ways of understanding relationships between parts of a system. In the case of a system such as a sentence like the one that follows, the syntagmatic relationships describe how a chain of signifiers (i.e., words) fit together based on a set of rules (i.e., grammar): I learned the truth. The paradigmatic relationships in the same system describe the options for which signifiers can be used, but not at the same time: We understand an opinion. Consider how these syntagmatic and paradigmatic relationships relate back to my opening anecdotes in the figures below.

Figure 1 describes a system of a sentence in which I have represented the essence of the issue presented to me by my son and his shoes. The syntagmatic reading of this system is "my shoes are uncomfortable." A paradigmatic reading of the system suggests other possibilities by imagining possible signs that might be substituted for those presented to me. Perhaps the problem is in my son's socks, not his shoes. Perhaps the issue has nothing to do with a physical problem like the shoe being too small or having a sharp protrusion, but is, instead, something that my son cannot or will not express, for example, that he dislikes the shoes because a friend made fun of them.

In the conversation with my high school friend, the system represented in Figure 2 shows that where he is seeing effort translating into success, opportunity, and enhanced reputation, I am considering these same outcomes as the result of privilege. According to Chandler (2002) "Temporally, syntagmatic relations refer intratextually to other signifiers co-present within the text, while paradigmatic relations refer intertextually to signifiers which are absent from the text" (p. 84). With this understanding, then, "paradigmatic" refers to a broader context within which any experience might be understood by comparing the signifiers that are observed to the others that might be observed in the same circumstances.

Paradigmatic thinking can be conceived as a toolbox of perspectives that can be brought to bear based on the thinker's understanding of the circumstances. Henry Louis Gates, Jr., for example, offers "signifyin(g)" as a substantially similar critical approach. Gates (1987) describes signifyin(g) as, an "indigenously black" rhetorical strategy that is based on a complex intertextual series of references (p. 48). In a later publication, Gates (2014) claims the sign, "signifyin(g)," is itself a signification on the difference between this Black linguistic use, which is at once confrontational and playful, and the standard English use, which suggests the more straightforward, syntagmatic understanding of meaning-making (p. 50).

FIGURE 1. SEMIOTIC ANALYSIS OF UNCOMFORTABLE SHOES

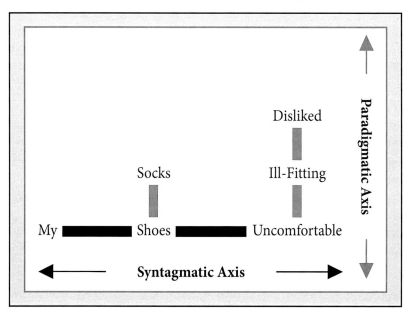

FIGURE 2. SEMIOTIC ANALYSIS OF PRIVILEGE

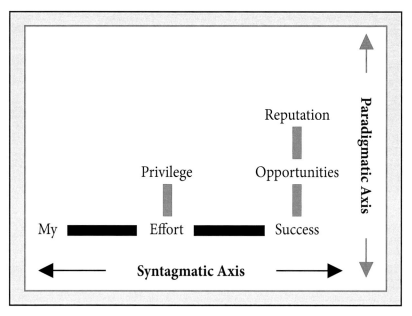

Elsewhere, I have conceived of a paradigmatic understanding of intelligence based on four premises:

> that relevant and useful behavior is pluralistically defined, that relevant and useful behavior is designated as intelligent, and the process of learning behavior(s) is environmentally mediated. Further, the environment in which behavior is learned and reinforced has cultural norms that not only designate intelligent behavior but also act (or not) in learning situations. (Kotinek, 2008, p. 2)

Paradigmatic intelligence and paradigmatic thinking may be useful constructs to help understand language as a technology or tool that actively shapes an individual's or a culture's perception of reality. The idea that meaning-making is culturally mediated has gained popular traction as evidenced by the publication of these ideas in the popular press such as *The Wall Street Journal*. For example, an online article there by Boroditsky (2010) titled "Lost in Translation" concludes that "structures that exist in our languages profoundly shape how we construct reality."

A major obstacle to reconciling our different perceptions about what is true is a lack of understanding about the subjective experience of reality or the conceptions about reality that we form from these perceptions. The differences are indiscernible without careful attention to the challenges of seeking understanding across cultural barriers. Language, or the technology we use to convey understanding about the world around us, is shaped by different cultural perspectives; therefore the effort of seeking understanding requires ongoing collaboration. One way to address the disconnect is to provide opportunities for learners to seek out alternative (even oppositional!) perspectives, triangulate where those perspectives overlap, and synthesize a shared understanding of truth.

POSITIVISM VS. CONSTRUCTIVISM

This section discusses postivism and constructivism before finally suggesting how critical thinking, paradigmatic intelligence, and constructivism might fit together to inform our pedagogies.

291

Popular culture is replete with observations about truth and the subjective nature of reality. Consider the following:

> Beauty is truth, truth beauty—that is all
> Ye know on earth, and all ye need to know.
> —John Keats, "Ode on a Grecian Urn"

> Luke, you're going to find that many of the truths we cling to depend greatly on your point of view.
> —Obi Wan Kenobi,
> *Star Wars Episode VI: Return of the Jedi*

> Memory is a complicated thing, a relative of truth but not its twin.
> —Barbara Kingsolver, *Animal Dreams*

> You never know just how you look through other people's eyes.
> —Butthole Surfers, "Pepper"

How is it that the culturally salient understanding of subjectivism does not translate to the academy and the sciences practiced within it? I argue below that the culture of the academy—and the historical course of what was deemed normal, natural, right, and good in the pursuit of knowledge—has been steered by syntagmatic, positivist perspectives.

John Médaille (2010), theologian-cum-political economist, highlights this influence in describing why the science of economics needs to be accountable to the values of the society it serves:

> *Every* science, insofar as it really is a science, is *both* positive and normative. Every science, insofar as it is a science, must be "normalized" to some criteria of truth. These truths arise from two sources: an internal and an external source. The internal criteria involve a science's proper subject matter and methodology. But these criteria are insufficient to found any science as a science. In addition, there must be external criteria of truth, and these truths can only come from one or more higher sciences. In the absence of such an external check, the science will merely be circular,

292

dependent on nothing but itself and disconnected from the hierarchy of truth. Thus, for example, biology is responsible to chemistry, chemistry to physics, physics to metaphysics. No biologist can violate the laws of chemistry, and no chemist can reach a conclusion contrary to physics. Thus every science is responsible to its own methodology (and therefore *positive*) and to the higher sciences (and therefore *normative*). (p. 24, emphasis in original)

Médaille asserts that determining what the object of study is—the physical world or the human person in relationship—is more useful than considering whether a science is normative or positive (p. 26). Since Médaille describes science as "knowledge organized into a hierarchy of truth," it follows, then, that knowledge in the humane sciences, including honors education, must take into account relationships and how these interact with what is normal, natural, right, and good (p. 25).

According to Schwandt (2013) positivism is concerned with physical realities that can be measured using human senses. It is characterized by realist ontology, objectivist epistemology, and interventionist methodology (p. 23). Nineteenth-century philosopher Auguste Comte is considered the progenitor of positivism. On this subject, Comte (1880) notes that "the first characteristic of Positive Philosophy is that it regards all phenomena as subjected to invariable natural *Laws*" (p. 29, emphasis in original). Comte's *The Course in Positive Philosophy* developed an interrelated philosophy of the physical and mathematical sciences, which he conceived of as a hierarchy of truths:

Thus we have before us Five fundamental Sciences in successive dependence—Astronomy, Physics, Chemistry, Physiology, and finally Social Physics. The first considers the most general, simple, abstract, and remote phenomena known to us and those that affect all others without being affected by them. The last considers the most particular, compound, concrete phenomena, and those that are the most interesting to Man. Between these two, the degrees

293

of speciality, of complexity, and individuality are in regular proportion to the place of the respective sciences in the scale exhibited. This—casting out everything arbitrary—we must regard as the true filiation of the sciences; and in it we find the plan of this work. (p. 28)

Émile Durkheim (1982), who, along with Comte, is considered a founder of the field of sociology, expanded on the hierarchy of truth established by Comte (1880) in *The Course in Positive Philosophy*. Writing in the preface to his *Rules of Sociological Method*, Durkheim says, "our rule implies no metaphysical conception, no speculation about the innermost depth of being. What it demands is that the sociologist should assume the state of mind of physicists, chemists, and physiologists when they venture into an as yet unexplored area of their scientific field" (p. 37).

The adoption of the positivist perspective in the fields of psychology and education is a result of skepticism and pushback from faculty in traditional fields. Consequently, according to Shavelson and Towne (2002), in their handbook for *Scientific Research in Education* from the National Research Council, research perspectives and methodology "were derived from the mechanistic, positivistic sciences" (p. 15). As they also note, despite recognition that more inclusive perspectives are needed and that "there is room in the mansion of science for more than one model," the positivist influence on educational psychology research, and therefore pedagogical practice, remains clear in the assumptions guiding what is normal, natural, right and good (p. 16). The following guidance from Shavelson and Towne provides little alternative to the realist ontology, objectivist epistemology, and interventionist methodology that define the positivistic perspective:

"What makes research scientific is not the motive, but manner in which it is carried out." (p. 20)

"We assume it is possible to describe the physical & social world scientifically so that . . . multiple observers can agree on what they see." (p. 25)

"Epistemological principles: seeking conceptual/theoretical understanding, posing empirically testable and refutable hypotheses, using observational methods linked to theory to enable other scientists to verify accuracy (reliability), recognizing the importance of independent replication and generalization." (p. 50)

According to King, Keohane, and Verba (1994), the constructivist perspective, in contrast to the positivist perspective informing the foregoing research guidelines, understands that inquiry in human sciences deals with non-quantifiable entities and depends on the lenses of culture and context" (p. 38). Ernst von Glasersfeld (2007) provides a useful overview of the history of constructivist thought in describing the development of his own theory, dubbed "Radical Constructivism" (von Glasersfeld and Larochelle p. 91). He identifies eighteenth-century thinkers Giambattista Vico and George Berkeley as first breaking "with the age-old philosophical belief that human knowledge must in some way provide a representation of an observer-independent reality" and proposing new conceptualizations of human knowledge and existence (von Glasersfeld and Larochelle pp. 92–93). Glasersfeld sees the work of twentieth-century theorist Jean Piaget encapsulating these new concepts in the epistemological principles that "knowledge is ... an accommodation to reality" and that "cognitive activity is adaptive" (von Glasersfeld and Larochelle p. 94).

The theoretical perspective called constructivism provides a framework for thinking about, pursuing, and ultimately learning from the subjective experience of others. A major tenet of constructivist thought is that the only way to discern this subjective experience is through an immersive series of dialogues—with stakeholders, with self, and with peers. This intense process of engagement renders monolithic understanding of any phenomenon impractical (if not laughable) and focuses on the connection between two or more people (see Alfrey on engagement in this volume, pp. 215–31).

Constructivism (originally naturalistic inquiry) is the name given to the paradigm developed by higher education scholars and qualitative methodologists Yvonna Lincoln and Egon Guba over the course of their respective careers. Their work has focused on explicating and refining qualitative research theory and methodology. In the process, one concern has been to answer criticism from the positivist establishment (i.e., funding agencies and journals) with respect to the legitimacy of qualitative research. Their answers are couched in the form of corollaries to positivist methodological criteria such as validity, reliability, and objectivity. For Lincoln and Guba (2013), the corresponding constructivist methodological criteria are credibility, transferability, dependability, and confirmability (p. 82). As Cohen and Crabtree (2006) explain: the credibility criterion can be met through prolonged engagement, persistent observation, triangulation, peer debriefing, negative case analysis, referential adequacy, and member-checking. The transferability criterion can be met through thick, rich description. The dependability criterion can be met through an inquiry audit. The confirmability criterion can be met through a confirmability audit, audit trail, triangulation, and a reflexive journal. While an exhaustive explanation of qualitative research methodology is beyond the scope of this chapter, the takeaway here is that methodological credibility, transferability, and dependability are established through investing significant time with research participants and in their environments, meticulously documenting details about the participants and research insights, and actively reflecting on the process and progress of research as it goes forward.[3]

Relativism is the basic ontological assumption of constructivism. This means that social reality, or the world as it is experienced by people, is relative. For Lincoln and Guba (2013), knowledge is conceived of as a relationship between the knower and the knowable, and it is non-quantifiable (p. 40). Transactional subjectivism is the basic epistemological presupposition of constructivism. The relationship between the knower and the knowable is highly personal and context-specific; thus, knowledge is created, not discovered (Lincoln and Guba, p. 40). Lincoln and Guba explain how the hermeneutic/dialectic is the basic methodological presupposition of constructivism and that constructivist methodology delves into minds and into the meaning-making and sense-making of the several knowers involved. The process involves first uncovering constructions and then confronting, comparing, and contrasting the constructions. Finally, the hermeneutic circle of going from part to whole and back again defines the constant-comparative methodology utilized in constructivist/naturalistic inquiry (Lincoln and Guba, p. 40).

Teaching constructivism as critical methodology, therefore, is a valuable contribution to the mission of diversity education because it provides learners a framework for recognizing their own biases and teaches an ethic of seeking alternative perspectives and valuing those in making decisions. This diversity of perspectives is crucial to honing the critical consciousness of honors students and truly everyone involved in the honors enterprise.

CURATORS OF THE PARTICULAR

How, then, can we teach constructivist thought and put it to work in the life of honors students? As discussed above, our experience of the world is subjective and colored by the values, expectations, and perspectives that are dominant in our respective cultures. Baltzly (2014) quotes Zeno of Citium, founder of the Greek Stoic school of philosophy, to show that the Stoics believed that there was only one true correspondence between physical reality and human understanding and that this could be discerned as a cognitive impression that "'arises from that which is; is stamped and impressed in accordance with that very thing; and of such a kind as could not arise from what is not.'" This perspective depends on a one-to-one correspondence between language and reality that is echoed throughout Western thought from the Enlightenment onward in the conflation of intelligence and the ability to write.

In contrast, semiotics provides a progressive understanding of language, which is informed by the understanding of the experience of reality and the relationship between signifier and signified as subjective. While Saussure (1963) himself noted that "the individual does not have the power to change a sign in any way once it has become established in the linguistic community" (p. 68), the example Gates (1987) provides of signifyin(g) shows that signs can be adapted to new meanings, given different perspectives and contexts. Further expansion of semiotics suggests that indeterminacy of meaning is well-accepted. Brown and Yule (1983) note that "however objective the notion of 'text' may appear . . . the perception and interpretation of each text is essentially subjective" (p. 11). This subjective perspective, more aligned with the constructivist worldview, helps us to understand that language represents a very tenuous agreement about our experience of the world. I might always perceive the color signified by "blue" in the same way, for example, but the way in which other people experience and decode the same refraction of light is dependent on their individual genetics and body chemistry.[4] Something that might seem as objectively discernable as the color of the sky, then, is only as true as our overlapping perceptions of the phenomenon. Indeed while Herbert (2015), in his lead essay for the *JNCHC* commemorating the 50th anniversary of the organization, asserts that "thoughts actually are something that people can have in common" (p. 8), this assertion follows several pages in which Herbert describes, in detail, the pains he had to take in two different organizations to seek out this shared understanding. The process of "thinking and rethinking" Herbert describes requires careful listening, restating, and willingness to find common ground (p. 5–7), and it is dangerous to assume that thoughts are held in common by default. A significant amount of work is needed to achieve those thoughts in common. What is needed, first of all, is an understanding of how individualized perceptions might be. Secondly, a desire to seek out and compare different perceptions is required. We will briefly consider how we encode perception before moving on to how we might employ this understanding in our pedagogies.

According to Broadbent (1958), information processing theory, a theory of learning that uses computers as a model for the way that humans process and store information, posits that we use schema to encode and organize new experience (p. 206). The mental organization of information in information processing theory includes both declarative knowledge (what) and procedural knowledge (how) (see Broadbent, 1964, p. 64; Hampson and Morris,

1996, p. 130).[5] If human information processing corresponds to computer information processing, such a theory does suggest that previous learning and experience are crucial to the retention of new information. It also gives an indication as to why experiential learning—the opportunity for a person to directly experience, encode, and associate stimuli—is an important part of education. Appropriately, most of what we call high-impact learning depends on this direct, hands-on learning experience. The way that we associate this new learning with previous learning is highly subjective and therefore highly personal. One's ability or inability to imagine the perspective of others also plays a role in this learning process as the following discussion of theory of mind explains.

"Theory of mind" is the psychological term for human self-awareness. In Jean Piaget's theory of cognitive development, an important part of the development of this theory of mind is the elimination of egocentrism or the inability to conceive that other people have different perspectives. Curiously, the concept of White privilege, the concept I introduced at the beginning of this chapter, seems to operate in much the same way as egocentrism works to preclude the possibility that the subjective experience of another person might contradict one's worldview. Studies that introduce different perspectives offer some hope that this "mindblindness," as the inability to eliminate egocentrism is sometimes called, may be positively influenced. According to Galinsky and Ku (2004), "Perspective-taking also appears to take advantage of the very cognitive processes that produce intergroup bias in the first place. Although ethnocentrism is a natural extension of egocentrism, perspective-taking utilizes egocentric tendencies—our proclivity for thinking highly of ourselves—to reduce bias rather than increase it" (p. 601; see also McCoy, 2010, in *Setting the Table for Diversity*, pp. 135–50). If our instinctual reactions to unfamiliar others can be conceived of as a schema in which the procedural knowledge of appropriate behavior kicks in, then it should be possible to retrain that response by recognizing it as a construct; contrasting the values present in the construct to an ideal of diversity, access, and inclusion; and then working to replace the response positively.

In an honors context, this exercise of recognizing one's perspective as a construct might be put into practice by creating a series of assignments in a first-year seminar in which students must interrogate received values and perspectives before being asked to evaluate values and perspectives that differ from their own. Students would receive instruction on how humans are socialized to a particular understanding of "normal, natural, right, and good," and then they would work through scenarios in which they are asked to evaluate their initial response to a situation critically by employing perspective-taking of the unfamiliar other (see Kotinek 2010). An important point to make in this educational exercise is that it will be exactly those things that students imagine need no explanation that, in fact, require the most careful explication. Future honors courses or reflective eportfolio assignments might be built on the understanding that students have established perspective-taking competence; additional assignments could then expand and enhance that competency in increasingly more complex ways and in different disciplinary contexts.

In this chapter, I have conceived of using the constructivist perspective to improve diversity, access, and inclusion in honors, but the utility of the method can be adapted further. The idiosyncratic overlap of our interests, abilities, and opportunities gives each of us the chance to be a niche specialist. The architecture student with an interest in healthcare, an engineering student taking a second major in philosophy, and the English student focused on social justice issues all come to a conversation about healthcare reform from different perspectives and with different strengths, but they may also be interested in working together to create a novel approach to the subject. If these students have been trained to actively seek different perspectives with an aim of creating better understanding, they will be better primed and prepared to engage in this work across disciplinary boundaries.

Presuming that people have taken the opportunity to ensure a good fit between their values and the work they set out to accomplish, the cultivation of this niche specialty gives them the ability to advocate for the cause of their choice. Cultivation of expertise entails building a base of knowledge through study and experience as well as drawing connections across disciplinary boundaries and critically evaluating sources from this insider/outsider perspective. Undertaking to explain, in detail, their assumptions and thought processes will make students more effective ambassadors for their ideas. Taken together with a culture that supports valuing others' perspectives through perspective-taking, efforts to encourage this kind of breadth and depth in honors students positions them to be change leaders. Everyone has a sphere of influence, and, as noted by singer-cum-activist Paul David Hewson (better known by his stage name, Bono), influence, no matter how localized, is "a kind of currency . . . you have to spend it wisely" (qtd. in Assayas, 2005, p. 93). We can and should encourage students to think of themselves as curators for their own idiosyncratic expertise and foster their continued efforts to build or curate that knowledge base as they seek out correspondences with other students whose interests, abilities, and opportunities border their own.

In closing this section, I want to clarify that I am not suggesting that students uncritically accept the opinion of others as verified fact, only that a constructivist approach provides an opportunity to discover perspectives and insights different from those we might draw on or take ourselves. In fact, I would suggest that we should also be giving our students license and experience to evaluate new perspectives critically, even as they graciously learn to have their own perspectives critically evaluated. The practice of this constructivist methodology leaves open the possibility of adding to their understanding of the world. Below I adapt some critical evaluation questions potentially useful for the promotion of a process of critical inquiry that appreciates different perspectives.

- What is the question/issue/problem that is being presented to me?

- What additional information do I need to answer this question?

- What information has been provided that I think is irrelevant? What makes me think that the information is irrelevant?

- Given the information presented, or the information that I already have, what do I think is the best answer or solution?

- How would changes in the situation affect my choice of a solution?

CONCLUSION

The need for perspective taking and critical evaluation are not mutually exclusive, although our students likely come to us with little experience—personal or vicarious—that prepares them to do this work simultaneously. For example, the 2016 election cycle saw an unprecedented proliferation of "fake news," a confluence of misinformation exacerbated by a current tendency in the United States for people to associate with like-minded others and depend on social media that agrees with their own personal opinion for their news, habits that effectively create echo chambers of the same. As noted by Kunda (1990), "people are not at liberty to believe anything they like; they are constrained by their prior beliefs" (p. 490). The ongoing problem with "fake news" provides evidence of the desperate need for the entire American electorate to develop both critical thinking and social awareness.

As an antidote to echo chambers of the same, we can encourage our students to be curators of the particular. Encouraging students to develop a niche of expertise that is a good reflection of their interests and values, as well as to look to each other as resources about topics of tangential interest, constitutes good first steps toward highlighting the diversity of thought and opinion in the world. When coupled with the habits of mind developed with a constructivist perspective—recognizing one's own biases, seeking disconfirming information, and valuing others' opinions in decision making—the development of curators of the particular can also serve to inoculate our future leaders to an increasingly polarized social and political world. In fact, in a recent research article in *Political Psychology*, Kahan, Landrum, Carpenter, Helft, and Jamieson (2016) have demonstrated that curiosity can counteract the politically motivated reasoning that is driving social polarization (p. 180).

An honors community and curriculum that provide social and emotional support, along with the intellectual challenge to seek disconfirming evidence as students develop their own perspectives, can bridge the experience gap and train culturally responsive intellectual leaders for their campus and our future world. Further, the sharing of diverse perspectives this chapter champions and the equity and inclusion to which such exercises can lead may be generalizable not only to the entire honors community but to the higher education community as a whole—faculty, staff, and administrators alike—in support of high-impact practices that can lead to diversity, equity, and inclusion for all.

NOTES

[1]For more detailed discussion of this elusive definition of honors, see Kotinek, Neuber, and Sindt, 2010; Digby and Kotinek, 2010.

[2]To read the elaborating document for the NCHC definition of honors education, click the hyperlinked word "document" on the definition webpage at <http://www.nchchonors.org/directors-faculty/definition-of-honors-education>.

[3]For further detail on qualitative research methodology, see the Qualitative Research Guidelines Project provided by Cohen and Crabtree (2006) at <http://qualres.org>.

[4]See Zand and Borhan's work on Rhodopsin and Cellular Retinotic Acid-binding Protein II <https://news.kettering.edu/news/seeing-red-or-green-chemistry-color-vision> as explanation for my assertions about individual perceptions of color.

[5]The "method of loci" mnemonic device described in ancient Greek and Roman treatises (and also popularized as "mind palaces" in Thomas Harris's *Hannibal* and BBC's *Sherlock*) are examples of highly developed mental schema.

REFERENCES

American Association of Colleges & Universities. (2017). Carol Geary Schneider. Washington, D.C.: Author. Retrieved from <https://www.aacu.org/contributor/carol-geary-schneider>

Assayas, M. (2005). *Bono: In conversation with Michka Assayas*. New York, NY: Riverhead Books.

Baltzly, D. (2014). Stoicism. In E. N. Zalta (Ed.), *The Stanford Encyclopedia of Philosophy*. Retrieved from <https://plato.stanford.edu/entries/stocism>

Boroditsky, L. (2010). Lost in translation. *The Wall Street Journal*, July 23, 2010. Retrieved from <http://www.wsj.com/articles/SB10001424052748703467304575383131592767868>

Bourdeau, M. (2015). Auguste Comte. In E. N. Zalta (Ed.), *The Stanford Encyclopedia of Philosophy*. Retrieved from <http://plato.stanford.edu/entries/comte>

Broadbent, D. E. (1958). *Perception and communication*. Oxford, UK: Pergamon Press.

Brown, G., & Yule, G. (1983). *Discourse analysis*. Cambridge, UK: Cambridge UP.

Chandler, D. (2002). *Semiotics: The basics*. Oxford, UK: Routledge Press.

Cohen, D., & Crabtree, B. (2006). Qualitative research guidelines project. Retrieved from <http://qualres.org>

Coleman, F. D. (2016). Hip hop culture: The fifth element. Class lecture slides.

Coleman, L. L. (2010). Introduction: Changing our selves, changing the world: *Setting the table for diversity*. In L. L. Coleman & J. D. Kotinek (Eds.). *Setting the table for diversity*. (pp. 11–18). Lincoln, NE: National Collegiate Honors Council. NCHC Monograph Series.

Coleman, L. L., & Kotinek, J. D. (Eds.). (2010). *Setting the table for diversity*. Lincoln, NE: National Collegiate Honors Council. NCHC Monograph Series.

Comte, A. (1880). *The course in positive philosophy*. H. Martineau, Trans. Chicago, IL: Belford-Clarke Co.

Digby, J., & Kotinek, J. D. (2010). Defining honors: Distilling meaning from a chorus of voices. Paper presented at the National Collegiate Honors Council Conference. Kansas City, MO.

Durkheim, É., & Lukes, S. (Ed.). (1982). Preface to the second edition. In *The rules of sociological method and selected texts on sociology and its method* (pp. 34–47). (W. D. Halls, Trans.). New York, NY: The Free Press. (Original work published in 1895)

Eliade, M. (1963). *Myth and reality*. Long Grove, IL: Waveland Press.

Galinsky, A. D., & Ku, G. (2004). The effects of perspective-taking on prejudice: The moderating role of self-evaluation. *Personality and Social Psychology Bulletin, 30*(5), 594–604. doi:10.1177/0146167203262802

Gates, Jr., H. L. (1987). *Figures in black: Words, signs, and the "racial" self*. New York, NY: Oxford University Press.

—. (2014). *The signifying monkey: A theory of African-American literary criticism*. New York, NY: Oxford University Press.

Gerace, A., Day, A., Casey, S., & Mohr, P. (2015). Perspective taking and empathy: Does having similar past experience to another person make it easier to take their perspective? *Journal of Relationships Research, 6*. doi:10.1017/jrr.2015.6

Hacking, I. (Ed.). (1981). *Scientific revolutions*. New York, NY: Oxford UP.

Halfpenny, P. (1982). *Positivism and sociology: Explaining social life*. London, UK: Allen and Unwin.

Hampson, P. J., & Morris, P. E. (1996). *Understanding cognition*. Cambridge, MA: Blackwell Publishers, Inc.

Herbert, J. (2015) Thinking and rethinking: The practical value of an honors education. *Journal of the National Collegiate Honors Council, 16*(2), 3–9.

Hubert, D., Pickavance, J., & Hyberger, A. (2015). Reflective e-portfolios: One HIP to rule them all? *Peer Review, 17*(14). Retrieved from <https://www.aacu.org/peerreview/2015/fall/hubert>

Kahan, D. M., Landrum, A., Carpenter, K., Helft, L., & Jamieson, K. H. (2016). Science, curiosity, and political information processing. *Political Psychology, 38*, 179–99. doi:10.1111/pops.12396

Kelly, S. K. (2013). Assessing success in honors: Getting beyond graduation rates. *Journal of the National Collegiate Honors Council, 14*(2), 25–30.

King, G., Keohane, R., & Verba, S. (1994). *Designing social inquiry: Scientific inference in qualitative research.* Princeton, NJ: Princeton University Press.

Kohlberg, L. (1976). Moral stages and moralization: The cognitive-developmental approach. In T. Lickona (Ed.), *Moral development and behavior* (pp. 31–53). New York, NY: Holt, Rinehart & Winston.

Kotinek, J. D. (2010). Passing for Black: White privilege and Black identity formation. In L. L. Coleman & J. D. Kotinek (Eds.), *Setting the table for diversity* (pp. 229–38). Lincoln, NE: National Collegiate Honors Council. NCHC Monograph Series.

—. (2008). Toward a theory of paradigmatic intelligence: Individual performance. Unpublished project completed for EPSY 648—Intelligence & Creativity. Texas A&M University.

Kotinek, J. D., Neuber, A., & Sindt, K. (2010). Gifted, high-achieving, honors: Is there a meaningful difference? Paper presented at the National Academic Advising Association National Conference. Orlando, FL.

Kuh, G. D. (2008). High-impact educational practices (Excerpt from *High-impact educational practices: What they are, who has access to them, and why they matter.*), Washington, D.C.:

Association of American Colleges and Universities. Retrieved from American Colleges and Universities website <https://www.aacu.org/leap/hips>

Kunda, Z. (1990). The case for motivated reasoning. *Psychological Bulletin, 108*(3), 480–98. doi:10.1037/0033-2909.108.3.480

Lanier, G., Reubel, J., Scott, R., Torda, E., & Kotinek, J. (2013). Definition of honors education. National Collegiate Honors Council Board of Directors Task Force. Lincoln, NE. Retrieved 01 March 2017 from <https://www.nchchonors.org/directors-faculty/definition-of-honors-education>

Lewis, C. S. (2002). Myth became fact. In L. Walmsley (Ed.), *C. S. Lewis essay collection: Faith, Christianity and the church* (pp. 138–42). London, UK: HarperCollins.

Lincoln, Y. S., & Guba, E. G. (2013). *The constructivist credo.* London, UK: Routledge Press.

Long, A. (2002). "Editor's introduction." in A. Long, D. Mullins & R. Rushton (Eds.). *Journal of the National Collegiate Honors Council, 3*(1), 9-11. Retrieved from <http://digitalcommons.unl.edu/nchcjournal/235>

Long, A., Mullins, D. & Rushton, R. (Eds.). (2002). *Journal of the National Collegiate Honors Council, 3*(1). Retrieved from <http://digitalcommons.unl.edu/nchcjournal/235>

Long, A., & Mullins, D. (Eds.). (2015). *Journal of the National Collegiate Honors Council, 16*(2). Retrieved from <http://digitalcommons.unl.edu/nchcjournal/487>

March, J. G., & Olsen, J. P. (1995). *Democratic governance.* New York, NY: Free Press.

McCoy, M. L. (2010). A place for diversity: Experiential projects in honors curricula. In L. L. Coleman & J. D. Kotinek (Eds.), *Setting the table for diversity* (pp. 135–50). Lincoln, NE: National Collegiate Honors Council. NCHC Monograph Series.

Médaille, J. (2010). *Toward a truly free market: A distributist perspective on the role of government, taxes, health care, deficits, and more.* Wilmington, DE: ISI Books.

Piaget, J. (1952). *The origins of intelligence in children* (M. Cook, Trans.). New York, NY: International Universities Press.

Rice, L. (2015). The impact of honors on the campus community. *Journal of the National Collegiate Honors Council, 16*(2). Retrieved from <http://digitalcommons.unl.edu/nchc journal/480>

Riek, E., & Sheridan, K. (2010). Setting the table for diversity. In L. L. Coleman & J. D. Kotinek (Eds.), *Setting the table for diversity* (pp. 21–29). Lincoln, NE: National Collegiate Honors Council. NCHC Monograph Series.

Saussure, F. de. (1983). *Course in general linguistics* (R. Harris, Trans.). London, UK: Duckworth. (Original work published 1916).

Schneider, C. G. (2015). The LEAP challenge: Transformative for students, essential for liberal education. Retrieved from <https://www.aacu.org/leap/hips>

Schneider, C. G. (2002). President's campaign for the advancement of liberal learning (CALL). Reprinted from Association of American Colleges and Universities (AAUP) website (Jan. 2002) in *Journal of the National Collegiate Honors Council, 3*(1), 33–35.

Schwandt, T. A. (1998). Constructivist, interpretivist approaches to human inquiry. In N. K. Denzin & Y. S. Lincoln (Eds.), *The landscape of qualitative research: Theories and issues* (pp. 118–37). Thousand Oaks, CA: Sage Publications.

Schwandt, T. A. (2013). Egon Guba: Observations on a journey to constructivism. In Y. S. Lincoln & E. G. Guba (Eds.), *The constructivist credo* (pp. 15–26). London, UK: Routledge Press.

Shavelson, R. I., & Towne, L. (Eds.). (2002). *Scientific research in education.* Committee on Scientific Principles for Education

Research. National Research Council Center for Education, Division of Behavioral and Social Sciences and Education. Washington, D.C.: National Academy Press.

Silverman, K. (1983). *The subject of semiotics*. New York, NY: Oxford University Press.

Sladek, R. M., Bond, M. J., & Phillips, P. A. (2010). Age and gender differences in preferences for rational and experiential thinking. *Personality and Individual Differences, 49*(8), 907–11. doi:10.1016/j.paid.2010.07.028

Stein, B., Haynes, A., & Redding, M. (2016). National dissemination of the CAT instrument: Lessons learned and implications. *Proceedings of the AAAS/NSF Envisioning the Future of Undergraduate STEM Education: Research and Practice Symposium.*

von Glasersfeld, E., & Larochelle, M. (Ed.). (2007). Aspects of constructivism: Vico, Berkeley, Piaget. *Key works in radical constructivism* (pp. 91–99). Rotterdam, Netherlands: Sense Publishers.

A Blueprint for Occupying Honors: Activism in Institutional Diversity, Equity, Inclusion, Social Justice, and Academic Excellence

Finnie D. Coleman
University of New Mexico

THE ORIGINS OF THE OCCUPY MOVEMENT

On 18 December 2010, 26-year-old fruit and vegetable vender Mohamed (Tarek) Bouazizi took his own life in the streets of Sidi Bouzid, Tunisia. Bouazizi's Tibetanesque protest against police brutality and widespread corruption led to the near immediate downfall of Tunisian President Zine El Abidine Ben Ali, a man who had held power since leading the Tunisian Revolution or the "medical coup d'état" of November 1987.[1] That this powerful dictator fell as the result of a single act by one frustrated and humiliated man is difficult to believe. Perhaps that is because the supposed cause and effect relationship between Bouazizi's suicide and the collapse of Ali's regime is not altogether accurate. When Ben Ali fled Tunisia on January 14, 2011, people around the world were given a powerful example of how an individual act committed in the pursuit of justice can literally change the world—but only if conditions are ripe for such change.

While Bouazizi's self-immolation was certainly a catalyst in Ben Ali's downfall, it was not the actual cause of the larger movement. Following his death, members of Bouazizi's family and some of his close friends held a small protest in open defiance of laws put in place to curb public demonstrations. Knowing that they faced beatings or worse, this small group of people found the courage to stand against Ben Ali's tyranny in spite of the potential consequences. In truth, it was the success of that small, defiant protest immediately following Bouazizi's immolation that sparked the Arab Spring, not the ritual sacrifice in and of itself.

Although numerous newspapers, Internet bloggers, so-called "Web-Activists," and international news outlets have claimed that the so-called Arab Spring began with Bouazizi's self-immolation, absent the risks taken by family and friends following his death, Bouazizi's desperate act would likely have gone unnoticed by the world in much the same way as the world has virtually ignored more than 145 similar acts in China's Sichuan Province since 2009.

Indeed, while it is likely that the impact of Bouazizi's act would not have been felt beyond the amazement of those who personally witnessed his charred and smoldering body lying in front of the provincial headquarters in Sidi Bouzid, Bouazizi's sacrifice and the small protest that followed tapped into deep and long-festering feelings of anger and unrest. In "Revolution and Counterrevolution in Tunisia," Tunis Al Manar University sociologist Mounir Saidani and his co-author R. A. Judy describe the chaos that followed this first small protest as a "dialectic of conflict and appeasement" that highlighted a process of "making, unmaking, and remaking" that was driven by "an intense ongoing struggle between emergent social forces and established political formations" (43).

Country after country entered the cycle of making (violent civil unrest), unmaking (the fall of long-standing dictatorships), and remaking (rebuilding government and social institutions). Egypt's President Hosni Mubarak resigned from office just four weeks after

Ben Ali fled Tunisia for Saudi Arabia. In March, the Syrian Civil War was sparked by protests in the ancient city of Darra that called for the ouster of President Bashar al-Assad. Six months after Ben Ali fled Tunisia, Muammar Gaddafi found himself on the run and was brutally killed in October 2011. Following Gaddafi's death, it was not surprising that Yemeni President Ali Abdullah Saleh agreed to give up power in the face of rising resistance. Following Saleh's lead, numerous leaders across the region proactively announced that they would not be running for reelection. Only the second leader since Algeria gained its independence from France in 1956, Ben Ali reigned for more than 23 years, Mubarak for 30 years, Saleh for 33, and Gaddafi for 42 years. Something was different now. . . . The blueprint for social upheaval had changed.

Political protests and civil unrest across the Arab world quickly spread to other parts of the planet. Countries large and small—powerful and not so powerful—were forced to countenance long-standing social, political, and economic injustices that fueled innumerable acts of resistance and outright rebellion against constituted state authority. The social unrest associated with the Arab Spring saw its first public manifestation in the United States of America on 17 September 2011when protestors "occupied" Zucotti Park (formerly Liberty Square) in New York City.

Members of the business community, political leaders, and many everyday citizens were almost evenly split over the Occupy Wall Street Movement. Some commentators lambasted the leaders of the movement as disorganized and opportunistic degenerates while others like 2012 presidential candidate Ron Paul openly praised the Occupy Movement, putting it on par philosophically with the then emerging Tea Party.[2] Few pundits, detractors or supporters, however, could have anticipated just how impactful and effective the movement would become.

There was some genius in the idea of what could be called its "decentralized organization." If nothing else, it allowed for activists of very different political stripes to come together to lobby for change at the local level where grassroots movements are especially effective. As if the invisible hand of an uber-mediator guided them, these individuals came to see that by temporarily abandoning their positions (the change that they wanted), they were able to discover their shared interests (why they wanted change).

The movement spread rapidly across the country, spawning numerous "secondary" Occupy Movements. Three of these movements, Occupy Colleges, Occupy Education, and Occupy Education Northern California, joined together with the New York Student Aid Alliance to stage one of the first coordinated, nationwide protests by high school and college students. During the "Day of Action," 1 March 2012, students went on strike, staged sit-ins, marched, and otherwise attempted to disrupt business as usual.[3] The antinomianism that galvanized Bouazizi's family and friends was alive and well in student activists on campuses across the country.[4]

The success of this "Day of Action" event forced many leaders in higher education to take notice of student unrest regarding tuition, quality of education, and faculty compensation. This nationwide rejection of the status quo in higher education was followed by innumerable sit-ins at local school board meetings, picketing of mayor's offices, protests in front of city halls, demonstrations at the Department of Education, and occupation of college campuses. From Boston to Berkeley, college students joined together to protest the rising cost of a college education. As the movement grew, students, faculty, staff, and administrators began to see more clearly that controlling costs was not just the right thing to do, it was good for business as well.

No matter which side one might have taken in the early debates concerning the motivations for the Occupy Movement or the efficacy of its platform, one could not help but marvel at the fact that unprecedented numbers of people from very different walks of life took notice and then took action. The healthy antinomianism on display during the Occupy Movement was not new to the United States; we saw similar energies at work during the Women's Liberation and Civil Rights Movements that dominated the latter half of the twentieth century and in the LGBT Rights Movement that ushered in the twenty-first century.

While the social energy, skepticism of constituted authority, and activist spirit that undergirded these movements were not new, the reliance on social media and Internet technologies to recruit new activists, to train those activists, and to coordinate their individual efforts in places like Tahrir Square was revolutionary. Disciplined indirection replaced phrases like "marching orders," broadly conceived goals displaced "lists of demands," and manipulating the rules of engagement by way of coyness and brinksmanship replaced the traditional "frontal assault." The Occupy Movement reflected the vibrancy of a new and very different blueprint for confronting power.

On 13 July 2013, George Zimmerman was acquitted of all charges related to the shooting death of seventeen-year-old Trayvon Martin, and another movement began. Anguished by this decision, social activist Alicia Garza posted "A Love Note to Black People" on Facebook that contained the phrase "Our Lives Matter, Black Lives Matter." Garza would go on to partner with fellow activists Patrice Cullors and April Tometi to found the Black Lives Matter Movement.[5]

Only slightly modifying the blueprint that led to dramatic change in the Arab world and feeding upon the same antinomianistic energy that fed the various Occupy Movements, Black Lives Matter quickly found itself at the head of the ongoing struggle for social justice in the United States. It is important to note that the energy that I am referring to is present across the political spectrum—it energizes the political left as much as it energizes the political right. The 2016 national election is the best example to date of how this energy is literally transforming American society.

Given the remarkable fluidity of terminology in social media, the idea of "Occupying Honors" may seem a bit anachronistic. I persist in using the term here not for its currency but for the locus of ideas and energies that we have come to associate with the term. Likewise, the terms "diversity," "equity," "inclusion," and "social justice" are dated terms—what we are after is the locus of ideas regarding social justice that have always undergirded these terms.

For the sake of discussion, "Occupying Honors" reflects our efforts to harness the transformative political and social energies circulating in our communities and on our campuses to address long-standing social justice issues on college campuses around our country. For reasons detailed below, honors programs and colleges are not merely interesting sites to revisit these issues, these programs are also the logical places to make the transition from theory to practice, to tap into the activist spirit that is afoot in our country and around the world.

TOWARD OCCUPYING HONORS

On 16 November 2012, the aforementioned "activist spirit" made an improbable appearance at the National Collegiate Honors Council's 47th Annual Conference. During a session titled "Diversity Forum 2012: Occupy Honors Education," honors faculty, students, and professional staff members asked themselves, "How can we *occupy* honors education in transformative and revolutionary ways that place honors education on the cutting edge of educational practice and promote the democratic values of diversity, equity, inclusion, and justice?"

Given the caliber of the question, the setting in which the question was asked, and the time frame allotted for discussion, responses were necessarily rhetorical and cursory. The question allowed participants to briefly plumb each other for nuggets of wisdom, best practices, and philosophical gems that might be brought back to home institutions for further consideration. And while the idea of occupying honors began as a somewhat rhetorical question, some in the honors community before, during, and after the conference wondered aloud about how we might actually move this question from rhetoric to reality.

In this essay I examine the implications of occupying honors and speculate about the methods and strategies we might deploy if in fact we see fit to move beyond merely asking whether we should or should not pursue the question any further. How would we go about occupying honors, what would we want to accomplish, and how will we know when we have succeeded? What, precisely, would a blueprint for occupying honors look like anyway? We must of course properly frame these and other questions so that they are no longer rhetorical, but answerable.

Assuming that we can successfully reframe these questions, we should be prepared for the reality that the answers we arrive at will vary to the same degree that our country's honors programs and colleges differ one from another in terms of character; organizational structure; positioning and prestige on campus; educational goals; faculty, student, and staff demographics; pedagogical practices; internal and executive leadership; donor relations; and facilities. This variability in methods and desired outcomes of course precludes a one-size-fits-all set of answers to how we might successfully occupy honors; just as our rationales and methods will vary from one institution to the next, our individual institutional outcomes will also vary.

The impracticality of hitting upon a common set of solutions does not mean that we cannot find common ground upon which to construct our particular blueprints. That common ground is found in the similarity of the institutional levers we use to produce institutional change. Commonalities in organizational structure, institutional priorities, leadership structure, and operational philosophies used by colleges and universities across the country will serve as common starting points if honors is to be successfully occupied. Because of these commonalities, the processes for creating and driving institutional change share many important similarities across academia regardless of the structure and scope of individual institutions.

Before laying out what I feel is a reasonable set of general strategies for fostering change in honors education, I offer a word on a more personal note about guiding principles and what is at stake in staging an Occupy Honors Movement. Understanding that the Occupy Movement conjures stereotypes about individuals engaged in openly belligerent and subversive behaviors, I hasten to add here that my intention in this essay is not to negatively criticize honors or to in any way foment unrest in our honors communities. I intend here only to challenge honors faculty, students, and staff to look beyond the *rhetoric* of occupation to develop strategies and plans that will lead to a specific set of positive outcomes: placing honors education on the cutting edge of educational practice and promoting the democratic values of diversity, equity, inclusion, and social justice.

I learned a great deal about these values and their importance to the success of our honors communities from an important mentor of mine, Dr. Edward Funkhouser, who led one of the nation's largest honors enterprises at one of the nation's most conservative institutions in higher education, Texas A&M University. Before touching upon these experiences at Texas A&M, I offer a summary discussion of an important set of terms and concepts relating to diversity.

NUANCES OF DIVERSITY: A TECHNICAL VOCABULARY

Across the country, colorful binders containing inch-thick diversity plans and strategies sit on bookshelves in the offices of senior administrators who almost daily find themselves perplexed by problems associated with diversity, equity, inclusion, and campus climate. Hidden in plain view, these plans range from the excellently conceived and plausible to the hastily constructed and impractical. They reflect investments of time, trust, resources, and goodwill that should never be squandered. Independent of their quality or practicality, far too many of these diversity plans merely offer talking points in abridged conversations about institutional change.

These plans should function as fresh beginnings of protracted conversations that guide the implementation of a carefully and thoughtfully crafted blueprint for action. Jean Ries, management consultant at Olive Grove, a leader in non-profit consulting, teaches us that our strategic plans must be "implementable and iterative," "integrated into the existing management structure," and, most important, "responsive to emergent conditions."[6] We do well to keep Ries's admonition in mind as we engage in fresh conversations about diversity.

Unfortunately, our conversations about diversity are often undermined by deficit model thinking—thinking rooted in the problems of diversity as opposed to the opportunities diversity provides. Our efforts are also damaged by contentious debates and intellectually truncated by zero-sum-game politics—the belief that improving conditions for one segment of society must mean a decline for some other segment in that society. Even among the best-intentioned actors on our campuses, these conversations may be sabotaged by the fact that very few of us in academia possess the technical vocabulary required to intelligently discuss the nuances of diversity.

More often than not, when we say diversity we mean numerical diversity, which is only one dimension of a complex multi-dimensional concept. Our discussions of diversity often become hopelessly muddled when we fail to realize that numerical or structural diversity is important to but not definitive of transactional diversity and that transactional diversity is more often than not the product of our efforts to enhance categorical diversity. If we throw in the personal and professional decisions that impact universal diversity, and explain why universal diversity is essentially a prerequisite for transformational diversity—and by extension the institution's value proposition—we find ourselves lost in worrisome discussions that are essentially ill-advised trips across jargon-choked shallows. This result is a shame because these complex conversations about diversity, which I address in detail below, are necessary if we are to successfully foster equity, inclusion, and social justice on our campuses. Again, occupying honors is essentially an effort to help our institutions to do just that. If honors communities intend to take the lead in these complex discussions, they must begin with their own understanding of the complexities of the term "diversity."

Institutions often focus almost exclusively on the measure of diversity. Demographics offer an easily understandable metric, but they do not tell us any more than the fact that the more perspectives we have on campus, the more likely we are to benefit from those perspectives. These numbers tell us nothing about whether or not we are in fact benefiting from diverse perspectives, and they provide no guidance as to how we might benefit from those important perspectives.

While **Structural Diversity** is clearly important and an understandably popular marker of institutional change or stasis, it is but the first of four pillars that support the fifth and most important manifestation of diversity. These four pillars are **Structural (Numerical) Diversity**, **Categorical Diversity**, **Transactional Diversity**, **and Universal Diversity**. We need all four of these pillars if we are to support our ultimate goal: achieving **Transformative Diversity** (see Figure 1).

PILLAR I: STRUCTURAL OR NUMERICAL DIVERSITY[7]

Structural diversity is essentially a census of an institution's gender, racial, and ethnic composition: a snapshot of an institution's demographic realities. "The Dominant Group" is a key term in understanding structural diversity. The dominant group is an institution's entrenched governing majority. Numerical superiority, institutional history, and tradition support this group's ability to dominate an institution's decision-making. In the United States, academic institutions are placed in categories that reflect the race or ethnicity of the dominant or numerically superior group: Predominantly White Institutions (PWIs), Historically Black Colleges and Universities (106 HBCUs), Hispanic Serving Institutions (356 HSIs), and Tribal Colleges and Universities (37 TCUs).

We might reasonably expect that sufficient numerical or structural diversity provides the variety of personal experiences institutions need if they are to successfully pursue other forms of diversity. It is important, however, that we recognize that numbers only provide the necessary foundation to succeed; numbers do not guarantee success in improving campus climate, improvements in our efforts to become more inclusive, or a positive impact on the number of equitable outcomes we achieve.

PILLAR II: CATEGORICAL DIVERSITY[8]

This form of diversity helps us to understand that ethnicity and race are but two of numerous categories of difference that we might value. Gender, sexual orientation, class distinctions, generational

FIGURE 1. THE RELATIONSHIP BETWEEN DIFFERENT MANIFESTATIONS OF DIVERSITY

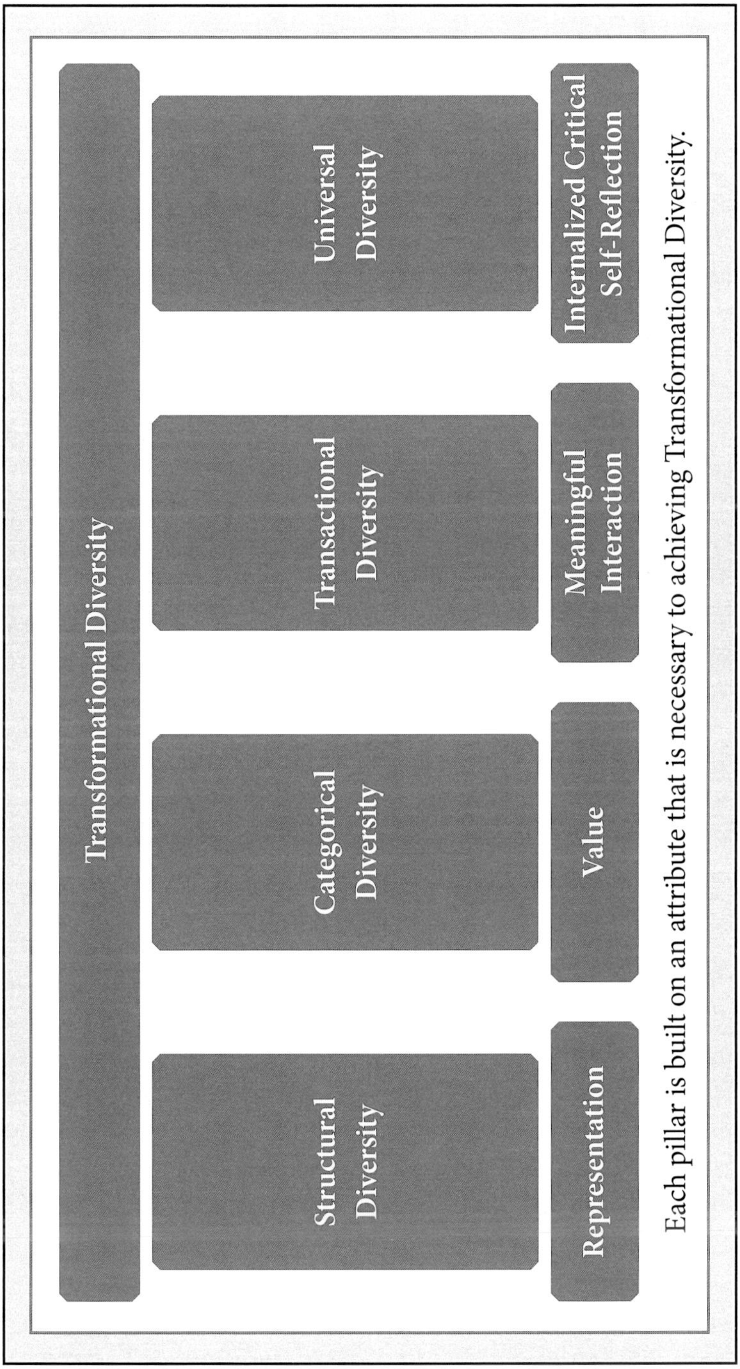

Transformational Diversity

Structural Diversity — Categorical Diversity — Transactional Diversity — Universal Diversity

Representation — Value — Meaningful Interaction — Internalized Critical Self-Reflection

Each pillar is built on an attribute that is necessary to achieving Transformational Diversity.

differences, age, or political leanings are other popular categories of difference. When fostering categorical diversity, we eschew focusing upon representation via numbers of a particular racial or ethnic group. Instead, we identify and come to celebrate what different cultural or social groups bring to the table.

How do we not just understand but benefit from the perspectives of Gays, Blacks, or Latinos? Categorical diversity moves beyond counting who is here to valuing who is here and inviting those different perspectives to tables of discussion (Inclusion). It is important to note that when properly practiced, categorical diversity does not privilege one group's perspectives over another's. These perspectives hold equal pride of place with other perspectives: they are not treated as thoughts from the margins.

Unfortunately, what we tend to do in the absence of truly engaged categorical diversity is to celebrate content. In those situations, difference is treated as a commodity. Culture, for example, is reduced to entertainment. We attend Feast Days not to understand the deeper meaning and history of Native American dance, for example, but to be entertained by the spectacle of their dance. We invite "them" in to entertain "us." Categorical diversity requires that we genuinely attempt to understand and include all elements of our socio-cultural communities in community-building discourse.

PILLAR III: TRANSACTIONAL DIVERSITY

Because transactional diversity is typically oriented around events and activities that celebrate interactions between people of different cultures or ethnicities, it is often conflated with categorical diversity. People often measure transactional diversity by the frequency with which different groups of people are given opportunities for genuine interaction. By bringing people of varying backgrounds together to celebrate a culture or an event, we learn from them and in the process improve our interpersonal skills. Too often people view transactional diversity as a mechanism by which "we" learn how to get along with "them." This perspective is unfortunate because we rarely challenge the essentialist notions of us-versus-them rhetoric in these exchanges. In transactional diversity we learn that our interactions should not be conducted for the sole benefit of one or another group but for the benefit of the community as a whole. Transactional diversity recognizes that community is the locus of all of these activities and that the community is comprised of different groups that interact on a regular basis.

PILLAR IV: UNIVERSAL DIVERSITY

Universal diversity recognizes that culture, race, and ethnicity are but part of a broader set of traits and characteristics that make people unique; diversity emanates from human difference . . . differences that can be capitalized upon. This definition is perhaps the stickiest of the ones I mention here. Universal diversity is perhaps the easiest to describe but the most difficult in terms of illuminating the potential problems associated with it. Several questions might help: What do we mean by diverse students? Do diverse students lose their status as diverse when they are at home or in their home environments? When we say "diverse students," don't we really mean "non-White" or "different from the majority?" We say "diverse students" because we are uncomfortable saying "different from White people." What are the implications of why White students are rarely if ever discussed as "diverse" students? Do we risk missing or losing the diversity that these individuals also bring to the table?

We somehow imagine diversity to have some sort of inverse or perhaps reciprocal relationship to race or ethnicity when the readily apparent absurdity of this construction should lead us to deeper questions about how we erroneously conflate race and pigmentation, which parallels gender issues and our concomitant tendency to conflate biological reality with performance of social roles. Universal diversity is the space where we interrogate the flimsiness of static definitions of diversity, realize the benefits of equity and inclusion, and mete out the deconstruction of us-versus-them logic and rhetoric. We recognize the inherent flaws in othering and pigeonholing in the name of diversity.

TRANSFORMATIVE DIVERSITY

Transformative diversity allows us to knowledgeably appreciate the manifold differences that set us apart and to earnestly celebrate the remarkable variety of traits, characteristics, beliefs, and values that bring us together. While structural diversity measures the number of underrepresented individuals on our campuses, in a number of articles, Sylvia Hurtado has argued that transformative diversity actively cultivates, nurtures, and values what these individuals have to offer.[9]

I want to take Hurtado's argument a step further: transformative diversity requires that we interrogate the historical, structural, behavioral, and psychological factors that are the principle factors in campus climate. In doing so we obliterate the notions of "we" and "they." Instead of "us" finding the time and resources to nurture "them," we recognize that it is important for all of us to assume equal footing in building a community that is nurturing for all of us. Herein lies the true power and possibility of diversity. To achieve it we must have successfully negotiated the four pillars of diversity upon which transformative diversity rests. This final stage is where we are able to truly and justly harness the strength of equity and inclusion. Beyond the important goals of fostering equity, inclusion, and social justice on our campuses, transformative diversity serves the important function of creating an environment where people are able to come together to address problems that their individual talents would not allow them to solve on their own. Here the dynamic shifts from providing utility to fostering synergy.[10]

THE FUNKHOUSER METHOD:
FROM EXCLUSIVITY TO INCLUSIVITY

For ten years Dr. Edward Funkhouser served as Executive Director of the Office of Honors Programs and Academic Scholarships at Texas A&M. Serving one of the nation's largest student bodies, this complex program was responsible for a remarkably wide range of activities that impacted thousands of honors-eligible as well as non-honors eligible students each semester. Funkhouser was responsible for guiding three distinct teams comprised of A&M students, faculty, and staff: the offices of Professional School Advising, Academic Scholarships, and Honors Programming.

Varying in age, personal politics, and work experience, these three diverse teams were responsible for recruiting prospective students, awarding academic scholarships, providing extracurricular programming, and housing honors. They were also responsible for coordinating honors instruction across the university, providing research opportunities for students and faculty, shepherding honors students into their graduate studies, and placing honors and non-honors students in their professions upon graduation.

Funkhouser was one of the first leaders in honors to understand that the real-world mission of honors went well beyond fostering excellence within honors communities. Early in his tenure as Executive Director, Funkhouser recognized the hidden impact that honors had on shaping campus climate; driving community relations; and fostering diversity, equity, and inclusion for faculty, staff and students across campus, not just in honors.

Arriving in honors with a background in business and the military, I was struck by Funkhouser's radical notion: "Honors should always be in the business of putting itself out of business." According to him, our responsibility in honors was to model the ideal education and champion innovative pedagogical practices such that how faculty members taught in honors could be emulated across the academic enterprise. Our ultimate success would not be measured in how well we served our cohort of honors students, but in how what we did in honors elevated educational experiences for all students; we would as a matter of course arrive at a point where the honors experience would become increasingly inclusive not exclusive. This perspective surprised me. My conceptualization of honors had always been that honors served as the ultimate exclusive enterprise of the many exclusive enterprises operating within academia.

Contrary to my notions of honors as a wellspring of unapologetic exclusivity in academia, Funkhouser developed strategies aimed at aggressively disrupting exclusionary pedagogies in honors. Our primary goal then was to imagine and construct a more inclusive future for higher education, a future where there would be no need for special classes designed for select groups of students. The academic side of honors, if successful, would render itself obsolete. What I did not realize before entering honors education was that this academic side was only part of what honors programs and colleges provide to academic communities across the country.

The most important point in Funkhouser's broad and forward-thinking vision for honors was that the pedagogical models that we embraced yesterday in honors had become stunningly archaic. Honors, like other aspects of the educational enterprise, Funkhouser felt, would have to evolve if it intended to survive. In this evolutionary process, honors would have to recognize the important role it has to play not just in fostering academic excellence but also in helping academic institutions to embrace the challenges borne of the natural evolution of higher education mores. All too few institutions of higher learning recognize the potential honors holds to impact and shape campus climate and to lead in the very transformation of an institution.

It is incumbent upon the honors community to recognize and more effectively communicate to administrators, faculty, students, and staff how our programs and colleges can serve as potent catalysts for institutional change. This role as catalyst will become increasingly important as dominant trends in higher education force institutions to become nimbler in their approaches to managing campus climate and institutional change as they strive to meet the increasingly sophisticated educational needs of future generations of students. Funkhouser understood intuitively that the future of academia hinged on the ability of institutions to understand that globalization was not merely a trend but an inevitable reality for American colleges and universities and that honors had a significant role to play in shaping that understanding.

Around the world, myriad studies on the future of higher education are helping us to understand that more is at stake in the battle for limited financial resources and a shrinking pool of high-achieving students than institutional footprint or reputation. In the near future, institutional survival will depend on how effectively institutions respond to changing demographics by embracing innovation and maintaining flexibility. The broader point is captured especially well in a sobering study from Universities UK, "Futures for Higher Education: Analyzing Trends." This study maps challenges that institutions of higher education must successfully negotiate between now and 2040 if they intend to remain viable. Noting the increasing pace of change in higher education, the study's authors argue that institutions are entering

> a period of significant change. This is being driven by a number of factors: political, cultural, economic, and technological. The trends are global in their scope, and far-reaching in their impact. They affect every aspect of university provision, the environment in which universities operate, what they will be required to deliver in future, and how they will be structured and funded. (Universities UK 2)

This study along with others argue that five factors will drive institutional success in this brave new future:

1. understanding the relationship between *"growth and investment"* (Universities UK 4);

2. anticipating the *"global demand for higher education"* (Universities UK 12) ;

3. embracing *"innovation"* in higher education delivery (Universities UK 18);

4. recognizing the importance of *flexibility in maintaining "Institutional Identity"* (Universities UK 24); and

5. perspicacity regarding *"'Global' Interconnectedness"*—the institution's specific role in an increasingly complex system of education that transcends national borders. (Universities UK 28, emphasis added).

Honors has always been an important site for negotiating these trends and factors and will remain so well into the future if administrators as well as faculty, students, and staff in honors are willing to accept the challenges that come of moving the occupation of honors from theory to practice in the near future. Funkhouser's guiding principles for honors education may prove invaluable to these efforts.

A BLUEPRINT FOR OCCUPYING HONORS

Pinching methodologically from Michel Foucault and his penchant for revising the original, I formulate the blueprint for occupying honors by examining, commenting on, and revising the questions the editors of this monograph formulated when they issued their call for papers.[11] I believe that the questions we ask tell us more than the answers we seek. The NCHC diversity monograph, *Occupy Honors Education*, is dedicated to answering the following questions:

1. How can students occupy or own their honors education?

2. What are the dreams and realities of diversity in honors?

3. How can honors occupy the canons of knowledge in ways that promote diversity?

4. Does honors have a specific responsibility to occupy the corridors of knowledge—to press for justice in the relations of educational institutions to state and corporate structures?

5. What physical practices, processes, or acts of diversity should take place in honors education?

6. How do different practices of diversity play a role in creating intellectual diversity?

7. What role does intellectual diversity play in fostering the conditions for a vibrant, critically reflective, and just democracy? (Coleman and Kotinek *Occupy Honors Education* CFP)

While I do not presume to answer the forgoing seven questions, I interrogate briefly and attempt to revise the first six of them with an eye toward making them a bit more introspective. I also suggest possible starting points for developing effective strategies for operationalizing them. In doing so I return to the familiar terrain of campus climate and the role diversity, equity, and inclusion play in controlling that climate. I will temporarily pass over question #7 to offer an eighth question and will return to question #7 at the conclusion of the essay.

1. Owning the Honors Experience

"How can students occupy or own their honors education?"

This question countenances the fact that within the honors community some students do not in fact own their honors education. How does this absence of ownership reinforce existing systems of thought that ostensibly require some form of intervention or occupation? To what degree does this absence of ownership actually contribute to or detract from the campus climate as far as diversity, equity, and inclusion are concerned? Does this absence of ownership suggest that honors students are complicit with the system that some of them seek to deconstruct, challenge, or change? The good news of course is that we recognize that this question is an important one to ask.

Any effort to change material conditions in honors should begin with the recognition that honors students will arguably play the most important roles in any occupy effort and that diversity must be understood as it functions synergistically with equity and inclusion. These roles range from canvassing and organizing fellow honors students to planning and executing strategies that bring concerns and potential solutions to the attention of the upper administration. It may make sense to re-imagine question 1 as follows: What are the institutional barriers and personal predispositions of honors students that have led some of them to fail to own their honors education and how do we systematically address those barriers and predispositions?

2. Understanding Honors and Its Role in Fostering Diversity, Equity, and Inclusion

What do we really mean when we ask: "What are the dreams and realities of diversity in honors?"

The realities about honors and numerical diversity can sometimes be quite surprising. In the early 2000s, for example, Texas A&M's Honors Program supported the Office of Academic Scholarships' Century Scholars Program. This program brought diverse groups of students to campus, often for the first time. Among programs that brought Black male students to campus as prospective students, the Century Scholars program had but one rival at Texas A&M, the University's Division I, Aggie Football program.

Remembering that numbers and demographics are only part of what we should be addressing, we might rephrase the original question about dreams and realities as follows: How can honors position itself such that it exerts greater influence upon conversations about improving diversity, equity, and inclusion on our various campuses? How might honors help to translate institutional aspirations for diversity, equity, and inclusion from institutional dream to institutional reality?

3. Canonicity and Diversity in Honors Education

"How can honors occupy the canons of knowledge in ways that promote diversity?"

In our attempts to answer this question, we might begin with a simpler question: "Is occupation of the canons of knowledge sufficient or even desirable?" Accepting uncritically the notion of canonical knowledge is to miss an opportunity to at least interrogate if not directly challenge the notoriously exclusive hegemonic processes of canon formation that dominate and in effect control whole schools of thought in higher education. We must consider the possibility that recognizing established canons of knowledge as sites worthy of occupation offers the hierarchies they support even further legitimacy. The circularity I am referring to here hints at a pathogenesis of premise that in turn calls into question the very possibility of occupation.

In *Cultural Capital: The Problem of Literary Canon Formation,* John Guillory closes his spirited discussion and complicated defense of the sociological aspects of canon formation with an oft-quoted passage from Pierre Bourdieu regarding hierarchy: "'To denounce hierarchy does not get us anywhere. What must be changed are the conditions that make this hierarchy exist both in reality and in minds'" (Bourdieu 84; qtd. in Guillory 340).[12] If we are not deliberate and careful with how we navigate the idea of canonicity, the exclusivity and privileging germane to canon formation may threaten our efforts to foster inclusive excellence.

It may be useful here to turn the question a bit. How might honors use its embrace of a broader diversity of ideas to broaden existing canons of knowledge? Of course, sufficiently broadening canons of knowledge defeats the purpose of having them in the first place. If I understand Guillory correctly, he would point out that the true power of canon formation begins with individual syllabi. The honors curriculum would be a more effective place to begin since the courses we choose to teach point the way to particular canons of knowledge and not the other way around. (See L. L. Coleman on the importance of curriculum change in this volume, pp. 233–79.)

4. Honors and the Corridors of Knowledge

"Does honors have a specific responsibility to occupy the corridors of knowledge—to press for justice in the relations of educational institutions to state and corporate structures?"

In the previous question we mention, but leave unresolved, seminal questions of legitimacy and the hegemonic practices that undergird canon formation. Here we must do the same with access and epistemological concerns regarding "corridors of knowledge." Assuming that these corridors exist in meaningful ways, honors certainly has a responsibility to occupy them, to press for justice in the relations of educational institutions to state and corporate structures. The question then is not if we in honors have a responsibility but how we might meet that responsibility. Our question then should be as follows:

"How, precisely, do we in honors use our access to the corridors of knowledge to successfully press for justice in the relations of educational institutions to state and corporate structures?"

5. Moving Beyond Transactional Diversity Within Honors Communities

"What physical practices, processes, or acts of diversity should take place in honors education?"

Writ more simply, "Where diversity is concerned, what is not happening in honors that should be happening?" Above and elsewhere I have referred to transactional diversity as being, in part, events and activities that celebrate interactions between people of different cultures or ethnicities. (See F. D. Coleman pp. 239–49 in *Setting the Table for Diversity*.) Transactional diversity is measured by the frequency with which different groups of people are given opportunities for genuine cultural and intellectual interaction. Curiously, transactional diversity is often treated as a mechanism by which "we" learn how to get along with "them." The chief benefit of these interactions is reduced to bringing people of varying backgrounds together to celebrate a culture or an event in which we learn from "them" and in the process improve "our" lot and perhaps even feel virtuous. This attitude re-inscribes the essentialist notion of "us" versus "them" rhetoric—social and cultural "othering."

While there is certainly a great deal of individual personal benefit to be had in these interactions, we must interact with different groups for mutual benefit. We must work to make sure that our physical practices, processes, and acts are not conducted for the benefit of one or another group but for the benefit of the community as a whole. In doing so we recognize that it is the locus of all of these activities that bridges the gaps between the various groups that comprise our community. Here we find deeper understanding of diversity.

We must see that diversity is much more than a series of practices, processes, and acts: *it is a way of thinking and being that deserves to be conscientiously woven into the fabric of our daily operations and interactions.* How might leaders in the honors community, students, faculty, and professional staff members lead the charge to have our institutional mission statements reflect an institutional commitment to fostering social justice as an integral part of the academic mission?

6. Honors and Intellectual Diversity

"How do different practices of diversity play a role in creating intellectual diversity?"

Strictly speaking, intellectual diversity is not suddenly being newly created; it already exists in some shape or form on our campuses. An institution's level of intellectual diversity—diversity of ideas and types of thinkers—depends upon two things, demographics and climate. No matter how supportive an environment may be, building a diverse community of thinkers requires bringing together people with different personal backgrounds and experiences. For those institutions that are fortunate enough to employ a diverse group of people, the full richness of the ideas that these individuals bring with them cannot be fully tapped if the institution's climate privileges certain types of intellectual exchanges or forecloses discussion outside of that which is privileged. We enhance intellectual diversity in two ways: by bringing together a wider range of thinkers and by improving the climate for the free exchange of ideas. Consequently, we must ask two questions:

1. What are the concrete steps in harnessing intellectual diversity to successfully foster a vibrant, critically reflective, and just campus climate that in turn fosters greater intellectual diversity?

2. How do we make our campuses more attractive to a wider range of thinkers and how do we get them to join us?

333

Question 8. Reflections on Courage and Wisdom

Revising the first six of the seven NCHC Monograph II questions leads us to a prickly eighth question:

"What must happen within academia for this generation of scholars to find the courage and wisdom required to succeed where preceding generations have struggled valiantly but in the end failed?"

Honestly assessing where we are and thinking critically and reasonably about where we want to go have great value. Acknowledging our shortcomings is often the most important step in moving beyond deficit model thinking. From these points of truth about ourselves, we are able to chart new paths and directions. While this process may sound simple, it takes courage and wisdom to arrive at the complex of answers required to transform our theories and dreams into realities. All of the foregoing questions require this courage and wisdom.

Perhaps as we revise the questions that we ask, we should also be re-imagining higher education more broadly. It makes sense to decenter our own experience in honors to ask questions, especially broader questions that speak more directly to the demographic realities, technological advances, social realities, and political inevitabilities that are shaping and will continue to shape higher education for the foreseeable future. We should also reconsider where we typically begin our assessments. Maybe it is misguided to expect success as we have come to understand it; perhaps we need a paradigm shift that is as effective as what we saw and continue to see in the Occupy Movement. It may appear counterintuitive to some, but sometimes rather than beginning with our shortcomings, we might be better off beginning with an interrogation of our supposed successes.

It is perhaps a truism that if a college or university is struggling to attract underrepresented students, that struggle is likely to be more pronounced for that institution's honors program. Across the country, honors colleges and programs have invested in recruiting strategies designed to yield more minority students within our programs. And while these thoughtful and commendable efforts are often successful, they do not interrogate historical trajectories or strike at the structural issues that produced the demographic disparities in the first place. More important is the rarely discussed ethical dilemma that these recruitment efforts can produce. These programs often correctly identify barriers to entry and help students to negotiate these barriers successfully. Once inside the institution, however, these students are then required to navigate, often on their own, virtually invisible barriers to their success. Research shows that mentorship is an important hedge against these barriers, but it is often difficult to come by. Even when it is available, mentorship often is not enough. It is a mistake to believe that this problem only exists at institutions that struggle to attract underrepresented students. Keeping in mind Mark Twain's admonition about relying too heavily on numbers to tell our stories—"lies, damned lies, and statistics"—I crunch some numbers to illuminate what we might label the problem of success.

THE PROBLEM OF SUCCESS

Based on data from the 2012–13 academic year, Robert Morse in *U.S. News and World Report* identified Rutgers University as the country's most diverse "national university." This influential news magazine came to its conclusion based on Rutgers' "Diversity Index." As adapted by *U.S. News and World Report,* the Diversity Index is used to calculate the likelihood that a student will encounter "others from different ethnic backgrounds." The Diversity Index was created by statisticians Philip Meyer and Shawn McIntosh in early 1992 to strengthen assessments of the wealth of ethnic data collected in the 1990 census.[13]

According to Kyle Reese-Cassal, demographer and writer of the Environmental Systems Research Institute (Esri) "White Paper," "2014/2019 Esri U.S. Diversity Index," the 2010 Census revealed that the 2014 Diversity Index for the U.S. would be 62.6 and 65.0 by 2019 (3). The nation's most diverse region, the West, would reach 74.6 in 2014 and 76.1 by 2019 (3). Ignoring reservations about the broader methodology of the Diversity Index in which international students are not counted, while domestic students declining to identify themselves racially or ethnically are classified as white, Rutgers' Diversity Index of 77.0 was simply astounding.

According to "We are Diverse," an article on the Rutger's fall 2014 website, more than 50% of Rutgers' incoming freshman class identified as "non-white." With a Diversity Index that mirrors the future of the country's most diverse region, Rutgers was justifiably proud when describing its numbers:

> more than half of our first-year students identify them-selves as nonwhite. 52.8 percent of students are women. Students from more than 115 countries come to Rutgers to study. Race/ethnicity enrollment statistics: White: 45.2 per-cent / Asian: 20.2 percent / Latino: 11.7 percent / African American: 10.2 percent / International: 6.3 percent / Other: 7 percent.

These numbers, coupled with the nation's highest Diversity Index, are a strong selling point for Rutgers as it continues its efforts to recruit high-achieving students of color. In spite of these encour-aging if not inspiring numbers for its incoming class, Rutgers University finds itself facing a vexing reality: the numerical diver-sity of its faculty does not match the numerical diversity of its incoming students. The Diversity Index as used currently helps us to understand the composition of a campus's student body but tells us precious little about the people who teach that student body. According to the "Analysis of Staffing Trends" as reported in the *2012–2013 Rutgers Fact Book*, this remarkably diverse incoming class at Rutgers will be taught by a faculty that is White: 66 percent / Asian: 11.2 percent / African American: 3.5 percent / Latino: 2.7 percent / International: 9 percent (79). (See Table 1.)

These numbers include individuals who declined to identify themselves racially or ethnically. For the population of faculty who did in fact self-identify, a slightly different picture emerges: White: 71.6 percent / Asian: 12.2 percent / Latino: 2.9 percent / African American: 3.8 percent / International: 9.5 percent ("Analysis of Staffing Trends"). If we were to employ the methodology used by *U.S. News and World Report*, where non-identified members of the sample are classified as White, the percentage of White faculty would be 73.2 percent. Whites make up 76.7 percent of tenured faculty at Rutgers and 80.1% of all full professors ("Analysis of Staffing Trends").

What do these numbers mean for mentorship opportunities in honors at Rutgers? The Rutgers School of Arts and Sciences Honors Program has developed a robust Faculty Mentor Program. Of the 89 mentors who serve this important program, 59 are male (66%), and they are mostly White. Students who come to Rutgers because of its "diversity" will find that they have been deceived if they made their choice believing that the demographics of the faculty are as diverse as the student body.

Using the statistical model that drives the existing Diversity Index for students, we might develop an "Institutional Diversity Index" that would assess the diversity of faculty, administration, and staff. Given existing research that demonstrates a strong positive correlation between mentorship and academic performance, we might benefit from an index that demonstrates the likelihood of students encountering a mentor from their own ethnic group within the faculty, staff, or administration. Without this measure, we are left to speculate about the size of the gap between Rutgers' Student Diversity Index and its Institutional Diversity Index, a gap that at first glance appears to be significant.[14] The point here, of course, is not that Rutgers University or the School of Arts and Sciences Honors Program is doing poorly—actually, just the opposite

TABLE 1. PERCENTAGE DIFFERENTIALS—RUTGERS FACULTY
AND STUDENTS

Race	Incoming Students %	All Rutgers Faculty %	Difference in %
White	45.0	66.0	+21.0
Asian	20.2	11.2	-9.0
African American	10.2	3.5	-6.7
Latino	11.7	2.7	-9.0
International	6.3	9.0	+2.7
Other or Unknown	7.0	8.6	+1.6

seems to be true. Even though Rutgers has been remarkably successful in fostering ethnic diversity on its various campuses, it nevertheless has significant work left in the struggle to diversify its faculty—and so does the rest of the nation. What we find is that while Rutgers has a way to go in terms of the structural diversity of its faculty, the institution is actually well ahead of where other universities find themselves around the country.

According to "Fast Facts," supplied in 2011 by the National Center for Education Statistics (NCES) for the U.S. Department of Education, an assessment of institutions from across the nation revealed that the percentages in degree-granting postsecondary institutions of full-time instructional faculty whose race/ethnicity was known were as follows: White: 79 percent / Asian: 9 percent / Latino: 4 percent / African American: 6 percent. At the same time, according to another NCES report authored by Scott A. Ginder and Janice E. Kelly-Reid, these faculty members taught a national student body that was significantly more diverse: White: 54.1 percent / Asian: 5.4 percent / African American: 13.5 percent / Latino: 13.8 percent. (See Table 2.)

The demographic tidings for honors are not good. Honors faculties tend to be more homogenous than the national average, and honors student bodies tend to be less diverse than the general student body (see Jones in this volume, 33–79). How will honors close the gap? We cannot simply hope that the gap closes just because the student body has become more diverse. As much as we long for and actively participate in the mythopoeic construction of post-racial America, we are faced with a stark reality to the contrary: race and

TABLE 2. NATIONAL NUMERICAL DIVERSITY COMPARISON OF STUDENTS
AND FACULTY

Race	Student Body %	Faculty %	Difference in %
White	54.1	79	+24.9
Asian	5.4	9	+3.6
African American	13.5	6	-7.5
Latino	13.8	4	-9.8

racism, gender bias and sexism, ageism, and homophobia are all alive and well even as America becomes more numerically diverse as a society.

If we fail to fully exorcise our demons from the past, this growing diversity promises to become as much of a curse as it may be a blessing. Closing the gap and becoming more inclusive mean directly confronting lingering problems regarding, access, inclusion, and equity that limit our ability to fully capitalize on the remarkable diversity of thought, talents, and experiences that obtain on a college campus. The pace of change in academia is painfully slow, but honors may serve as an important catalyst.

Yes, there is some irony at the crux of the matter: honors, one of academia's most exclusive spaces, has an opportunity to take the lead in making academia more inclusive. If honors does want to change, it must continue to pay attention to the demographic profiles of incoming student bodies, but that focus cannot be singular. Those efforts must be complemented with a more rigorous interrogation of the diversity of honors faculty, staff, and administrators. Yes, even though:

1. honors colleges and programs attract a less diverse student body; and

2. honors faculty, staff, and administration are typically less numerically diverse than the rest of the institution, honors remains fertile ground for the type of institutional change needed across academia.

NEXT STEPS—TOWARD OCCUPYING HONORS EDUCATION

If honors education is to be occupied, then at a minimum we must be certain that honors does in fact want to change or serve as an agent of change. The Occupy Movement offers many positive and negative lessons about what we should and should not do to foster the change we desire. We should at every opportunity build upon critical lessons learned from the Occupy Movement. One of the most promising aspects of occupying honors is that our success will hinge on how well we engage our peers and colleagues in discussion and at times heated debate. Our mutual goal is the betterment of academia. This means that there will be friction at times.

DOES HONORS REALLY WANT TO CHANGE?

As I have suggested, honors is fertile ground for the type of thoughtful internal organizational change that begets institutional change, but before honors can presume to effect institutional change, it must look closely at itself and tell the truth about what it sees. It is indeed tempting to embrace the privileges that accrue to honors while turning a blind eye and deaf ear to issues of social justice, meaningful inclusion, and equitable outcomes that less-privileged members of our academic communities struggle to achieve. Honors colleges and programs are rarely innocent bystanders in these processes. More often than not, they are actually complicit with the maintenance of long-standing and exclusionary systems of privilege.

Those who would presume to occupy honors must be intellectually honest about what honors has become and understand that for a variety of reasons not everyone living and working within honors is interested in change. When we look at honors curricula, faculty demographics, and structural diversity of the honors student body, what do we see? Are those of us in honors functioning within what some would consider self-perpetuating bastions of privilege, or can we lay honest claim to inhabiting self-guided halls of justice, equity, and inclusion? Before we presume to occupy honors, we must be clear on why honors education needs to be occupied. What about this exemplary education needs to change and how and where do these changes intersect with our efforts to foster diversity, equity, and inclusion on our campuses?

We might gauge whether or not honors is seriously interested in changing not by measuring the numerical diversity of honors students but the degree to which we commit to addressing underrepresentation within honors faculty, staff, and administration. If we are up to that important first task, then perhaps we will have the courage to recognize that this first step is what we should be doing as a matter of course (see Jones in this volume, pp. 33–79). There is nothing special about doing what we should be doing in the first place. Occupying honors means moving beyond that first step.

Occupying honors is the first step in the potentially lengthy trek toward eliminating the aforementioned virtually invisible barriers to student success and creatively undermining the trenchant prejudices and hatreds that far too many people bring to campus. Occupying honors means creating blueprints that will allow honors to lead in identifying and systematically and expeditiously eliminating these obstacles and barriers, thus extirpating the demons that previous generations weakened but could not destroy.

If we arrive at this point, we must then be careful to fully grasp another important point; it is a trap for us in honors to approach diversity, equity, and inclusion with the idea that we are performing a charitable act in which we attempt to help "needy" students meet their needs (see Brown and Cope in this volume, pp. 107–34). We must embark upon this quest because it is what we should be doing as conscientious members of our academic communities.

WHAT CRITICAL LESSONS CAN WE TAKE FROM THE OCCUPY MOVEMENT?

When discussing inequities in academia and other American institutions, a curious strain of aphasia prevents us from naming the thing directly. In truth, the majority of the inequities that continue to haunt academia are the legacy of White Supremacy and centuries of unchecked gender prejudice. We are reluctant to invoke these terms because we have little desire to invoke the demons of our past, never suspecting or perhaps never wanting to suspect that the demons of our past are the demons of our present. Acknowledging their presence is the first step in preventing them from continuing as the demons of our collective future. We must have the courage to name the thing. And while there is great power bound up in the Adamic naming process, there is not enough power there to simply name our demons out of existence.

We cannot with any intellectual honesty believe that merely naming our moment "post racial" eliminates racism. Even though traditional semiotics teaches that within the dyadic sign, the relationship between the signifier and the signified is arbitrary, we cannot hope that merely changing the signifier will actually ensure that the signified will follow suit. As we gain greater clarity in expressing what the problem is that we wish to solve, we must also be able to imagine into being the resolutions that we desire. Occupying honors requires imagination not just in what we want to do but also in what we want to accomplish. The future that we desire must be imagined into being. Goals? The Occupy Movement has taught us much in this regard.

As we attempt to foster diversity, equity, and inclusion on our campuses, we are brought face-to-face with lingering issues of social justice that we cannot shy away from. We cannot allow academia to recoil from its responsibility to foster social justice. Our success in challenging institutional power requires that we understand three critical lessons from the Occupy Movement with great clarity.

First, occupying honors is challenging what Michel Foucault would call ubiquitous and all-encompassing power: power that may mask itself at times but is nevertheless real. We must understand that we may challenge structures, strategies, and methodologies, but we cannot wholly negate the dark energy that is power. Advancing in the struggle does not require the overthrow of those in power. The goal has to be to reshape material realties such that it does not matter who is in power.

Second, occupying honors means understanding and accepting that we will probably fall short of achieving all that we desire. It is absolutely normal to stop a campaign once immediate needs have been met, but we must avoid the trap of stopping. The Occupy Movement demonstrated the importance of becoming comfortable with asymptotic approaches to change. We may strive for diversity, equity, and inclusion on our campuses, but we must understand that, by definition, these ideals will always remain on the horizon, just out of reach; we cannot ever fully and finally achieve diversity, equity, and inclusion. As intimated above, the goal is to develop enough energy, will, and desire for diversity, equity, and inclusion that we are motivated to continue striving for them even after we have met our individual or programmatic needs.

Finally, we must be cognizant of the fact that our desires for diversity, equity, and inclusion are understandably threatening to those in power who have been taught that to embrace diversity, equity, and inclusion is tantamount to threatening the scaffolding upon which rests their own privilege and power and that the desire for social justice will challenge their supremacy, their right to stand where they stand. These notions are, of course, false conceits, self-generated fears, and specious concerns in the main.

Those who would occupy honors should never doubt that it is the very falseness of these concerns that has been critical to the maintenance of race-conscious systems of privilege, not just in our historical moment, but across the expanse of human existence. Occupying honors can only succeed if we recognize the historical dimensions of the problems that we are facing. More than that, we must be absolutely clear about what the military calls the rules of engagement.

WHAT ARE THE RULES OF ENGAGEMENT?

Institutional change is difficult and potentially dangerous to force into being when campus climate and campus leadership are aligned against it. The exchanges that take place between disgruntled students and the leadership of their academic institutions can become contentious if not outright acrimonious. As the Occupy Education and Occupy Colleges Movements gained strength, we could not help but remember "Bloody Thursday" at Berkeley in May of 1969 or the unfathomable tragedy of the Kent State University shootings in May of 1970. While we might like to think that violence of this type is unimaginable today, the usage of pepper spray and batons at Berkeley in 2011 demonstrates otherwise.[15]

Any responsible blueprint for occupying honors must take this unfortunate reality into account and guard against incidents or exchanges that might escalate into violent confrontation. Those blueprints should also countenance the fact that student activism simply does not work when it is rooted too closely to either passive resistance or open rebellion. Neither moral suasion nor open threats are effective at generating meaningful institutional change that moves beyond conciliatory stopgap measures that are rarely capable of or even intended to address systemic institutional dysfunction. In fact, if not managed skillfully, resistance can lead to greater entrenchment of the very ideas and practices the activist hopes to change or eliminate.

Lasting and meaningful change should be accomplished within the bounds of civil discourse and in keeping with ostensible efforts made by academic administrations to the ongoing improvement of academic excellence. Occupying honors is not a hostile occupation; neither is it nor can it be completely spontaneous. Fostering change on today's college campus requires a more sophisticated set of strategies than either/or ultimatums; it requires careful planning and hard work that begin with understanding the mechanisms that govern campus climate, diversity, equity, inclusion, and academic excellence. It does not matter whether desired outcomes are esoteric or reflective of a significant paradigmatic shift; creating institutional change begins with understanding the engines of institutional change and how members of the honors community may positively impact both the speed and direction of those engines.

HOW DO INSTITUTIONAL VALUES AND LEVERS OF INSTITUTIONAL CHANGE FUNCTION?

We must avoid confusing what institutions say they value with what they actually value. Relying on an institution's mission statement, value proposition, or its strategic plan to gauge what the institution truly values is a mistake. These documents explain what the institution believes that it accomplishes (mission), what it offers in exchange for tuition dollars (value proposition), or what the institution plans to do in the future (strategic plan). These documents are ephemeral and may change from one administration to the next.

As it should be, an academic institution's values almost always transcend the proclamations of its executive leadership. More important, even if these documents and the executive leadership that produced them are in perfect alignment concerning institutional values, these values are not what we are after: we need to know what the institution values. The former tells us what an institution believes; the latter tells us what it is willing to invest in. Institutional values are typically lofty enough that an institution is always in pursuit of its values. While institutional values may be annoyingly opaque, we find absolute clarity when it comes to discerning what institutions of higher education are willing to invest in.

Setting aside for the moment questions of infrastructure and physical plant, academic institutions usually invest in three distinct areas: what the institution decides to teach (curriculum), who the institution hires to teach (faculty demographics), and who the institution recruits to learn what it has decided to teach (demographic profile of the student body). These three realities above all others bring into relief what we might call the veritable image of an institution: the college or university that the institution has actually become as opposed to the institution that the college or university imagines itself to be or wants to become.

Within this veritable image we encounter the institutionalization of strictures on curriculum and barriers to entry for particular groups; these are strictures and barriers that the institution may disavow to the degree that they conflict with a vigilantly maintained public image of the institution. In this nether region between the institution's veritable image and its public image, we find the leverage to affect meaningful institutional change; here we may shape and mold the structures and practices that generate what so many academic consultants and diversity specialists call campus climate. What then are the challenges to entering this space and how do we overcome them? How do we successfully occupy honors?

HOW DO WE BUILD SUSTAINABILITY AND ACCOUNTABILITY?

Remembering the unsung efforts made by Bouazizi's family and friends behind the scenes, honors community activists must differentiate between the stagecraft of protest—the symbolic acts of resistance that bring attention to a movement or cause—and the often difficult and thankless work that occurs behind the scenes. It takes courage to commit meaningfully to that work and in many cases to sustain the dogged persistence required to see it through.

It is important then that honors students play a prominent role in this process of imagining things into being; setting goals; and planning, organizing, and executing actions needed at the university if it is to change, but this imperative is also a fairly obvious point of weakness. The pace of change on a college campus is so slow that student-led efforts to create lasting change fall victim to the fact that a student's event horizon is typically only four or five years. Institutions or administrations that are resistant or averse to student-led change can simply wait them out.

Sustainability is something that we must build into any efforts to change institutions in the long-term. This sustainability hinges upon two complementary efforts. In the first we must actively recruit incoming students who have similar interests in institutional change. This tactic of course requires conscientious mentorship of junior students. The second and perhaps more important effort is that honors students must continue to think about these issues when they become alumni as opposed to just being activists as sophomores, juniors, or seniors.

CONCLUSION

We should anticipate then that the blueprints of an Occupy Honors Movement must necessarily vary from institution to institution; no single plan will work for all institutions. Even so, all plans will likely share several points. As we endeavor to answer our original eight questions, we might return to the prescient wisdom of Edward Funkhouser for another set of questions to keep in the back of our minds, questions that are beguilingly more complex than they may appear at first blush: How are the solutions that we seek for honors students any different than what we should be seeking for all students? What institutional changes are needed that would apply solely to the honors experience? If there are such things, will pursuing them positively or negatively impact the changes we seek? I use this binary here because I find it implausible that the effects of such measures or initiatives would be wholly neutral in their impact. We must understand that while all of our blueprints will be different, the overarching goal will be same. As promised, I want to return to question 7 of the Call for Proposals for *Occupy Honors Education*:

"What role does intellectual diversity play in fostering the conditions for a vibrant, critically reflective, and just democracy?"

The answer to this question is fairly straightforward: even conceiving of a vibrant, critically reflective, and just democracy is nigh impossible. Given the fact that honors programs across the country are committed to fostering intellectual diversity, we might revise this question to read:

"How would the absence or even the truncation of intellectual diversity impact conditions for a vibrant, critically reflective, and just democracy?"

In answering this question we must realize that honors has a vital leadership role to play in shaping and directing academia in general and that academia must continue to play a vital role in shaping and directing our democracy and in crafting a just democracy. Question 7 is invaluable because it should prompt us to continue asking difficult questions, revising those questions, and seeking intellectually honest answers.

Moving forward we must ask how existing structures within academia will need to change to meet the demands not just of individual students but the demands of a global society. How might those shifts begin in honors? Edward Funkhouser was successful for so many years because he conscientiously made honors into a place where it was safe to try the uncommon. He also recognized that the true power of diversity rests in the fact that no one group alone can solve the complex problems facing the world and that no problems are so complex that the combination of our individual talents cannot solve them. Pinching from a sign that he saw in a hospital elevator in New Jersey, Funkhouser insisted that everyone in honors understand that beyond our various core missions, our work was essentially about celebrating the similarities that bring us together and understanding, honoring, and respecting the differences that set us apart. Perhaps our occupation of honors should begin with celebrating and understanding.

NOTES

[1]On November 6, 1987, Ben Ali convened a panel of seven doctors who pronounced then "President for Life" Habib Bourguiba incompetent. Like Bourguiba, Ben Ali moved unscrupulously from his role of Prime Minister to that of President. See "Habib Bourguiba" in *The Economist*, April 13, 2000.

[2]For more on Ron Paul's views on Occupy and the Tea Party, see John McCormack's "Ron Paul Praises Occupy Wall Street."

[3]For an announcement of the National Day of Action, 1 March, 2012, see "Letter from the General Assembly to the Campus Community" under "Student Protests" on the University of California Santa Cruz Faculty Association website.

[4]I do not intend the more common Medieval Latin derived usage of antinomianism regarding faith and the dispensation of grace and their relation and freedom from adherence to moral law. I use antinomianism here as a referent to healthy skepticism and mistrust of constituted authority. My usage is closer to the ancient Greek, "one who is against (*anti*) the law (*nómos*)."

[5]For insight into this movement, see Herbert G. Ruffin's "Black Lives Matter: The Growth of a New Social Justice Movement" on the BlackPast.org website.

[6]For more on strategic planning, see Jean Ries, "The Strategic Planning Process: How to Avoid a Plan That Just Sits on the Shelf," in which she explains how flexibility, malleability, creativity, and sustainability are all hallmarks of successful strategic plans.

[7]Dr. Sylvia Hurtado is one of the foremost experts in diversity studies. In "Diversity and Higher Education: Theory and Impact on Educational Outcomes" (Gurin et al.), Hurtado teams with Patricia Gurin, Eric Dey, and Gerald Gurin to discuss three different types

of diversity that students encounter on college campuses: structural diversity, informal interactional diversity, and what they term classroom diversity.

[8]For categorical, transactional, and universal diversity, I draw upon Haluk Soydan's fine work in *Social Work and Minorities: European Perspectives* (2002).

[9]Sylvia Hurtado and Rona Halualani argue that "institution-wide change requires organizational learning and authentic forms of professional development that empower faculty (both full- and part-time) and all levels of staff to implement transformative practices that advance diversity and student success." For more on this topic, see *Hispanic-Serving Institutions: Advancing Research and Transformative Practice* by Anne-Marie Nuñez, Sylvia Hurtado, and Emily Calderón Galdeano.

[10]The body of scholarship dedicated to the five aforementioned types of diversity is substantial. What I have offered above is a necessarily truncated summary of that scholarship. Time and space do not allow for a similar summary of the equally robust body of scholarship dedicated to equity and inclusion.

[11]The NCHC Diversity Monograph II Call for Papers included the following introduction from Lisa L. Coleman and Jonathan D. Kotinek prior to its list of seven questions:

> Published in 2010, NCHC Diversity Monograph I, *Setting the Table for Diversity*, discussed the value of preparing a place for diversity at the honors table. Today, inspired by the 2012 NCHC Conference theme, "Challenging Structures," we are issuing a call for papers for the next diversity monograph. In sum, *Occupy Honors Education* will ask:

> How can *we* (students, faculty and professional staff members) *occupy* Honors Education in transformative and revolutionary ways that place honors education on the cutting edge of educational practice and promote the democratic values of diversity, equity, inclusion, and justice? (Emphasis added).

[12]See also, Pierre Bourdieu and Loïc J. D. Wacquant's *An Invitation to Reflexive Sociology* (1992).

[13]See also Philip Meyer and Shawn McIntosh's 1992 journal article, "The *USA Today* Index of Ethnic Diversity."

[14]We also know from the engaging study by Katherine L. Milkman et al., "What Happens Before? A Field Experiment Exploring How Pay and Representation Differentially Shape Bias on the Pathway into Organizations," that university faculty members decline opportunities to mentor women and minorities at a higher rate than for Caucasian males.

[15]See Carly Schwartz's video, "Occupy U.C. Berkeley Protesters Face Violent Confrontation with Campus Police" and Victoria Colliver's coverage of police violence and student protests at the City College of San Francisco for the *San Francisco Chronicle,* in "Violent Protest at City College of San Francisco."

REFERENCES

"Analysis of Staffing Trends." *2012–2013 Rutgers Fact Book.* Rutgers University Office of Academic Planning and Research, n.d. Web. 05 May 2014.

Bourdieu, Pierre, and Loïc J. D. Wacquant. *An Invitation to Reflexive Sociology.* Chicago: University of Chicago Press, 1992. Print.

Coleman, Finnie D. "The Problem with Diversity: Moving Past the Numbers." *Setting the Table for Diversity.* Ed. Lisa L. Coleman and Jonathan D. Kotinek. Lincoln: National Collegiate Honors Council, 2010. 239–49. NCHC Monograph Series. Print.

Coleman, Lisa L., and Jonathan D. Kotinek. "National Collegiate Honors Council Diversity Monograph II: *Occupy Honors Education* Call For Papers." 2012. Lisa L. Coleman Personal Collection. Typescript.

Colliver, Victoria. "Violent Protest at City College of San Francisco." *SFGate*.com. *San Francisco Chronicle,* 14 Mar. 2014. Web. 29 Mar. 2017.

"Fast Facts." U.S. Department of Education. Washington, D.C.: National Center for Education Statistics (NCES), n.d. Web. 17 Aug. 2014.

Ginder, Scott A., and Janice E. Kelly-Reid. "Enrollment in Postsecondary Institutions, Fall 2012; Financial Statistics, Fiscal Year 2012; Graduation Rates, Selected Cohorts, 2004–09; and Employees in Postsecondary Institutions, Fall 2012: First Look (Provisional Data) (NCES 2013–183)." U.S. Department of Education. Washington, D.C.: National Center for Education Statistics (NCES), 2013. Web. 29 Mar. 2017.

Guillory, John. *Cultural Capital: The Problem of Literary Canon Formation.* Chicago: University of Chicago Press, 1993.

Gurin, Patricia, Eric Dey, Sylvia Hurtado, and Gerald Gurin. "Diversity and Higher Education: Theory and Impact on Educational Outcomes." *Harvard Educational Review* 72.3 (2002): 330–67. Web. 27 Mar. 2017.

"Habib Bourguiba." *The Economist.* The Economist Newspaper, Ltd., 13 Apr. 2000. Web. 27 Mar. 2017.

Hurtado, Sylvia, and Rona Halualani. "Diversity Assessment, Accountability, and Action: Going Beyond the Numbers." *Diversity and Democracy.* Association of American Colleges & Universities, 29 Dec. 2014. Web. 27 Mar. 2017.

"Letter from the General Assembly to the Campus Community." "Student Protests." UCSCFA.org. University of California Santa Cruz Faculty Association, 23 Feb. 2012. Web. 27 Mar. 2017.

McCormack, John. "Ron Paul Praises Occupy Wall Street." *The Weekly Standard.* The Weekly Standard, 29 Dec. 2011. Web. 22 June 2014.

Meyer, Philip, and Shawn McIntosh. "The *USA Today* Index of Ethnic Diversity." *International Journal of Public Opinion Research* 4.1 (Spring 1992), 51–58. Web. 29 Mar. 2017.

Milkman, Katherine L., Modupe Akinola, and Dolly Chugh. "What Happens Before? A Field Experiment Exploring How Pay and

Representation Differentially Shape Bias on the Pathway into Organizations." *Journal of Applied Psychology* 100.6 (Apr. 2015): 1678–712. Web. 28 Mar. 2017.

Morse, Robert. "Campus Ethnic Diversity Methodology." *US News & World Report*, 09 Sept. 2013. Web. 17 Aug. 2014.

Nuñez, Anne-Marie, Sylvia Hurtado, and Emily Calderón Galdeano. *Hispanic-Serving Institutions: Advancing Research and Transformative Practice.* New York: Routledge, 2015. Print.

Reese-Cassal, Kyle. "2014/2019 Esri U.S. Diversity Index: An Esri® White Paper." Environmental Systems Research Institute, Inc., Sept. 2014. Web. 28 Mar. 2017.

Ries, Jean. "How To Avoid A Strategic Plan That Sits On The Shelf." *The Olive Grove*, n.d. Web. 08 Mar. 2017.

Ruffin, Herbert G. "Black Lives Matter: The Growth of a New Social Justice Movement." BlackPast.org. *The Black Past: Remembered and Reclaimed*, 2015. Web. 26 Mar. 2017.

Saidani, Mounir, and R. A. Judy. "Revolution and Counterrevolution in Tunisia: The Forty Days That Shook the Country." *Boundary 2* 39.1 (2012): 43–54. Web. 27 Mar. 2017.

Schwartz, Carly. "Occupy U.C. Berkeley Protesters Face Violent Confrontation with Campus Police." TheHuffingtonPost.com. *The Huffington Post*, 10 Nov. 2011. Web. 22 July 2014. Video.

Soydan, Haluk. *Social Work and Minorities: European Perspectives.* London: Routledge, 2002.

Universities UK. "Futures for Higher Education: Analyzing Trends." Jan. 2012. Web. 28 Mar. 2017.

"We Are Diverse." *Rutgers, The State University of New Jersey*, n.d. Web. 17 Aug. 2014.

ABOUT THE AUTHORS

SHAWN ALFREY is Associate Director of the University Honors Program at the University of Denver, where she has worked and taught since 2007. Her publications include *The Sublime of Intense Sociability: Emily Dickinson, H.D., and Gertrude Stein* and several articles. Her most recent publication concerns the implications of Slavoj Zizek's work for literary study. She has presented several times at NCHC conferences.

LOPAMUDRA BASU is Professor of English at the University of Wisconsin-Stout. She served as Director of UW-Stout's Honors College from 2011–16. She also served as elected Board Member of NCHC from 2014–16. She is the co-editor of *Passage to Manhattan: Critical Essays on Meena Alexander*, Cambridge Scholars Publishing, UK, 2009. Her research on postcolonial literature has been widely published.

STEPHANIE BROWN is Associate Professor of English and Assistant Dean at Ohio State University at Newark. She has been developing and leading education abroad programs for the past twelve years. Her publications include *The Postwar African American Novel: Protest and Discontent, 1945–1950*; *Engaging Tradition, Making It New: Essays on Teaching Recent African-American Literature*; and numerous other articles.

PHAME CAMARENA is Director of the University Honors Program and Professor of Human Development at Central Michigan University. He is a member of the American Psychological Association and studies the overlap of self-development, diversity, and educational achievement across adolescence and emerging adulthood. He serves on the NCHC Publications Board and the NCHC Committee on Diversity Issues.

RACHEL CHILDERS is a student at Southeastern Oklahoma State University (SE). She is an English and history double major and heavily involved in the SE Honors Program as well as in the local chapters of Sigma Tau Delta and Phi Alpha Theta. She serves as an editor for the university's literary journal, *Green Eggs and Hamlet,* and she has presented at an NCHC conference and at a MEMNTO conference.

FINNIE D. COLEMAN, Associate Professor in the Department of English Language and Literature at the University of New Mexico, teaches courses in American and African American literature, history, and culture (including Underground Hip Hop and Black Lives Matter). He is an American Council on Education Fellow (University of Miami) and served as Director of Africana Studies and Interim Dean of University College.

LISA L. COLEMAN served as Coordinator and Director of the Southeastern Oklahoma State University Honors Program from 1998 until her retirement in 2016. She co-edited the NCHC monograph *Setting the Table for Diversity* (2010). A former member of the NCHC Board of Directors, she has chaired or co-chaired the NCHC Committee on Diversity Issues since 2004 and has served on the NCHC Publications Board since 1999.

VIRGINIA COPE, Associate Professor of English at Ohio State University, is Associate Dean at the OSU Newark campus, where she directs the Honors, Outreach, and Education Abroad programs. Her publications include *Property, Education and Identity in Late Eighteenth-Century Fiction* and articles on the multiethnic 2012 Broadway production of *A Streetcar Named Desire* and *Incidents in the Life of a Slave Girl* by Harriet Jacobs.

AMBERLY DZIESINSKI is a PhD student studying higher education in the Department of Leadership, Organization, and Policy Studies at Vanderbilt University. She graduated with a BS in sociology from Central Michigan University. As an active member of the CMU honors community, Dziesinski participated in honors student organizations, wrote for the honors news publication, and presented at MEHA.

SAMANTHA FAUDREE is a senior at Southeastern Oklahoma State University (SE) pursuing a BBA in marketing. She is active in the SE Honors Program as a student worker and as the president of the Honors Advisory Council. In addition, she is a member of the Cardinal Key National Honor Society, the Alpha Chi Honor Society, and Beta Gamma Sigma, and she was recognized as a Top Ten Freshman. Faudree presented at NCHC in 2015.

CAITLIN HOMRICH-KNIELING, a community organizer at Michigan United, engages community members in participatory democracy. She earned an MA in anthropology from the University of Massachusetts Amherst; her thesis focused on anti-racist and anti-oppression political mobilizations. While in the Central Michigan University Honors Program, she participated in research on first-generation college students.

DAVID M. JONES is Professor of English and Honors Education and Director of the University Honors Program at the University of Wisconsin at Eau Claire, where he has served for twenty years. He is also a professional musician and songwriter. His courses examine African American literature and culture, popular music, and gender studies. Publications include *Coming Out to the Mainstream: New Queer Cinema in the 21st Century*.

JONATHAN D. KOTINEK is Associate Director for the University Honors Program at Texas A&M University, where he has worked since 2003. He co-edited the NCHC monograph *Setting the Table for Diversity* (2010), and he served as co-chair of the NCHC Committee on Diversity Issues from 2006–16. A former member of the NCHC Board of Directors, Kotinek earned his PhD in educational psychology from Texas A&M in 2013.

HYUN SEO (HANNAH) LEE is a native of Korea. She graduated with her BA in psychology from Azusa Pacific University, receiving the department's Outstanding Senior Award. She is currently a research assistant at the university.

JAKE MARTIN, a rising senior at Southeastern Oklahoma State University (SE), is pursuing a bachelor's degree in history. He served two years on the SE Honors Advisory Council and has presented at NCHC. In 2017, the Leadership Alliance awarded Martin an internship during which he curated the exhibit *Songs of a Secret Country* for the Kluge-Ruhe Art Collection at the University of Virginia in Charlottesville.

ALAN Y. ODA (PhD, University of California, Riverside) is Professor of Psychology at Azusa Pacific University. He is Co-Chair of the Diversity Committee for the National Collegiate Honors Council. Oda is also a disaster relief consultant and volunteer with OperationSAFE International and CRASH (Christian Relief, Assistance, Support and Hope) Japan.

YE EUN (GRACE) OH is a native of Korea. She graduated with her Bachelor of Science Degree in nursing from Azusa Pacific University. She is a member of the Sigma Theta Tau Nursing Honors Society.

AARON STOLLER serves as Director of the First-Year Experience Program at Colorado College. From 2010–16, he was Associate Director of the North Carolina State University Honors Program and was a member of the NCHC Committee on Diversity Issues. As a philosopher and educational theorist, he specializes in the work of John Dewey and is the author of *Knowing and Learning as Creative Action* (2014).

NANCY M. WEST is Professor of English and a former director of the Honors College at the University of Missouri, where she teaches a range of courses in film and television studies and Victorian literature and culture.

ABOUT THE NCHC MONOGRAPH SERIES

The Publications Board of the National Collegiate Honors Council typically publishes two to three monographs a year. The subject matter and style range widely: from handbooks on nuts-and-bolts practices and discussions of honors pedagogy to anthologies on diverse topics addressing honors education and issues relevant to higher education.

The Publications Board encourages people with expertise interested in writing such a monograph to submit a prospectus. Prospective authors or editors of an anthology should submit a proposal discussing the purpose or scope of the manuscript; a prospectus that includes a chapter by chapter summary; a brief writing sample, preferably a draft of the introduction or an early chapter; and a *curriculum vitae*. All monograph proposals will be reviewed by the NCHC Publications Board.

Direct all proposals, manuscripts, and inquiries about submitting a proposal to the General Editor of the Monograph Series:

Dr. Jeffrey A. Portnoy
General Editor, Monograph Series
Honors College
Perimeter College
Georgia State University
555 N. Indian Creek Drive
Clarkston, GA 30021-2396

jportnoy@gsu.edu

(678) 891-3620

NCHC Monographs & Journals

Assessing and Evaluating Honors Programs and Honors Colleges: A Practical Handbook by Rosalie Otero and Robert Spurrier (2005, 98pp). This monograph includes an overview of assessment and evaluation practices and strategies. It explores the process for conducting self-studies and discusses the differences between using consultants and external reviewers. It provides a guide to conducting external reviews along with information about how to become an NCHC-Recommended Site Visitor. A dozen appendices provide examples of "best practices."

Beginning in Honors: A Handbook by Samuel Schuman (Fourth Edition, 2006, 80pp). Advice on starting a new honors program. Covers budgets, recruiting students and faculty, physical plant, administrative concerns, curriculum design, and descriptions of some model programs.

Fundrai$ing for Honor$: A Handbook by Larry R. Andrews (2009, 160pp). Offers information and advice on raising money for honors, beginning with easy first steps and progressing to more sophisticated and ambitious fundraising activities.

A Handbook for Honors Administrators by Ada Long (1995, 117pp). Everything an honors administrator needs to know, including a description of some models of honors administration.

A Handbook for Honors Programs at Two-Year Colleges by Theresa James (2006, 136pp). A useful handbook for two-year schools contemplating beginning or redesigning their honors program and for four-year schools doing likewise or wanting to increase awareness about two-year programs and articulation agreements. Contains extensive appendices about honors contracts and a comprehensive bibliography on honors education.

The Honors College Phenomenon edited by Peter C. Sederberg (2008, 172pp). This monograph examines the growth of honors colleges since 1990: historical and descriptive characterizations of the trend, alternative models that include determining whether becoming a college is appropriate, and stories of creation and recreation. Leaders whose institutions are contemplating or taking this step as well as those directing established colleges should find these essays valuable.

Honors Composition: Historical Perspectives and Contemporary Practices by Annmarie Guzy (2003, 182pp). Parallel historical developments in honors and composition studies; contemporary honors writing projects ranging from admission essays to theses as reported by over 300 NCHC members.

Honors Programs at Smaller Colleges by Samuel Schuman (Third Edition, 2011, 80pp). Practical and comprehensive advice on creating and managing honors programs with particular emphasis on colleges with fewer than 4,000 students.

The Honors Thesis: A Handbook for Honors Directors, Deans, and Faculty Advisors by Mark Anderson, Karen Lyons, and Norman Weiner (2014, 176pp). To all those who design, administer, and implement an honors thesis program, this handbook offers a range of options, models, best practices, and philosophies that illustrate how to evaluate an honors thesis program, solve pressing problems, select effective requirements and procedures, or introduce a new honors thesis program.

Housing Honors edited by Linda Frost, Lisa W. Kay, and Rachael Poe (2015, 352pp). This collection of essays addresses the issues of where honors lives and how honors space influences educators and students. This volume includes the results of a survey of over 400 institutions; essays on the acquisition, construction, renovation, development, and even the loss of honors space; a forum offering a range of perspectives on residential space for honors students; and a section featuring student perspectives.

If Honors Students Were People: Holistic Honors Education by Samuel Schuman (2013, 256pp). What if honors students were people? What if they were not disembodied intellects but whole persons with physical bodies and questing spirits? Of course . . . they are. This monograph examines the spiritual yearnings of college students and the relationship between exercise and learning.

Inspiring Exemplary Teaching and Learning: Perspectives on Teaching Academically Talented College Students edited by Larry Clark and John Zubizarreta (2008, 216pp). This rich collection of essays offers valuable insights into innovative teaching and significant learning in the context of academically challenging classrooms and programs. The volume provides theoretical, descriptive, and practical resources, including models of effective instructional practices, examples of successful courses designed for enhanced learning, and a list of online links to teaching and learning centers and educational databases worldwide.

Occupy Honors Education edited by Lisa L. Coleman, Jonathan D. Kotinek, and Alan Y. Oda (2017, 394pp). This collection of essays issues a call to honors to make diversity, equity, and inclusive excellence its central mission and ongoing state of mind. Echoing the AAC&U declaration "without inclusion there is no true excellence," the authors discuss transformational diversity, why it is essential, and how to achieve it.

NCHC Monographs & Journals

The Other Culture: Science and Mathematics Education in Honors edited by Ellen B. Buckner and Keith Garbutt (2012, 296pp). A collection of essays about teaching science and math in an honors context: topics include science in society, strategies for science and non-science majors, the threat of pseudoscience, chemistry, interdisciplinary science, scientific literacy, philosophy of science, thesis development, calculus, and statistics.

Partners in the Parks: Field Guide to an Experiential Program in the National Parks by Joan Digby with reflective essays on theory and practice by student and faculty participants and National Park Service personnel (First Edition, 2010, 272pp). This monograph explores an experiential-learning program that fosters immersion in and stewardship of the national parks. The topics include program designs, group dynamics, philosophical and political issues, photography, wilderness exploration, and assessment.

Partners in the Parks: Field Guide to an Experiential Program in the National Parks edited by Heather Thiessen-Reily and Joan Digby (Second Edition, 2016, 268pp). This collection of recent photographs and essays by students, faculty, and National Park Service rangers reflects upon PITP experiential-learning projects in new NPS locations, offers significant refinements in programming and curriculum for revisited projects, and provides strategies and tools for assessing PITP adventures.

Place as Text: Approaches to Active Learning edited by Bernice Braid and Ada Long (Second Edition, 2010, 128pp). Updated theory, information, and advice on experiential pedagogies developed within NCHC during the past 35 years, including Honors Semesters and City as Text™, along with suggested adaptations to multiple educational contexts.

Preparing Tomorrow's Global Leaders: Honors International Education edited by Mary Kay Mulvaney and Kim Klein (2013, 400pp). A valuable resource for initiating or expanding honors study abroad programs, these essays examine theoretical issues, curricular and faculty development, assessment, funding, and security. The monograph also provides models of successful programs that incorporate high-impact educational practices, including City as Text™ pedagogy, service learning, and undergraduate research.

Setting the Table for Diversity edited by Lisa L. Coleman and Jonathan D. Kotinek (2010, 288pp). This collection of essays provides definitions of diversity in honors, explores the challenges and opportunities diversity brings to honors education, and depicts the transformative nature of diversity when coupled with equity and inclusion. These essays discuss African American, Latina/o, international, and first-generation students as well as students with disabilities. Other issues include experiential and service learning, the politics of diversity, and the psychological resistance to it. Appendices relating to NCHC member institutions contain diversity statements and a structural diversity survey.

Shatter the Glassy Stare: Implementing Experiential Learning in Higher Education edited by Peter A. Machonis (2008, 160pp). A companion piece to *Place as Text*, focusing on recent, innovative applications of City as Text™ teaching strategies. Chapters on campus as text, local neighborhoods, study abroad, science courses, writing exercises, and philosophical considerations, with practical materials for instituting this pedagogy.

Teaching and Learning in Honors edited by Cheryl L. Fuiks and Larry Clark (2000, 128pp). Presents a variety of perspectives on teaching and learning useful to anyone developing new or renovating established honors curricula.

Writing on Your Feet: Reflective Practices in City as Text™ edited by Ada Long (2014, 160pp). A sequel to the NCHC monographs *Place as Text: Approaches to Active Learning* and *Shatter the Glassy Stare: Implementing Experiential Learning in Higher Education*, this volume explores the role of reflective writing in the process of active learning while also paying homage to the City as Text™ approach to experiential education that has been pioneered by Bernice Braid and sponsored by NCHC during the past four decades.

Journal of the National Collegiate Honors Council (*JNCHC*) is a semi-annual periodical featuring scholarly articles on honors education. Articles may include analyses of trends in teaching methodology, articles on interdisciplinary efforts, discussions of problems common to honors programs, items on the national higher education agenda, and presentations of emergent issues relevant to honors education.

Honors in Practice (*HIP*) is an annual journal that accommodates the need and desire for articles about nuts-and-bolts practices by featuring practical and descriptive essays on topics such as successful honors courses, suggestions for out-of-class experiences, administrative issues, and other topics of interest to honors administrators, faculty, and students.

NCHC Publications Order Form

Purchases may be made by calling 402-472-9150, emailing nchc@unl.edu, visiting our website <http://www.nchchonors.org>, or mailing a check or money order payable to: NCHC • 1100 Neihardt Residence Center • University of Nebraska–Lincoln • 540 N. 16th Street • Lincoln, NE 68588-0627.   FEIN 52–1188042

	Member	Non-Member	No. of Copies	Amount This Item
Monographs:				
Assessing and Evaluating Honors Programs and Honors Colleges: A Practical Handbook	$25.00	$45.00		
Beginning in Honors: A Handbook (4th Ed.)	$25.00	$45.00		
Fundrai$ing for Honor$: A Handbook	$25.00	$45.00		
A Handbook for Honors Administrators	$25.00	$45.00		
A Handbook for Honors Programs at Two-Year Colleges	$25.00	$45.00		
The Honors College Phenomenon	$25.00	$45.00		
Honors Composition: Historical Perspectives and Contemporary Practices	$25.00	$45.00		
Honors Programs at Smaller Colleges (3rd Ed.)	$25.00	$45.00		
The Honors Thesis: A Handbook for Honors Directors, Deans, and Faculty Advisors	$25.00	$45.00		
Housing Honors	$25.00	$45.00		
If Honors Students Were People: Holistic Honors Education	$25.00	$45.00		
Inspiring Exemplary Teaching and Learning: Perspectives on Teaching Academically Talented College Students	$25.00	$45.00		
Occupy Honors Education	$25.00	$45.00		
The Other Culture: Science and Mathematics Education in Honors	$25.00	$45.00		
Partners in the Parks: Field Guide to an Experiential Program in the National Parks (1st Ed.)	$25.00	$45.00		
Partners in the Parks: Field Guide to an Experiential Program in the National Parks (2nd Ed.)	$25.00	$45.00		
Place as Text: Approaches to Active Learning (2nd Ed.)	$25.00	$45.00		
Preparing Tomorrow's Global Leaders: Honors International Education	$25.00	$45.00		
Setting the Table for Diversity	$25.00	$45.00		
Shatter the Glassy Stare: Implementing Experiential Learning in Higher Education	$25.00	$45.00		
Teaching and Learning in Honors	$25.00	$45.00		
Writing on Your Feet: Reflective Practices in City as Text™	$25.00	$45.00		
Journals:				
Journal of the National Collegiate Honors Council (JNCHC) Specify Vol/Issue ___/___	$25.00	$45.00		
Honors in Practice (HIP) Specify Vol ____	$25.00	$45.00		
Total Copies Ordered and Total Amount Paid:				$

Name_____ Institution _____
Address _____ City, State, Zip_____
Phone _____ Fax_____ Email _____

Print-on-Demand publications will be delivered in 4-6 weeks. Shipping costs will be calculated on the number of items purchased. Apply a 20% discount if 10+ copies are purchased.